FROMME

EasyGuide

To

The Virgin Islands

By

Alexis Lipsitz Flippin

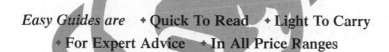

Easy Guides are ✦ Quick To Read ✦ Light To Carry
✦ For Expert Advice ✦ In All Price Ranges

FrommerMedia LLC

Published by
FROMMER MEDIA LLC

Copyright (c) 2014 by Frommer Media LLC, New York City, New York. All rights reserved. No part of this publication may be reproduced, stored in a retrieval system, or transmitted in any form or by any means, electronic, mechanical, photocopying, recording, scanning or otherwise, except as permitted under Sections 107 or 108 of the 1976 United States Copyright Act, without the prior written permission of the Publisher. Requests to the Publisher for permission should be addressed to the Permissions Department, Frommer Media LLC, 44 West 62nd Street, New York, NY 10023, or online at http://www.frommers.com/permissions.

Frommer's is a registered trademark of Arthur Frommer. Used under license. All other trademarks are the property of their respective owners. Frommer Media LLC is not associated with any product or vendor mentioned in this book.

ISBN 978-1-62887-068-8 (paper), 978-1-62887-069-5 (e-book)

Editorial Director: Pauline Frommer
Editor: Pauline Frommer
Production Editor: Heather Wilcox
Cartographer: Roberta Stockwell
Page Compositor: Lissa Auciello-Brogan
Cover Design: Howard Grossman

For information on our other products or services, see www.frommers.com.

Frommer Media LLC also publishes its books in a variety of electronic formats. Some content that appears in print may not be available in electronic formats.

Manufactured in the United States of America

5 4 3 2 1

ABOUT THE AUTHOR

Alexis Lipsitz Flippin is the author of "Frommer's Turks & Caicos," "Frommer's St. Maarten/ St. Martin," "Anguilla & St. Barts," "The Food Lovers' Guide to Manhattan," and "Frommer's NYC with Kids" and the co-author of "Frommer's 500 Extraordinary Islands," "Frommer's Caribbean," and "Frommer's Carolinas & Georgia." She has written for numerous magazines and webzines, including CNN.com, MSNBC.com, Zagat.com, and AARP.com and is a former Senior Editor of the Frommer's travel guides.

ABOUT THE FROMMER'S TRAVEL GUIDES

For most of the past 50 years, Frommer's has been the leading series of travel guides in North America, accounting for as many as 24 percent of all guidebooks sold. I think I know why.

Although we hope our books are entertaining, we nevertheless deal with travel in a serious fashion. Our guidebooks have never looked on such journeys as a mere recreation, but as a far more important human function, a time of learning and introspection, an essential part of a civilized life. We stress the culture, lifestyle, history, and beliefs of the destinations we cover and urge our readers to seek out people and new ideas as the chief rewards of travel.

We have never shied from controversy. We have, from the beginning, encouraged our authors to be intensely judgmental, critical—both pro and con—in their comments, and wholly independent. Our only clients are our readers, and we have triggered the ire of countless prominent sorts, from a tourist newspaper we called "practically worthless" (it unsuccessfully sued us) to the many rip-offs we've condemned.

And because we believe that travel should be available to everyone regardless of their incomes, we have always been cost-conscious at every level of expenditure. Although we have broadened our recommendations beyond the budget category, we insist that every lodging we include be sensibly priced. We use every form of media to assist our readers and are particularly proud of our feisty daily website, the award-winning Frommers.com.

I have high hopes for the future of Frommer's. May these guidebooks, in all the years ahead, continue to reflect the joy of travel and the freedom that travel represents. May they always pursue a cost-conscious path, so that people of all incomes can enjoy the rewards of travel. And may they create, for both the traveler and the persons among whom we travel, a community of friends, where all human beings live in harmony and peace.

Arthur Frommer

THE BEST OF THE VIRGIN ISLANDS

Mountainous and luminously green, the Virgin Islands number about 100, some governed by the United States and others by Great Britain. The larger islands appear as mossy green hills rising dramatically out of turquoise seas; others are little more than rocky outcroppings rimmed by whispery white-sand beaches waiting for Robinson Crusoe to call. The former haunt of derring-do sea captains and pirate marauders, today many of the Virgin Islands are invaded by thousands of visitors, arriving by plane and cruise ship, suntan lotion in hand.

The region's major islands include the three United States territories: Bustling **St. Thomas** attracts the most visitors, many of them disembarking from some of the biggest cruise ships in the business; the "plantation island," **St. Croix** is the Virgins' largest island and some say its cultural heart; and the lush beauty known as **St. John,** at 9 miles long and 5 miles wide, is the smallest of the three. No matter where you're traveling from, St. Thomas is for many people the gateway to the Virgins. With the busiest cruise-ship harbor in the Caribbean, St. Thomas bustles with duty-free shopping and global dining. **St. Croix** is more laid-back than St. Thomas, with well-preserved colonial towns and verdant countryside dotted with plantation ruins. Little **St. John** is positively sleepy, two-thirds of its acreage taken up by one of America's most beautiful national parks.

With its dizzying mountain topography and scalloped coastline of shimmering blue coves and powdery beaches, the B.V.I. remains a pristine retreat for yachties and visitors who want to a true escape from the scrum of modern civilization. With steady tradewinds and scores of protected deep-water harbors, the B.V.I. offer some of the best sailing grounds in the Caribbean. Many boaters base themselves on **Tortola,** the largest island in the B.V.I. and its capital—it's a relaxed spot with something for everyone. Beautiful and sparsely populated **Virgin Gorda** is the place to go for luxury stays in secluded resorts. Dotted about the main islands are private island retreats and uninhabited islands perfect for castaway day-tripping.

For beach lovers, the Virgin Islands contain some of the most celebrated white-sand beaches in the West Indies, including **Magens Bay** on St. Thomas, **Trunk Bay** on St. John, and **Cane Garden Bay** on Tortola. Swimming and snorkeling await you at every cove—and in the vibrant coral reef ringing **Buck Island,** St. Croix has America's only underwater national monument. Throughout the island archipelago are also miles of idyllic hiking trails, tracing the sinous curves of these scenic volcanic wonders.

THE most authentic EXPERIENCES

o **Island-Hopping by Sea:** Whether you're traveling the liquid expanse of the local waterways by ferry, sailboat, or mega yacht, seeing the Virgin Islands by sea feels like the way nature intended it. Most visitors take to the waters at some point in their trip, cruising to big-shouldered islands or exploring uninhabited cays. For many, it's the most peaceful and relaxing way to travel the Virgins.

o **Waking Up to Tropical Birdsong and Roosters Crowing:** No matter where you are on the islands, you will be accompanied by the musical chatter of tropical birdsong, from the twittering of colorful birds to the morning, noon, and night cock-a-doodle-dooing of roadside roosters in splendid plumage of gold, green, and blue.

o **Swimming with Turtles and Starfish:** The Virgins' undersea marine habitat is as beauteous as its scenic topography, making this a stupendous place to sightsee beneath the waves. Look for hawksbill turtles grazing on seagrass, angelfish darting in and out of rocks, and starfish stretching out on sandy sea bottoms.

o **Kicking Back with Serious Views:** The islands' curvaceous terrain is truly swoon-worthy, and practically every island has restaurants, cafes, and bars that take full advantage of the panoramic views. Claim your perch (and a cool rum punch) at places like the **Mafolie restaurant,** overlooking the glittering harbor in Charlotte Amalie (St. Thomas; p. 62); **Bananakeet,** 400 feet above the north shore beaches of Tortola (p. 163); or the **Hilltop Restaurant at Biras Creek,** on Virgin Gorda, high over the inky-blue North Sound (p. 178).

o **Celebrating the Solstice with Full-Moon Beach Parties:** Locals and visitors come out to play for the islands' monthly full-moon celebrations. The most celebrated are on Tortola, from **Bomba's Full Moon Party** on Cappoon Bay (p. 171) to artist Aragorn's **Fireball Full Moon Party** at Trellis Bay (p. 171).

THE best BEACHES

The Virgin Islands are known for beautiful beaches of soft white sand and azure seas. Best of all, every beach is open to the public and, with a few exceptions, free. Even private resorts—which often command some of the prettiest stretches of sand—are required to offer public access to their beaches.

o **Magens Bay Beach** (St. Thomas): This long, half-mile stretch of soft sand, boasting remarkably calm waters, is the most popular and picturesque beach on St. Thomas. Two peninsulas protect the shore from erosion and strong waves, making Magens an ideal spot for swimming. Expect a crowd in the high season. See p. 67.

o **Lindquist Beach** (St. Thomas): A lovely, undeveloped beach on the East End, Lindquist is only reachable by a dirt road; it's a favorite of locals who make Sundays here a lively beach day. See p. 69.

o **Trunk Bay** (St. John): St. John has so many good beaches it's almost impossible to pick the best, but this, the island's most popular beach, is protected by the U.S. National Park Service and has an underwater snorkeling trail. See p. 136.

o **Sandy Point** (St. Croix): The biggest beach in the U.S. Virgin Islands, Sandy Point is a beauty—the final, redemptive scene of "The Shawshank Redemption" was filmed here. Because the beach is a protected reserve and a nesting spot for

If you're trying to decide which Virgin Island to visit, consider the following basics:

o American citizens don't need a **passport** to enter the U.S. Virgins, but everyone needs a passport to enter the British Virgin Islands.

o The U.S. Virgin Islands are **easier to reach** for most people. Currently, there are no direct flights on commercial carriers from North America or Europe to Tortola or any of the other British Virgin Islands. St. Thomas is the gateway to the islands, with major carriers connecting into the island's international airport.

o You'll have **more hotels and resorts** to choose from in the U.S. Virgin Islands, of all sizes and price ranges, than are in the B.V.I.

o The **U.S. dollar** is the official currency for both island chains, and **English** is the official language.

The obvious issues aside, American and British cultures have left different imprints on the Virgin Islands. The classic knock on the U.S. Virgins is that they're overbuilt and over-commercialized and not "virgins" anymore. Yes, **St. Thomas** offers a somewhat Americanized hurly-burly, with easy access to familiar global brands and a wide range of goods and services. But this is no fast-paced megalopolis—chickens still skitter along

hillsides and tropical foliage blankets the landscape with a fetching unruliness.

St. Croix has big commercial chains like Home Depot and K-Mart, but it also has bucolic stretches of rural countryside, a uniquely rich culture, and an earthy sensuality. With two-thirds of its terrain protected national parkland, **St. John** is a haven of undeveloped tranquillity.

Still, the **British Virgin Islands** are noticeably sleepier and less developed. Many of them recall the way the Caribbean was before the advent of high-rise condos, fast-food chains, and mega cruise ships—and being a little remote hasn't hurt. **Tortola** is where the B.V.I. action is, limited as its shopping and nightlife may be (although traffic gridlock has found its ornery way here, particularly in the B.V.I. capital, Road Town, on cruise-ship days). To the east, beautiful, pristine **Virgin Gorda** has just 3,000 inhabitants but most of the Virgin Islands' top resorts. Crime is minimal here. You'll find an even more laidback vibe on less-populated islands like **Jost Van Dyke** and **Anegada**, as well as uninhabited isles with hidden coves and beaches where you may be the only sunbather. It's a sailor's paradise.

In truth, the days of traveling to one versus the other are pretty much history. Most people who visit the Virgins touch down on both U.S. and British soil. Plus, the region's dependency on tourism has made it increasingly easier to hop between islands. For suggested itineraries between the islands, see chapter 2.

endangered sea turtles, it's open to the public only on Saturdays and Sundays from 10am to 4pm. See p. 106.

o **Cane Garden Bay** (Tortola): A scenic beauty, Cane Garden Bay is the most popular beach on Tortola. Its translucent waters and sugar-white sands attract crowds (especially when cruise ships drop off van loads of beachgoers), but it offers plenty of sand to play on. Across the water is Jost Van Dyke; rising behind the beach are green hillsides dotted with villas. See p. 165.

o **Smuggler's Cove** (Tortola): This fetching West End beach is reached by driving down a (largely) dirt road through a grove of mature palm trees. It's got good snorkeling but no facilities.

o **Savannah Bay** (Virgin Gorda): Just around the corner from the beach at Little Dix Bay is this often-deserted gem, with gin-clear waters and a crescent slice of soft white sand.

o **Anegada:** The second-largest island in the B.V.I. is the most remote of the Virgins and home to only 200 permanent citizens. It's the island chain's only coral island as well, which makes it one big, beautiful stretch of (largely undeveloped) powdery sand.

o **White Bay,** Guana Island (Guana Island): This pretty-as-a-picture ivory beach is fringed in palm trees and rising green hills.

THE best SNORKELING SPOTS

o **Coki Point Beach** (St. Thomas): On the north shore of St. Thomas, Coki Point offers superb year-round snorkeling. Explore the coral ledges near Coral World's underwater tower. See p. 68.

o **Hurricane Hole** (St. John): You may not immediately think of a mangrove forest as a great place to snorkel, but here coral grows in abundance on the mangrove roots—attended by huge starfish, sponges (and the hawksbills that eat them), and anemones. It's magical. **SerenaSea** runs snorkeling and sightseeing tours out of Coral Bay to Hurricane Hole (http://serenasea.com). See p. 139.

o **Waterlemon Cay/Leinster Bay** (St. John): Easily accessible Leinster Bay, on the northern shore of St. John, offers calm, clear, uncrowded waters teeming with sea life. See p. 139.

o **Haulover Bay** (St. John): A favorite with locals, this small bay is rougher than Leinster, with a pebbly beach. The snorkeling, however, is dramatic, with ledges, walls, and nooks to explore. See p. 139.

o **Cane Bay** (St. Croix): One of the island's best diving and snorkeling sites is off this breezy, north-shore beach. On a good day, you can swim out 450 feet to see the Cane Bay Wall, which drops dramatically off to the deep waters below. Multicolored fish, plus elkhorn and brain coral, flourish here. See p. 106.

o **Buck Island** (off St. Croix): This tiny island, whose land and offshore waters together are classified as a national monument, lies 2 miles off the north coast of St. Croix. More than 250 recorded species of fish swim through its reef system. A variety of sponges, corals, and crustaceans also inhabit the area. See p. 119.

o **Norman Island & the Indians** (B.V.I.): Snorkel the calm waters of the Bight near Norman Island. Bring some bread to draw reef fish to the surface when you snorkel the deep waters around the Indians—four fingers of rock jutting out of the sea and only accessible by boat. See p. 170.

o **The Baths** (Virgin Gorda): It's often overrun with boats, but the Baths—and nearby beaches, Spring Bay and Devil's Bay—are still mind-blowingly beautiful and the shallow crystalline seas and caves a fun place to explore by snorkel. See p. 179.

THE best DIVE SITES

o **Cow and Calf Rocks** (St. Thomas): This site, off the southeast end of St. Thomas (about a 45-min. boat ride from Charlotte Amalie), is the island's best diving spot.

It's also a good bet for snorkeling. You'll discover a network of coral tunnels filled with caves, reefs, and ancient boulders encrusted with coral. See p. 71.

o **The Cane Bay Wall** (St. Croix): Walk right off the beach into one of the most awesome dives in the Virgins. It's just a 100-yard swim to the 3,000-foot vertical wall at Cane Bay. Even at depths of 30 feet, you'll see coral gardens abloom with fantastical formations and colorful tropical life. See p. 106.

o **Frederiksted Pier** (St. Croix): The Fredriksted pier is one of the best spots in the islands for an electric night dive, where you plunge right offshore into a world of exotic creatures, including sea horses, lobster, and octopuses. See p. 109.

o **The Wreck of the RMS _Rhone_** (off Salt Island, B.V.I.): Many people think the _Rhone_ wreck is the premier dive site not only in the Virgin Islands, but in the entire Caribbean. This royal mail steamer, which went down in 1867, was featured in the film "The Deep." See p. 169.

o **_Chikuzen_** (off Tortola): Although it's not the _Rhone_ (see above), this 269-foot steel-hulled refrigerator ship, which sank off the island's east end in 1981, is one of the British Virgin Islands' most fascinating dive sites. The hull—still intact under about 24m (79 ft.) of water—is now home to a vast array of tropical fish, including yellowtail, barracuda, black-tip sharks, octopus, and drum fish. See p. 169.

o **Alice in Wonderland** (Ginger Island, off Tortola): This brilliant coral wall, off the shore of a tiny island, slopes from 12m (39 ft.) to a sandy bottom at 30m (98 ft.). Divers often refer to the site as "a fantasy" because of its monstrous overhangs, vibrant colors, gigantic mushroom-shaped corals, and wide variety of sea creatures—everything from conch and garden eels to long-nose butterfly fish. See p. 169.

THE best NATURE WALKS

o **The Annaberg Historic Trail** (St. John): This paved walk is only .25 miles long, but it's a highlight of the 10,000-acre U.S. Virgin Islands National Park. The trail traverses the ruins of what was once the most important sugar-cane plantation on the island. Slaves' quarters, a windmill tower, and ballast-brick buildings are remnants of a long-vanished era. Stunning views look toward Tortola and Jost Van Dyke on the opposite side of Sir Francis Drake Passage. See p. 140.

o **The "Rain Forest" Hike** (St. Croix): At the northwestern end of St. Croix lies the 15-acre "rain forest," dense with magnificent tropical foliage. The little-traveled four-wheel-drive roads through the area make great hiking paths. See p. 107.

o **Virgin Gorda Peak** (Virgin Gorda): Trek to the top of the island's highest peak, Virgin Gorda (414m/1,359 ft.), on this 50-minute round-trip hike through tropical forest. The views from the top are utterly breathtaking—you'll have views of both the Caribbean and Atlantic oceans. See p. 180.

o **The Sage Mountain National Park Hike** (Tortola): This 3- to 4-hour hike is one of the most dramatic in the British Virgins. It goes from Brewer's Bay to the top of Mount Sage, the highest peak in the Virgin Islands, at 523m (1,716 ft.). Along the way, you'll see intriguing ruins of old homes in addition to the beautiful flora and fauna of the park's primeval forest. See p. 168.

THE best RESORTS

o **The Buccaneer** (St. Croix): Family-owned and built around the historic ruins of an old sugar plantation, this St. Croix resort is a class act, stretching over so many rolling acres that it comfortably encompasses an 18-hole golf course, eight championship tennis courts, a spa and health club, a 2-mile jogging trail, and three scenic beaches. See p. 93.

o **Caneel Bay** (St. John): Laurance S. Rockefeller created Caneel Bay as the Caribbean's first eco-resort back in the days when no one knew what that word meant. It's an understated classic, an outpost of refinement without ostentation, and operating at the top of its game. The resort's low-rise, low-impact structures front some of the island's best beaches. See p. 125.

o **Biras Creek Resort** (Virgin Gorda): The ultimate in serene privacy, this resort is built around an old hillside fortress that's high up overlooking the liquid expanse of North Sound. It's an escapist's hideaway, no question, with luxe rooms, bicycles to breeze around in, and Boston whalers to comb North Sound on your very own. There are no phones or TVs, but who needs it when you've got iguanas, chickens, brilliant Atlantic Ocean surf, and a thousand stars above to sing you to sleep? See p. 174.

o **The Ritz-Carlton** (St. Thomas): This is the top-tier place to stay on St. Thomas. Overseen by a grand Italianate palazzo and fronted by white-sand beaches, this full-service resort offers the kind of manicured comfort that's luxurious if somewhat generic; still, rooms and suites are spacious and outfitted with sumptuous bathrooms and top-of-the-line amenities. See p. 56.

o **Bitter End Yacht Club** (Virgin Gorda): Entertaining a lively scrum of sailors, families, and beach lovers, this sailing and diving resort opens onto North Sound, one of the most unspoiled deepwater harbors in the Caribbean. It feels a little like a rakish colonial outpost, with boats coming and going and an open-air lobby straight out of a Somerset Maugham tale, but it's also a peaceful getaway, with luxury treehouse-style lodgings high above the seas. See p. 175.

o **Frenchmans B.V.I.** (Tortola): The top lodging on Tortola, this small boutique property combines all the perks of a resort—including a topnotch restaurant—with the seclusion of a private villa. All cottages face the blue sweep of Frenchman's Bay, with pelicans whirling and diving and terraces kissed by warm tradewinds. See p. 158.

o **Guana Island** (Guana Island): Of all the very fine resorts in the B.V.I., this private island eco-retreat may be *ne plus ultra* in terms of sheer comfort and romantic seclusion, even if it's a glorious and gracious throwback to the days before technological intrusions ruled daily life. This is rustic old-school luxury, where the service is hushed and impeccable, and the sea breezes are the best air-conditioning you'll ever need. See p. 189.

o **Rosewood Little Dix Bay** (Virgin Gorda): Warm service and understated elegance make this wonderful, 494-acre resort popular with families, older couples, and honeymooners alike. It celebrated its 50th anniversary in 2014. This impeccably run property offers sporting activities galore, the best spa in the Virgin Islands, and, in the beautiful wooden Pavilion, the bonhomie heart of the resort, a fizzy and convivial place to wine and dine. See p. 176.

THE best FAMILY RESORTS

o **Bolongo Bay Beach Resort** (St. Thomas): This fun and laidback place, right on the beach, has lots of sand to run around on, water sports aplenty, and a happening restaurant with a lively weekly Carnival. All of the 62 rooms face the beachfront, each with balcony or terrace. See p. 56.

o **Westin St. John Resort & Villas** (St. John): This contemporary mega-resort, set on 34 acres of neatly landscaped grounds and fronting a nice beach with gentle seas, offers some of the best children's programs on the island and good watersports. See p. 128.

o **The Buccaneer** (St. Croix): This longtime family favorite resort is packed with on-site facilities for just about every sport you can think of, including tennis, golf, swimming, jogging, sailing, scuba diving, and snorkeling. Children's programs include a half-day sail to Buck Island Reef and nature walks through tropical foliage, where kids can taste local fruit in the wild. See p. 93.

o **The Palms at Pelican Cove** (St. Croix): This small resort has something for everyone, but it has a lot to offer families, including the fact that all kids 17 and under stay for free in their parent's rooms And kids 10 and over are treated to complimentary scuba lessons. The resident iguana and pelican don't hurt either. See p. 105.

o **Long Bay Beach Club** (Tortola): Downsized to a boutique resort with just 42 rooms, this resort is spread out along a wonderful sandy beach licked by gentle waves—you can snorkel right off the beach. Its deluxe beachfront rooms can sleep five, and adjoining suites are available. Beachfront suites have full kitchens, and all rooms come with personal grills for impromptu family barbecues. See p. 159.

o **Bitter End Yacht Club** (Virgin Gorda): This lively resort is very kid-friendly, and its festive main restaurant, the Clubhouse, is ideal for noisy, chattering families planning a big day of water play. Most children's programs are geared toward those ages 6 and over and involve all the typical watersports: sailing, windsurfing, snorkeling, swimming, and more. See p. 175.

THE best BAREFOOT RETREATS

Some lodgings don't even try to tart up the place, preferring unvarnished barefoot charm to fancy frills, luxury amenities, and hermetically sealed interiors. It helps, of course, to have a glorious natural setting to prop up those bare feet. Old-school, the Caribbean the way it used to be, relaxed and comfortably rustic: The following places hum to the rhythms of the natural world.

o **Concordia Eco-Tents** (St. John): Overlooking Salt Pond Bay, these tent-cottages high up on a secluded hillside are kept cool by the constant trade winds. The resort is quiet and serene: You're pillowed in hundreds of acres of green national parkland. Got any complaints? See p. 126.

o **Cooper Island Beach Club** (Cooper Island): This escapist's retreat on remote Cooper Island is smartly designed and very comfortable, with 10 rooms in simple cottages built of reclaimed timber. It's "fan-ventilated"—that is, no A/C—and don't expect TV either. Do expect yachties and divers dropping in at the lively bar and restaurant. See p. 157.

o **Sandcastle Hotel** (Jost Van Dyke): This funky, unpolished hotel is perfect for devotees of laid-back getaways. The six phone- and TV-free cottages nestled in bougainvillea enjoy panoramic views of an idyllic white-sand beach. When you're not padding the beach in your bare feet, you can hit the famed beachside bar, the Soggy Dollar, home of the Painkiller cocktail. See p. 182.

o **Anegada Reef Hotel** (Anegada): This 20-room hotel is located on a flat mass of coral and limestone, one of the most remote spots in the entire Virgin Islands. Yes, rooms have been nicely freshened up, and you can blast the air-conditioning if you prefer it to ceiling fans. But it's still the kind of place where, if the bartender isn't around, you make your own cocktails and write down what you had. See p. 186.

THE best RESTAURANTS

o **Havana Blue** (Morning Star Beach Club at the Marriott Frenchman's Reef, St. Thomas): You would be forgiven if you thought the food would be relegated to a secondary role at this beachside restaurant, given the bombshell bar staff, sexy blue lighting, and thumping soundtrack. But someone very talented is in the kitchen. Yes, miso-glazed fish has been done since the dawn of time, but Havana Blue's iteration (with sea bass and lemongrass) is melt-in-the-mouth perfection. See p. 66.

o **Gladys' Cafe** (Charlotte Amalie, St. Thomas): Smack dab in the middle of tourist central, this local treasure is hidden away in plain sight in the maze of cobblestoned alleyways of Royal Dane Mall. Inside 18th-century walls of native stone, you'll dine on refined versions of Caribbean specialties (conch fritters, jerk fish, peas and rice) and surefire winners like avocado stuffed with lobster salad. Plus, Gladys makes her own hot sauce and even breaks into robust song whenever she feels like it. See p. 64.

o **Mafolie Restaurant** (Mafolie Hotel, St. Thomas): High up in the hills above Charlotte Amalie, with soul-stirring views of the twinkling lights of the harbor and beyond, this restaurant is a real find. Chef Manny Thompson is a masterful cook, and the owners are committed to the island's burgeoning farm-to-table movement. And those views! See p. 62.

o **Sunset Grille** (Secret Harbour Resort, St. Thomas): Serving some of the most flavorful and innovative dishes on the island, the Sunset Grille offers upscale dining in a quintessentially romantic Caribbean setting: overlooking the sandy beach and gentle waters of Secret Harbour. See p. 67.

o **ZoZo's** (Caneel Bay Resort, St. John): This marriage of superstars in late 2013 installed St. John's best Italian restaurant in one of the island's most thrilling locations: atop the ruins of an 18th-century sugar mill at Caneel Bay resort. It's a real mashup, where colonial Caribbean meets Frank Lloyd Wright and pumps out a sizzling Sixties-era James Bond vibe. See p. 133.

o **Kendrick's** (St. Croix): Kendrick's brings a light Continental touch to richly flavored dishes in a historic Danish building in Christiansted. See p. 102.

o **Brandywine** (Tortola): You'll find it down a winding dirt road along Brandywine Bay, an elegant stone treehouse serving equally elegant Mediterranean fare. See p. 164.

o **The Dove** (Tortola): One of the top special-occasion restaurants in Road Town is also one of the best restaurants in the entire Virgin Islands, serving a seasonal menu of continental classics. See p. 161.

o **Bananakeet** (Tortola): It's got stupendous views from its perch high up on Windy Hill, but the food and service keep folks raving. Plan at least one sunset dinner here. See p. 163.

o **The Pavilion** (Little Dix Bay, Virgin Gorda): Each night a different themed buffet is served in this soaring alfresco space—and it's all utterly fresh and absolutely delicious. See p. 178.

o **Hilltop Restaurant** (Biras Creek, Virgin Gorda): Dine on impeccably prepared continental classics (with Caribbean influences) as you practically touch the stars from your perch above North Sound. See p. 178.

THE best LOCAL BUYS

The U.S. Virgin Islands are rightfully known as the shopping mecca of the Caribbean. It's tempting indeed to comb the historic streets of St. Thomas's capital, Charlotte Amalie, in search of bargains amid the global outposts of "luxury" goods, those international brands of china and crystal, jewelry, and cosmetics that blanket every cruise port. The incentives are strong: Every person gets a $1,600 duty-free allowance and no sales tax is tacked on. But for those seeking original, artisanal gifts made by the people who actually live here, the following is a sampling of our favorite Virgin Islands mementos.

o **Aragorn's metal fireballs:** Any search for wonderful local art should start at **Aragorn's Studio** (p. 170) on Trellis Bay, Tortola. Tortola-born Aragorn is a printmaker, potter, and sculptor; his giant "fireballs"—silhouetted metal sculptures—are set ablaze during the monthly Fireball Full Moon Parties on Trellis Bay. Look for miniature fire balls (candle holders), beautiful original prints, pottery, jewelry, and gifts, the work of Aragorn, inhouse artisans, and regional artists.

o **Hot sauce:** Virgin Islanders love their hot sauce (aka "pepper" sauce), and many island cooks prepare and bottle their own. Look for local favorites like **Miss Anna's** (St. John), **Blind Betty's** (St. Croix), **Jerome's** (St. Thomas), and **ValleyDoll** (St. John), sold in gift shops and food stores around the islands. It's a real taste of the islands.

o **Moko Jumbie holiday ornaments:** A traditional presence at Carnival in St. Croix, Moko Jumbies are masked and costumed revelers on stilts. Glittery home-made Moko Jumbie ornaments are the handiwork of Cruzan native and "scrap-art designer" Sandra Michael; you can find her work in shops like **Franklin's on the Waterfront** in Fredriksted (p. 118).

o **Hand-blown recycled glass gifts:** Founded by local nonprofit GreenVI, this outdoor glass-blowing studio on Cane Garden Bay in Tortola recycles bottles of beer and booze discarded from the local beach bars to fashion beautiful hand-blown glass delicacies, from starfish paperweights to turtle ornaments to flower glass sculptures. The **GreenVI Glass Studio** has trained a number of locals in the intricacies of glass-blowing, and a local octogenarian makes cloth bags out of donated clothing to carry them home in (p. 170).

o **Local art:** Look for genre paintings by the accomplished artist **Joseph Hodge,** who has a studio in the **Craft Alive** artisans' village in Road Town, Tortola (p. 169). In Christiansted, St. Croix, the 40-year-old **Many Hands** gallery continues to feature original work by local artists and craftspeople (p. 117). In St. Thomas, you can find the latest work of local artisans (dolls, jewelry, soaps) in the **Native Arts and Crafts Cooperative** (p. 83).

SUGGESTED ITINERARIES

2

Sprinkled scattershot between the Caribbean and Atlantic oceans, the Virgin Islands mark the easternmost point of the Lesser Antilles. They're part of a necklace of islands that stretches southeast from Cuba and curls back west again at Trinidad and Tobago. Despite being the progeny of two different nations, the U.S. and British Virgin Islands have a brotherly closeness—not only are the islands a breezy ferry ride or plane hop away from one another, but you're almost always eyeballing another Virgin no matter where you are. From Jost Van Dyke you can watch the glittering lights of cars weave along the coastal road of St. Thomas; from Tortola's West End the broad-shouldered hills of St. John are a comforting constant. The two island chains share the same sparkling waterways, the same vibrant marine playgrounds, the same balmy tradewinds. The history of both the U.S. and British Virgins is inextricably linked with sugarcane and the slave trade—centuries-old plantation ruins throughout the islands tell part of the tale. You'll find the same classic island dishes on restaurant menus and hear the same lilting rhythms in ramshackle beach bars.

All of which is to say, no matter how long your Virgins vacation, you will most likely be touching down on both U.S. and British soil. It's easy to do so: Ferries connecting St. Thomas, St. John, Tortola, and Virgin Gorda run on a regular basis in season and even link some of the smaller islands, such as Anegada and Jost Van Dyke, albeit on a limited basis. (You'll need to fly or sail by private boat or charter to reach the more remote islands of the BVI.) Still, it's a stretch to say that everything here runs with the efficiency of a Swiss clock, so be sure to plot your itineraries around the frequency of public and private ferry schedules and interisland flights. Use the following suggested itineraries to kick-start your Virgin Islands vacation.

THE U.S. VIRGIN ISLANDS IN 10 DAYS

You could easily spend a week or more in each of the U.S. Virgins—St. Thomas, St. Croix, and St. John—and still have plenty more to do and see. But 3 days on each should give you a good sense of the flavorful character of each island. Refer to the individual chapters in this book to find the lodgings and restaurants best suited for you. Keep in mind that ferries between St. Thomas and St. John run regularly all day long (it's just a 20-min. trip from Red Hook on St. Thomas), but you will need to fly between St. Thomas and St. Croix—at least until regular ferry service between the two islands is rebooted.

Day 1: Arrive in St. Thomas

Check into your hotel and spend whatever time you have upon arrival relaxing or hitting the beach. If you're staying in Charlotte Amalie, call a taxi for dinner at the restaurant at **Mafolie Hotel** (p. 54), with stunning views of the glittering harbor below, or **Havana Blue** (p. 66), beachside at Marriott Frenchman's Reef.

Day 2: Take an Island Tour & Hit the Beach

Get the lay of the land on a full island tour with a tour operator or taxi driver. We recommend the services of taxi driver/tour guide extraordinaire **Campbell Rey** (✆ **340/771-1568**). Spend the afternoon on the beach. The island's top beach, **Magens Bay** (p. 67), is recommended if you like clear, gentle seas in a spectacular setting (and who doesn't?). If you want to snorkel, head to **Secret Harbour** (p. 68) or **Coki Beach** (p. 72). If you have kids in tow (and even if you don't), make time after exploring Coki Beach to visit **Coral World** (p. 78), the fun-filled aquarium next door.

Day 3: Shop the Historic District & Ride the Zipline

If shopping and historic architecture are high on your to-do list, spend the morning touring the cobblestone lanes in Charlotte Amalie—an especially easy proposition if you're staying in the area. Have lunch with the locals at **Gladys' Café** (p. 64) or the waterfront **Petite Pump Room** (p. 62), near the Charlotte Amalie ferry terminal. If you're game for adventure, you can spend the afternoon at the **Tree Limin' Extreme** (p. 72), a ziplining canopy tour in the rain forest of St. Peter Mountain; you'll have views of Magen's Bay and even Tortola and Jost Van Dyke. Combine a ziplining adventure with a visit to the tropical gardens of the **St. Peter Great House & Botanical Gardens** (p. 72), just across the street. It's a great spot for a sunset cocktail and even dinner.

Day 4: St. Croix ★★★ & West End Attractions

Take a morning flight from St. Thomas to St. Croix; air time: 25 minutes. If you're traveling by seaplane (from the St. Thomas seaport), you'll land right on the Christiansted waterfront—and you should explore the island's East End from here (see "Day 5," below). If you fly on regular air shuttle into the St. Croix airport, you'll be closer to West End must-see attractions like the **Estate Whim Plantation** (p. 116), the **St. George Village Botanical Garden** (p. 117), the **Ridge to Reef** rain-forest farm (p. 98), and the **Cruzan Rum Factory** (p. 116). In any event, arrange an airport pickup and island tour with one of the island's expert taxi driver/tour operators, such **Ames Joseph** (✆ **340/277-6133**). If it's a Saturday or Sunday, stop off (and take a dip at) at the beautiful beach at **Sandy Point** (p. 115; the wildlife refuge is only open on weekends, and is closed 7 days a week during turtle nesting season Apr–Sept). If you're staying at a beach resort, spend the rest of your afternoon swimming and relaxing.

Suggested Itineraries: The Virgin Islands

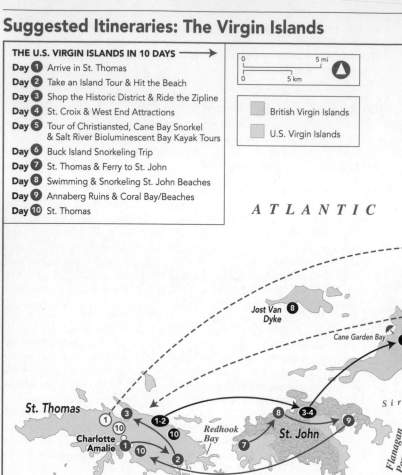

THE U.S. VIRGIN ISLANDS IN 10 DAYS ⟶

Day 1 Arrive in St. Thomas
Day 2 Take an Island Tour & Hit the Beach
Day 3 Shop the Historic District & Ride the Zipline
Day 4 St. Croix & West End Attractions
Day 5 Tour of Christiansted, Cane Bay Snorkel & Salt River Bioluminescent Bay Kayak Tours
Day 6 Buck Island Snorkeling Trip
Day 7 St. Thomas & Ferry to St. John
Day 8 Swimming & Snorkeling St. John Beaches
Day 9 Annaberg Ruins & Coral Bay/Beaches
Day 10 St. Thomas

British Virgin Islands
U.S. Virgin Islands

ATLANTIC

Jost Van Dyke

Cane Garden Bay

St. Thomas

Charlotte Amalie

Redhook Bay

St. John

Sir

Flanagan Passage

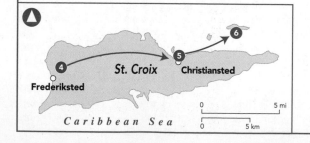

St. Croix

Frederiksted

Christiansted

Caribbean Sea

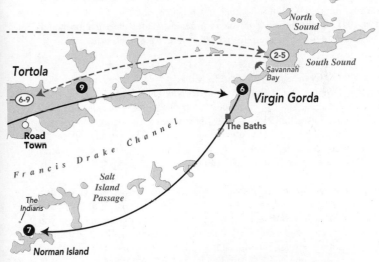

THE BRITISH VIRGIN ISLANDS IN 10 DAYS - - - - →

Day (1) Arrive in St. Thomas

Days (2-5) Virgin Gorda

Day (6-9) Tortola

Day (10) St. Thomas

Anegada

O C E A N

North Sound

(2-5) *South Sound*

Savannah Bay

Tortola

9

(6-9) ◄ **Virgin Gorda**

6

■ **The Baths**

○ **Road Town**

F r a n c i s   D r a k e   C h a n n e l

Salt Island Passage

The Indians

7 ◄

Norman Island

C a r i b b e a n   S e a

ISLAND HOPPING FOR 10 DAYS ⟶

Days 1-2 St. Thomas

Days 3-4 St. John

Day 5 Tortola: Road Town Tour & Cane Garden Bay

Day 6 Island Hop #1: The Baths & Savannah Bay

Day 7 Island Hop #2: Dive "Wreck Alley" or Snorkel Norman Island & the Indians

Day 8 Jost Van Dyke & Soper's Hole

Day 9 The East End & Shopping Trellis Bay

Day 10 St. Thomas

Day 5: Tour of Christiansted ★★, Cane Bay Snorkel ★★ & Salt River Bioluminescent Bay Kayak Tours ★★

Take a walking tour of historic Christiansted with an expert guide from **Crucian, Heritage & Nature Tourism** (**Chant;** p. 110) and have lunch in town. Alternatively, if you're an avid diver or snorkeler, you should spend the morning at **Cane Bay beach** (p. 106), on the island's north shore, where you can snorkel off the reefs or swim out 100 yards to a steep dropoff. If the moon cycle is right, schedule a see-through-kayak tour of the **bioluminescent bay** in the **Salt River National Historical Park and Ecological Reserve** (p. 115).

Day 6: Buck Island Snorkeling Trip ★★★

The only marine national park in the United States is well worth a day-trip of fine snorkeling, swimming, and hiking. A number of excursion companies, including **Big Beard's Adventure Tours** (p. 120), offer full and half-day sails to Buck Island National Reef Monument that often include beach barbecues. If you have time on your return, do a little shopping in Christiansted or head south to **ART-Farm** (p. 105), a combination vegetable farm stand and art gallery that opened in 2000 on an old cattle ranch along the island's picturesque south side.

Day 7: St. Thomas & Ferry to St. John ★★★

You may want to fly the seaplane out of St. Croix, which conveniently arrives at the seaplane terminal in Charlotte Amalie, located next door to the Charlotte Amalie ferry terminal. You can easily take a ferry to St. John from here or from the island's East End at Red Hook—that way you avoid a sometimes traffic-ridden taxi ride from the airport. If you plan to return to St. Thomas and stay on the island's East End for a night before flying out, schedule your round-trip ferry between Red Hook and St. John. The ferry from Red Hook to St. John is a pleasant 20-minute ride.

Depending on when you arrive, you may want to explore **Cruz Bay** (p. 123), the island's main town and your arrival point. It has lots of shops and waterfront eateries. St. John is a great place to rent a car for a few days, so you can fully explore its wonderful beaches and national parkland. But if you aren't renting a car, arrange ferry pickup/transfer—and an island tour—with a local taxi driver. We highly recommend Kenneth Lewis (✆ **340/776-6865**).

Day 8: Swimming & Snorkeling St. John Beaches ★★★

This is the day to **beach it,** and the island has an abundance of excellent strands of sand for swimming, snorkeling, and exploring. The island's most famous beach, **Trunk Bay** (p. 136), has an underwater snorkeling trail. Go to chapter 6 for more great beaches on St. John.

Day 9: Annaberg Ruins ★★ & Coral Bay/Beaches ★★

In the morning, take a tour of the **Annaberg sugar plantation ruins** (p. 136). Then hit the beach. Close to the ruins is **Waterlemon Cay** (p. 137), with great snorkeling and turtles; on the island's eastern side is **Hurricane Hole** (p. 139), where you can snorkel among a coral reef growing on mangroves—or head south to the quiet beach at **Little Lameshur Bay** (p. 137). Have a late lunch in the quaint little settlement of **Coral Bay,** about a 20-minute drive from Cruz Bay.

Sample homemade pulled-pork sandwiches and a rum punch at **Tourist Trap** (p. 142); juicy burgers in the honky-tonk atmosphere of **Skinny Legs** (p. 143); or the grilled jerk fish at **Shipwreck Landing.**

Day 10: St. Thomas

Plan your ferry trip back to St. Thomas around your departure itinerary.

THE BRITISH VIRGIN ISLANDS IN 10 DAYS

We guarantee that a 8-day week exploring the British Virgin Islands should erase all the stresses of modern civilization. Ten days to 2 weeks: Even better.

Day 1: Arrive in St. Thomas

Currently there are no direct flights into Tortola, the B.V.I.'s main island, from North America or Europe. For many people, St. Thomas (or, increasingly, San Juan) is the gateway to the British Virgin Islands. Remember to build time into your schedule to make the ferry or plane connections to your B.V.I. destination. Depending on your arrival into St. Thomas (or San Juan), that may include a night's stay-over.

Days 2–5: Virgin Gorda ★★★

We suggest starting your B.V.I. trip in Virgin Gorda, if the ferries (or plane connections) comply. If you're relying on ferries, you may have to take a ferry first to Tortola and then catch a second ferry to Virgin Gorda—the entire trip can take an hour or two, but being on the beautiful Virgin Islands waterways is a wonderful way to ease into the laidback island mentality.

Break up your Virgin Gorda stay into two parts: the Valley and the North Sound. We recommend first exploring the attractions in and around The Valley—the **Baths** (p. 179), **Savannah Bay** (p. 180), **Mahoe Bay** (p. 180)—with a stay in wonderful **Little Dix Bay** resort (p. 176), which also happens to have the **best spa** in the region. Then spend 2 nights exploring the island's other end with a stay at a North Sound resort—whether **Biras Creek** (p. 174), **Bitter End** (p. 175), or **Saba Rock** (p. 177). From there you can sail the North Sound, sunbathe on Prickley Pear Island,

Days 6–9: Tortola ★★★

The British Virgin Islands' largest and most populous island, Tortola has a leisurely sensibility, uncrowded beaches, and interesting historical attractions in its capital, **Road Town** (p. 149). Base yourself in the cliffside cottages at **Frenchmans Cay** (p. 158) or down on the beach at the **Long Bay Beach Club** (p. 159). Spend a couple of days exploring the island, swimming the gorgeous beach at **Cane Garden Bay** (p. 165), snorkeling at **Smuggler's Cove** (p. 23), or taking an island tour. We highly recommend the services of taxi driver/tour guide Wayne Robinson (ⓒ **284/494-4097**).

Tortola is also a great base from which to **island-hop ★★★**. Take a day-trip to **Norman Island and the Indians** (p. 167), **Jost Van Dyke** (p. 167), **Anegada** (p. 167), or any number of uninhabited isles just waiting for a castaway soul.

Day 10: St. Thomas

Fly or take a short (45- to 60-min.) ferry ride from Tortola to St. Thomas. Plan your return ferry trip back around your departure itinerary. Keep in mind that the Charlotte Amalie ferry terminal is much closer to the airport than the Red Hook terminal, and traffic gridlock between the island's East End and West End (where the St. Thomas airport is located) is not uncommon.

ISLAND-HOPPING FOR 10 DAYS

Anyone visiting the Virgin Islands for any length of time will want to take advantage of the region's smorgasbord of attractions and activities. Here's a 10-day trip for those who want to hit the highlights of both the U.S. and British Virgin Islands

Days 1 & 2: St. Thomas

Follow Days 2 and 3 in the "U.S. Virgins in 10 Days" itinerary, above.

Days 3 & 4: St. John

Take a ferry from St. Thomas (leaving from either the Charlotte Amalie or Red Hook terminals) to Cruz Bay on St. John. Follow Days 8 and 9 in the "U.S. Virgins in 10 Days" itinerary, above

Day 5: Tortola

Take a ferry from Cruz Bay in St. John to Tortola. If you're traveling between Cruz Bay and Tortola's West End, the total trip time should be under 30 minutes. Once on Tortola, take an island tour (see "The British Virgin Islands in 10 Days," above) and then settle in on one of the beaches close to your lodging. Use Tortola as a base for the rest of your B.V.I. trip. We recommend staying at one of the West End resorts or renting a villa for a week.

Day 5: Road Town Tour ★ & Cane Garden Bay ★★★

Take the morning to visit some of the Road Town's historical attractions, including the circa-1780 **SugarWorks museum** (p. 167), the **J. R. Neal Botanical Gardens** (p. 166), and old **Government House.** Don't miss the **mural** high up on Fahie Road (p. 166). Then grab your swimsuit and hit the beach at Cane Garden Bay, enjoying a late lunch on conch fritters and grilled fish at **Quito's Gazebo** (p. 164). Walk over to the **GreenVI Glass Studio,** the outdoor glass-blowing studio where recycled bottles of beer and booze are fashioned into beautiful hand-blown glass delicacies (p. 170). If the moon is full, join the monthly Full Moon Party at **Bomba Surfside Shack** (p. 171), in nearby Cappoons Bay.

Day 6: Island-Hop #1: The Baths ★★★ & Savannah Bay ★★★

Take a day-trip by boat from Tortola to the beaches in The Valley on Virgin Gorda. Explore the caves and boulders of the world-famous **Baths** and swim in the sparkling seas around **Devil's Bay** and **Spring Bay** (p. 180). For utter seclusion, round the bend and swim in the beautiful, clear seas of **Savannah Bay** and **Mahoe Bay** (p. 180).

Day 7: Island-Hop #2: Dive "Wreck Alley" ★★★ or Snorkel Norman Island & the Indians ★★★

Scuba divers can make a beeline (by boat or tour operator) to the area between Cooper and Salt islands known as **"Wreck Alley"**—a world-class diving spot filled with shipwrecks including the famed RMS *Rhone,* which went down in a hurricane in 1867 (p. 169). Snorkelers, on the other hand, can head to Norman Island, where they can snorkel the caves around "Treasure Isle" and the deep waters around the four fingers of rock known as the Indians. Have lunch on the beach at **Pirate's Bight** restaurant (p. 170).

Day 8: Jost Van Dyke ★★★ & Soper's Hole

Take a day-trip to the barefoot beaches of Jost Van Dyke or Anegada, both sparsely populated islands in the B.V.I. chain. Both islands have laidback restaurants and bars right on the beach; be sure to sample a Painkiller, the cocktail created at famed **Foxy's** (p. 184) in Jost. On your return to Soper's Hole, stop in and shop the marina stores.

Day 9: The East End & Shopping Trellis Bay

Spend a last leisurely day on Tortola by traveling the coastal highway to the island's East End, where you can shop the regional arts-and-crafts treasures at **Aragorn's Studio** (p. 170). If it's full moon time, don't miss the Fireball Full Moon Party here. On your way back west, stop in at **Brandywine Estate restaurant** (p. 164) for an elegant lunch or early dinner and maybe a dip in the calm waters of Brandywine Bay. Or just head to your West End resort and have a fabulous dinner nearby at the **Clubhouse at Frenchmans** (p. 162), the **Sugar Mill restaurant** (p. 163), or **Bananakeet** (p. 163).

Day 10: St. Thomas

Fly or take the short (45- to 60-min.) ferry ride from Tortola to St. Thomas. Plan your return ferry trip back around your departure itinerary. Keep in mind that the Charlotte Amalie ferry terminal is much closer to the airport than the Red Hook terminal, and traffic gridlock between the island's East End and West End (where the St. Thomas airport is located) is not uncommon.

THE VIRGIN ISLANDS IN CONTEXT

3

G olden beaches shaded by palm trees and crystalline waters teeming with rainbow-hued marine life are undoubtedly the main attractions in both the U.S. and British Virgin Islands. Most visitors will likely spend their days hanging out on the beach, playing in the blue seas, browsing boutiques, and savoring fresh-caught fish. But beneath the Carnival costumes and tourism baubles lies a fascinating history and rich culture. Like so many other islands in the Caribbean, the Virgin Islands were inextricably intertwined with the colonial ambitions of Western Europe and the slave trade in North America. This chapter offers a peek at the cultural and historical influences coursing just beneath the surface of any modern-day escape to the Virgin Islands. It also includes tips about the best times to visit and the myriad activities and tours available to you.

THE ISLANDS IN BRIEF

The islands described in detail below are the main inhabited islands and the most frequently visited in both the U.S. and British Virgin Islands. Use the information to help guide you to your own idea of paradise.

A few words about islands that aren't mentioned below: For those who really crave a secluded getaway, the British Virgin Islands have a number of escapist-friendly island islands such as **Peter Island, Necker Island,** and **Guana Island.** These are virtually private hideaways and the sole domain of expensive resorts. Two remote British Virgin Islands with small populations and limited commercial activity (but more democratically priced hotels) are **Anegada** and **Jost Van Dyke.** For more information on these islands, go to chapter 7.

No matter where you're staying in the Virgin Islands, you will definitely want to go **island-hopping** to visit the lesser-known islands—and even the more popular spots, like the Baths (Virgin Gorda), that are B.V.I. must-sees.

The U.S. Virgin Islands are located some 90 miles east of Puerto Rico, with a combined landmass roughly twice the size of Washington, D.C. Lying just 97km (60 miles) to the east of Puerto Rico, the British Virgin Islands comprise a total landmass of 153 sq. km (59 sq. miles), a little smaller than Washington, D.C.

The U.S. Virgin Islands

The U.S. Virgin Islands consist of three main islands: St. Thomas, St. John, St. Croix, plus a little islet called Water Island and several smaller islets.

ST. THOMAS

St. Thomas may be, as some say, the most "unvirgin" of the Virgin Islands, but few can deny the island's substantial physical attributes. The most developed of the U.S. Virgin Islands, St. Thomas is sprawling and mountainous, with breathtaking vistas and palm-fringed beaches. It's the commercial heart of the Virgin Islands, but it offers something for everyone, from duty-free shopping to sizzling nightlife to laidback aeries far from the hustling scrum. The harbor at Charlotte Amalie, the capital, bustles with the energy of a small city, especially when cruise ships are in port. This is one of the largest cruise-ship ports in the Caribbean. Do as the locals do and avoid the harbor area at rush hour or when the cruise-ship passengers disembark—when a long lineup of taxi drivers in big vans and open-air "safari" buses idle alongside the docks to spirit passengers to excursions around the island. The cruise-ship traffic also herds to the city's shopping bazaars and malls, chasing down some of the Caribbean's hottest duty-free shopping. Much of the retail action is found in the labyrinth of cobblestoned streets in the city's historic section, where the narrow lanes and picturesque old stone alleyways (built by the Danish) are packed with taxi vans and touts inviting shoppers in for a look. It's an intense beehive of activity during cruise-ship hours (roughly around 8am–4pm) and in high season, but every afternoon before dark the big ships slip back out to sea, and the city belongs once more to the locals and non-cruise-ship visitors.

St. Thomas may have a cosmopolitan sheen, but it's got a distinctively Caribbean pulse. Even here, where everyone seems to be breathlessly chasing the almighty dollar, island time rules. Yes, **Magens Bay Beach,** with its tranquil waves and long sweep of sugar-white sand, is likely to be packed on heavy cruise-ship days, but it's still a fetching swath of beach, surrounded on three sides by rising green hills. And if peace, quiet, and seclusion you're after, you'll find plenty of opportunity to relax and soak up the scenery, whether you've got your feet up on a powdery East End beach or enveloped in rain forest foliage on a mountain trail.

Yachts and boats anchor at **Yacht Haven Grande Marina** in Charlotte Amalie and at **American Yacht Harbor** in Red Hook on the island's eastern tip. The island attracts snorkelers and scuba divers—and there are outfitters aplenty offering equipment, excursions, and instruction. Kayaking and parasailing also draw beach bums into the gin-clear seas. The island also has a surprisingly good surfing spots, including Hull Bay.

St. Thomas has one of the most eclectic and sophisticated **restaurant scenes** in the Virgin Islands. Emphasis is on French and Continental fare, but the wide selection of

The Virgin Islands

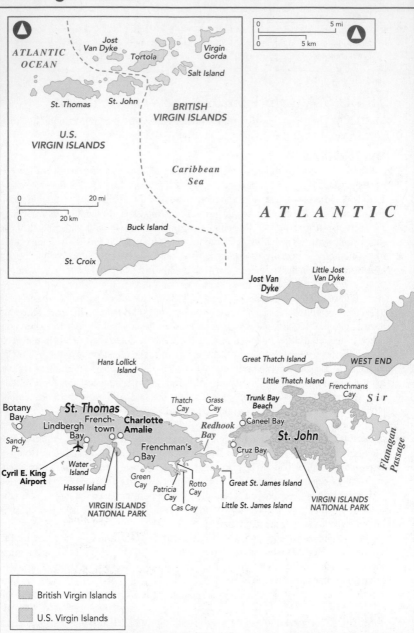

ATLANTIC OCEAN

Jost Van Dyke

Tortola

Virgin Gorda

Salt Island

St. Thomas   St. John

BRITISH VIRGIN ISLANDS

U.S. VIRGIN ISLANDS

Caribbean Sea

0   20 mi
0   20 km

0   5 mi
0   5 km

Buck Island

St. Croix

ATLANTIC

Jost Van Dyke

Little Jost Van Dyke

Great Thatch Island

WEST END

Little Thatch Island

Frenchmans Cay

Sir

Hans Lollick Island

Trunk Bay Beach

Botany Bay

St. Thomas

Thatch Cay

Grass Cay

Caneel Bay

Lindbergh Bay

French-town

Charlotte Amalie

Redhook Bay

St. John

Sandy Pt.

Frenchman's Bay

Cruz Bay

Flanagan Passage

Cyril E. King Airport

Water Island

Green Cay

Rotto Cay

Great St. James Island

Hassel Island

Patricia Cay

Cas Cay

Little St. James Island

VIRGIN ISLANDS NATIONAL PARK

VIRGIN ISLANDS NATIONAL PARK

British Virgin Islands

U.S. Virgin Islands

FLORIDA

BAHAMA
ISLANDS

*ATLANTIC
OCEAN*

0   300 mi

0   300 km

TURKS & CAICOS
ISLANDS

CUBA

VIRGIN ISLANDS

CAYMAN
ISLANDS

HAITI

DOMINICA
N REPUBLIC

PUERTO
RICO

JAMAICA

Caribbean Sea

Anegada

The Settlement

Prickly
Pear
Island

Necker Island

OCEAN

Mosquito
Island

*North
Sound*

Eustatia

Seal Dogs

George Dog

Great Camanoe

West Dog

Guana
Island

Scrub
Island

Great Dog

South Sound

Little
Camanoe

Marina Cay

Spanish
Town

Virgin Gorda

Tortola

EAST
END

Beef
Island

Francis Drake Channel

Fallen
Jerusalem

**Road
Town**

Cooper
Island

Round
Rock

*Salt
Island
Passage*

Ginger
Island

The
Indians

Salt
Island

Pelican
Island

Peter
Island

Norman Island

Caribbean   Sea

0   5 mi

0   5 km

Buck Island

Protestant
Cay

Green Cay

Frederiksted

St. Croix

Christiansted

**Henry E.
Rohlsen
Airport**

Caribbean Sea

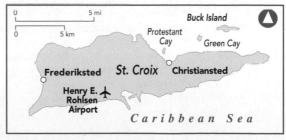

restaurants also includes options from West Indian and Italian to Asian. St. Thomas pays more for its imported (usually European) chefs and secures the freshest of ingredients from mainland or Puerto Rican markets. The island also hosts a number of American chain franchises, from Wendy's to Hooters—especially near the cruise-ship piers.

St. Thomas has a wide variety of **accommodations,** from small, historic B&Bs tucked into the hills overlooking glittering Charlotte Amalie to the full-service, manicured beachfront resorts in the East End. Apartment and villa rentals abound.

ST. CROIX

At 82 square miles, St. Croix is the largest island in the U.S. Virgins but it's sparsely populated for its size (some 54,000 people live here). It's mainly reached by plane, even from neighboring islands (it's more than an hour by boat from St. Thomas, a journey through deep and sometimes rough seas). St. Croix is developed, with good roads and the kinds of stores found in American suburbs, but it also has large swaths of rural farmland and a remote feel. Its two historic towns, **Frederiksted** and the capital, **Christiansted,** were built by the Danes during the sugarcane-plantation days, and Frederiksted's deep-water port brings a small number of cruise ships weekly to the island. St. Croix is also the only island that has a casino. Despite its nod to modernity, many of St. Croix's true West Indian–style buildings have been preserved, along with its rich cultural traditions.

One of the best reasons to take a trip to St. Croix, even if only for a day, is to visit **Buck Island National Park,** just 1½ miles off St. Croix's northeast coast. The island's offshore reef attracts snorkelers and divers. Signs posted along the ocean floor guide you through a forest of staghorn coral swarming with flamboyant fish.

St. Croix is a world-class diving destination, with a deep trench for wall-diving offshore and good diving (and snorkeling) around the cruise-ship pier in Frederiksted. It's also the premier golfing destination in the Virgin Islands, mainly because it boasts **Carambola,** the archipelago's most challenging 18-hole course. St. Croix is a tennis mecca, too: The **Buccaneer Hotel** has some of the best courts in the Virgin Islands and hosts several annual tournaments. Other sports for active vacationers include horseback riding, parasailing, sportsfishing, and water-skiing. It has one of the world's few healthy bioluminescent bays.

St. Croix is also gaining traction as a health-and-wellness destination, and practices what it preaches, with a growing presence in solar and wind energy and a boom in sustainable and organic farming.

The restaurants on St. Croix reflect the island's intriguing multicultural mix—the citizenry is comprised of a large Latino population (many Puerto Ricans and Dominicans migrated here in the mid–20th c.), the descendants of black slaves (Afro-Caribbean), mestivos, and expats from around the world. (It's the home of a healthy gay population as well.) You will find plenty of small, creative local eateries serving up dishes and snacks ranging from West Indian curries to French croissants. Life after dark is mostly confined to a handful of bars in Christiansted.

St. Croix has few fine hotels, but it does have attractive inns and B&Bs. Still, many people opt to rent villas and condos at often-reasonable weekly rates.

ST. JOHN

St. John is one breathtakingly beautiful island, with some of the most pristine beaches in the entire Caribbean. And it will likely stay that way: Two-thirds of the island are protected parkland, the **U.S. Virgin Islands National Park.** Guided walks and safari bus tours are available to help you navigate the park, which is full of secret coves, hiking trails, and the ghostly remains of sugar-cane plantations. A third of the park is underwater. **Trunk Bay,** which also boasts one of the island's finest beaches, has an amazing underwater snorkeling trail. As you can imagine, scuba diving is another major attraction on St. John.

St. John has a smattering of upscale restaurants, but for the most part you'll dine well in colorful West Indian eateries, many located on the charming little harbor of the island's main town, **Cruz Bay,** and many serving the region's fresh seafood. Nightlife isn't a major attraction here; it usually consists of sipping rum drinks in a bar in Cruz Bay, and maybe listening to a local calypso band. After spending a day outdoors, most visitors on St. John are happy to turn in early.

St. John has only two deluxe hotels and a sprinkling of charming inns. Most people who visit the island rent villas, houses, or condos or stay in one of the island's plethora of campgrounds. St. John is a popular day-trip for visitors to the other Virgin Islands, but it's not a cruise-ship destination per se—its port cannot accommodate the big ships. Cruise-ship passengers are usually day-trippers arriving by passenger ferry from ships anchored in St. Thomas.

The British Virgin Islands

The British Virgin Islands comprise some 60 islands, among them 15 inhabited. The total population of the B.V.I. is around 27,000 people.

TORTOLA

Tortola is the hub of the British Virgin Islands and a wonderful place to stay and use as your base to day-trip to outlying islands. Yes, Virgin Gorda (see below) is less developed and has better (and pricier) resorts and restaurants, and **Road Town,** the B.V.I. capital, is fairly charmless, with minor shopping, routine restaurants, and uninspired architecture—and the daily arrival of two or three cruise ships makes the morning traffic a real slog. But head west or east out of Road Town, and you'll find an alluring place, with some of the warmest and most soulful people in the islands and a dramatic topography, where the roads do racy arabesques around green peaks, and the vistas from on high are utterly ravishing.

The island's best and most unspoiled beaches, including **Smuggler's Cove** (with its secluded collection of snorkeling reefs), lie at the island's western tip and along the northern shoreline. Tortola's premier beach is **Cane Garden Bay,** a 2.4km (1½-mile) stretch of white sand bookended by rising green hills. Because of the clean, gentle surf and the smooth sand bottom, it's one of the safest places for families with small children—and there's plenty of ocean for everyone even on the busiest cruise-ship days. For hikers on Tortola, exploring **Sage Mountain National Park,** where trails lead to a 543m (1,781-ft.) peak that offers panoramic views, is a highlight. The park is rich in flora and fauna, from mamey trees to cooing mountain doves.

Although many visitors to the Caribbean look forward to fishing, hiking, horseback riding, snorkeling, and surfing, what makes Tortola exceptional is boating. It is *the* boating center of the British Virgin Islands, which are among the most cherished sailing territories on the planet. The island offers some 100 charter yachts and 300 bareboats, and its marina and shore facilities are the most up-to-date and extensive in the Caribbean Basin. It's a big reason why Tortola makes a great base from which to go island-hopping.

The food in Tortola is simple and straightforward, with menu staples of local fish, conch fritters, and fresh fruit juices (laced with rum, island-style). The nightlife is laidback, with **full-moon parties** on the beach and a roster of local musicians playing places like **Myett's** and **Quito's,** on Cane Garden Bay.

Tortola has just a couple of fine resorts and a few very basic hotels; many people who stay a while choose to rent villas, houses, or condos.

VIRGIN GORDA

Virgin Gorda is the third-largest member of the B.V.I. archipelago, with a permanent population of about 3,000 lucky souls. Virgin Gorda is uncrowded and incredibly scenic, with swooping roads that lace the tops of emerald peaks and some of the cleanest and clearest water on the planet. In fact, being on the water, whether under sail or with snorkel and mask, is the default mode on Virgin Gorda. It's a sun-and-sea worshiper's dream come true.

Many visitors come over just for a day to check out the **Baths,** an astounding collection of gigantic boulders and crystalline tide pools on the southern tip. Crafted by volcanic pressures millions of years ago, the rocks have eroded into almost sculptural shapes—and you can snorkel in turquoise pools that snake through the big boulders.

It may be small and its population sparse, but Virgin Gorda is home to some of the best hotels in the Virgin Islands and among the world's finest, including **Little Dix Bay** and **Biras Creek.** One caveat: You will pay dearly for the privilege of staying at one of these expensive resorts. Outside the upscale hotels, restaurants tend to be simple places serving local West Indian cuisine. No one takes nightlife too seriously on Virgin Gorda, so there isn't very much of it.

THE VIRGIN ISLANDS TODAY

The American way of life prevails today in the U.S. Virgin Islands, and it has swept across to the British Virgin Islands, as well. The region's traditional recipes and remedies, as well as many of the self-reliant arts of fishing, boat-building, farming, and even hunting, are fading away. When islanders need something, they have it shipped from Miami. In clothes, cars, food, and entertainment, America, not Great Britain, rules the seas around both archipelagos. The British Virgins even use the U.S. dollar as their official currency, instead of British pounds.

Like the rest of the world, the Virgin Islands have felt the effects of the global recession. Tourism is rebounding, but the islands—like the rest of the Caribbean—have not seen the same number of visitors as they had prior to the recession. To attract tourists, the government officials have come to realize that the natural environment must be protected. During the 1980s, the islands, especially St. Thomas, experienced a real estate boom, and much of the island's natural terrain was converted into shopping malls and condo complexes. Caroline Brown, of the Environmental Association of St. Thomas, even issued a dire warning that islanders may find themselves one day "living in a concrete jungle." Today, awareness of the perils of overdevelopment has seeped into the collective consciousness, and protecting the environment—and curbing overdevelopment—has become a primary concern in the Virgin Islands. The B.V.I., for example, has done added 10 new parks, including the Anegada Nature Reserve, to its

A 51ST state?

The U.S. Virgin Islands are an unincorporated territory administered by the U.S. Department of the Interior. Politically speaking, the Virgin Islands, like Puerto Rico, remain outside the family of the United States. They are only permitted to send a nonvoting delegate to the U.S. House of Representatives. U.S. Virgin Islanders are not allowed to vote in national elections, a sore spot among some of the local residents. Many hope to see another star added to the American flag in the near future—feeling that only full statehood will provide the respect, power, and influence needed to turn the islands into more than just a "colony." Progress in this direction moves sluggishly along, if at all.

When the 1936 Organic Act of the Virgin Islands was passed under the Roosevelt administration, residents ages 21 and over were granted suffrage and could elect two municipal councils and a legislative assembly for the islands. In 1946, the first black governor of the islands, William Hastie, was appointed. By 1970, the U.S. Virgin Islanders had the right to elect their own governor and lieutenant governor.

existing national park system, which includes the Gorda Peak National Park and the Devil's Bay National Park on Virgin Gorda and the Sage Mountain National Park on Tortola. St. John, the smallest of the U.S. Virgin Islands, is the most protected landmass in the Caribbean, with some 60 percent of its acreage directly controlled by the U.S. National Park Service (and more parcels added on an ongoing basis).

On St. Thomas, the friction between developers and environmentalists was recently encapsulated in the battle over the future of the 400 acres surrounding Botany Bay. The area, on the western end of St. Thomas, has long been a refuge from the bustle of Charlotte Amalie, the capital. This undeveloped property (a private estate closed to the public for some 80 years) was a conservation area of sorts for deer, and a nesting ground for sea turtles, ringed by some of the healthiest coral reefs around St. Thomas. When it was first proposed in 2001, the development of a gated beachfront resort complex—The Preserve at Botany Bay—with a luxury hotel, timeshare condos, and sprawling home sites, was greeted with opposition from environmentalists and became a hot-button political topic. It felt as if much of the future of the islands was riding on what happened at Botany Bay. Some 5 years later, after developers reduced the density of the development and agreed to specific Coastal Zone Management division (CZM), requests (such as providing a walking path for public shoreline access and producing a booklet for future homeowners on preserving and protecting the area's unique environment), the U.S.V.I. Dept. of Planning & Natural Resources gave the green light to the development of the multi-use Preserve at Botany Bay.

Flash forward to late 2013: Although the hotel arm of the project remained at a standstill, a number of villas and homes had been completed, many commanding the hillsides overlooking Botany Bay. "The Wall Street Journal" reported that a "pirate-themed" six-bedroom villa in the Preserve at Botany Bay was on the market for $35 million.

LOOKING BACK: VIRGIN ISLANDS HISTORY

A Brief History

Christopher Columbus is credited with "discovering" the Virgin Islands in 1493, but, in fact, they had already been inhabited for 3,000 years. It is believed that the original settlers were the nomadic Ciboney Indians, who migrated from the mainland of South America and lived off the islands' fish and vegetation. The first real homesteaders were the peaceful Arawak Indians, who arrived from Venezuela, presumably in dugout canoes with sails.

For about 500 years, the Arawaks occupied the Virgin Islands, until the arrival of the cannibalistic Carib Indians in the 15th century. The Caribs destroyed the Arawaks, either by working them to death as slaves or by eating them. With the advent of European explorers and their diseases, these tribes were completely wiped out.

The Age of Colonization

In November 1493, on his second voyage to the New World, Columbus spotted the Virgin Islands, naming them *Las Once Mil Virgenes,* after the Christian St. Ursula and her martyred maidens. Short of drinking water, he decided to anchor at what is now Salt River on St. Croix's north shore. His men were greeted by a rainfall of arrows. Embittered, Columbus called that part of the island *Cabo de Flechas,* or "Cape of the Arrows," and sailed toward Puerto Rico.

As the sponsor of Columbus's voyage, Spain claimed the Virgin Islands; however, with more interest in the Greater Antilles, Spain chose not to colonize the Virgins, leaving the door open to other European powers. In 1625, both the English and the Dutch established opposing frontier outposts on St. Croix. Struggles between the two nations for control of the island continued for about 20 years, until the English prevailed (for the time being).

DATELINE

1493 Columbus sails by the Virgin Islands, lands on St. Croix, and is attacked by Carib Indians.

1625 Dutch and English establish frontier outposts on St. Croix.

1650 Spanish forces from Puerto Rico overrun English garrison on St. Croix.

1653 St. Croix taken over by the Knights of Malta.

1671 Danes begin settlement of St. Thomas.

1672 England adds British Virgin Islands to its empire.

1674 King Louis XIV of France makes St. Croix part of his empire.

1717 Danish planters from St. Thomas cultivate plantations on St. John.

1724 St. Thomas is declared a free port.

1733 Danish West India Company purchases St. Croix from France; slaves revolt on St. John.

As the struggle among European powers widened, the islands continued to function as a battleground. In 1650, Spanish forces from Puerto Rico overran the British garrison on St. Croix. Soon after, the Dutch invaded; in 1653, the island fell into the hands of the Knights of Malta, who gave St. Croix its name.

However, these aristocratic French cavaliers weren't exactly prepared for West Indian plantation life, and their debts quickly mounted. By 1674, King Louis XIV of France took control of St. Croix and made it part of his kingdom.

The English continued to fight Dutch settlers in Tortola, which was considered the most important of the British Virgin Islands. It wasn't until 1672 that England added the entire archipelago to its growing empire.

A year before, in March 1671, the Danish West India Company made an attempt to settle St. Thomas. The company sent two ships, but only one, the *Pharaoh,* completed the voyage, with about a third of its crew. Eventually, reinforcements arrived, and by 1679, at least 156 Europeans were reported to be living on St. Thomas, along with their slaves. Captain Kidd, Sir Francis Drake, Blackbeard, and other legendary pirates of the West Indies continued to use St. Thomas as their base for maritime raids in the area. Its harbor also became famous for its slave market.

In 1717, Danish planters sailed to St. John from St. Thomas to begin cultivating plantations. By 1733, an estimated 100 sugar, tobacco, and cotton plantations were operating on the island. That same year, the slaves rebelled against their colonial masters, taking control of the island for about 6 months and killing many Europeans. It took hundreds of French troops to quell the rebellion.

3

THE VIRGIN ISLANDS IN CONTEXT | Looking Back: Virgin Islands History

1792 Denmark announces plans to abandon the slave trade.

1807–15 England occupies Danish Virgin Islands.

1820s Sugar plantations on the Virgin Islands begin to see a loss in profits.

1834 England frees 5,133 slaves living in British Virgin Islands.

1848 Under pressure, the governor of St. Croix grants slaves emancipation.

1867 First attempt by the United States to purchase the Virgin Islands from the Danish.

1872 British Virgin Islands put under administration of the Federation of the Leeward Islands.

1916 Denmark signs treaty with the U.S. and sells islands for $25 million.

1917 Virgin Islands fall under the control of the U.S. Navy for 14 years.

1927 United States grants citizenship to island residents.

continues

In that same year, France sold St. Croix to the Danish West India Company, which divided the island into plantations, boosting the already flourishing slave trade. Some historians say that nearly 250,000 slaves were sold on the auction blocks at Charlotte Amalie before being sent elsewhere, often to America's South. By 1792, Denmark changed its tune and announced that it officially planned to end the slave trade. It was not until 1848, however, that it did so. The British had freed their 5,133 slaves in 1834.

The great economic boom that resulted from the Virgin Islands plantations began to wilt by the 1820s. The introduction of the sugar beet virtually bankrupted plantation owners, as the demand for cane sugar drastically declined. Cuba eventually took over the sugar market in the Caribbean. By 1872, the British had so little interest in the British Virgins that they placed them in the loosely conceived and administered Federation of the Leeward Islands.

Enter the United States

In 1867, the United States attempted to purchase the islands from Denmark, but the treaty was rejected by the U.S. Senate in 1870; the asking price was $7.5 million. Following its acquisition of Puerto Rico in 1902, the United States expressed renewed interest in acquiring the Danish islands. This time, the United States offered to pay only $5 million, and the Danish parliament spurned the offer.

On the eve of its entry into World War I, the U.S. Navy began to fear a possible German takeover of the islands. The United States was concerned that the Kaiser's navy, using the islands as a base, might prey on shipping through the Panama Canal. After renewed attempts by the United States to purchase the islands, Denmark agreed to sell them in 1916 for $25 million, a staggering sum to pay for island real estate in those days.

By 1917, the United States was in full control of the islands, and Denmark retreated from the Caribbean after a legacy of nearly 2½ centuries. The U.S. Navy looked after the islands for 14 years, and in 1954, they came under the sovereignty of the U.S. Department of the Interior.

1936 Under Franklin Roosevelt, the first Organic Act is passed, granting voting rights to U.S. Virgin Islanders.

1940 Population of U.S. Virgin Islands increases for the first time since 1860 because of its use as a port during World War II.

1946 First black governor of the U.S.V.I., William Hastie, is appointed.

1954 Revised Organic Act passed; the U.S.V.I. fall under jurisdiction of Department of the Interior.

1956 British Virgins released from the Federation of the Leeward Islands.

1966 Queen Elizabeth II visits the British Virgin Islands.

1967 B.V.I. get a new constitution.

1980s U.S.V.I. see major development and construction, putting natural resources at risk.

1989 Hurricane Hugo rips through the islands, hitting St. Croix especially hard.

Some money was diverted to the area during the Prohibition era, as some islanders made rum and shipped it illegally to the United States, often through Freeport, in the Bahamas. In 1927, the United States granted citizenship to the island residents. In 1936, under Franklin Roosevelt, the first Organic Act was passed, giving the islanders voting rights in local elections. This act was revised in 1954, granting them a greater degree of self-government.

Jobs generated by World War II finally woke the islands from their long economic slumber. The U.S.V.I. were used as a port during the war, and visitors first started to appear on the islands. In the postwar economic boom that swept across America, the Virgin Islands at long last found a replacement for sugar cane.

The British Virgin Islands Develop

The British Virgin Islands were finally freed from the Leeward Islands Federation in 1956, and in 1966, Queen Elizabeth II visited this remote colonial outpost. By 1967, the British Virgin Islands had received a new constitution. Tourism was slower to come to the British Virgins than to the U.S. Virgin Islands, but it is now the mainstay of the economy.

In 2000, the British government issued a report that found that nearly 41 percent of offshore companies in the world were formed in the British Virgin Islands. By 2011, the B.V.I. was one of the world's leading offshore financial centers, and the local population boasted one of the highest incomes per capita in the Caribbean—at around $40,000 per family.

Tourism & the Economy Today

The economy of both the British and the U.S. Virgins has been one of the most stable and prosperous in the Caribbean. All of the islands felt the impact of the worldwide economic slump, however, with a falloff in tourism and revenues.

In the meantime, the governments of both the British Virgins and the U.S. Virgins continue to struggle with unemployment as they mount ongoing struggles to reduce crime and to protect the environment. The U.S. Virgin Islands were awarded $364

1995 Hurricane Marilyn causes millions of dollars of damage and leaves thousands homeless.

1996 Water Island, off the coast of St. Thomas, is officially declared the fourth U.S. Virgin Island; U.S. Senate grants permission for two casino hotels to be built on St. Croix.

2000 St. Croix becomes the first "casino island" in the Virgin Islands.

2005 Plans stall for grand development of St. Thomas.

2008 B.V.I. become one of the world's leading offshore financial centers.

2009 Islands experience drop-off in tourism as U.S. economy goes into recession.

2010 U.S.V.I. officials tackle environmental problems.

THE DANES ARE GONE BUT THEIR
architecture STILL STANDS

Some of the architectural legacy left by the colonizing Danes still remains in the islands, especially in Christiansted and Frederiksted on St. Croix, and in Charlotte Amalie on St. Thomas.

Many of the commercial buildings constructed in downtown Charlotte Amalie are restrained in ornamentation. Pilasters and classical cornices were commonplace on many buildings. Most door arches and windows were framed in brick. To "dress up" a building, ornamentation, such as cornices, was added in the final stages. The walls were covered with plaster, but in recent decades this plaster and stucco have been stripped from the walls. Underneath the rubble, well-designed shapes and patterns of old brick and "blue bitch"—a native stone made of volcanic tuff—were discovered. The old masons may have known what they were doing. Once stripped of their plaster coating, the walls don't stand up well in the Caribbean sun and salt air. Cast-iron grillwork on some of the second-floor overhanging balconies adds a certain architectural flair. Many of the buildings in St. Thomas originally had courtyards, or still do. These added to the living space on the second floor. In the courtyard were kitchens and, almost more vital, cisterns to capture precious rainwater.

Similar building techniques were used on structures that went up on St. Croix.

Christiansted remains one of the most historically authentic towns in the West Indies, true to its original Danish colonial flavor. The basic style was a revival of the European classic look of the 18th century, but with variations to accommodate the tropical climate. As early as 1747, the Danes adopted a strict building code, which spared Christiansted from some of the violent fires that virtually wiped out Charlotte Amalie. Frederiksted, the other major town of St. Croix, has a well-designed waterfront, with blocks of arcaded sidewalks. The quarter is protected by the government as part of Frederiksted's National Historic District.

Great architecture was never the forte of the British Virgin Islands. During a time when major buildings might have been created, the B.V.I. were too economically depressed to find the funds for major structures of lasting significance. Therefore, for much of its history, its people have lived in typical West Indies shanties, with an occasional public building constructed that vaguely imitated 18th-century Europe in style. Curiously enough, although the B.V.I. didn't leave the world any lasting architectural heritage, it did produce a native son, William Thornton, whose designs were used for the U.S. Capitol building in Washington.

million in federal stimulus funding in 2009, and the funding is being used to stimulate the local economy during the recession. One of the major and predictable goals of the stimulus package is in job creation. Some of the money has been earmarked for upgrading the ferry service between Cruz Bay on St. John and Red Hook on St. Thomas.

In 2010, officials in the U.S. Virgin Islands developed closer contact with the U.S. Environmental Protection Agency. The aim is to help the territory solve some of its longstanding problems, such as the best way to address the solid waste problem and how to preserve healthy air standards.

THE VIRGIN ISLANDS IN POPULAR CULTURE

Books

FICTION

Herman Wouk's "Don't Stop the Carnival" (Little Brown & Co., 1992) is "the Caribbean classic," and all readers contemplating a visit to the Virgin Islands might want to pick it up. Wouk lived in St. Thomas in the 1950s, and his novel is based on actual people he met during that time. Bob Shacochis's "Easy in the Islands" (Grove, 2004) giddily re-creates the flavor of the West Indies with short stories. "Tales of St. John & the Caribbean," by Gerald Singer (Sombrero Publishing Co., 2001), is an easy read: a collection of amusing and insightful stories, and the best volume if you'd like a behind-the-scenes look at St. John after the tourists have taken the ferry back to St. Thomas for the night.

"My Name Is Not Angelica," by Scott O'Dell (Yearling Books, 1990), is a young-adult historical novel based in the Virgin Islands in the early 18th century. It tells the saga of a slave girl, Raisha, who escapes bondage; the grim realities of slavery are depicted.

Robert Louis Stevenson is said to have used Norman Island, in the B.V.I., as a fictional setting for his 1883 classic "Treasure Island." This swashbuckling adventure has intrigued readers for years with such characters as the immortal Long John Silver. The book, which gave rise to such memorable lines as "shiver me timbers," continues to find new generations of readers.

COOKBOOKS

A number of books are devoted to recipes of the Caribbean, including "The Sugar Mill Caribbean Cookbook: Casual and Elegant Recipes Inspired by the Islands," by Jinx and Jefferson Morgan (Harvard Common Press, 1996). The Morgans run the Sugar Mill on Tortola. With this book, you can learn the secrets of many of the Sugar Mill's signature dishes, including Rasta Pasta, rum-glazed chicken wings, and lobster and christophine curry.

"Food & Folklore of the Virgin Islands" (Romik, 1990) was penned by Arona Petersen, a well-known St. Thomas writer and folklorist born in 1908. The regional flavor of Virgin Islands fare is captured in her recipes, and the idiomatic dialogues of island people are perfectly re-created as she spins old island tales and wisdom. In her story "What Does Tomorrow Mean? In any Language, Wait" appears this passage: "Wat I trying to say is dat waitin is wat life is about. Everybody waitin fo something or udder, mannin or nite. Tain get wan purson wat, livin ain waitin-fo a bus, fo a taxi, fo a airplane, fo a steamer, fo a letter to come back. Some doan even know wat dey waiting for but dey still waitin." Her books are sold in local shops.

HISTORY BOOKS

The concise "History of the Virgin Islands" (University Press of the West Indies, 2000) is a bit scholarly for some tastes, but if you're seriously interested in the islands, this is the best-researched survey of what was going on before your arrival. "Caribbean Pirates," by Warren Alleyne (Macmillan-Caribbean, 1986), is a good read for preteen travelers and attempts to separate fact from fiction in the sagas of the most notorious pirates in history. Some of the material is based on published letters and documents.

OUTDOOR ADVENTURE BOOKS

Sailing enthusiasts say you shouldn't set out to explore the islets, cays, coral reefs, and islands of the B.V.I. without John Rousmanière's well-researched "The Sailing Lifestyle" (Fireside, 1988).

"Exploring St. Croix," by Shirley Imsand and Richard Philobosian (Travelers Information Press, 1987), is a very detailed activity guide of this island. The authors take you to 49 beaches, 34 snorkeling and scuba-diving sites, and 22 bird-watching areas, and lead you on 20 different hikes.

"A Guide to the Birds of Puerto Rico & the Virgin Islands," by Herbert A. Raffaele, Cindy J. House, and John Wiessinger (Princeton University Press, 1989), is for birdwatchers. The illustrations alone are worth a look, with 273 depictions of the 284 documented species on the islands.

Film

Film production reached its heyday on St. Thomas in the '70s and '80s, when major TV shows, such as "Charlie's Angels," "The Love Boat," and "All My Children," were shot here.

Many movies have been shot in the Virgin Islands, including "Open Water" (2003), the hair-raising adventure story of a couple stranded in shark-infested waters (based on a true story) and "The Deep," shot around the wreck of the RMS *Rhone* near Salt Island, the B.V.I. The final scene of "The Shawshank Redemption" (1994), when Andy Dufresne escapes the harsh Shawshank Prison for an idyllic tropical island, was filmed on Sandy Point, in St. Croix. The final island scene in "Trading Places" (1983), starring Eddie Murphy and Jamie Lee Curtis, was also shot in St. Croix. A 1980s film classic, "The Four Seasons" (1981), was filmed in part in the Virgin Islands; the film is a tender-sweet melodrama that stars Carol Burnett and Alan Alda.

The 1990 television remake of Ernest Hemingway's "The Old Man and the Sea," starring Anthony Quinn, was filmed on the half-moon bay at Smuggler's Cove, on Tortola in the B.V.I. The ruins of the movie set still remain.

The true classic of the archipelago is "Virgin Island" (1958), starring John Cassavetes and Sidney Poitier. Filmed in the British Virgin Islands, it is a fairy-tale type of story about a young man and woman who buy a small, uninhabited island and go there to find their dream. The film was based on the actual experiences of novelist Robb White, who with his wife bought Marina Cay in 1937 for $60 and decided to pursue a Robinson Crusoe existence on the islands. He wrote about it in three memoirs: "In Privateers Bay," "Our Virgin Island," and "Two on the Isle."

Essential Guide to Sailing the Virgin Islands

For more than a quarter of a century, "Yachtsman's Guide to the Virgin Islands" has been the classic cruising guide to this area (it's now in its 13th edition). The detailed, 288-page text is supplemented by 27 hand-drawn sketch charts, aerial photographs, and numerous landfall sketches showing harbors, channels, landmarks, and such. Subjects covered include piloting, anchoring, communication, weather, fishing, and more. The guide also covers the eastern end of Puerto Rico, Vieques, and Culebra. Copies are available at major marine outlets, bookstores, and direct from **Yachtman's Guide** (ⓒ **877/923-9653**; www.yachtsmansguide.com).

Don't Let the Jumbies Get Ya!

"Don't let the Jumbies get ya!" is an often-heard phrase in the Virgin Islands, particularly when people are leaving their hosts and heading home in the dark. Jumbies, capable of good or evil, are supernatural beings that are believed to live around households. It is said that new settlers from the mainland of the United States never see these Jumbies and, therefore, need not fear them. But many islanders believe in their existence and, if queried, may enthrall you with tales of sightings.

No one seems to agree on exactly what a Jumbie is. Some claim it's the spirit of a dead person that didn't go where it belonged. Others disagree. "They're the souls of live people," one islander told us, "but they live in the body of the dead." The most prominent Jumbies are "moko jumbies," colorful stilt walkers seen at all carnival parades.

Music

As the Caribbean rhythms go, the Virgin Islands encompass it all, from reggae to classical to steel drums to spiritual hymns, but soca, reggae, calypso, and steel pan beats seem to dominate the night.

Though it originated in Trinidad, **calypso** has its unique sounds in the Virgins. It is famously known for expressing political commentary through satire.

If you add a little soul music to calypso, you have **soca,** a music form that also made its way north to the Virgin Islands from Trinidad. **Reggae** originated on Jamaica, but is alive and well in the Virgins. Virgin Islanders have put a unique stamp on reggae, making it their own.

Scratch bands are popular in the British Virgins, in the musical form known as **fungi. Merengue** is also heard in the Virgins, having "floated over" from Puerto Rico and the Dominican Republic.

Throughout the year in various bars, clubs, reggae concerts, steel-pan shows, and jazz concerts, you can hear the music of the islands, including **zouk,** dance music from Martinique. Find out what's happening by reading the local newspapers.

Of course, the leading musicians of the islands make recordings, including the hypnotic and tantalizing roots-reggae stylings of St. Croix native **Dezarie,** whose albums, including "Gracious Mama Africa" and her latest, "Fourth Book," have earned her the title of St. Croix's Roots Empress. Another St. Croix–born singer is **Mada Nile** (http://madafyahnile.com), known for her poignant lyrics.

A vocal rival of both Dezarie and Mada Nile is **Sistah Joyce,** a reggae artist from Virgin Gorda who is acclaimed for her hard-hitting lyrics as evoked by her recording of "Remembah." She scored a hit with her debut album, "H.Y.P.O.C.R.I.C.Y."

Island-bred reggae bands, such as **Midnite** (from St. Croix) and **Inner Visions** (from St. John), have never been more popular, although they've been around since the '80s. "Midnite Intense Pressure," Midnite's debut album, firmly established them as a force in roots music; the group is known for its fiery lyrics. Its latest album is "Lion out of Zion" (http://midniteband.com). The albums of Inner Visions (www.innervisionsreggae.com) demonstrate the group's refined musical abilities, which distinguish them from the more "raw roots" style of many other rival artists. The band is made up of first- and second-generation members of the Pickering family, with names like Grasshopper and Jupiter.

3

THE VIRGIN ISLANDS IN CONTEXT

The Virgin Islands in Popular Culture

33

EATING & DRINKING

Overall, you will eat very well in the islands. Many fine talents, both local and imported, are ensconced in kitchens throughout the region, and competition breeds excellence. In addition, traditional Caribbean cuisine is alive and well in the Virgin Islands, and many classic island dishes are staples on restaurant menus, and not just the laidback local spots. Even upscale resorts serving an international clientele favor menus with an island spin, fomenting a Caribbean/continental fusion.

Dining in the Virgin Islands is generally more expensive than it is in North America because much of the food has to be imported. Whenever possible, take advantage of fresh regional foods, like **locally caught fish,** especially mahimahi, wahoo, yellowtail, grouper, and red snapper. The sweet **Caribbean lobster** is another local specialty. More and more, **farm-fresh produce** is making a reappearance, and you'll even find local fruits and vegetables sold in the island's grocery stores—fresh avocadoes, bananas, sweet potatoes, cassava, you name it.

Tips on Dining

TIPPING   A 10 percent to 15 percent service charge is automatically added to most restaurant tabs. If the service is good, you should tip a bit extra.

WHAT TO WEAR   In some of the posher resorts, such as Caneel Bay on St. John, it is customary for men to wear a jacket, but in summer, virtually no establishment requires it. If in doubt, ask the restaurant beforehand. At the better places, women's evening attire is casual-chic. During the day it is always proper to wear something over your bathing suit if you're in a restaurant.

RESERVATIONS   Most places require reservations, especially in high season. But even in the slower seasons (or shoulder seasons), many of the smaller restaurants need to know how many people to expect for the evening's meal, so reservations may be required there as well.

The Cuisine

You may want to start your meal with a bowl of *kallaloo,* or **callaloo,** a West Indian–style gumbo made in an infinite number of ways with a leafy green vegetable similar to spinach. It may come flavored with hot peppers, a ham bone, fresh seafood, okra, onions, and spices. We've also eaten a wonderful breakfast dish of steamed callaloo with sauteed mushrooms, onions, and halved cherry tomatoes.

Saltfish salad is traditionally served on Maundy Thursday or Good Friday in the Virgin Islands. It consists of boneless salt fish, potatoes, onions, boiled eggs, and an oil-and-vinegar dressing.

Herring gundy is another old-time island favorite; it's a salad made with salt herring, potatoes, onions, green sweet and hot peppers, olives, diced beets, raw carrots, herbs, and boiled eggs.

The classic vegetable dish, which some families eat every night, is **peas and rice.** It usually consists of pigeon peas flavored with ham or salt meat, onion, tomatoes, herbs, and sometimes slices of pumpkin. Pigeon peas, one of the most common vegetables in the islands, are sometimes called congo peas or *gunga.*

Many local joints serve a sweet and savory **island slaw,** often made with raisins and sweet peppers.

Fungi is a simple cornmeal dish not unlike grits, made more interesting with the addition of okra and other ingredients. Sweet *fungi* is served as a dessert, with sugar, milk, cinnamon, and raisins.

Okra (often spelled *ochroe* in the islands) is a mainstay vegetable, usually accompanying beef, fish, or chicken. It's often fried and flavored with hot peppers, tomatoes, onions, garlic, and bacon fat or butter. **Accra,** a popular dish, is made with okra, black-eyed peas, salt, and pepper, all fried until they're golden brown.

Way back when, locals gave colorful names to the various fish brought home for dinner, everything from "ole wife" to "doctors," both of which are whitefish. "Porgies and grunts," along with yellowtail, kingfish, and bonito, also show up on many Caribbean dinner tables. Fish is often boiled in a lime-flavored brew seasoned with hot peppers and herbs, and is commonly served with a Creole sauce of peppers, tomatoes, and onions, among other ingredients. **Salt fish and rice** is an excellent low-cost dish; the fish is flavored with onion, tomatoes, shortening, garlic, and green peppers.

Conch shows up on the menu in all sorts of interesting manifestations. Every restaurant has its own version of **conch fritters. Conch Creole** is a savory brew, seasoned with onions, garlic, spices, hot peppers, and salt pork. Another West Indian favorite is chicken and rice, usually made with Spanish peppers. More adventurous diners might try **curried goat,** the longtime classic West Indian dinner prepared with herbs, cardamom pods, and onions.

The famous **johnnycakes** that accompany many of these fish and meat dishes are made with flour, baking powder, shortening, and salt, then fried or baked.

On the B.V.I., you'll find a number of inexpensive **roti** joints, serving up East Indian-style turnovers stuffed with curried chicken, fish, or potatoes and peas.

For dessert, **sweet potato pie** is a Virgin Islands classic, made with sugar, eggs, butter, milk, salt, cinnamon, raisins, and chopped raw almonds. The exotic **fruits** of the islands lend themselves to various homemade ice creams, including mango, guava, soursop (a tangy fruit), banana, carambola (star fruit), pineapple, and papaya. Sometimes dumplings made with guava, peach, plum, gooseberry, cherry, or apple are served for dessert.

Some Like It Hot

Virgin Islanders like their hot sauce (aka "pepper" sauce), in any number of creative variations, and many island cooks prepare and bottle their own, a number of which are available for sale in stores around the islands. Foodies and bloggers have a field day defending their favorites, including **Miss Anna's** (St. John), **Blind Betty's** (St. Croix), **Jerome's** (St. Thomas), and **ValleyDoll** (St. John). At Little Dix Bay in Virgin Gorda, one of the resort's longtime servers, Venita Chapman, creates her own saucy concoction with mangos, papayas, and peppers, **Venita's Hot Pepper Sauce,** sold right there at the resort. Even Miss Gladys, proprietor of **Gladys' Café** in St. Thomas, makes and bottles her own divine hot-sauce concoctions (in such flavors as mango, mustard, and tomato) and sells them in her restaurant. If you're a hot-sauce aficionado, you'll find an exhaustive selection of these and more at **St. John Spice** (http://stjohnspice.com), on the harbor in Cruz Bay. They make great gifts to take home, but be sure to pack them in your luggage and not your carryon.

Drinks

The islands' true poison is **rum.** To help stimulate the local economy, U.S. Customs allows you to bring home an extra bottle of local rum, in addition to your usual 5-liter liquor allowance.

Long before the arrival of Coca-Cola and Pepsi, many islanders concocted their own fruit drinks using whatever fruit was in season. Fresh fruit concoctions are ubiquitous on menus today. American sodas and beer are sold in both the U.S. Virgin Islands and the British Virgin Islands. Wine is sold, too, but it can be expensive.

Water is generally safe to drink on the islands. Much of the water is stored in cisterns and filtered before it's served. Still, delicate stomachs should stick to bottled water or club soda. Some resorts have their own desalination plants, providing water that is delicious and highly drinkable.

WHEN TO GO
Weather

Sunshine and warm temperatures are practically an everyday affair in the Virgin Islands. Temperatures climb into the 80s (high 20s Celsius) during the day, and drop into the more comfortable 70s (low 20s Celsius) at night. Winter is generally the dry season in the islands, but rainfall can occur at any time of the year. You don't have to worry too much, though—tropical showers usually come and go so quickly you won't even really notice. November is traditionally the wettest month—if you're out exploring for the day, you may want to bring an umbrella or rain hat just in case.

HURRICANES The hurricane season, the dark side of the Caribbean's beautiful weather, officially lasts from June to November. It peaks in September and October. The Virgin Islands chain lies in the main pathway of many a hurricane raging through the Caribbean, and the islands are often hit. If you're planning a vacation in hurricane season, stay abreast of weather conditions and consider investing in trip-cancellation insurance.

Islanders certainly don't stand around waiting for a hurricane to strike. Satellite forecasts generally give adequate warning to both residents and visitors. And of course, there's always prayer: Islanders have a legal holiday in the third week of July called Supplication Day, when they ask to be spared from devastating storms. In late October, locals celebrate the end of the season on Hurricane Thanksgiving Day.

Average Temperatures & Rainfall (in.) for St. Thomas

	JAN	FEB	MAR	APR	MAY	JUNE	JULY	AUG	SEPT	OCT	NOV	DEC
TEMP (°F)	77	77	77	79	79	82	82	83	82	83	81	77
TEMP (°C)	25	25	25	26	26	28	28	28	28	28	27	25
PRECIP.	1.86	.95	.97	8.32	9.25	1.62	2.25	3.6	2.04	4.43	7.77	2.46

The High Season & the Off Season

High season (or winter season) in the Virgin Islands, when hotel rates are at their peak, runs roughly from mid-December to mid-April. However, package and resort rates are sometimes lower in January, as a tourist slump usually occurs right after the Christmas holidays. February is the busiest month. If you're planning on visiting during the winter months, make reservations as far in advance as possible.

Off season begins when North America starts to warm up, and vacationers, assuming that temperatures in the Virgin Islands are soaring into the 100s (upper 30s

Celsius), head for less tropical local beaches. However, the Virgin Islands are actually quite balmy year-round, thanks to the fabled trade winds—with temperatures varying little more than 5° between winter and summer.

There are many advantages to off-season travel in the Virgin Islands. First, from mid-April to mid-December, hotel rates are slashed—often in half. Second, you're less likely to encounter crowds at beaches, resorts, restaurants, and shops. A slower pace prevails in the off season, especially in St. Croix and St. Thomas, and you'll have a better chance to appreciate the local culture and cuisine. Of course, there are disadvantages to off-season travel, too: Many hotels use the slower months for construction and/or restoration, fewer facilities are likely to be open, and some hotels and restaurants may close completely when business is really slow.

Additionally, if you're planning a trip during the off season and traveling alone, ask for the hotel's occupancy rate—you may want crowds. The social scene in both the B.V.I. and the U.S.V.I. is intense from mid-December to mid-April. After that, it slumbers a bit. If you seek escape from the world and its masses, summer is the way to go, especially if you aren't depending on meeting others.

Holidays

In addition to the standard legal holidays observed in the United States, **U.S. Virgin Islanders** also observe the following holidays: Three Kings' Day (Jan 6); Transfer Day, commemorating the transfer of the Danish Virgin Islands to the Americans (Mar 31); Organic Act Day, honoring the legislation that granted voting rights to the islanders (June 20); Emancipation Day, celebrating the freeing of the slaves by the Danish in 1848 (July 3); Hurricane Supplication Day (July 25); Hurricane Thanksgiving Day (Oct 17); Liberty Day (Nov 1); and Christmas Second Day (Dec 26). The islands also celebrate 2 carnival days on the last Friday and Saturday in April: Children's Carnival Parade and the Grand Carnival Parade.

In the **British Virgin Islands,** public holidays include the following: New Year's Day, Commonwealth Day (Mar 12), Good Friday, Easter Monday, Whitmonday (sometime in July), Territory Day Sunday (usually July 1), Festival Monday and Tuesday (during the first week of Aug), St. Ursula's Day (Oct 21), Birthday of the Heir to the Throne (Nov 14), Christmas Day, and Boxing Day (Dec 26).

The Virgin Islands Calendar of Events

JANUARY

Estate Bordeaux Agricultural & Cultural Food Fair, St. Thomas. Weekend-long farm fair in the hills of Estate Bordeaux, with reggae music, crafts, farm tours, and more served up from 10am to midnight. Contact We Grow Food (www.facebook.com/WEGROWFOOD). January 19 and 20.

FEBRUARY

St. Croix House Tours, St. Croix. Two separate weekends of house tours, each in a different St. Croix neighborhood, are held to raise funds for the St. Croix Landmarks Society. Go to www.stcroixlandmarks.com for details. Two weekends in mid-February.

Agrifest: St. Croix Agricultural Fair, St. Croix. Held at the Rudolph Shulterbrandt Agricultural Complex, Estate Lower Love, this 3-day festival is one of the island's highlights, a family-friendly event featuring music, crafts, and lots of locally made food and island-grown produce. Go to www.viagrifest.org for details. Presidents' Day weekend.

MARCH

Mardi Gras Annual Parade, St. Croix. The scenic north shore of St. Croix becomes one big colorful party at Mardi Gras, with a parade to Cane Bay. For information, check www.stcroixtourism.com. First Saturday before Fat Tuesday, usually early March.

St. Thomas International Regatta, St. Thomas. This is one of three regattas in the Caribbean Ocean Racing Triangle (CORT) series. Top-ranked international racers come to St. Thomas to compete in front of the world's yachting press. The St. Thomas Yacht Club hosts the 3-day event. Call ☎ **340/775-4701,** or visit www.rolexcupregatta.com. Late March.

Transfer Day, U.S. Virgin Islands. This holiday commemorates the day the U.S. Virgins were transferred from Denmark to the United States. On this day, vendors sell Danish products, and visits to the remains of Danish ruins and forts are arranged. Call ☎ **340/772-0598,** or visit www.stcroix landmarks.com. March 31.

APRIL

B.V.I. Spring Regatta & Sailing Festival, Tortola. This is the third of the CORT events (see St. Thomas International Regatta, above). A range of talents, from the most dedicated racers to bareboat crews out for "rum and reggae," participate in the 4-day race. Contact the B.V.I. Spring Regatta Committee in Tortola at ☎ **284/541-6732,** or sail over to www.bvispringregatta.org for information. Early April.

Virgin Gorda Easter Festival, Virgin Gorda. Easter weekend is a big event on Virgin Gorda, featuring street parades, a beauty pageant, and nonstop partying. Arrive on Good Friday, Holy Saturday, or Easter Sunday, and you should have no trouble finding the party. Easter weekend.

St. Croix Food & Wine Experience, St. Croix. It's a weeklong food party on St. Croix, where the island's culinary delights are highlighted with city food crawls, wine events, sunset BBQs, and the chance to sample local creations at the "Taste of St. Croix." Go to www.stcroixfoodandwine.com. April 16–21.

Virgin Islands Carnival, St. Thomas. This annual celebration on St. Thomas, with origins in Africa, is the most spectacular and fun carnival in the Virgin Islands. "Mocko Jumbies," people dressed as spirits, parade through the streets on stilts nearly 20 feet high. Steel and fungi bands, "jump-ups," and parades are part of the festivities. Over

the years, interestingly, the festivities have become more and more Christianized. Events take place islandwide, but most of the action is on the streets of Charlotte Amalie. For information, call ☎ **340/776-3112,** or visit www.vicarnival.com for a schedule of events. After Easter.

MAY

B.V.I. Music Festival, Tortola. Music—mostly reggae—drowns out the sea at this music festival on Cane Garden Bay in Tortola, the island's best beach. Musicians come from all over the West Indies to perform. For more information, visit www.bvimusicfestival.com. Late May.

JUNE

St John Festival, St. John. Known also as "Carnival," this month-long cultural event takes place on St. John, with steel-pan concerts, calypso shows, parades, beauty pageants, and fireworks displays. For more information, call **800/372-USVI** [8784]. The carnival begins the first week of June and lasts until July 4.

JULY

Mango Melee and Tropical Fruit Festival, St. Croix. Mango aficionados and devotees of other tropical fruit converge here for tastings, cooking demonstrations, and contests at the St. George Village Botanical Gardens. For more information, call ☎ **340/692-2874.** Early July.

Independence Day, St. John. The elements of Carnival are combined with emancipation and independence celebrations in this festive event, which culminates on July 4 with a big parade. Thousands of St. Thomas residents flock to St. John for the parades, calypso bands, colorful costumes, and events leading up to the selection of Ms. St. John and the King of the Carnival. Call the St. John tourist office at ☎ **340/776-6201** for more details. July 4.

AUGUST

B.V.I. Emancipation Celebrations, Tortola. Many visitors from other Caribbean islands hop over to Road Town, in Tortola, for this 2-week party. Join locals as they dance to fungi and reggae bands, and take part in the Emancipation Day Parade and other carnival activities and festivities. For information, call the B.V.I. Tourist Board Office at ℂ **284/494-3701.** Early August.

U.S. Virgin Islands Open/Atlantic Blue Marlin Tournament, St. Thomas. This prestigious St. Thomas–centered charity event (proceeds go to the Boy Scouts) is also eco-friendly—trophies are based on the number of blue marlin caught, tagged, and released. The tournament is open to anyone who's interested, and sportsfishers come from around the world to participate. For more information, call the VI Council of the Boy Scouts of America at ℂ **888/234-7484** or 340/775-9500; www.abmt.vi. Mid-August.

OCTOBER

Virgin Islands Fashion Week, St. Thomas. Aspiring designers from across the Caribbean, the United States, and even West Africa fly into St. Thomas to showcase their latest fashion designs. At the Caribbean Catwalk Runway show, beach and casual fashions are the draw. Nearly all events, including rap party, are open to the public. For more information, call ℂ **340/344-6078.** Five days in October, dates vary.

NOVEMBER

St. Thomas-St. John Agriculture and Food Fair, St. Thomas and St. John. Produce and livestock, along with local vendors selling arts and crafts, are the focus of this agriculture and food fair held on the grounds of the University of Virgin Islands' Reichhold Center for the Arts. Saturday, November 3, and Sunday, November 4 (10am–5pm).

Annual St. Croix International Regatta, St. Croix. Held at the St. Croix Yacht Club on Teague Bay, this 3-day regatta celebrated its 21st year in 2013. It draws serious yachties from the B.V.I., the U.S.V.I., and Florida. Call St. Croix Yacht Club at ℂ **340/773-9531,** or visit www.stcroixyc.com for details. Mid-November.

Paradise Jam College Basketball Tournament, St. Thomas. Catch big-time college hoops action at this men's and women's basketball tournament held at the University of the Virgin Islands Sports & Fitness Center. Teams have included Kansas, Duke, Providence, and Maryland. For information, go

to www.paradisejam.com or call ℂ **340/693-1056.**

BVI Restaurant Week, the British Virgin Islands. If you're in the British Virgin Islands around Thanksgiving, take advantage of the island-wide Restaurant Week, where some 40 participating restaurants throughout the B.V.I. feature prix-fixe dinners. Go to www.bvitourism.com. Last week in November.

Art in the Garden Arts & Crafts Festival, St. Thomas. This annual 3-day festival, which takes place in Tillett Gardens in St. Thomas, includes displays from more than 30 local artists, along with live music and entertainment and free activities for kids. For information, visit www.tillettfoundation.org. Last weekend in November.

Anegada Lobster Festival, the British Virgin Islands. It's a 2-day beach party on the white sands of Anegada for the November Lobster Festival, celebrating the island's famously sweet Caribbean lobster. Eight of the island's restaurants feature sampler plates of lobster dishes. Smiths Ferry (http://bviferryservices.com) and Road Town Fast Ferry (www.roadtownfastferry.com) offer special runs to and from the island, with the last ferries leaving at 9pm. Call ℂ **284/494-3134.** Last weekend in November.

DECEMBER

Christmas in St. Croix. This major event launches the beginning of a 12-day celebration that includes **Crucian Christmas Carnival** (www.stxcarnival.com)—with calypso music, parades, horse races, food fairs, and fireworks—Christmas Day, Christmas Second Day (Dec 26), New Year's Eve (called "Old Year's Day"), and New Year's Day. It ends on January 6, the Feast of the Three Kings, with a parade of flamboyantly attired merrymakers. For information, call the U.S. Virgin Islands Department of Tourism office in Christiansted at ℂ **340/773-0495.**

Foxy's Old Year's Night, Jost Van Dyke, B.V.I. It's a mega-party on Jost's Great Harbour as Foxy rings in the New Year with weekend-long events, from a Caribbean barbecue to DJ music on the beach to a headliner concert that in 2013 showcased Bunny Wailer. For information, go to http://foxysbar.com.

RESPONSIBLE TRAVEL

Many of the islands were clear-cut in the 1700s to make way for sugar plantations, destroying much of the natural landscape. All through the 1900s, while real estate developments on St. Thomas continued to mushroom, little concern was given to preserving and sustaining the natural resources of the U.S.V.I. Today, there is a very different attitude toward the ecosystem of the Virgin Islands among permanent residents and visitors alike.

The sparkling marine waters of the Virgin Islands require special stewardship, and the B.V.I. is a leader in environment regulations regarding the islands' pristine seas. The country has banned the use of **jet skis** (also not allowed in the marine parkland around St. John) and requires that any jet skis or WaveRunners brought into the country be declared at Customs upon entry. Penalties for jet-ski use include confiscation of the jet skis and a $5,000 fine. The National Parks Act of 2006 prohibits sewage disposal and the removing of any living or dead coral from any coastal area, among other regulations.

In this **sailing and boating paradise,** boaters are asked to anchor using mooring balls or if you must anchor, look for a sandy bottom that's clear of coral or seagrass meadows where sea turtles feed. Do not anchor or tie your boat to mangroves. Don't drag dinghies onto the beach; look for dinghy moorings or docks. Never throw trash, particularly plastic, overboard (turtles choke on plastic bags). Divers and snorkelers should take care not to touch or accidentally brush up against delicate coral. If you see environmental disturbances (or turtle nesting activity), call the **B.V.I. Conservation & Fisheries Department** (✆ 284/494-3429). An invaluable resource is the online "Marine Awareness Guide" at **www.bvimarineawareness.com**.

Low-impact activities like **hiking, snorkeling, and kayaking** are hugely popular in the Virgin Islands. While on St. Croix, contact the **St. Croix Environmental Association** (p. 108), which hosts hikes, tours of research facilities, and events based around the hatching of baby sea turtles. Aside from the many companies that offer tours, the St. Thomas–based **Virgin Islands Ecotours** (✆ 877/845-2925; http://viecotours.com) offers tours with professional naturalists of the mangrove lagoon and nature reserve at Cas Cay, St. Thomas, and snorkeling and hiking tours in Caneel Bay, St. John. **B.V.I. Eco-Tours** (✆ 284/495-0271; www.bvi-ecotours.com) offers a variety of guided tours, including snorkeling, bird-watching, sightseeing, diving, and general tours of the British Virgin Islands.

Sustainable Eating

It takes a whole lot of fossil fuels to import food onto these remote islands. That's why it's heartening to see the rebirth of small farms and sustainable farming throughout the Virgins, a movement that is catching fire in particular on St. Croix, with its farmer's markets, farm co-ops, and **Virgin Islands Sustainable Farm Institute** (http://vi.locallygrown. net) and on St. Thomas, where West End farms in Estate Bordeaux are using government grants to increase capacity in the loamy volcanic soil, where as one farmer said, "you can grow anything." You can do your part in saving energy by eating local: dining on seafood caught in and around the waters of Virgin Islands and buying produce and fruit from the weekly farmer's markets and produce stands

A number of truly eco-friendly lodgings are found on the islands, including campsites. St. John, which is almost entirely a national park, has numerous campsites, including those run by the National Park Service. Alas, the beloved 114-unit **Maho Bay Camp** eco-resort closed in summer 2013 (sold for $13.95 million to an unknown buyer), but its sister eco-resort **Estate Concordia Preserve** may expand beyond its 42 campsites. On St. Croix, there is **Mount Victory Camp** (p. 99), which relies on renewable energy to power its cottages. The British Virgin Islands are less developed than their American cousins, and lodgings tend to be more eco-friendly by nature. You don't have to camp out to stay in eco-sensitive lodging, however. The **Cooper Island Beach Club** (p. 157) meets the middle ground between luxury and roughing it. All of **Guana Island** (p. 189), a private resort, is a wildlife sanctuary watched over by the attentive owners (it even has its own organic orchard and a smattering of flamingoes in the salt pond). The **Bitter End Yacht Club** (p. 175), sustainably run by necessity in its early days, continues its green ways by generating its own electricity and collecting and distilling its own water. In fact, many resorts around the islands have their own desalination plants, making highly potable fresh water out of seawater.

St. Thomas, with all its development and modern conveniences, faces the biggest challenges in regard to sustainable development. To learn more, see the section "The Virgin Islands Today," earlier in this chapter.

ST. THOMAS

The cosmopolitan hub of the Virgin Islands, St. Thomas is known for its brassy commercial hustle. But with sparkling turquoise seas and peaceful mountain aeries, it's easy to leave the hubbub far behind. Yes, the 32-square-mile island is home to the busiest cruise-ship harbor in the West Indies, and its historic capital, Charlotte Amalie, is the beating commercial heart of the region. But just minutes from the action are serene beaches and pampering retreats. More than any other Virgin Island, St. Thomas has something for everyone: Join the market throngs by day and swing to reggae rhythms at night—or simply forget your cares on a sun-kissed, palm-fringed beach.

ESSENTIALS

Getting There

BY PLANE

If you're flying to St. Thomas, you will land at the **Cyril E. King Airport** (© **340/774-5100;** http://saint-thomas-airport.com; airport code STT), 3 miles (about a 15-min. drive) to the west of the central business district in Charlotte Amalie on Route 30. From here, you can easily grab a taxi to your hotel or villa. Chances are you will be staying east of Charlotte Amalie, so keep in mind that getting through town often involves long delays and traffic jams during rush hours.

Many people flying in from mainland cities in North America and from overseas connect through Miami or San Juan. Flight time from Miami is about 2½ hours. Flight time from San Juan to St. Thomas is approximately 30 minutes. Flight time between St. Thomas and St. Croix is only 20 minutes.

Direct flights to the U.S. Virgin Islands are available on **American Airlines** (© **800/433-7300** in the U.S.; www.aa.com) from New York City, Boston, Miami, and San Juan. Flights from NYC take 3¾ hours. **Continental Airlines** (© **800/231-0856** in the U.S.; www.continental.com) has daily flights from Newark International Airport, in New Jersey, to St. Thomas. **Delta** (© **800/241-4141** in the U.S.; www.delta.com) offers two daily non-stop flights between Atlanta and St. Thomas. **US Airways** (© **800/428-4322** in the U.S.; www.usairways.com) has direct flights from Philadelphia and Charlotte. **JetBlue** (© **800/538-2583;** www.jetblue.com) has direct flights from Boston. **United Airlines** (© **800/538-2929** in the U.S.; www.united.com) has direct flights into St. Thomas from Chicago, Dulles (Washington, D.C.), and Newark. **Spirit Airlines** (© **800/772-7117;** www.spirit.com) has direct flights from Fort Lauderdale.

Cape Air (© **866/227-3247** in the U.S. and U.S.V.I.; www.capeair.com) offers daily service between St. Thomas and San Juan, Puerto Rico, and

St. Thomas

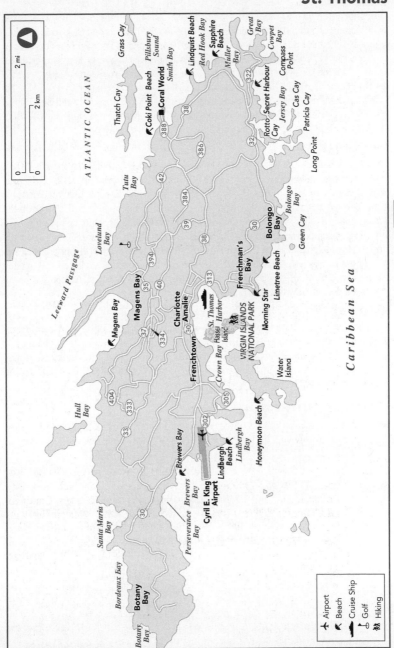

4

ST. THOMAS | Essentials

43

has expanded its service to include flights between St. Thomas and both St. Croix and Tortola.

Seaborne Airlines (📞 **866/359-8784** or 340/773-6442 in the U.S.V.I, www.seaborne airlines.com) is currently the major carrier between St. Thomas and St. Croix, offering regularly scheduled daily flights on 34-seat turboprop planes and seaplanes capable of carrying 15 to 17 passengers. Its regular planes fly between Cyril E. King airport in St. Thomas and the Henry E. Rahlsen airport in St. Croix. Seaborne seaplanes fly between the St. Thomas seaplane base (next to the Charlotte Amalie ferry terminal) and the St. Croix seaplane seaport in the Christiansted waterfront. Flight time between St. Thomas and St. Croix is 20 to 25 minutes. Seaborne also flies between St. Thomas and Beef Island, Tortola.

BY CRUISE SHIP

Charlotte Amalie is one of the world's busiest cruise ports and the Caribbean's largest duty-free port, welcoming nearly 1,800,000 cruise passengers in 2012 (2013 was unavailable as we went to press). Most of the major cruise lines include regular stops in St. Thomas on their Caribbean itineraries, including the biggest cruise ships in the world, floating "cities at sea" capable of holding up to 6,000 passengers at a time.

Cruise ships dock at one of two major piers, each with room for two mega-ships at a time: **Havensight Pier** and **Crown Bay.** In addition, during the cruising high season, it's not unusual to have an additional one, two, even three ships anchored just outside the harbor, delivering cruise-ship passengers to shore in tenders. At press time an expansion was in the works for the Crown Bay pier.

BY BOAT

Ferry service from Puerto Rico to St. Thomas, with a stop in St. John, is available only during Carnival. Trip time between Fajardo and Charlotte Amalie (St. Thomas) is about 1¾ hours, with the departure Saturday morning and the return Sunday afternoon. The cost is $100 one-way, $125 round-trip. For more information, call **Transportation Services** at 📞 **340/776-6282.**

Visitor Information

The U.S. Virgin Islands tourist board **Welcome Center,** in Havensight Mall, on the Waterfront in downtown Charlotte Amalie (📞 **340/774-8784;** www.visitusvi.com), is

---

St. Thomas: Gateway to the Other Virgins

Most people who visit the other Virgin Islands—both U.S. and British—must travel through St. Thomas to get there. Even if you plan to stay in St. Thomas your entire trip, day-trips to one or several other islands should be high on your vacation agenda. A robust ferry system delivers passengers between the islands (except for St. Croix, which is better reached by plane). For details on ferry departure times, check in any recent issue of the free weekly publication "This Week," or go to **www.bestofbvi. com/info/info_bviferry.htm**, with updated ferry times. For a list of ferry companies and contact information, go to p. 193. St. Thomas has two ferry terminals: **Marine Terminal,** in Charlotte Amalie, and **Red Hook,** on the island's east end. Keep in mind that everyone—including U.K. citizens—traveling to the British Virgin Islands needs a passport and must pay a $15-per-person passenger tax at departure.

open Monday to Friday 8am to 5pm and Saturday 8am to 2pm. You can get maps, brochures, and even a list of legal shoreline fishing sites throughout the islands here.

Island Layout
CHARLOTTE AMALIE
For a map of the landmarks and attractions discussed below, see "Walking Tour: Charlotte Amalie," on p. 73.

Charlotte Amalie, the capital of St. Thomas, is the only town on the island. Its seaside promenade is called **Waterfront Highway,** or simply, the **Waterfront.** From here, you can take any of the streets or alleyways into town to **Main Street** (also called Dronningens Gade). Principal links between Main Street and the Waterfront include **Raadets Gade, Tolbod Gade, Store Tvaer Gade,** and **Strand Gade.**

Main Street is home to all of the major shops. The western end (near the intersection with Strand Gade) is known as **Market Square.** Once the site of the biggest slave market auctions in the Caribbean Basin, today it's an open-air cluster of stalls where local farmers and gardeners—many from the Estate Bordeaux farms on the island's West End—gather to sell their produce; Saturday is their big day. Go early in the morning to see the market at its best.

Running parallel to and north of Main Street is **Back Street** (also known as Vimmelskaft Gade), which is also lined with stores, including some of the less expensive choices. *Note:* It can be dangerous to walk along Back Street at night, but it's reasonably safe for daytime shopping.

In the eastern part of town, between Tolbod Gade and Fort Pladsen (northwest of Fort Christian), lies **Emancipation Park,** commemorating the liberation of the slaves in 1848. Most of the major historic buildings, including the Legislature, Fort Christian, and Government House, lie within a short walk of this park.

Southeast of the park looms **Fort Christian.** Crowned by a clock tower and painted rusty red, it was constructed by the Danes in 1671. The **Legislative Building,** seat of the elected government of the U.S. Virgin Islands, lies on the harbor side of the fort.

Kongens Gade (or King's Street) leads to **Government Hill,** which overlooks the town and St. Thomas Harbor. **Government House,** a white brick building dating from 1867, stands atop the hill.

Between **Hotel 1829** (a mansion built that year by a French sea captain) and Government House is a stone staircase known as the **Street of 99 Steps.** Actually, someone miscounted: It should be called the Street of 103 Steps. Regardless, the steps lead to the summit of Government Hill.

WEST OF CHARLOTTE AMALIE
The most important of the outlying neighborhoods to the west of Charlotte Amalie is **Frenchtown.** Some of the older islanders still speak a distinctive Norman-French dialect here. Because the heart of Charlotte Amalie can be less safe at night, Frenchtown, with its finer restaurants and interesting bars, has become the place to go after dark. To reach Frenchtown, take Veterans Drive west of town along the Waterfront, turning left (shortly after passing the Windward Passage Hotel on your right) at the sign pointing to the Villa Olga.

The mid-grade hotels that lie to the immediate west of Charlotte Amalie attract visitors who are seeking more moderate hotel rates than those charged at the mega-resorts that dot the gold-plated South Coast. The disadvantage is that you may have to depend on public transportation to reach the sands. The biggest attraction is that you're on the very doorstep of Charlotte Amalie, filled with restaurants, bars, shopping, and other amusements.

EAST OF CHARLOTTE AMALIE

Traveling east from Charlotte Amalie, along a traffic-clogged highway, you'll see St. Thomas Harbor on your right. If you stay in this area, you'll be in a tranquil setting just a short car or taxi ride from the bustle of Charlotte Amalie. The major disadvantage is that you must reach the sands by some form of transportation; if you want to run out of your hotel-room door onto the beach, look elsewhere.

THE SOUTH COAST

This fabled strip, with its good, sandy beaches, has put St. Thomas on the tourist maps of the Caribbean. Many visitors prefer the full-service resorts on the South Coast and East End to the hustle and bustle of Charlotte Amalie, especially during the day, when it's overrun by cruise-ship passengers. But if you feel the need for a shopping binge, cars, hotel shuttles, and taxis can quickly deliver you to Charlotte Amalie.

THE EAST END

The East End is reached by traversing a long, twisting, traffic-clogged road east of Charlotte Amalie. Once you're here, you can enjoy sea, sand, and sun with little to disturb you (the East End offers even more isolation than the South Coast). This is the site of such lovely beaches as Sapphire Beach and Lindquist Beach. This section of bays and golden sands is where you'll find the the luxe Ritz-Carlton resort as well as a smattering of smaller, less-expensive resorts and condos. The settlement at **Red Hook** is a bustling community with raffish charm and lots of seaside bars and affordable eateries. It is also the departure point for ferries to St. John.

THE NORTH COAST

The renowned beach at **Magens Bay** lies on the lush North Coast. Be aware that the beach is often overrun with visitors, especially when cruise-ship arrivals are heavy. The North Coast has few buildings and not much traffic, but what it does have are scenic vistas, among the most panoramic on the island. Note that traveling the roads can be like a ride on a rollercoaster—the roads have no shoulders and can be especially scary for those not familiar with driving on the left. A lot of the northwest coast, especially at Botany Bay, Bordeaux Bay, and Santa Maria Bay, isn't linked to any roads. Estate Bordeaux has some beautiful, rural stretches of lush mountain farmland, where farmers raise produce and livestock in the loamy green hills.

Getting Around

Renting a car is a great way to see the island and save money on taxi fares. On average, a taxi costs $8 per person per trip, which can add up if you plan a couple of outings from your resort every day. On the other hand, roads on the island can be steep, narrow, poorly lit, and twisting (and often not in the best of shape), so driving St. Thomas can be a challenge for inexperienced drivers—particularly at night. Plus, driving on the left can be somewhat of an adjustment for those used to driving on the right. One local advised thinking "shoulder to shoulder"—your left shoulder should be to the shoulder of the road.

Also keep in mind that normal **traffic congestion** at rush hours in Charlotte Amalie is only compounded by the morning arrival of sometimes thousands of cruise-ship passengers and the taxis and safari vans there to deliver them to their day's excursions. The good news is that waterfront traffic should be transformed in the next few years, when the harborfront road is expanded from two to a luxurious four lanes.

BY CAR

St. Thomas has many leading North American **car-rental firms** at the airport, and competition is stiff. Before you go, compare the rates of the "big three": **Avis** (℃ **800/331-1212** or 340/774-1468; www.avis.com), **Budget** (℃ **800/626-4516** or 340/776-5774; www.budgetstt.com), and **Hertz** (℃ **800/654-3131** or 340/774-1879; www.hertz.com). You can often save money by renting from a local agency, although vehicles may be older, with more wear and tear. Recommended agencies include **Dependable Car Rental,** 3901 B Altona, Welgunst, behind the Bank of Nova Scotia and the Medical Arts Complex (℃ **800/522-3076** or 340/774-2253; www.dependablecar.com), which provides free pickup and drop-off anywhere on St. Thomas and offers a 12 percent discount when you mention that you saw them on the Internet; and the aptly named **Discount Car Rental,** 14 Harwood Hwy., located just outside the airport on the main highway (℃ **877/478-2833** or 340/776-4858; www.discountcar.vi), which offers a 12 percent discount when you book online or through its Facebook page—and advertises "clean, new cars."

Note: Gas (petrol) was hovering close to $5 a gallon at press time.

DRIVING RULES *Always drive on the left.* The speed limit is 20 mph in town, 35 mph outside town. Seat belts are required by law, and it's illegal to talk on cellphones while driving.

PARKING Because Charlotte Amalie is a labyrinth of congested one-way streets, don't try to drive in town looking for a parking spot. If you can't find a place to park along the Waterfront (free), go to the sprawling lot to the east of Fort Christian, across from the Legislature Building. Parking fees are nominal here, and you can park your car and walk northwest toward Emancipation Park, or along the Waterfront, until you reach the shops and attractions.

BY TAXI

Taxi rates are set by the island's Taxi Association and fares are widely posted, even in taxis; check out the official fares in the free magazine "This Week" offered in most businesses. Look for officially licensed taxis only: You can spot them by their dome lights and the letters TP on the license plate. Still, be sure to confirm the rate with the driver before you get into the taxi. A typical fare from Charlotte Amalie to Sapphire Beach is $13 per person; from the airport to the Marriot Frenchman's Reef is $10 per person. We took a taxi one night from the Ritz-Carlton to Secret Harbour for dinner and were charged $5 a person. Surcharges are added after midnight. Add on $2 per bag for luggage (and a $1 surcharge for trips June 1–Sept 1).

Taxi vans and **open-air safaris** (converted truck beds with open-air seating) are ubiquitous around the island. Taxi vans are equipped to transport approximately 8 to 12 passengers to multiple destinations on the island, while safaris can often fit up to 25 people. It's cheaper to hop on a van or safari than ride a taxi on your own if you're going between your hotel and the airport, but keep in mind you will be making stops along the way—an exhausting proposition if you have arrived on a late flight. The cost for luggage ranges from $1 to $2 per bag. Call ℃ **340/774-7457** to order a taxi van.

If you don't plan to rent a car, it's easy to find taxi drivers. Just have your hotel or restaurant call a taxi for you, no matter where you are. Even better: Get the card of a favorite taxi driver and let him or her know your itinerary—or call the drivers we recommend below. Taxi drivers also make wonderful **sightseeing guides.** Expect to pay about $50 for a single-passenger tour or $25 per person for two or more passengers for 2 hours of sightseeing in a shared car.

If you're looking for a thoroughly engaging and wonderfully informative taxi driver/ tour guide, look no further than **Campbell Rey** (℃ 340/771-1568), the unofficial "mayor" of the island—we highly recommend his services. We also highly recommend **Llewelyn Powell** (℃ 340/771-1568 or 776-3887). For 24-hour radio-dispatch taxi service, call ℃ **340/774-7457.**

BY WATER TAXI

Getting around by **water taxi** is another way to travel. **Dohm's Water Taxi** is an inter-island water taxi service that will take you anywhere in the Virgin Islands you want to go in custom-built catamaran powerboats. It's a smart alternative if you're staying off island and your flight arrives in St. Thomas too late to catch a public ferry. Dohm's also offers water-taxi service directly between the Ritz-Carlton or Marriott Frenchman's Reef and St. John ($50 and $30 per person, respectively, with a five-person minimum). Go to www.watertaxi-vi.com or call ℃ **340/775-6501.**

BY BUS

Public buses run in the city and the country between 5:15am and 8pm daily, but waits can be very long and this is a difficult way to get about. A ride within Charlotte Amalie is 75¢; a ride to anywhere else is $1. For schedule and bus-stop information, call ℃ **340/774-5678.**

ON FOOT

Walking is the best way to explore the historic section of Charlotte Amalie during the day. However, you will need a car or driver to reach many other island attractions, including Coral World and Magens Bay.

[FastFACTS] ST. THOMAS

Banks FirstBank Virgin Islands (℃ **340/775-7777;** www.firstbankvi.com) has six locations on the island, with 24-hour ATMs at Crown Bay Center, East End Plaza, FirstBank Plaza, the Waterfront, and Yacht Haven. **Scotiabank** (℃ **340/776-5880;** www.scotiabank.com) has six locations on St. Thomas, including Havensight Mall and Tutu Park Mall; all branches have ATMs. **Banco Popular** ℃ **800/724-3655;** www.popular.com/vi) has branches in Charlotte Amalie and Red Hook. Most island banks are open Monday to Thursday 8:30am to 3pm, and Friday 8:30am to 4pm. The banks are your only option if you need to

exchange currency. More than 50 ATMs are available on the island.

Business Hours Typical business and store hours are Monday to Friday 9am to 5pm and Saturday 9am to 1pm. Some shops open Sunday for cruise-ship arrivals. Bars are usually open daily 11am to midnight or 1am, although some hot spots stay open later.

Dentists The V.I. Dental Center, Foothills Professional Building, 9151 Estate Thomas, Ste. 203 (℃ **340/ 772-6000;** http://vidental center.com), has a team of dentists that are members of the American Dental Association. Call for information or an appointment.

Doctors Schneider Regional Medical Center, 9048 Sugar Estate, Charlotte Amalie (℃ **340/776-8311;** www.rlshospital.org), provides services for locals and visitors.

Drugstores Go to **Havensight Pharmacy,** Havensight Mall, Building 4, Charlotte Amalie (℃ **340/ 777-5313**).

Emergencies For the police, call ℃ **911;** ambulance, ℃ **911;** fire, ℃ **921.**

Hospitals/Clinics The **Schneider Regional Medical Center** is at 9048 Sugar Estate, Charlotte Amalie (℃ **340/776-8311;** www. rlshospital.org). For 24-hour medical care call the **Red Hook Family Practice**

(✆ 340/775-2303) or **Doctors on Duty** (✆ 340/776-7966).

Hot Lines Call the **police** at ✆ **911** in case of emergency. If you have or witness a boating mishap, call the **U.S. Coast Guard Rescue** (✆ 787/729-6800), which operates out of San Juan, Puerto Rico. Scuba divers should note the number of a **decompression chamber** (✆ 340/776-8311) at the **Schneider Regional Medical Center** on St. Thomas.

Internet Most hotels and resorts now offer free Wi-Fi in the lobby. Many bars and restaurants also offer free Wi-Fi.

Laundry & Dry Cleaning The major hotels provide laundry service, but it's more expensive than a Laundromat. For dry cleaning, go to **One-Hour Martinizing,** Barbel Plaza, Charlotte Amalie (✆ 340/774-5452).

Mail Postage rates are the same as on the U.S. mainland: 34¢ for a postcard and 49¢ for a letter to U.S. addresses. For international mail, a first-class postcard or letter stamp costs $1.15.

Maps See "Visitor Information," earlier in this chapter.

Newspapers & Magazines Copies of U.S. mainland newspapers, such as "The New York Times," "USA Today," and "The Miami Herald," arrive daily in St. Thomas and sold at newsstands. "The Virgin Island Daily News" (http://virginislandsdailynews.com) covers local, national, and international events. "St. Thomas This Week," packed with visitor information, is distributed free on the island.

Police The main police headquarters is currently located in the Alexander Farrelly Criminal Justice Center in Charlotte Amalie (✆ 340/774-2211). The Crime Line phone number is ✆ 340/777-8700.

Post Office The main post office is at 9846 Estate Thomas, Charlotte Amalie (✆ 340/774-1950), and is open Monday to Friday 7:30am to 5pm and Saturday 7:30am to noon.

Safety The Virgin Islands are a relatively safe destination. The small permanent populations are generally friendly and welcoming. That being said, **St. Thomas** is no longer as safe as it once was. Crime, especially muggings, is on the rise in Charlotte Amalie. Wandering the town at night, especially on the back streets (particularly on Back St.), is not recommended. Avoid frequenting Charlotte Amalie's bars alone at night. Guard your valuables. Store them in hotel safes if possible, and make sure you keep your doors and windows shut at night.

Taxes The only local tax is an 10 percent hotel tax. St. Thomas has no sales or luxury taxes.

Telephone All island phone numbers have seven digits. It is not necessary to use the 340 area code when dialing within St. Thomas. Numbers for all three islands, including St. John and St. Croix, are found in the U.S. Virgin Islands phone book.

Tipping Go to "Fast Facts," in Chapter 8 for tipping guidelines.

Toilets You'll find public toilets at beaches and at the airport, but they are limited in town. Most visitors use the facilities of a bar or restaurant.

Transit Information Call ✆ 340/774-7457 to order a taxi 24 hours a day. Call ✆ 340/774-5100 for airport information and ✆ 340/776-6282 for information about ferry departures for St. John.

Weather For emergency (hurricane and disaster) weather reports, call **Vietema** at ✆ 340/774-2244.

WHERE TO STAY

The choice of hotels on St. Thomas divides almost evenly between small inns and B&Bs in Charlotte Amalie and full-service resorts along the East End and South Coast that front fabulous beaches. There are advantages and disadvantages to both.

renting A CONDO, APARTMENT, OR VILLA

Many visitors prefer renting a condo, apartment, or villa when they visit the island—particularly for the self-catering capabilities. We've found that **Calypso Realty** (© 800/747-4858 or 340/774-1620; www.calypsorealty.com) often has the best offers, especially on rentals from April to mid-December. A condo goes for $1,200 to $4,000 per week, with a 7-day minimum stay.

Another good source is **McLaughlin Anderson Luxury Caribbean Villas** (© 800/537-6246 or 340/776-0635; www.mclaughlinanderson.com), which has beautiful rentals not only on St. Thomas but also on St. John, St. Croix, and various other Caribbean isles. A two-bedroom villa begins at $2,000 per week in winter, with off-season rates beginning at $1,449.

Antilles Resorts (© 800/874-7897 or 340/775-6100; www.antillesresorts.com)

is a hit among habitual island-goers to St. Thomas and St. Croix, enjoying a repeat business for its wide range of properties, from economical to luxury.

You can also find excellent deals on popular owner-rented vacation lodging websites, including **VRBO** (www.vrbo.com) and **HomeAway** (www.homeaway.com); both websites list numerous attractive villas and condos throughout the Virgins. What you will *not* get with these rentals is service (unless advertised) or even guarantees that the rental is what is appears to be. Both VRBO and Home-Away sell rental guarantee insurance ($39 and up) that guarantees your money back under certain circumstances (the property has been double-booked or grossly misrepresented, for example)—so you may want to weigh that extra fee against the low rental rates.

If you want to be within close proximity to the island's best shopping, the widest choice of restaurants and bars, and most historic attractions, Charlotte Amalie is the place to be. And if you're looking for budget accommodations, or a choice of moderately priced inns, you'll need to be in or near Charlotte Amalie. The downside to staying here is that you'll have to take a shuttle or taxi ride over to a good beach, a ride of no more than 10 to 15 minutes from most Charlotte Amalie properties. The one exception to this rule is Marriott Frenchman's Reef, which offers the isolation of a beachside resort along with proximity to all of Charlotte Amalie's attractions and shops.

If your dream is to arrive in St. Thomas and anchor yourself directly on a beach, then the East End is the place to be. Beachfront resorts and condominiums on the East End and along the South Coast offer many perks, among them a measure of serenity and security. Expect a range of watersports, in-house spas and dining options. But almost without exception, the East End beachfront resorts are the most expensive properties on island. In spite of the cost, these hotels attract customers who want the full-service resort life that you simply won't find at the inns and B&Bs of Charlotte Amalie. The downside is that if you want to experience some of the island's best restaurants, you'll have to depend on taxis or risk driving along narrow, dark, and unfamiliar roads at night. To those who opt to stay resort-bound for most of their stay, we say call a taxi for a night out from the resort at least once while you're here.

Hotels in the Virgin Islands slash their prices in summer by 20 percent to 60 percent.

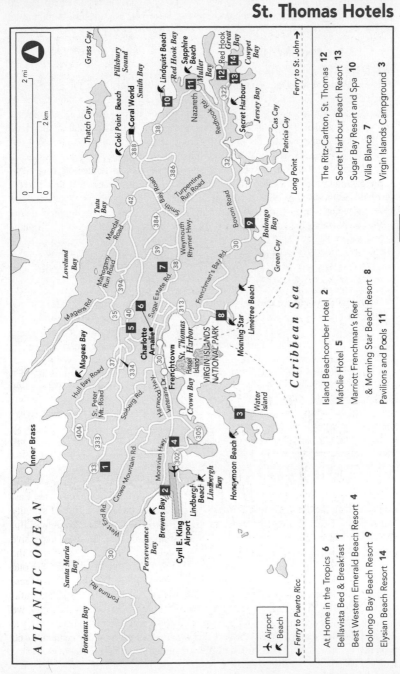

4

The Ritz-Carlton, St. Thomas **12**

Secret Harbour Beach Resort **13**

Sugar Bay Resort and Spa **10**

Villa Blanca **7**

Virgin Islands Campground **3**

Island Beachcomber Hotel **2**

Mafolie Hotel **5**

Marriott Frenchman's Reef
& Morning Star Beach Resort **8**

Pavilions and Pools **11**

At Home in the Tropics **6**

Bellavista Bed & Breakfast **1**

Best Western Emerald Beach Resort **4**

Bolongo Bay Beach Resort **9**

Elysian Beach Resort **14**

51

Two important notes on rates: Unless otherwise noted, the rates listed below do not include the 10 percent government hotel tax. Also note that most of the high-end resorts also tack on daily resort fees, from $35 to $50.

In Charlotte Amalie

MODERATE

Villa Santana ★★ Done up in Mexican clay tiles and stonework, this is the reconstructed palace of the exiled, former president of Mexico, General Antonio Lopez de Santa Anna of Mexico, who built it in the 1850s (the original burned in a fire in 1985). Pillowed in a garden of hibiscus and bougainvillea, Villa Santana has panoramic views of Charlotte Amalie and the St. Thomas harbor and six charming, handsomely furnished guest suites. La Mansion, in the villa's former library, is a duplex with a full kitchen; La Terraza is another split-level room with a spacious terrace offering views of the glittering harbor. La Torre has its own outdoor dining patio next to a gazebo. Many of the rooms have original rock walls and four-poster beds (one, rumor has it, was used by the General himself—the frame, not the mattress!). The shopping district in Charlotte Amalie is just a 5-minute walk away; Magens Bay Beach is a 15-minute drive north.

2602 Bjere Gade, No. 2D. ℂ **340/776-1311.** www.villasantana.com. 6 units. Winter $150–$245; off season $120–$176. Rates based on 3-night minimum; surcharge may be added for shorter stays. **Amenities:** Outdoor pool; Wi-Fi (free).

Windward Passage Hotel ★ This blocky hotel originated as a Holiday Inn and looks it. But despite its chain-hotel bones it's favored by business travelers and locals in transit to and from the other Virgin Islands. We think that's because it's well-maintained and friendly, but its location, just across the street from the Charlotte Amalie ferry docks, probably doesn't hurt, either. Rooms are dated but very clean (a renovation was in the works when we visited in early 2014), each with its own private balcony. Book a harbor-view room to fully appreciate the size and heft of the cruise ships slipping in and out of port.

Veterans Dr. ℂ **800/524-7389** or 340/774-5200. www.windwardpassage.com. 150 units. Winter $231–$275 double, $331–$375 suite; off season $150–$245 double, $274–$311 suite. **Amenities:** Restaurant; bar; babysitting; off-site health club ($25 per day); freshwater pool; putt-putt golf; spa; watersports equipment/rentals; Wi-Fi (free).

At Home in the Tropics ★★ This award-winning guesthouse is one of the best B&Bs in Charlotte Amalie, a traditional West Indian house where each room opens onto splendid views of Charlotte Amalie harbor. Dating from 1803 (it was the barracks for the guard of the Danish Governor), the inn feels exclusive and quite private, with a small harborside pool and attractively furnished rooms with tile floors and breeze-filled windows. It's up on Blackbeard's Hill (a swank neighborhood) and an easy walk to downtown and the shops of Charlotte Amalie—but those with mobility issues might have trouble navigating the stairs back up the hill. Closed from June 1 to November 1.

Blackbeard's Hill, 1680 Dronningens Gade. ℂ **340/777-9857.** http://athomeinthetropics.com. Winter $245–$265 double; off season $225–$245 double. Rates include breakfast. Children under 12 discouraged. **Amenities:** Outdoor swimming pool; Wi-Fi (free).

Bellavista Bed & Breakfast ★★ This wonderful four-room West Indian–style property is our favorite B&B in Charlotte Amalie. It's nestled on Denmark Hill, a restored island estate overlooking the city harbor and just a 5-minute walk into town.

Charlotte Amalie Hotels & Restaurants

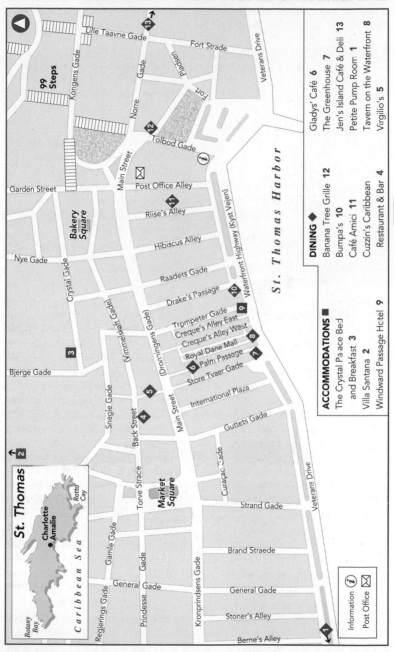

DINING ◆

Banana Tree Grille **12**
Bumpa's **10**
Café Amici **11**
Cuzzin's Caribbean
Restaurant & Bar **4**
Gladys' Café **6**
The Greenhouse **7**
Jen's Island Café & Deli **13**
Petite Pump Room **1**
Tavern on the Waterfront **8**
Virgilio's **5**

ACCOMMODATIONS ■

The Crystal Palace Bed
and Breakfast **3**
Villa Santana **2**
Windward Passage Hotel **9**

Information ⓘ
Post Office ⊠

St. Thomas Harbor

4

ST. THOMAS | Where to Stay

Rooms are dreamy, with slatted wood ceilings, wood floors, and tastefully done tropical hues. You can relax after a day of touring on the sun-dappled pool deck or in the breezy open-air living room, framed in lush foliage. Reserve early; this place books up. *Note:* Do not confuse this B&B with the Bellavista Scott hotel in Estate Thomas, which offers much more basic accommodations.

2713 Murphy Gade 12–14. ℂ **888/333-3063** or 340/714-5706. www.bellavista-bnb.com. 4 units. Winter $220–$295 double; summer $195–$270 double. Rates include breakfast. **Amenities:** Concierge; outdoor pool; Wi-Fi (free).

INEXPENSIVE

The Crystal Palace Bed and Breakfast ★ This stately old colonial home, filled with antiques, West Indian relics, and family flotsam and jetsam, is overseen by owner Ronnie Lockhart, who grew up here. It has plenty of old-world personality, with elegant and airy parlor rooms, some with walls lined with early-19th-century stonework. Rooms are oversized and high-ceilinged but not particularly fancy. Three of the five accommodations have shared facilities in the corridors; of the two rooms with private baths, one is downstairs and the other is up (both have queen four-posters). Stay here if you appreciate old-school languor…or look forward to soaking in views of the harbor from the veranda while sipping a cocktail from the honor bar.

12 Crystal Gade. ℂ **866/502-2277** or 340/777-2277. www.crystalpalaceusvi.com. 5 units, 2 with bathrooms. Winter $139 double without bathroom, $169 double with bathroom; off season $119 double without bathroom, $139 double with bathroom. Extra person $20/night. Rates include breakfast. **Amenities:** Wi-Fi (free).

Mafolie Hotel ★ This good-value gem sits high in the hills above Charlotte Amalie and its sparkling harbor—the views are splendid during the day but off-the-charts gorgeous at night. It has a congenial proprietor in Adam Israel, and the superb **Mafolie Restaurant** (p. 62) is one of the island's best, a big proponent of the island's farm-to-table movement with a menu featuring farm-grown produce and fresh-caught seafood. Each room is pleasantly furnished; none are swank by any means, in fact, some are on the smallish side, and a little dark, and a handful are only entered on the road side of the resort. But all are comfortable, with quality beds. Of the 22 rooms, 10 will have outdoor balconies by the time you read this, with those glittering harbor views at your feet, and five are suites. You can take a dip in the pool, which enjoys the same panoramic vista, or simply drink in the views at the pool bar.

7091 Estate Mafolie. ℂ **340/774-2790.** www.mafolie.com. 22 units. Winter $144–$160 double; off season $105–$125 double. Rates include continental breakfast. Up to 2 children 12 and under stay free in parent's room. Extra person $15. Ask about island packages. **Amenities:** Restaurant; 2 bars; concierge; pool; Wi-Fi (free).

Villa Blanca ★ Set on 3 acres of lush hilltop just 1½ miles east of Charlotte Amalie, the Villa Blanca provides killer views of the harbor and mossy hills rising out of blue seas. It's nestled in lovingly tended gardens. Each room comes with a well-equipped kitchenette, tile floors, good beds, and a private balcony or terrace with views either eastward to St. John or westward to the Charlotte Amalie harbor and the cruise-ship docks. Take a dip in the freshwater pool or watch the sun set from the villa's lounge deck. Charlotte Amalie shopping is just a 5-minute taxi ride away.

4 Raphune Hill, Rte. 38. ℂ **800/231-0034** or 340/776-0749. www.villablancahotel.com. 14 units. Winter $135–$145 double; off season $95–$105 double. Rates include continental breakfast. Children 9 and under stay free in parent's room. Extra person $15/night. **Amenities:** Pool (outdoor); Wi-Fi, in lobby (free).

West of Charlotte Amalie

EXPENSIVE

Best Western Emerald Beach Resort ★   Yes, this Best Western is located just across from the airport, but it's also set on a pretty white-sand beach, with beachfront views from every room. Lying 2 miles to the west of Charlotte Amalie, to which it is linked by free shuttle service. Emerald Beach attracts both businesspeople and families for its location close to the airport and town. The rooms are outfitted in standard Best Western furnishings, but everything is clean and comfortable, with king-size beds in every room. If this is booked, try its sister property, **Best Western Carib Beach Resort** (© **800/792-2742** in the U.S. or 340/774-2525; www.caribbeachresort.com), just a 5-minute walk away at 70C Lindbergh Bay, with affordable oceanview rooms with private terraces.

8070 Lindbergh Bay. © **800/233-4936** in the U.S., or 340/777-8800. www.emeraldbeach.com. 90 units. Winter $200–$327 double; off season $159 and up double. Children 11 and under stay free in parent's room. **Amenities:** Restaurant; 2 bars; fitness center; high-speed Internet (free); pool; tennis court (lit); watersports.

MODERATE

Island Beachcomber Hotel ★   The island's first beachfront hotel opened up on Lindbergh Bay in 1956 and was once frequented by the likes of Cecil B. DeMille and Vivian Vance (Ethel Mertz from "I Love Lucy"). Yes, this hotel has seen glitzier days, and it's fairly standard-issue in every way today, but you can't beat the location on beauteous Lindbergh Bay. This is a good place to stay if you're in transit by air or ferry and you don't want to spend a lot of money—and it's surprisingly comfortable and tropical-beachy. Look for medium-size rooms, many with patios just steps from the beach.

8071 Lindbergh Beach Rd. © **340/774-5250.** www.islandbeachcomber.net. 48 units. Winter $199–$225 double; off season $130–$169 double. Extra person $15. **Amenities:** Restaurant; bar; Wi-Fi (free).

The South Coast

EXPENSIVE

Marriott Frenchman's Reef & Morning Star Beach Resort ★★   If you like a full-service American-style resort with plenty of onsite entertainment and dining options—and a fetching sweep of white-sand beach—this resort should fit the bill. As the only major resort in close proximity to Charlotte Amalie (it's just 3 miles east), it's a beehive of activity and, some say, the heartbeat of the island's south shore. If you're looking for better-quality rooms and a more luxurious ambience, head to the **Ritz-Carlton** (p. 56). But if you want to be where the action is in Charlotte Amalie, this is the spot.

This is the largest hotel in the U.S. Virgin Islands, made up of two separate parts, Frenchman's Reef and Morning Star, that were joined into one mega-resort in 2005 in an excellent location on a bluff overlooking both the harbor and the Caribbean. Around the corner is **Frenchman's Cove,** the 220-room timeshare section of the resort, with luxury two- and three-bedroom villas. (And yes, you may be asked to learn more about the timeshares during your stay: In the Marriott lobby, a booth offers rum punches and other enticements to get people to attend timeshare promotions. Don't be shy about saying "no" if you're not interested and they'll let you be.)

The rooms at Frenchman's Reef are traditionally furnished and comfortable (with the Marriott's signature silky linens and bedding), if uninspired. Those at the Morning Star are more spacious, some opening up right onto the beach with dreamy water views from patios or balconies (non-sea-view balconies have views of the green hills opposite). Note that the resorts are a half-mile apart, and getting from one to another is a bit of a hike (nearly 100 steps uphill from Morning Star to Frenchman's Reef); a shuttle runs guests between the two sections as well.

The in-house dining is exceptional, and you won't go wrong with dinner at the excellent **Havana Blue** (p. 66), a Miami-style beachfront boîte at Morning Star with a truly inspired menu. The Marriott also has a well-respected in-house tour operator, **Adventure Center** (www.adventurecenters.net), which offers snorkeling, sailing, and kayak excursions (the latter in clear see-through kayaks).

Note that daily **water-taxi service** in a gondola-style boat is available straight from the Marriott dock to the shopping hub in Charlotte Amalie. The boat leaves the resort every 30 minutes between 8:30am and 5pm (one-way: $7 adults, $4 children 3–12).

No. 5 Estate Bakkeroe. © **888/236-2427** or 340/776-8500. www.marriott.com. 478 units. Winter $475–$745 double, from $760 suite; off season $300–$630 double, from $600 suite. Children 12 and under stay free in parent's room. Daily resort fee $35. **Amenities:** 5 restaurants; 2 bars; coffeehouse; deli; babysitting; health club and spa; room service; 2 tennis courts (lit); watersports equipment/rentals; Wi-Fi (included in $35-a-day resort fee).

MODERATE

Bolongo Bay Beach Resort ★ This family-run resort is a casual, barefoot place to stay. A complex of pink two-story buildings, it's built around a crescent-shaped beach on the sands of Bolongo Bay. That means plenty of watersports activities (even scuba-diving lessons), so many guests check in on the European Plan, which includes watersports activities and even a scuba-diving lesson. Others opt for all-inclusive plans that include all meals, drinks, excursions, and more. Both are good values, especially for St. Thomas. Rooms are simple, summery, and filled with comfortable furniture and a fridge—and all face the beach, with a balcony or terrace opening up onto the beach. Nine two-bedroom condos, in a three-story building, have full kitchens and are ideal for families of up to five. Onsite are two lively restaurants, including **Iggies** (p. 66). A final enticement? The resort is known for its Wednesday-night **Carnival,** held from November through Labor Day, with a Caribbean buffet, calypso music, and Moko Jumbie stilt dancers.

7150 Bolongo. © **800/524-4746** or 340/775-1800. www.bolongobay.com. 80 units. Winter $250–$415 double, $570–$620 condo; off season $145–$350 double, $350–$520 condo. Extra person $25 per day. Children 12 and under $15 per day. Resort fee 7%. Ask about the resort's all-inclusive plans. **Amenities:** 2 restaurants, including Iggies Beach Bar & Grill (p. 66); 2 bars; babysitting; children's programs (ages 4–12); exercise room; 2 pools (outdoor); 2 tennis courts (lit); watersports equipment/rentals; Wi-Fi by pool (free).

The East End

The shuttered **Grand Beach Palace,** closed up tight for almost 10 years, is expected to reopen in late 2014 as a full-service 262-unit **Wyndham Margaritaville Vacation Club resort.** The former Renaissance hotel fronts one of the island's prettiest beaches, Grand Beach, opening onto Smith Bay.

EXPENSIVE

The Ritz-Carlton, St. Thomas ★★★ This is the island's one true luxury resort. Fronted by white-sand beaches and the protected turquoise seas of Great Bay, the Ritz covers a sprawling 30 acres of oceanfront on the southeastern tip of St. Thomas, 4 miles (a 30-min. drive) from Charlotte Amalie. Its centerpiece is a Venetian-style palazzo, surrounded by terraced gardens. Pathways lead down to the curving infinity pool (home to two resident ducks) and a beach with canopied chairs and a bustling food and beverage service.

All day long, the resort's water-sports toys see plenty of use on Great Bay, from stand-up paddleboards to Hobie Cats to kayaks to snorkel equipment—it's a veritable kids' playground, with a full-service dive shop, Patagon Dive Center, right on property. (The bay bottom is somewhat grassy and pebbly, however.) The terrific Ritz Kids activities are part of the resident Jean-Michel Cousteau's "Ambassadors of the Environment" program, with excursions for all ages, including explorations of the coral reef, island mangroves, and constellations. Adults can try night snorkeling in Great Bay or sign up for ocean kayak adventures in clear-bottom kayaks. If you've always wanted to learn to sail, take advantage of the on-site certified sailing school, Island Sol. Finally, the property has its own private 53-foot catamaran, *Lady Lynsey*, in which guests can take full and half-day sailing excursions.

The resort's main lobby has a generic feel in spite of its elegant appointments, but the Ritz rooms are the island's best, supremely comfortable and spacious, with great big bathrooms (tubs and rain showers) and top-of-the-line amenities throughout. The resort features an extensive spa with luxurious treatment rooms and open-air cabanas. Of the restaurants, **Bleuwater** (p. 66) is chillingly expensive but a real special-occasion spot. Finally, the warm and friendly Ritz staff is unparalleled on an island that still has a few things to learn about personal service. In addition to the 180 hotel rooms, the resort also holds a number of Ritz-Carlton Destination Club timeshare villas.

6900 Great Bay ⓒ **800/241-3333** or 340/775-3333. www.ritzcarlton.com. 100 units. Winter $660–$880 double, from $1,290 suite; off season $380–$570 double, from $700 suite. Daily resort fee $50. **Amenities:** 4 restaurants; 3 bars; ATM; babysitting; children's programs; concierge; full-service health club and spa; 2 pools (outdoor); room service; sailing school; 2 tennis courts (lit); watersports equipment/rentals; Wi-Fi (free).

Sugar Bay Resort and Spa ★★   No longer a Wyndham property, this 294-room all-inclusive resort has undergone exciting renovations, with recent refreshments of all rooms, the lobby, and the main restaurant, which by press time, should be a fully operating Japanese teppanyaki steakhouse. It's an impressive, well-maintained property, on one of the island's prettiest perches, a 32-acre plot of sloping terrain just 5 minutes from the ferry terminal at Red Hook. From its position atop a rocky promontory, guests are treated to panoramic views out over the sea. At its feet is a pretty, secluded beach that's smallish but excellent for snorkeling and swimming. It's a fine family resort, with a wonderful pool/beach/restaurant area called the **Mangroves** right on the beach (reached via a steep walk 99 steps down from the hotel; those with mobility issues can reach it by hotel shuttle). On Thursday the Mangroves rocks with a Carnival party, and the daily activities are many and varied (sunrise Pilates, pool volleyball, iguana feedings). Rooms are attractively furnished but are more utilitarian than luxe, each with a small balcony—the only thing that distinguishes one room from another is the view, so if you want to guarantee those amazing ocean vistas, request it when booking. Still, the 2013 renovations have given the rooms a pleasant new look, with tile floors replacing carpet, marble counters in bathrooms, and a beachy blue-and-white palette. Those who want to splash out, so to speak, go for the properties cushier 475-square-foot suites. Sugar Bay offers both all-inclusive plans and room-only rates;

the all-inclusive plans make sense for those who prefer to stay put during their vacation—and with Sugar Bay's lineup of good restaurants, full complement of water sports, and ongoing daily activities, you may never have to leave the premises.

6500 Estate Smith Bay. (C) **800/927-7100** or 340/777-7100. www.sugarbayresortandspa.com. 294 units. Winter $310–$700 double, from $1,250 suite; off season $238–$530 double, from $1,050 suite. Check the website for all-inclusive plans; all-inclusives include 15% service charge. **Amenities:** 3 restaurants; 2 bars; babysitting; basketball court; boat dock; children's programs; exercise room; miniature golf; 3 pools; 4 tennis courts (lit); watersports (canoes, kayaks, sailboats, snorkeling gear); Wi-Fi (free).

Elysian Beach Resort ★   This resort overlooks its own secluded cove bobbing with boats and white-sand beach on Cowpet Bay, a 30-minute drive from Charlotte Amalie. It's not luxurious like the Ritz next door, but it's tranquil and secluded, and the exquisite white-sand beach and free-form swimming pool sweeten the deal. The one-bedroom condos (which can hold up to four people) contain kitchenettes and balconies, and 14 offer sleeping lofts that are reached by a spiral staircase. Look for standard-issue tropical decor, with rattan and bamboo furnishings, ceiling fans, and natural-wood ceilings. Rooms in buildings V to Z are some distance from the beach, so try to avoid them when booking. The resort has two good restaurants, including the **Caribbean Fish Market** (p. 66), a fun spot with tables right on the beach, serving creative West Indian cuisine since 2012.

6800 Estate Nazareth. (C) **866/620-7994** or 340/775-1000. www.elysianbeachresort.net. 180 units. Winter $220–$265 double, $459 suite; off season $215–$260 double, $399 suite. **Amenities:** 2 restaurants; 2 bars; exercise room; pool (outdoor); small spa; tennis court (lit); watersports equipment/rentals, Wi-Fi (free; lobby only).

Pavilions and Pools ★   If absolute seclusion is on your wish list, this 25-unit condominium resort might be just the ticket: Each villa opens onto its own private

Camping Out on Water Island

St. Thomas has its own bucolic pocket of rusticity—and it's just off the hustle and bustle of the Charlotte Amalie harbor. Called the **Virgin Islands Campground** on **Water Island** ((C) **340/776-5488;** www.virginislandscampground.com), guests stay in the most eco-sensitive lodgings in St. Thomas. They're hardly roughing it: The digs are wood-frame-and-canvas cabins (cottages) with wind-drawn electricity, nice beds, and crisp linens. Each opens onto private, ocean-view terraces. The campground has no restaurant, but you can grill your own meals in the common area known as the **Pavilion;** you can also store your food in a refrigerator or freezer. From the campgrounds, it's a 5-minute walk to the island's idyllic **Honeymoon Beach,** where you can take a swim, snorkel or just nurse a nice tan. Regular ferry service runs between Water Island and St. Thomas (trip time: 7 min.).

A 3-night minimum stay is required; cabins cost $165 per night in winter and $115 per night in the off season. Cabins accommodate up to 3 adults and 2 children. The campground also has a special suite with a fully equipped kitchen and its own private bath and deck ($149–$200 per night).

Water Island is very small; to get around, simply hike along the island's pristine trails. You can also take bike rides (see chapter 8). For more on visiting Water Island, see p. 79.

swimming pool. Sure the pools are smallish, but each has a tile deck with loungers that's walled off and pillowed in tropical greenery. Need more privacy? There's no need to dine out: Here you can cook your own meals in a well-equipped kitchen, or dine on affordable Mexican fare in the resort's open-air restaurant, **Torcido Taco.** Villas are generally comfortable and spacious (the International Pool Villas have 1,400 sq. ft. of space; Caribbean Pool Villas 1,200 sq. ft.), though they each have an individual look as they're all privately owned. The resort is just 1 mile from the bars and restaurants of Red Hook and 7 miles east of Charlotte Amalie. One of the island's best beaches and watersports concessions, Sapphire Bay, is a (steep uphill) walk away—but you may never feel like venturing out of your bubble of quiet seclusion.

6400 Estate Smith Bay. © **800/524-2001** or 340/775-6110. www.pavilionsandpools.com. 25 units. Winter $240–$350 double; off season $200–$280 double. Extra person $25 per night. Rates include continental breakfast. **Amenities:** Restaurant; private pools; watersports equipment/rentals; Wi-Fi (free in lobby).

Secret Harbour Beach Resort ★

This boutique all-suites condo resort sits on the white-sand beach at Nazareth Bay, near Red Hook Marina, with excellent snorkeling just outside your door. The four low-rise buildings have southwestern exposure (great sunsets!), and each room is beachfront or oceanview, mere steps from the sand (some bottom-floor suites even have outdoor showers on their patios). Each room and suite comes a private deck or patio and a fully equipped kitchen. The resort rooms are individually owned, so it's impossible to say what the decor will be like, though most owners go for attractive furnishings. There are three types of accommodations: studio suites, one-bedroom suites, and two-bedroom suites. Each one- and two-bedroom suite has a pullout couch. All rooms have king-size beds; the two-bedroom suites may have one king and two twins. Secret Harbour is also home to one of the best restaurants on the island, the **Sunset Grille** (p. 67). The resort has a full-service dive site on the premises, **Aqua Action Dive Center** (© **340/775-6285;** www.aadivers.com), which offers PADI courses, snorkeling equipment, and snorkeling outings.

6280 Estate Nazareth. © **800/524-2250** or 340/775-6550. www.secretharbourvi.com. 60 units. Winter $355–$435 double, $385–$505 1-bedroom suite, $635–$765 2-bedroom suite; off season $255–$305 double, $285–$375 1-bedroom suite, $535–$635 2-bedroom suite. Children 12 and under stay free in parent's room. Each additional guest $35 per day. **Amenities:** Restaurant; bar; dive shop; exercise room; pool (outdoor); 3 tennis courts (lit); watersports equipment/rentals; Wi-Fi (free).

WHERE TO EAT

The dining scene in St. Thomas these days is among the best in the West Indies, but it has its drawbacks: Fine dining—and even not-so-fine dining—tends to be expensive, and you may have to travel by taxi or car to reach some of the best spots.

You'll find an eclectic mix of global cuisines on St. Thomas, including Italian, Mexican, Asian, and French. American fast-food franchises, pizza joints, and East Indian roti shacks are also part of the scene. But some of the best food on St. Thomas is island-bred: West Indian–style cuisine and interesting fusions thereof. We particularly like those places that take advantage of the island's natural bounty, menus featuring fresh-caught seafood, fresh fruit, and locally grown produce. Finally, go where the locals go: They know the best spots and are happy to recommend their favorites.

St. Thomas Restaurants

A Room with a View **8**
Bleuwater **15**
Blue Orchid **2**
The Caribbean Fish Market **16**
Caribbean Saloon **14**

Epernay Bistro **3**
Fish Tails **13**
Frenchtown Deli **4**
Havana Blue **9**
Hook, Line & Sinker **4**

Hull Bay Hideaway **1**
Iggies Beach Bar & Grill **10**
Latitude 18 **14**
Mafolie Restaurant **6**
Margaritaville **11**

Oceana **5**
The Old Stone Farmhouse **7**
Sunset Grille **17**
Señor Pizza **12**

FARM-FRESH produce ON ESTATE BORDEAUX

In 1984 a Vietnam vet named Myron ("Buddy") Henneman found solace in a serene spot high up in the green hills of the island's western end, with vistas of blue seas and robin's-egg skies. In the loamy volcanic soil, once tended by French farmers who immigrated here from St. Barts, he planted a chemical-free garden, and pretty soon the government was offering him agricultural land leases. Today, the **Green Ridge Guava-berry Farm** is thriving, part of the island's burgeoning agrarian renaissance. Some 20 Estate Bordeaux farms now grow crops of astonishing diversity in these quiet green hills, an edenic haven from the scrum of civilization far down below. "Once you train the land," says Henneman, "the land will grow any-thing." And it does, including peas, Asian dragonfruit, okra, cashews, even the healing "tree of life," the meranga bush (said to be good for the liver). A whopping 17-pound cauliflower was recently plucked from the soil, beneath which had been growing a 200-pound pumpkin. A number of Rastafarian gardeners work the land throughout the islands, and lunch is some delicious con-coction: roasted wild salmon or pumpkin soup made in a big clay pot over a fire. You can buy produce from this and other Estate Bordeaux farms, as well as fresh-baked bread, eggs, honey, and exotic island juices, in the **Saturday morning market** at Market Square, in Charlotte Amalie, and on the second and last Sun-day of every month at the **Bordeaux farmer's market** (10am–4pm), in an open-air pavilion near the entrance to the Preserve at Botany Bay. In January (usually around Jan. 19 and 20) the farms hold the weekend-long **Agricultural & Cultural Food Fair,** where some 2,000 visitors enjoy reggae music, crafts, farm tours, and more on the farms themselves from 10am to midnight. Contact the Bor-deaux Farmers' Market at ✆ **340/774-4204.** The farmer's market and farm fair are in part sponsored by the nonprofit organization **We Grow Food** (www.facebook.com/WEGROWFOOD), which hopes to reclaim some 400 acres of Estate Bordeaux land for growing food.

In Charlotte Amalie
EXPENSIVE

Amalia Café ★ SPANISH   Set on an alfresco terrace on Palm Passage in the center of Charlotte Amalie, this long-established spot serves up some of the most savory Spanish cuisine in town. You can order one of the hearty entrees (paella Valenciana, say, or *zarzuela de mariscos,* seafood casserole) or make a meal out of tapas, flavorful small plates that might include garlic shrimp, chorizo sautéed in cider, or clams in a green sauce. Wash it all down with the Amalia's signature sangria.

24 Palm Passage. ✆ **340/714-7373.** http://amaliacafe.com. Reservations recommended. Main courses lunch $15–$23, dinner $28–$49. Mon–Sat 11am–10pm; Sun 11am–3pm (winter only).

Banana Tree Grille ★★ INTERNATIONAL   Dine in an atmosphere of informal elegance with views over the bustling harbor at this longtime favorite in Bluebeard's Castle timeshare resort. It's a special-occasion spot (with prices to match), but the views are sublime. The real surprise is the equally elegant food, overseen by a trans-planted New Orleans chef. We recommend the grouper stuffed with crab imperial, and the meltingly tender, grass-fed Banana Tree filet mignon in a bérnaise sauce. Breads are also a specialty, particularly the "Oh My" Gorgonzola loaf (garlicky Ciabatta with a Gorgonzola dipping sauce). The fantastic desserts include a nod to the Big Easy: bananas Foster cheesecake drizzled in homemade chocolate sauce.

In Bluebeard's Castle, Bluebeard's Hill. ✆ **340/776-4050.** www.bananatreegrille.com. Reservations recommended. Main courses $20–$56. Tues–Sun 5:30–9:30pm.

Mafolie Restaurant ★★ CARIBBEAN/INTERNATIONAL This is one of the island's top restaurants—and you get your money's worth, from the terrific island fare to the breathtaking views of the Charlotte Amalie harbor below from the open-air dining room. The Caribbean specialties include a classic kalaloo soup, here brimming with shrimp, crab, and okra; and conch fritters served with sweet mango Scotch bonnet honey. Chef Manny Thompson has a deft touch: For a main course, try the jambalaya; it has a subtle fire and perfectly caramelized vegetables. Fresh-caught fish and Water Island lobster are also highly recommended—the proprietor and his bartender often do morning lobster fishing for the night's meal. Look for traditional island sides like fungi (thickened cornmeal polenta), breadfruit mash, and sweet potato dumplings.

7091 Estate Mafolie. ✆ **340/774-2790.** www.mafolie.com. Entrees $27–$39. Daily 6–10pm.

Petite Pump Room ★★ WEST INDIAN/INTERNATIONAL Join the locals for a reliably tasty St. Thomas breakfast and lunch at this second-floor harborside spot in the ferryboat terminal in Charlotte Amalie. Located on the harbor since 1970, it serves some of the island's most flavorful West Indian cooking, with a menu of callaloo greens, conch fritters (a house specialty), and daily specials like fried potfish or conch sauteed in butter sauce. Sides include pigeon peas and rice, fungi with vegetables, and fried plantains. It's a convenient spot for a bite if you're waiting for a ferry. Snag a seat on the seaside deck and watch ships cruise into the harbor.

In the Edward Wilmoth Blyden Building, Veterans Dr. ✆ **340/776-2976.** www.petitepumproom. com. Breakfast $7–$13; sandwiches and salads $8–$18; platters $14–$20. Daily 7am–4:30pm.

A Room with a View ★★ INTERNATIONAL Just east of Charlotte Amalie, this topnotch restaurant serves up international classics and wraparound harbor views from open floor-to-ceiling windows. Kick off your dinner with one of the specialty martinis (Grand Marnier martini, melon martini) and smoked salmon on toast points or grilled portobello mushrooms with goat cheese. Main courses include one of several house pastas (Alfredo, pesto, meat sauce); chicken in a creamy curry sauce; shrimp Creole; or a New York strip steak *au poivre.*

In Bluebeard's Castle, Bluebeard's Hill. ✆ **340/774-2377.** Reservations recommended. Main courses $19–$42. Mon–Sat 5–11pm.

Tavern on the Waterfront ★ MODERN EUROPEAN/CARIBBEAN How's this for a global mashup: a nightclub/restaurant that serves inventive French and Polish dishes with West Indies inflections in a glittering setting on the St. Thomas waterfront. Sounds odd, but it works. So you might pinball from Polish pierogies to garlic escargots to "Down Island" conch chowder. Recommended entrees include the house babyback ribs; an almond-and-hazelnut-crusted grouper; and a jumbo vegetable pot pie. Come for live jazz on Friday nights or a tropical cocktail at the upstairs bar.

Waterfront at Royal Dane Mall, 30 Dronningens Gade. ✆ **340/776-4328.** www.tavernonthewaterfront.com. Reservations required. Main courses $14–$37 (Caribbean lobster $53). Mon–Sat 11am–3pm; Mon–Thurs 5–9pm; Fri–Sat 5–10pm.

groceries, markets & more:
PROVISIONING RESOURCES ON ST. THOMAS

More than any other Virgin Island, St. Thomas has no lack of stores to find what you need to eat and drink and stock your pantry. That's because it's a prime provisioning stop for boaters, and the many people who visit the island stay in rented houses, villas, and condo (even resorts) with full kitchens. Here's a sampling of resources:

Groceries: Open daily, the chain grocery **Pueblo** has three locations on St. Thomas including Rumer Drive in Charlotte Amalie (**℄ 340/774-4200**). In Red Hook, the **Food Center** (**℄ 340/777-8806**; www. foodcentervi.com) is the largest grocery on the East End; it's open daily. Also open daily is the local favorite **Plaza Extra,** Tutu Park Mall (**℄ 340/775-5646**; http://plazaextra.com).

Fresh Seafood: S&P Seafoods, 3801 Crown Bay (**℄ 340/774-5280**), is a full-service fishmonger. You can also buy fresh-off-the-boat fish at the docks at Frenchtown when the fishing boats return around 3pm or 4pm.

Fresh Produce/Fruit: St. Thomas has a number of small farmer's markets, including the Saturday market at **Market Square** in Charlotte Amalie, and the **Bordeaux farmer's market** on the second and last Sunday of each month in Estate Bordeaux, on the island's west end.

Liquor: Liquor stores abound along Main Street in Charlotte Amalie, and liquor, wine, and beer are sold in most grocery stores throughout the island. **Al Cohen's Discount Liquors,** Long Bay Road (**℄ 340/774-3690**; www.rumanyone. com/AlCohen.htm): One of St. Thomas's most famous outlets occupies a big warehouse at Havensight, across from the West Indian Company docks, where cruise-ship passengers disembark. Inside is a huge storehouse of liquor and wine.

Virgilio's ★★ ITALIAN   The best Italian restaurants on island, Virgilio's serves up Sicilian classics and homemade pastas and risottos, including a hearty "Lasagna de Maria," from a Virgilio family recipe. You can also get traditional veal and chicken dishes, as well as a sprinkling of fresh-made pizzas, including a terrific *pizza del mare*, with shrimp and calamari. The restaurant's old-world charm is enhanced by wood beams and vaulted brick. Paintings in ornate frames line buttery-yellow walls. Look for Virgilio's tucked in an alley between Main and Back streets.

18 Dronningens Gade (entrance on a narrow alley running btw. Main and Back sts.) **℄ 340/776-4920.** www.virgiliosvi.com. Reservations recommended. Main courses lunch $18–$30, dinner $23–$48. Mon–Sat 11:30am–10pm; closed Sun.

MODERATE

Cuzzin's Caribbean Restaurant & Bar ★ CARIBBEAN   For authentic Caribbean cooking, head to this casual old-school lunch spot in a former 18th-century stable on Back Street. The brick-and-wood dining room has windows looking onto the street and a comfortable feel. Look for classic island dishes with an emphasis on seafood, especially lobster and fresh-caught fish. Conch comes in a variety of preparations, from curried conch to conch Creole to conch fritters. You can make a genuine West Indies meal out of the sides alone, which include fungi (cornmeal grits), peas and rice, fried plantains, and island coleslaw.

7 Wimmelskafts Gade (Back St.). **℄ 340/777-4711.** www.cuzzinsvi.com. Reservations recommended. Main courses $9–$22. Mon–Sat 11am–4:30pm.

Gladys' Café ★★ CARIBBEAN/AMERICAN   Dine on local favorites prepared to perfection at Gladys's Café, a lively spot housed in a 1700 pump house smack-dab in the middle Charlotte Amalie's historic district. It's open for breakfast or lunch only. Sample jerk mahi-mahi, curry chicken roti, creamy conch chowder, and kalaloo soup. Entrees come with peas and rice or fungi, a local cornmeal-based specialty similar to polenta or grits. A house specialty is the colorful and nutritious Caribbean lobster salad in a homegrown avocado—you can also get it with tuna or chicken salad. The owner, Gladys, is in the house daily—if you're lucky you will hear her occasionally burst into song. Don't leave without taking home a bottle of Gladys' homemade hot sauce, made with local peppers.

Royal Dane Mall. ℂ **340/774-6604.** http://gladyscafe.com. Reservations required for groups of 6 or more. Breakfast $3.75–$19; lunch main courses $10–$25. Daily 7am–5pm.

INEXPENSIVE

Bumpa's ★ AMERICAN   A deli-style joint, Bumpa's is perfect when you want something simple but well-made. Many people, locals and visitors alike, stop in early in the morning to breakfast on terrific oatmeal banana pancakes, omelets, bagels, and lemonade. Lunch features burgers and sandwiches. Bumpa's is located on the second floor of a building that faces the busy highway along the harbor.

38-A Waterfront Hwy. ℂ **340/776-5674.** http://bumpas.travelstthomasusvi.com. Main courses $7–$14. Daily 7:30am–5pm.

Café Amici ★ ITALIAN/CARIBBEAN   A reliable spot for lunch during a shopping expedition in Charlotte Amalie's historic district, Café Amici is located on an elevated patio in an old stone alley. It's known for its creative brick-oven-baked pizzas (including a Caribbean jerk pizza and a crab-cake pizza with mango-tomato relish) and satisfying pastas (such as a shrimp scampi pasta). Wraps, and sandwiches are also on the menu. Nutritious choices include hearty salads and veggie-rich Italian soups.

A.H. Riise's Alley. ℂ **340/714-7704.** www.cafeamicivi.com. Lunch specials $9.95–$13; pizza $14–$18. Daily 10:30am–3:30pm.

Jen's Island Café & Deli ★ DELI/CARIBBEAN   The food is good and tasty, the welcome warm, and the prices reasonable at this cafe/deli in Charlotte Amalie's downtown shopping district, right across from Emancipation Garden. In addition, the cafe has quite an extensive menu, from breakfast eggs to American-style deli sandwiches to burgers and salads. Jen even does classic island dishes, such as conch fritters, rotis, and local chicken soup with dumplings. The lobster and shrimp quesadillas are made with Cruzan rum–soaked onions.

Grand Hotel, 43–46 Norre Gade. ℂ **340/777-4611** or 514-5345. http://jensdeli.com. Breakfast $5–$10; main courses $6.75–$9. Mon–Fri 7am–5pm; Sat 10:30am–4pm.

North of Charlotte Amalie
EXPENSIVE

The Old Stone Farmhouse ★★★ INTERNATIONAL   Set in the centuries-old field house of a restored Danish sugar plantation, the newly revitalized Old Stone Farmhouse is a special-occasion treat. Part of the fun is visiting the kitchen to pick out your meat or fish and hobnob with the chefs. But it's just a kitchen, after all; you'll want to spend as much time as possible in the atmospheric dining rooms, whether you're seated outside in the courtyard or inside, with wood-plank floors and flickering candlelight casting shadows on native stone walls. It's the perfect setting to enjoy one of the finest culinary experiences on the island, whether you choose to dine on some kind of exotic wild game (New Zealand elk, say, or wild boar) or a perfect, cooked-to-order steak or fish dish.

Mahogany Run. © **340/777-6277.** http://oldstonefarmhouse.com. Reservations recommended. Main courses $24–$36. Mon–Sat 6–10pm.

MODERATE

Blue Orchid ★ CARIBBEAN/SMALL PLATES Bringing the trend of small plates to the rain-forest peaks of St. Thomas, Blue Orchid, at the Historic St. Peter Greathouse, is a winning combination of flavorful Caribbean-inspired dishes and insanely scenic vistas. Order a frothy cocktail and some of the delicious small plates; you and your party might graze on tuna tartare, lobster dip, duck confit sliders, or crab salad nachos, to name a few of the choices. The limited menu of entrees include steaks, seafood pastas, and pan-seared grouper. Come early (the bar opens at 4pm), so you can sip sunset drinks and point out the array of Virgin Islands, large and small, from the observation deck before nightfall.

Historic St. Peter Greathouse, at the corner of Rte. 40 (6A St. Peter Mountain Rd.) and Barrett Hill Rd. © **340/774-4999.** www.blueorchidvi.com. Reservations recommended. Main courses $22–$31. Mon–Sat 5–10:30pm.

Frenchtown
EXPENSIVE

Oceana ★★★ GLOBAL/ISLAND This buzzy local favorite is ensconced in the restored West Indian great house of an estate known as Villa Olga, which served as the island's Russian embassy in the late 1800s. It's right on the water's edge, with sweeping views of the Charlotte Amalie harbor. Inside the walls are blanketed with colorful local and global art. The chefs specialize in creative twists on the island bounty, so you'll have seared scallops served with a papaya pear relish and local honey gastrique, or Maryland crab cakes with a fresh mango salsa. The Oceana bouillabaisse comes brimming with Caribbean lobster, and a New Zealand lamb shank is accompanied by goat-cheese polenta. It's all beautifully prepared, in a memorable setting.

In the Villa Olga, 8 Honduras. © **340/774-4262.** www.oceana.vi. Reservations required. Main courses $27–$48; Caribbean lobster $58. Daily 5:30–9:30pm.

MODERATE

Hook, Line & Sinker ★ AMERICAN This lively spot is set right on the water, with a New England seaport feel: whitewashed wood, French doors, and windows with shimmering harbor views. Well-prepared standards are the name of the game, such as steamed mussels, Caesar salad, or mushrooms stuffed with crabmeat and cheese for starters; and burgers, pastas (pomodoro, Arrabbiata, primavera), chicken, steak, and seafood specials (such as fresh grilled shrimp) for mains.

62 Honduras. © **340/776-9708.** www.hooklineandsinkervi.com. Main courses lunch $9–$15, dinner $14–$28. Mon–Sat 11:30am–4pm and 6–10pm; Sun 10am–2:30pm.

INEXPENSIVE

Frenchtown Deli ★ DELI In addition to a full coffee bar, the Frenchtown Deli has some of the island's best deli-style sandwiches, along with bagels and smoked salmon, homemade soups, and salads. Eat in or take out.

24-A Honduras, Frenchtown Mall. © **340/776-7211.** Sandwiches $6.50–$12; salads $4–$15. Mon–Fri 7am–8pm; Sat 7am–5pm; Sun 7am–4pm.

The South Coast

Havana Blue ★★★ CUBAN FUSION   This Miami-style venue at the Marriott enjoys a beachfront ambience and an inspired menu. An inventive crew is in the kitchen, and out in the dining room, the party is rocking with sexy blue lights, a thumping soundtrack, and a bombshell bartenders serving up blueberry mojitos and mambo margaritas. Ignore the hubbub and get to work: This is some serious food. Start with the black-bean hummus or the tuna tartare with soy-lime vinaigrette. For a main, try the house specialty: miso-lemongrass-glazed sea bass, which comes with wasabi mashed potatoes and garlic spinach. Yes, miso cod, and so forth, has been done to death. No, it doesn't matter: You will find this iteration utterly delicious. ©

In Marriott Frenchman's Reef & Morning Star Beach Resort (p. 55), 5 Estate Bakkeroe. © **340/715-2583.** www.havanabluerestaurant.com. Reservations required. Main courses $30–$52. Daily 5:30–10:30pm.

Iggies Beach Bar & Grill ★ AMERICAN/CONTINENTAL   This action-packed seaside grill is an island hot spot (see "Nightlife," below), but it's also a fine place to take the family to dine. The menu features a plethora of pub-style appetizers plus steaks, ribs, and seafood, but every night is theme night; Wednesday is **Cruzan Carnival Night,** with a Caribbean buffet that opens at 6pm, music at 7pm, and a Carnival show at 8pm ($38 adults, $15 children 11 and under). Tuesday the special is steamed crabs and beer, and Thursday is seafood night; on Friday Iggies serves up tacos and margaritas, and Sunday it's BBQ ribs and chicken night.

At the Bolongo Bay Beach Resort (p. 56), 7150 Bolongo (Rte. 30). © **340/693-2600.** www.iggies beachbar.com. Burgers and sandwiches $6.50–$15; dinner main courses $18–$34. Daily 11am–11pm.

The East End
EXPENSIVE

Bleuwater ★★ SEAFOOD/STEAK   The Ritz's showcase restaurant fashions elegant, creative turns on classic dishes. That might mean a lobster and truffle mac-n-cheese, or plantain gnocchi with Maine lobster and English peas. Fresh Virgin Islands seafood is highlighted—we devoured a pan-seared local Queen snapper with conch and jasmine rice here recently—but this is also the place to come for a big, juicy, perfectly cooked steak. Guests can dine in the elegant and expansive dining room or out on the waterfront patio under a sky peppered with stars. And hurray: The kids' menu has more variation than most.

In the Ritz-Carlton (p. 56), 6900 Great Bay. © **340/775-3333.** Reservations required. Main courses $40–$65. Wed–Sun 6:30–9:30pm.

The Caribbean Fish Market ★ SEAFOOD/WEST INDIAN   Breezy and bright, this indoor/outdoor seafood eatery sits right on the beach at the Elysian Beach Resort, looking out onto the sapphire seas of Cowpet Bay. It's also right next door to the Ritz-Carlton, making it a very convenient place for Ritz guests to enjoy a solid seafood dinner if they don't want to pay Ritz prices to dine (and don't want to have to take a taxi to get somewhere else). Most order the fresh catch of the day, which is cooked any number of ways. Grilled Caribbean lobster and such upscale treats as goat-cheese gnocchi, coconut shrimp lettuce wrap, and lobster and wild mushroom ravioli are also good choices. Sunday brunch is from 8am to 2pm.

In the Elysian Beach Resort (p. 58), 6800 Estate Nazareth. ℂ **340/714-7874.** http://caribbeanfish marketvi.com. Reservations recommended. Main courses $25–$45. Mon–Sun 5–10pm; Sun brunch 8am–2pm.

Sunset Grille ★★★ AMERICAN   This may be the island's best new restaurant, with a waterside setting that's both breezy and seductive, and a menu with plenty of flavorful turns. Such as the prawns tempura, lightly fried shrimp in a sweet soy glaze served on long skewers, or the tomato-based conch chowder (a switch from the mainly creamy version most often found on island). Overall, it's a surf-or-turf kind of place: from a bevy of gloriously fresh fish to grilled steaks, jerk chicken, and lamb "lolli-pops." And as I said at the start its a gorgeous setting: The last time we dined here, we watched the orange sun set over the protected cove; then, as night crawled in, we spied lights snaking beneath the inky black seas—a posse of night snorkelers out exploring the marine wonders of the Caribbean sea.

In the Secret Harbour Beach Resort, 6280 Estate Nazareth. ℂ **340/714-7874.** www.secret harbourvi.com. Reservations required. Main courses $24–$48. Daily 5:30–10:30pm.

MODERATE

Fish Tails ★ SEAFOOD   If you're looking for a casual, friendly seafood spot right on the water, Fish Tails should nicely fit the bill. You'll dine alfresco on a wooden deck overlooking Vessup Bay and its symphony of fishing boats. It's open practically all day long, serving up island treats like shrimp and eggs (with potatoes) for breakfast and fish cake, seared tuna, grilled wahoo, and Caribbean lobster for lunch and dinner. It's a nice place to bring the family, but it works well for a sunset cocktail, too—and it's a local favorite for breakfast.

Next door to Red Hook ferry terminal, Red Hook. ℂ **340/714-3188.** http://fishtailsvi.com. Main courses $15–$30. Daily 7am–10pm.

INEXPENSIVE

Señor Pizza ★ PIZZA   If you're burned out on conch (and even if you're not), you'll be quite satisfied with the big, cheesy pizza pies served at Senor Pizza. Slices are oversized, so one might be all you need for a tasty, filling lunch. They also deliver.

Red Hook Plaza (across from the ferry dock). ℂ **340/775-3030.** http://senorpizza.cbt.cc/index. html. Slice $3; whole pizza $16–$18. No credit cards. Daily 11am–9pm.

EXPLORING ST. THOMAS

Beaches

St. Thomas's beaches are renowned for their powdery white sand and clear azure waters, including the very best of them all, Magens Bay. Chances are that your hotel is right on the beach, or very close to one. Keep in mind that all the beaches in the Virgin Islands are public—even the resort beaches—and most St. Thomas beaches lie anywhere from 2 to 5 miles from Charlotte Amalie.

THE NORTH COAST

The gorgeous white sands of **Magens Bay** ★★—the family favorite of St. Thomas— lie between two mountains 3 miles north of the capital. The turquoise waters here are calm and ideal for swimming, though the snorkeling isn't that good. The beach is no secret, and it's usually overcrowded, though it gets better in the midafternoon. There is no public transportation to get here (although some hotels provide shuttle buses). A taxi from Charlotte Amalie costs about $8.50 per person. If you've rented a car, from Charlotte Amalie take Route 35 north all the way. The gates to the beach are open daily from 6am to 6pm. After 4pm, you'll need insect repellent. Admission is $1 per person and $1 per car. You can rent beach chairs ($7), loungers ($5), towels ($8), and snorkel and masks ($9) right there at the beach. Don't bring valuables, and don't leave anything of value in your parked car. For a bite to eat (try its famous authentic Greek pizza) or a cool libation, **Magens Bay Beach Bar & Café** (*©* **340/777-6270;** daily 9:30am–5pm) is the local favorite.

A marked trail leads to **Little Magens Bay,** a separate, clothing-optional beach that's especially popular with gay and lesbian visitors. This is former U.S. President Clinton's preferred beach on St. Thomas (no, he doesn't go nude).

Coki Point Beach, in the northeast near Coral World, is good but narrow and often crowded with both singles and families. It's noted for its warm, crystal-clear water and excellent snorkeling; you'll see thousands of rainbow-hued fish swimming among the beautiful corals. Vendors even sell small bags of fish food to feed the sea creatures while you're snorkeling. From the beach, there's a panoramic view of offshore Thatch Cay. Concessions can arrange everything from water-skiing to parasailing. **Coki Dive Center** (www.cokidive.com) has locker rentals onsite so you don't have to worry about your valuables.

Also on the north side of the island is luscious **Grand Beach,** one of St. Thomas's most beautiful, attracting families and couples. It opens onto Smith Bay and is near Coral World. Many watersports are available here. The beach is right off Route 38.

THE EAST END

Small and calm, **Secret Harbour** ★ fronts the Secret Harbour Beach Resort and a collection of condos. With its white sand and coconut palms, it's a lovely little spot. The snorkeling near the rocks is some of the best on the island—and night snorkeling is also available. You can rent equipment or sign up for a 60-minute "Discover Snorkeling" course (all ages welcome) on-site at the Secret Harbour Beach Resort with **Aqua Action Dive Center** (*©* **340/775-6285**). It's an easy taxi ride east of Charlotte Amalie heading toward Red Hook.

Sapphire Beach ★ is set against the backdrop of the Sapphire Beach Resort and Marina (somewhat dilapidated the last time we visited). Still, like Magens Bay Beach, this wide, safe beach is one of the most frequented by families. You'll have good views of St. John, Tortola, Jost Van Dyke, and offshore cays, and a large reef is close to the shore. Windsurfers like this beach a lot. You can rent all kinds of watersports

HOT surfing SPOTS

Surfers come from miles around to test the swells at **Hull Bay,** on the north shore, just west of Magens Bay, particularly the waves along the western tip. It's also where local fishermen anchor in the more tranquil areas. Don't expect much in the way of watersports outfitters. There is a combined restaurant and open-air bar. If you're relying on taxis, it costs about $15 per person to reach the bay. Two other beaches have good surfing, **Perserverance Bay** and **Caret Bay,** but these are the unofficial territory of French locals, who as one surfer said, "let you know if they don't like you."

equipment right there on the beach at **DIVE IN!** (© **866/434-8346,** ext. 2144, in the U.S., or 340/777-5255; www.diveinusvi.com).

White-sand **Lindquist Beach** ★★ isn't a long strip, but it's one of the island's prettiest beaches. It's between Wyndham Sugar Bay Resort & Spa and the Sapphire Beach Resort. Many films and TV commercials have used this photogenic beach as a backdrop. It's not likely to be crowded, as it's not very well known. It has no beach bar or cafe, but you can actually have a pizza delivered here!

THE SOUTH COAST

Morning Star ★★—also known as Frenchman's Bay Beach—fronts the Morning Star section of the Marriott Frenchman's Reef & Morning Star beach resort, about 2 miles east of Charlotte Amalie. It's a lovely spot, with gentle swells. Sailboats, snorkeling equipment, and lounge chairs are available for rent. If you're not staying at Morning Star, you can reach the beach by a cliff-front elevator at Frenchman's Reef or by walking the cliffside walk down to the beach.

WEST OF CHARLOTTE AMALIE

Near the University of the Virgin Islands, in the southwest, **Brewers Bay** is one of the island's most popular beaches for families. The strip of white coral sand is almost as long as the beach at Magens Bay. Unfortunately, this isn't a good place for snorkeling. Vendors here sell light meals and drinks. From Charlotte Amalie, take the Fortuna bus heading west; get off at the edge of Brewers Bay, across from the Reichhold Center.

Lindbergh Beach, with a lifeguard, restrooms, and a bathhouse, is at the Island Beachcomber Hotel (p. 55) and is used extensively by locals, who stage events from political rallies to Carnival parties here. Beach-loving couples are also attracted to this beach. It's not good for snorkeling. Drinks are served on the beach. Take the Fortuna bus route west from Charlotte Amalie.

Watersports & Outdoor Adventures

BOAT CHARTERING/BAREBOATING Yacht Haven Grande St. Thomas, 9100 Port of Sale, Charlotte Amalie (© **340/774-9500**), is the premier marine facility for mega-yachts in the Caribbean. Located alongside Charlotte Amalie harbor, it encompasses a 48-slip facility, with dining, entertainment, and recreational options. **American Yacht Harbor** ★★, Red Hook (© **340/775-6454;** www.igy-american yachtharbor.com), can refer both bareboat and fully crewed charters. It leaves from the east end of St. Thomas in Vessup Bay. The harbor is home to numerous boat companies, including day-trippers, fishing boats, and sailing charters. There are also five restaurants on the property, serving everything from Continental to Caribbean cuisine. Another reliable outfitter is **Charteryacht League,** at Gregory East (© **800/524-2061** in the U.S., or 340/774-3944; www.vicl.org).

Sailors may want to check out the "Yachtsman's Guide to the Virgin Islands," available at major marine outlets, at bookstores, through catalog merchandisers, or directly from **Tropical Publishers** (© **877/923-9653;** www.yachtsmansguide.com).

DAY SAILING Sail the U.S. and British Virgin Islands on the beautiful 44-foot clipper-bowed ketch *Independence* (© **340/775-1408;** www.sailingvirginislands.net) with Captain Pat Stoeken. Based at the American Yacht Harbor in Red Hook, the *Independence* takes a maximum of six passengers on personally customized full- and half-day sails, including a hot lunch. Full-day rates are $140 adults, $125 children; half-day rates $90 adults, $80 children.

Another sail excursion that lets you avoid the crowds is aboard the *Fantasy,* 6100 Leeward Way, no. 28 (℃ **340/775-5652;** www.daysailfantasy.com), which departs daily from the American Yacht Harbor at Red Hook at 9:30am and returns at 3pm. The boat takes a maximum of six passengers to St. John and nearby islands for swimming, snorkeling, and beachcombing. Snorkel gear and expert instruction are provided, as is a champagne lunch. The full-day trip costs $140 per person for adults and children. A half-day sail, usually offered only during the low season, lasts 3 hours and costs $100 for adults and children.

The 50-foot *Yacht Nightwind,* Sapphire Marina (℃ **340/775-7017;** www.stjohnday sail.com), offers full-day sails to St. John and the outer islands. The $125 price includes continental breakfast, a champagne buffet lunch, and an open bar aboard. You're also given free snorkeling equipment and instruction.

New Horizons, 6501 Red Hook Plaza, Ste. 16, Red Hook (℃ **800/808-7604** or 340/775-1171; www.newhorizonsvi.com), offers windborne excursions amid the cays and reefs of the Virgin Islands. The two-masted, 65-foot sloop has circumnavigated the globe, and has even been used as a design prototype for other boats. Owned and operated by Canadian Tim Krygsveld, it contains a hot-water shower, serves a specialty drink called a New Horizons Nooner, and carries a complete line of snorkeling equipment for adults and children. A full-day excursion with a continental breakfast, an Italian buffet lunch, and an open bar costs $120 per person ($80 for children ages 2–12). Excursions depart daily, weather permitting, from the Sapphire Beach Resort and Marina. Call ahead for reservations. New Horizons also offers *New Horizons II* (℃ **340/775-1171;** www.newhorizonscharters.com), a 44-foot custom-made speedboat that takes you on a full-day trip, from 7am to 5pm, to some of the most scenic highlights of the British Virgin Islands. Trips cost $145 for adults or $95 for children ages 2 to 12. You will need your passport and will have to pay an additional $15-per-person Customs fee. *New Horizons II* leaves from the Sapphire Beach Resort at 7:15am and from the People Ferries' Dock in St. John at 7:45am.

FISHING   The U.S. Virgins have excellent deep-sea fishing—some 19 world records (eight for blue marlin) have been set in these waters. Outfitters abound at the major marinas like Red Hook. **Peanut Gallery Fishing Charters,** 8168 Crown Bay Marina, Ste. 310 (℃ **340/642-7423;** www.fishingstthomas.com), offers both light-tackle inshore sportsfishing and deep-sea sportsfishing. Your captain will be Captain David Pearsall. The vessels provide inshore fishing year-round for the likes of barracuda, bonefish, kingfish, mackerel, and tarpon. The cost for 4 hours is $575; 6 hours, $700; and 8 hours, $900.

You can also line-fish from the rocky shore along Mandahl Beach on the north coast. The tourist office in Charlotte Amalie should have a listing of legal spots for line fishing around the island.

GOLF   **Mahogany Run,** on the north shore at Mahogany Run Road (℃ **800/253-7103;** www.mahoganyrungolf.com), is an 18-hole, par-70 course. The course rises and drops like a roller coaster on its journey to the sea; cliffs and crashing sea waves are the ultimate hazards at the 13th and 14th holes. Greens fees are $125 to $165 for 18 holes. Carts are included. Club rental costs $70.

KAYAK TOURS   **Virgin Islands Ecotours** (℃ **340/779-2155;** www.viecotours.com) offers 2½-, 3-, and 5-hour kayak trips through the Cas Cay mangrove lagoon on the southern coastline. The cost is $69, $79, and $139 per person respectively (children 12 and under $39, $49, $79). The tour is led by professional naturalists who allow for 30 to 40 minutes of snorkeling.

Another new but increasingly popular trip is the **clear kayak night tour** leaving around sunset daily from the Marriott Frenchman's Reef resort. You paddle out to Pirate Point in clear see-through kayaks and turn on the boat's special LED lights— giving you views of the nocturnal marine world. Offered by the Marriott's on-property tour operator **Adventure Center,** which also has snorkel and sailing excursions, the 1½-hour trip costs $45 per person (𝒞 **866/868-7784;** www.adventurecenters.net).

SCUBA DIVING/SNUBA The best scuba-diving site off St. Thomas, especially for novices, is **Cow and Calf Rocks,** off the southeast end (45 min. from Charlotte Amalie by boat); here, you'll discover a network of coral tunnels filled with caves, reefs, and ancient boulders encrusted with coral. The *Cartanser Sr.,* a sunken World War II cargo ship that lies in about 35 feet of water, is beautifully encrusted with coral and is home to myriad colorful resident fish. Another popular wreck dive is the *Maj. General Rogers,* the stripped-down hull of a former Coast Guard cutter.

Experienced divers may want to dive at exposed sheer rock pinnacles like **Sail Rock** and **French Cap Pinnacle,** which are encrusted with hard and soft corals, and are frequented by lobsters and green and hawksbill turtles. Both spots are exposed to open-ocean currents, making these very challenging dives.

Many think the **St. Thomas Diving Club,** 7147 Bolongo Bay (𝒞 **877/538-8734** in the U.S., or 340/776-2381; www.stthomasdivingclub.com), is the best on the island. This full-service, PADI five-star IDC center offers open-water certification courses for $425 to $595. Advanced open-water certification courses go for $400 to $475. You can also enjoy a half-day snorkeling trip for $55.

Coki Dive Center, Coki Beach (𝒞 **340/775-4220;** www.cokidive.com), a PADI center, offers scuba-diving courses and guided dive tours for beginners and certified divers alike. You can also rent diving and snorkeling gear here. A PADI Discover Scuba Diving Course is $79. Night dives are $65.

Day-Tripping to St. John

Most visitors to St. Thomas include a day-trip to beautiful sister island St. John for swimming, snorkeling, hiking, or just hanging out on one of the island beaches. Ferries to St. John leave every hour on the hour from Red Hook ($6 per person) and last only 15 to 20 minutes; you can also catch less frequent ferries from the Charlotte Amalie ferry terminal. It's easy to make a day of it: The last ferry returning from Cruz Bay, St. John, is at 11pm. Car ferries also run between Red Hook and Cruz Bay, traveling from 7am to 7pm daily every half-hour; book ahead on one of three carriers: **Boyson** (𝒞 **340/776-6294**); **Love City** (𝒞 **340/779-4000**); or **Global Marine** (𝒞 **340/779-1739**). Car-ferry rates run from $42 to $50 round-trip; arrive at least 15 minutes before departure. If you don't have a car, have taxi driver **Kenneth Lewis** (𝒞 **340/776-6865**) or one of his cohorts meet you at the ferry terminal in St. John for transportation to and from the beach, the park, or wherever you decide to spend the day. At the end of your day, you return to Cruz Bay for shopping and dinner and catch the ferry home right there on the harborfront.

DIVE IN!, in the Sapphire Beach Resort and Marina, Smith Bay Road, Route 36 (© **866/434-8346,** ext. 2144, in the U.S., or 340/777-5255; www.diveinusvi.com), is a complete diving center offering professional instruction (beginner to advanced), daily beach and boat dives, custom dive packages, snorkeling trips, and a full-service PADI dive center. An introductory resort course costs $90, with a one-dive afternoon trip going for $75 and two-dive morning trip costing $96. A six-dive pass costs $255.

Non-divers and beginning swimmers can still have a diving experience with **Virgin Islands Snuba Excursions** (© **340/693-8063;** www.visnuba.com) These special excursions are offered both at Coral World on St. Thomas and at Trunk Bay on St. John. With Snuba's equipment—an air line that attaches to an air tank floating on the surface—even novices can breathe easily underwater without the use of heavy restrictive dive gear. The Snuba operations begin in waist-deep water and make a gradual descent to a depth of 20 feet. This is fun for the whole family, as kids ages 8 and up can participate, and no snorkeling or scuba experience is needed. Most orientation and guided underwater tours take 1½ hours, costing $70 per person on St. John. On St. Thomas, a pass to **Coral World** (p. 78) is included, and the rate is $74 for adults and $70 for children 8 to 12. Reservations are required.

SNORKELING   The island's best snorkeling spots include the rocks around **Coki Beach;** you can rent snorkeling gear from the **Coki Dive Center,** Coki Beach (© **340/775-4220;** www.cokidive.com); day snorkel rentals are $10 and locker rentals are $5. Another great spot to snorkel is **Secret Harbor;** you can rent equipment or sign up for a 60-minute "Discover Snorkeling" course (all ages welcome) on-site at the Secret Harbour Beach Resort with **Aqua Action Dive Center** (© **340/775-6285;** www.aadivers.com). Another popular snorkeling spot is **Sapphire Beach**—where you can rent snorkeling equipment right there on the beach at **DIVE IN!** (© **866/434-8346,** ext. 2144, in the U.S., or 340/777-5255; www.diveinusvi.com).

ZIPLINING   One of the newer outdoor adventure on island is **Tree Limin' Extreme** (© **340/777-9477;** www.ziplinestthomas.com), a ziplining canopy tour in the rain forest of St. Peter Mountain, with six ziplines (including a "yo-yo" zip—which gives riders, as the name implies, a yo-yo-style zipline ride). If you can take your eyes off your (secure) zipline, you'll have views of Magen's Bay and even Tortola and Jost Van Dyke. You can combine a ziplining adventure with a tour of the tropical gardens of the **St. Peter Great House & Botanical Gardens** (http://greathousevi.com; see below), just across the street.

Seeing the Sights

In 1733, the Danish government acquired the Virgin Islands from the Danish West India Company. The Danes did not find land suitable for agriculture, and St. Thomas became a bustling port instead. It also became a center for transporting slaves.

The Virgin Islands remained under Danish rule until 1917, when the U.S., fearing German infiltration in the Caribbean during World War I, purchased the islands from Denmark. Today the U.S. Virgin Islands claims the highest per-capita income in the Caribbean, with some 50,000 settlers of varying ethnicity making their home in St. Thomas alone. The port is also the busiest cruise-ship harbor in the West Indies, outranking Puerto Rico.

Today you can see many vestiges of the island's history in the capital, **Charlotte Amalie,** whose architecture reflects the island's culturally diverse past: You'll pass Dutch doors, Danish red-tile roofs, French iron grillwork, and Spanish-style patios.

With its white houses and bright red roofs glistening in the sun, the city is terraced along the green hills surrounding the harbor. The town is filled with historic sights, like **Fort Christian,** an intriguing 17th-century building constructed by the Danes.

The best way to see the sights is by **taxi tour.** Expect to pay about $50 for a single-passenger tour or $25 per person for two or more passengers for 2 hours of sightseeing in a shared car. We highly recommend **Campbell Rey** (𝒞 340/771-1568), the unofficial "mayor" of the island and a true gentleman. Rey has an open safari bus that can hold up to 27 people, and a smaller van that comfortably seats 12 or so. Another recommended taxi driver is **Llewelyn Powell** (𝒞 340/771-1568 or 340/776-3887).

Tropic Tours, 14AB the Guardian Building (𝒞 800/524-4334 or 340/774-1855; www.tropictoursusvi.com), offers a tour of St. Thomas that includes Drake's Seat, the Estate St. Peter Greathouse, and Charlotte Amalie shopping. The cost is $49 per person, $36 for children 12 and under.

For dramatic views of Charlotte Amalie's harbor, take a ride on the **Paradise Point Tram** (𝒞 866/868-7784; www.adventurecenters.net) to a 700-foot peak. The tram, similar to those used at ski resorts, operates six cars, each with an eight-person capacity, for the 15-minute round-trip ride. It transports customers from the Havensight area to Paradise Point, where you can disembark to visit shops and the popular restaurant and bar. The tramway runs daily 9am to 5pm. Reservations are required; the cost is $21 per adult round-trip, $12 round-trip for children 6 to 12, and free for children 5 and under.

The walking tour below will give you a good basic feel for the historic district of Charlotte Amalie.

WALKING TOUR: CHARLOTTE AMALIE

START:	**King's Wharf.**
FINISH:	**Waterfront.**
TIME:	**2½ hours.**
BEST TIME:	**Before 10am to avoid cruise-ship passengers.**
WORST TIME:	**Around midday to 4pm, when traffic and pedestrians are at their most plentiful.**

Even with the crowds and shops, it is easy to see how the natural colors and charm of the Caribbean come to life in the waterfront town of Charlotte Amalie. The capital of St. Thomas once attracted seafarers from all over the globe. At one time, St. Thomas was the biggest slave market in the world. Today, the old warehouses, once used for storing stolen pirate goods, have been converted to shops. In fact, the main streets, called "gade" (a reflection of their Danish heritage), now coalesce into a virtual shopping mall, one that is often packed with cruise-ship hordes. Sandwiched among these shops are a few historic buildings, most of which can be seen on foot in about 2 hours. Start your walking tour along the eastern harborfront at King's Wharf.

1 King's Wharf

This is the site of the Virgin Islands Legislature. The apple-green two-story structure was first built in 1824 as a military barracks for the Danish Police. The current building dates from 1874. It was in a ceremony on this site in 1917 that ownership of the Virgin Islands was officially transferred from the Danish West Indies to the U.S.—bought for a then-pretty price of $25 million.

From here, walk away from the harbor up Fort Pladsen to:

2 Fort Christian

Dating from 1680 and named after the Danish king Christian V, this handsome (if crumbling) salmon-red structure is the oldest standing building in the entire U.S. Virgin Islands. It has been a fort (with 3- to 6-ft.-thick walls), a governor's residence, a prison (with a downstairs dungeon), a police station, and a court until it was named a National Historic Landmark in 1977. Unfortunately, restoration efforts of both the fort and its museum have dragged on since 2005, when it was closed to the public for renovations.

Continue walking up Fort Pladsen to:

3 Emancipation Park

This is where a proclamation freeing African slaves and indentured European servants was read on July 3, 1848. The park is now mostly a picnic area for local workers and visitors.

Near the park is the:

4 Grand Galleria

From here, a visitor center dispenses valuable travel information about the island. When it opened as a hotel in 1837, it was a grand address, but it later fell into decay, and finally closed in 1975. The former guest rooms upstairs have been turned into offices and a restaurant.

Northwest of the park, at Main Street and Tolbod Gade, stands the:

5 Central Post Office

On display here are floor-to-ceiling murals by Stephen Dohanos, who became famous as an artist for "The Saturday Evening Post."

From the post office, walk east along Norre Gade to the:

6 Frederik Lutheran Church

This, the island's oldest church building, was built between 1780 and 1793. The original Georgian-style building, financed by a free black parishioner, Jean Reeneaus, was refurbished in 1826 and again in 1870 with Gothic and gabled flourishes. It has a "welcoming arms" entrance stairway, and is recognizable by its distinctive yellow-gold hue.

Exiting the church, walk east along Norre Gade to Lille Taarne Gade. Turn left (north) and climb to Kongens Gade (King St.), passing through a neighborhood of law firms, to:

7 Government House

This handsome neoclassical building is the administrative headquarters for the U.S. Virgin Islands. It's been the center of political life in the islands since it was built, around the time of the American Civil War, in 1867, for the Danish Colonial Council. The first two floors are open to the public and contain vintage West

Walking Tour: Charlotte Amalie

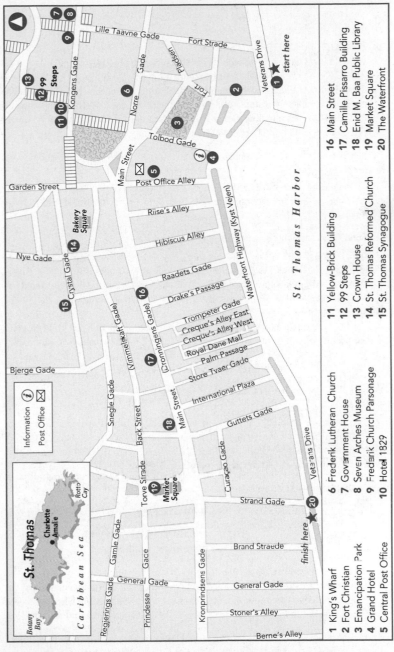

1 King's Wharf
2 Fort Christian
3 Emancipation Park
4 Grand Hotel
5 Central Post Office

6 Frederik Lutheran Church
7 Government House
8 Seven Arches Museum
9 Frederik Church Parsonage
10 Hotel 1829

11 Yellow-Brick Building
12 99 Steps
13 Crown House
14 St. Thomas Reformed Church
15 St. Thomas Synagogue

16 Main Street
17 Camille Pissarro Building
18 Enid M. Baa Public Library
19 Market Square
20 The Waterfront

Indian furniture and works of art by native son (and vaunted Impressionist) Camille Pisarro.

After leaving Government House, turn immediately to your left and look for the sign for:

8 Seven Arches Museum

Browsers and gapers love checking out this museum at Government Hill (© 340/ 774-9295; http://sevenarchesmuseum.com), the private home of longtime residents Philibert Fluck and Barbara Demaras. This 2-centuries-old Danish house has been completely restored and furnished with antiques. Walk through the yellow ballast arches into the Great Room, which has a wonderful view of the Caribbean's busiest harbor. It's open by appointment only.

After visiting the museum, return to Government House. Next to the building is:

9 Frederik Church Parsonage

This building dates from 1725. It's one of the oldest houses on the island, and the only structure in the Government Hill district to retain its simple 18th-century lines.

Continue west along Kongens Gade until you reach:

10 Hotel 1829

Formerly known as the Lavalette House (and now known officially as Blackbeard's Castle), this place was designed in 1829 by one of the leading merchants of Charlotte Amalie. This landmark building has views over Charlotte Amalie and the harbor.

This is also a great place to take a break. If the bar is open, Hotel 1829 provides the perfect veranda, with a spectacular view, for a midday drink or a sundowner. You may just fall in love with the place, abandon this tour, and stick around for dinner. The bar is open Monday to Saturday 4 to 11pm.

Next door (still on the same side of the street), observe the:

11 Yellow-Brick Building

This structure was built in 1854 in what local architects called "the style of Copenhagen"—it's square and squat, with colorful wooden shutters and a roof tiled of marble. It was built of ballast brick (brought over as ballast in the ship). You can go inside and browse the many shops within.

At this point, you might want to double back slightly on Kongens Gade to climb the famous:

12 99 Steps

These steps (actually 103 in total) were erected in the early 1700s, and take you to the summit of Government Hill, from where you'll see the 18th-century:

13 Crown House

This stately private house is immediately to your right, on the south side of the street. This was the home of von Scholten, the Danish ruler who issued the famous proclamation of emancipation in 1848 (see Emancipation Park, above).

Walk back down the steps and continue right (west) along Kongens Gade, then down a pair of old brick steps until you reach Garden Street. Go right (north) on Garden

Street and take a left onto Crystal Gade. On your left, at the corner of Nye Gade and Crystal Gade, you'll see:

14 St. Thomas Reformed Church

This building is from 1844, but it holds one of the oldest congregations in the Virgin Islands, established by Dutch traders around 1660. The church has been buffeted by fire and natural disasters: Fire destroyed two early-19th-century itera-tions (and a 1995 hurricane, Marilyn, damaged the sanctuary), but much of the 1844 structure, designed like a Greek temple, has been beautifully restored.

Continue up Crystal Gade. On your right (north side), you'll come to:

15 St. Thomas Synagogue

This is the oldest synagogue in continuous use under the American flag, and the second oldest in the Western Hemisphere. Nine Sephardic Jewish families founded the congregation in 1796, and the current building was erected in 1833. It still maintains the tradition of having sand on the floor, said to have muffled the sounds of worshippers' footsteps during the persecution of Jews during the Span-ish Inquisition (many communities of Sephardic Jews flourished in the Caribbean after being expulsed from Spain in 1492). The structure is made of local stone, ballast brick from Denmark, and mortar made of molasses and sand. It's open to visitors Monday to Thursday 9am to 4pm, Friday 9am to 3pm and Saturday dur-ing services. Next door, the **Weibel Museum** showcases 300 years of Jewish history. It keeps the same hours.

Retrace your steps (east) to Raadets Gade and turn south toward the water, crossing the famous Vimmelskaft Gade or "Back Street" (it can get a bit seedy at night, so be aware if you are walking after dark). Continue along Raadets Gade until you reach:

16 Main Street

This is Charlotte Amalie's major artery and most famous shopping street. Turn right (west) and walk along Main Street until you come to the mid-19th-century:

17 Camille Pissarro Building

This structure will be on your right, at the Amsterdam Sauer Jewelry Store. Pis-sarro, a Spanish Jew who became one of the founders of French Impressionism, was born in this building as Jacob Pizarro in 1830. Before moving to Paris, he worked for his father in a store on Main Street. Also housed in the building is **Gallery Camille Pissarro,** with a few Pissarro paintings on display and prints by local artists for sale.

Continuing west along Main Street, you will pass on your right the:

18 Enid M. Baa Public Library

This building, formerly the von Bretton House, dates from 1818.

Keep heading west until you reach:

19 Market Square

This was the center of a large slave-trading market before the 1848 emancipation and is officially called Rothschild Francis Square. Today it's an open-air fruit and vegetable market, selling, among other items, *genips* (grape-type fruit; to eat one, break open the skin and suck the pulp off the pit). The wrought-iron roof covered a railway station at the turn of the 20th century. The market is open Monday to Saturday, but Saturday is its busiest day; hours vary, but generally 9am to 3pm.

If the *genip* doesn't satisfy you, take Strand Gade down (south) to:

20 The Waterfront

Also known as Kyst Vejen, this is where you can purchase a fresh coconut. One of the vendors here will whack off the top with a machete so that you can drink the sweet milk from its hull. You'll have an up-close view of one of the most scenic harbors in the West Indies, even when it's filled with cruise ships.

ATTRACTIONS AROUND THE ISLAND

Route 30 (Veterans Dr.) will take you west of Charlotte Amalie to **Frenchtown** (turn left at the sign to the Admiral's Inn). Early French-speaking settlers arrived on St. Thomas from St. Barts after they were uprooted by the Swedes. Many of today's island residents are the direct descendants of those long-ago immigrants, who were known for speaking a distinctive French patois. This colorful village contains a bevy of restaurants and taverns. Because Charlotte Amalie has become somewhat dangerous at night, Frenchtown has picked up its after-dark business and is the best spot for dancing, drinking, and other local entertainment.

Farther west, Harwood Highway (Rte. 308) will lead you to **Crown Mountain Road,** a scenic drive opening onto the best views of the hills, beaches, and crystal-clear waters around St. Thomas.

Coral World Ocean Park ★ AQUARIUM   St. Thomas's number-one tourist attraction features a three-story underwater observation tower 100 feet offshore. Inside, you'll spy sea sponges, fish, coral, and other aquatic creatures in their natural state. An 80,000-gallon reef tank features exotic marine life of the Caribbean; another tank is devoted to sea predators, with circling sharks and giant moray eels. Among the exciting new activities are the **Sea Lion Splash** ($125 adult, $117 child; includes Coral World admission), where you actually get to swim with sea lions; the **Sea Lion Encounter** ($86 adult, $77 child; includes Coral World admission), where you interact with sea lions without gettting wet; the **Turtle Encounter** ($53 adult, $44 child; includes Coral World admission), where participants have up-close encounters with large sea turtles; and the **Shark Encounter** ($53 adult, $44 child; includes Coral World admission), where you have the chance to enter a shallow pool with juvenile sharks. Age and/or height and weight restrictions apply to all activities.

Nondivers can get some of the thrill long known to scuba aficionados by participating in **Sea Trek,** which is slightly different from **Snuba** (p. 71). For $79, or $70 for children, you can get a full immersion undersea with no experience necessary. Participants are given a helmet and a tube to breathe through. The tube is attached to an air source at the observatory tower. You then enjoy a 20-minute stroll in water that's 18 feet deep, observing rainbow-hued tropical fish and the coral reefs as you move along the seafloor. It's a marvelous way to experience the world through the eyes of a fish. *Note:* Reservations are required, so call ahead or log on to the park's website.

Coral World's guests can take advantage of adjacent **Coki Beach** for snorkel rentals, scuba lessons, or simply swimming and snorkeling. Lockers are available. Also included in the marine park are a seaside cafe, duty-free shops, and a nature trail.

6450 Estates Smith Bay, a 20-min. drive from Charlotte Amalie off Rte. 38. ℭ **340/775-1555.** http://coralworldvi.com. Admission $19 adults, $10 children ages 3–12. Daily 9am–4pm.

Estate St. Peter Greathouse & Botanical Gardens ★ GARDENS   Set on the island's northern rim 1,000 feet above sea level, this 11-acre estate was long ago

WATER ISLAND lore & history

To the native residents of St. Thomas, Water Island remains a land of legend and lore, having been settled by the Arawak Indians in the early 15th century. In the days of Caribbean piracy, as evoked by Disney's "Pirates of the Caribbean" movies, the island was used for both anchorage and fresh water, as pirates found numerous freshwater ponds here. Islanders on St. Thomas claim that millions of dollars in pirate treasure remain buried on Water Island, but so far no one has dug it up. An old leather trunk was once discovered, but it was empty except for one gold doubloon.

When European colonization arrived in the late 17th century, many Danes tried to use the island for raising cows and goats. White plantation owners and colonists shunned the island because of its arid land, so unlike the rest of the Caribbean, Water Island was farmed by nonwhite plantation owners. These were freed men of color who operated the plantations, like Jean Renaud, a free mulatto who owned the entire island in 1769, working it with 18 slaves.

In 1944, the United States bought the island for $10,000. The military began planning Fort Segarra here, but the war ended before it could be built. Traces of "the fort that never was" can still be seen today.

In 1950, the Department of the Interior leased the island to Water Phillips, a developer, for $3,000 annually. He built homes and a 100-room hotel. Popular in the 1950s, the hotel became the setting for Herman Wouk's 1965 novel, "Don't Stop the Carnival." (Incidentally, native residents of St. Croix claim that the novel was based on a hotel being built in the harbor of Christiansted.) The novel was turned into a short-lived musical by Jimmy Buffet in 1997. In 1989, Hurricane Hugo severely damaged the hotel, and it was shut down. It lies dormant today. The lease Phillips signed ran out 3 years later, and in 1996, Water Island was transferred to the federal government, in whose hands it remains today. At present (and likely to remain so for a long time to come), no foundations have been poured on Water Island. Nothing has been inaugurated. The cost of developing roads, irrigation, and sewage lines in this eco-sensitive environment is a daunting challenge and a dream that, for the immediate future, remains too expensive an undertaking.

part of the Plantation St. Peter. Today its gardens, restaurant, and event space is pillowed in oversize rain-forest foliage, with a tropical bird aviary and self-guided nature trails through a jungle of orchids. See the hump-backed islands of the B.V.I. from the panoramic deck above the gardens. The entry fee gets you panoramic views and a complimentary rum punch.

At the corner of Rte. 40 (6A St. Peter Mountain Rd.) and Barrett Hill Rd. (C) **340/774-4999.** http://greathousevi.com. Admission $8 adults, $5 children 11 and under. Daily 9am–4pm.

Excursions from St. Thomas
WATER ISLAND

Water Island, ¾ mile off the coast from the harbor at Charlotte Amalie, is the fourth-largest island in the U.S. Virgins, with nearly 500 acres of land. Irregular in shape, 2½-mile-long Water Island is filled with many bays and peninsulas, and studded with several good, sandy beaches along with secluded coves and rocky headlands. Established as the fourth U.S. Virgin Island in 1996, Water Island was once a part of a peninsula jutting out from St. Thomas, but a channel was cut through, allowing U.S. submarines to reach their base in a bay to the west. The island has a rich history that includes freed slaves, Herman Wouk, and Jimmy Buffett; see below.

At palm-shaded **Honeymoon Beach,** you can swim, snorkel, sail, water-ski, or sunbathe. The beach has been significantly improved in the past few years, as loads of rocks and gravel were hauled off and trees and brush removed. The sand was sifted to get rid of debris, and a dredge removed the seaweed and deposited white sand on the shore. Today it looks quite beautiful.

There is no commerce on the island—no taxis, gas stations, hotels, shops, or even a main town. Residents are totally dependent on Charlotte Amalie, lying a half-mile away. It you're planning on a visit, bring water and your own food supplies and other needs. Don't count on it, but a food cart sometimes shows up on Honeymoon Beach, serving surprisingly good meals, including an all-steak lunch.

The **Water Island Ferry** (𝒞 **340/690-4159;** http://waterislandferry.com) runs between Crown Bay Marina and Phillip's Landing on Water Island several times a day for $5 one-way, $10 round-trip (Crown Bay Marina is part of the St. Thomas submarine base).

If you prefer a guided tour, we recommend a bike tour with **Water Island Adventures** (𝒞 **340/714-2186;** www.waterislandadventures.com; $65 per person, including transportation and equipment). Beach and swimming time is included in the 3½ hours of the tour. Departures are from the dock at Havensight Mall or Crown Bay Marina.

HASSEL ISLAND

In the same bay as Water Island, and even closer to shore, is 136-acre **Hassel Island** (www.hasselisland.org). This island is almost completely deserted and protected as part of the Virgin Islands National Park, which prohibits most forms of development. There are no hotels or services of any kind here.

This island was connected to the mainland of St. Thomas until 1865 (end of the Civil War), when a channel was dug for easier passages of ships. During the early 19th century's Napoleonic Wars, the British occupied the island, and the ruins of two forts that the troops constructed here, Willoughby and Shipley, can be seen today. You can explore these ruins.

Hassel Island was once used by the Danes to defend the port of Charlotte Amalie. In 1840, the Danes built a marine railway operation for boat and sail repairs. As late as the 1960s, the marine railway was still in operation. It was one of the earliest steam-powered marine railways in the Western Hemisphere, as well as the oldest surviving example of a steam-powered marine railway in the world.

In 1978, some 95 percent of Hassel Island was sold to the U. S. National Park Service by its owners, the Paiewonski family. For almost 30 years, the island sat untouched and deteriorating until it was discovered by MTV location scouts as the ideal setting for the 27th season of the network's popular "Real World" franchise. "Real World: St. Thomas" debuted in 2012, with the participants living in an old estate.

Today, the MTV crew is long gone, but you can visit Hassel through **Virgin Islands Ecotours** (𝒞 **877/845-2925;** http://viecotours.com), the only concessionaire allowed to bring visitors to explore the island. It offers 3- and 5-hour kayak, hike, and snorkel tours of the island ($89/3 hr. and $143/5 hr.; the latter includes lunch), leaving from the Frenchtown marina. Trails take you across gentle hills with dry woods, lots of plants, and plenty of cacti—you'll think you're in the Arizona desert. The western shore has white sands shaded by sea grapes. The rather barren island has little shade, so bring along hats and plenty of sunscreen.

SHOPPING

The discounted, duty-free shopping in the Virgin Islands makes St. Thomas a shopping mecca. It's possible to find well-known brand names here at savings of up to 60 percent off mainland prices. And each U.S. resident is given a $1,600 duty-free allowance—even kids. Even better: St. Thomas has no sales tax. But be warned—savings are not always guaranteed, so make sure you know the price of the item back home to determine if you are truly getting a good deal. Having sounded that warning, we mention some St. Thomas shops in the listings below where we have indeed found good buys. For more help, the local publications "This Week in St. Thomas" and "Places to Explore" have updates on sales and shop openings.

Most shops are open Monday to Saturday 9am to 5pm. Some stores are open Sunday and holidays if a cruise ship is in port.

The Best Buys & Where to Find Them

The best buys on St. Thomas include china, crystal, perfumes, jewelry (especially emeralds), Haitian art, clothing, watches, and items made of wood. St. Thomas is also the best place in the Caribbean for discounts in porcelain, but remember that U.S. brands may often be purchased for 25 percent off the retail price on the mainland. Look for imported patterns for the biggest savings. Cameras and electronic items, based on our experience, are not the good buys they're reputed to be.

Nearly all the major shopping in St. Thomas is along the harbor of Charlotte Amalie. Cruise-ship passengers mainly shop at the **Havensight Mall,** right on the cruise-ship dock at the eastern edge of Charlotte Amalie. It has 100 retail stores selling goods at duty-free prices, but you'll see little here you won't find at most other Caribbean duty-free ports. The principal shopping street is **Main Street,** or Dronningens Gade (the old Danish name). Some of the shops occupy former pirate warehouses. To the north is another merchandise-loaded street called **Back Street** or Vimmelskaft. Many shops are also spread along the **Waterfront Highway** (also called Kyst Vejen). Between these major streets is a series of side streets, walkways, and stone alleys—each one packed to the gills with shops. Other shopping streets are Tolbod Gade, Raadets Gade, Royal Dane Mall, Palm Passage, Storetvaer Gade, and Strand Gade.

It is illegal for most street vendors (food vendors are about the only exception) to ply their trades outside of the designated area called **Vendors Plaza,** at the corner of Veterans Drive and Tolbod Gade. Hundreds of vendors converge here Monday through Saturday at 7:30am; they usually pack up around 5:30pm. (Very few hawk their wares on Sun, unless a cruise ship is scheduled to arrive.)

When you tire of French perfumes and Swiss watches, head for **Market Square,** as it's called locally, or more formally, Rothschild Francis Square. Here, on the site of a former slave market and under a Victorian tin roof, locals with machetes slice open fresh coconuts so you can drink the milk, and women sell ackee, cassava, and breadfruit.

Other big shopping areas include **Yacht Haven Grande,** within walking distance of Havensight Mall; and **Crown Bay Center,** near the Crown Bay cruise-ship dock and marina. If you're looking for original artworks, **Tillett Gardens** is a virtual oasis of arts and crafts—pottery, silk-screened fabrics, candles, watercolors, jewelry, and more—located on the highway across from Four Winds Shopping Center.

All the major stores in St. Thomas are located by number on an excellent map in the center of the publication "St. Thomas This Week," distributed free to all arriving plane and boat passengers, and available at the visitor center. A lot of the stores on the island don't have street numbers or don't display them, so look for their signs instead.

Shopping A to Z

In the 300-year-old historic district of Charlotte Amalie along Main Street and in the warren of old Danish alleyways (and, it goes without saying, in the Havensink and Crown Bay areas around the cruise-ship piers), you will find many of the same shops you see in other duty-free Caribbean ports and cruise-ship centers—as one visitor noted, the street is paved with "jewels and booze." When the cruise-ships are in, taxi vans crowd the streets and shop owners ratchet up the hard sell. Plenty of international names are strung along Main Street (Dronningens Gade in Danish), from **Tiffany & Co.,** 5 Dronningens Gade (www.tiffany.com) to **David Yurman,** 38 Dronningens Gade (www.davidyurman.com). If you poke around the cobblestoned alleyways between Main Street and the harbor, you may find a gem that's a little off the standard tourist radar.

For **jewelry and watches,** the choices around Main Street and near the cruise-ship piers at Havensight Mall and Crown Bay are practically endless, with an emphasis on high-end rocks. **Diamonds International ★**, Dronningens Gade, has the largest selection of diamonds on the island (② 800/444-4025; www.diamondsinternational.com; six other locations on St. Thomas); **H. Stern Jewelers,** 5332 Dronningens Gade, one of the most respected international jewelers in the world (② 340/776-1146; www.hstern.net); and **Cardow Jewelers,** 5195 Dronningens Gade, often called the Tiffany's of the Caribbean, with one of the largest selections of fine jewelry in the world (② 800/227-2117; www.cardow.com; two other locations in St. Thomas).

For **electronics,** the reliable dealers include **Boolchand's,** 31 Main St. (② 340/776-0794; www.boolchand.com) and **Royal Caribbean,** 33 and 35 Main St. (② 340/776-4110; http://royalcaribbeanvi.com; three other branches on St. Thomas).

For **crystal and china,** the family-run **Crystal Shoppe ★**, 14 Main St., offers a dazzling array of crystal from around the world (② 800/323-7232; http://crystal-shoppe.net). Ubiquitous in the Caribbean, **Little Switzerland,** 5 Dronningens Gade, offers some of the finest crystal sold on the island, as well as fine jewelry and watches (② 340/776-2010; www.littleswitzerland.com; six other locations in St. Thomas).

ANTIQUES

S.O.S. Antiques ★ This gallery is packed with antique maritime collectibles, including maps and charts, prints, sextants, and barometers. It also stocks a number of weapons, including antique and reproduction cannons, swords, pistols, and daggers. The highlight: genuine shipwreck salvage, such as actual pieces of eight mounted in 14-karat and 18-karat gold (you can also buy them unset). 5132 Dronningens Gade 1. ② **340/774-2074.**

ART

The Color of Joy ★   The vivid watercolors of Corinne Van Rensselaer are on display in this little gallery, where you can also buy original prints by local artists, crafts, and gifts, including batiks, cards, and prints, along with glass and larimar (volcanic stone) jewelry. There is also a selection of ceramics, coral sculptures (much of it done locally), and Haitian artwork. American Yacht Harbor, 6100 Red Hook Quarters. © **340/775-4020.** http://thecolorofjoyvi.com.

Gallery Camille Pissarro ★   This gallery is worth a visit just to see where the Impressionist artist Camille Pissarro was born in 1830 and lived until he was 26. Inside the circa-1811 building are prints and originals by local artists in three high-ceilinged rooms. It's just opposite the Royal Dane Mall at the top of a flight of uneven steps. 14 Main St. © **340/774-4621.** www.pissarro.vi.

Gallery St. Thomas ★   This gallery highlights Virgin Islands painters and "Caribbean-inspired" artworks. 5143 Palm Passage, Suite A-13. © **877/797-6363** or 340/777-6363. http://gallerystthomas.com.

Mango Tango Art Gallery ★   One of the island's largest art galleries offers both original artwork (many from Haiti) and less-expensive art prints, posters, and decorative maps. Look for Steffen Larsen's distinctive photographs of Cuba street scenes. Al Cohen Plaza, Raphune Hill, Rte. 38. © **340/777-3060.** www.mangotango-art.com.

Native Arts & Crafts Cooperative ★★   Housed inside the V.I. Welcome Center, the slightly dilapidated 19th-century brick former headquarters of the U.S. District Court, this is one of the few places on island that specializes in locally made, non-art items and gifts, from hot sauces and handmade dolls to wooden crafts and jewelry. Tabor Gade 1. © **340/777-1153.**

Shaka-Man Zulu ★   Selling handcrafted art and jewelry from Africa, this little shop has some interesting gift ideas. Look for the owner dressed in full Zulu costume prowling the streets. 33 Raadets Gade. © **340/514-8975.**

Tillett Gardens Center for the Arts ★★   This old Danish cattle farm has been one of the island's top arts-and-crafts centers since 1959. It's an indoor/outdoor complex of buildings housing studios, galleries, a drum museum, a live performing theater, a hostel, and two restaurants. It's now also home to the Arts Alive Foundation, which displays original artworks from from oils and watercolors to acrylics. Tillett Gardens, 4126 Anna's Retreat. © **340/775-1405.** www.tillettgardens.com. Take Rte. 38 east from Charlotte Amalie.

In His Footsteps: Camille Pissarro (1830–1903)

The dean of the French Impressionist painters was the most famous resident ever born on the island of St. Thomas. Attracted by the work of Camille Corot and, later, Gustave Courbet, Pissarro moved in a lofty artistic circle of friends that included Monet, Cézanne, and Renoir. He painted landscapes and scenes of rural life and some portraits.

o **Birthplace:** Danish St. Thomas, July 10, 1830, son of Jewish parents of French/Spanish extraction

o **Residences:** The Pissarro Building, off Main Street in Charlotte Amalie; Paris

o **Resting Place:** Paris

Jewelry is the most common item for sale in St. Thomas. Look carefully over the selections of gold and gemstones (emeralds are traditionally considered the finest savings). Gold that is marked 24-karat in the United States and Can-ada is marked 999 (or 99.9 percent pure gold) on European items. Gold marked 18-karat in the United States and Can-ada has a European marking of 750 (or 75 percent pure), and 14-karat gold is marked 585 (or 58.5 percent pure).

FOOD

The Belgian Chocolate Factory ★ Get your handmade Belgian chocolates—some made with local fruits like mango and papaya—at this bustling factory/store in the Charlotte Amalie historic district. 5093 Dronningens Gade, Ste. 3. ℭ **340/777-5247.** www.thebelgianchocolatefactory.com.

Gladys' Café ★ Be sure to enjoy local favorites like creamy conch chowder and jerk fish in this 30-year-old restaurant, but you don't have to dine to purchase a bottle of Gladys' delicious homemade hot sauce, in flavors from mango to mustard to tomato. Royal Dane Mall. ℭ **340/774-6604.** http://gladyscafe.com.

LINENS

Mr. Tablecloth ★ This shop has the best selection of tablecloths and accessories, plus doilies, in Charlotte Amalie. In addition to fine-linen tablecloths, the shops sells microfiber stain-resistant tablecloths. 6 Main St. ℭ **340/774-4343.** www.mrtablecloth-vi.com.

SANDALS

Zora of St. Thomas ★ Zora has been making hand-crafted sandals for nearly 50 years. In addition to classic looking, full-grain leather sandals, Zora also offers a line of solidly practical, toe-enclosed footware that the islanders call "limin' shoes." The store carries canvas backpacks, luggage, and even purses and briefcases made of that fabric. 5040 Norre Gade, Ste. 2. ℭ **340/774-2559.** www.zoraofstthomas.com.

ST. THOMAS AFTER DARK

St. Thomas has a whole lot more nightlife than any other island in the U.S. or British Virgin Islands, but it's not as extensive as you might think. Charlotte Amalie is no longer the swinging town it used to be. Many of the city's streets have become danger-ous after dark, so visitors have stopped visiting the area for nightlife, with the excep-tion of a few places. Much of the Charlotte Amalie action has shifted to nearby **Frenchtown,** which has some great restaurants and bars and is generally safer at night. However, just as in Charlotte Amalie, some of these little hot spots lie along dark, badly lit roads, so keep a watchful eye.

You'll find the real action in **Red Hook,** on the island's east end, where a number of bars and casual seaside eateries feature live music. Things are jumping at the island's hotels and resorts as well, particularly **Marriott Frenchman's Reef & Morn-ing Star, Bolongo Bay,** and **Secret Harbour,** each with lively after-dark scenes.

The Performing Arts

Pistarckle Theater ★ On the grounds of **Tillett Gardens Center for the Arts** (p. 83), this professional theater presents six full-length plays yearly as part of its subscription season. Occupying a vacant print shop, the 100-seat theater is air-conditioned. There is also a summer drama camp for children. Tillett Gardens, 4126 Anna's Retreat. © **340/775-7877.** www.pistarckletheater.vi. Tickets $20–$50.

Reichhold Center for the Arts ★★ The premier performing arts venue in the Caribbean lies west of Charlotte Amalie. Past performances have included the Alvin Ailey American Dance Theater and Al Jarreau. Call the theater or check with the tourist office to see what's on at the time of your visit. The lobby displays a frequently changing free exhibit of paintings and sculptures by Caribbean artists. A Japanese-inspired amphitheater, permeated by the scent of gardenias, is set into a natural valley, with seating space for 1,196. Performances usually begin at 8pm. University of the Virgin Islands, 2 John Brewers Bay. © **340/693-1559.** www.reichholdcenter.com. Tickets $15–$75.

Beach Bars, Bars & Clubs

Caribbean Saloon ★ This is a popular spot to drink, eat, watch sports on wide-screen TVs, or listen to live or DJ music on the weekends. It's one of the jumpin'est joints in Red Hook. Frozen concoctions, like the lethal Buckwackers (light and dark rum, Bailey's, Kahlua, Frangelico, Amaretto, and coconut), are priced to move at $6.50. It's open daily 11am to 10:30pm and serves an extensive menu of pub grub, burgers, and bar noshes. American Yacht Harbor, Red Hook. © **340/775-7060.** www.caribbeansaloon.com.

Duffy's Love Shack ★ Mingle with the locals at what has been called the coolest parking-lot bar in the Caribbean. Yep, it's pretty casual, which means you will probably be dancing with brand-new best friends by evening's end. It's open daily 11:30am till 2am. 6500 Red Hook Plaza, Rte. 38. © **340/779-2080.** www.duffysloveshack.com.

Epernay Bistro & Wine Bar ★★ This cozy and stylish bistro is a touch of France in the tropics, with candlelit wood tables and walls lined with wine bottles and gleaming glasses. Tapas is served during the 5- to 7pm happy hour, a nice time to stop in for a good glass of vino. Have a bite to eat while you're there; the food is good and elegantly presented. 24A Honduras. © **340/774-5348.**

The Greenhouse ★ This longtime waterfront bar and restaurant (the sister restaurant of the two equally lively Greenhouses in St. Maarten) is one of the few places we recommend in downtown Charlotte Amalie. (You can park nearby and walk to the entrance.) It's a cruise-ship hangout during the day, but after the ships slip away before dusk, the Greenhouse regroups with a daily happy hour (4:30–7pm) that offers two-for-one drinks and discounted appetizers. The Greenhouse is open daily 11am until the last customer leaves. Veterans Dr. © **340/774-7998.** www.thegreenhouserestaurant.com.

Hull Bay Hideaway ★ This 30-year mainstay in an open-air pavilion is just a short stroll from one of the best surfing beaches on island. It's a friendly, rustic spot that attracts an eclectic crowd, from surfer dudes to beach lovers. Many locals and regulars like to spend lazy Sunday afternoons here. It's got lots of good, cheap eats—look for fish tacos and hot dogs and hamburgers. Daily hours are 10am to 10pm. 10 Estate Hull Bay. © **340/777-1898.**

Iggies Beach Bar ★★★ During the day, Iggies is your typical family-friendly, informal, open-air seaside restaurant serving hamburgers, sandwiches, and salads. In the evening, it's an ongoing Caribbean party, with karaoke, beach bonfires, and a Wednesday-night Cruzan Carnival extravaganza, with live calypso music and Moko Jumbie stiltwalkers (Nov to Labor Day). Saturdays are reggae nights. Bolongo Bay Beach Resort, 7150 Bolongo. © **340/693-2600.** www.iggiesbeachbar.com.

Latitude 18 ★   This open-air waterfront spot is located down a dirt road near the Red Hook Marina, where the ferryboats depart for St. John. It's a casual restaurant and bar that sizzles with live entertainment every night from 7:30 to 10:30pm (including Reggae Sundays). It's a good cheap place to eat as well, serving up hot rotis, BBQ ribs, burgers, and catch of the day. It's open daily from 11am to 11pm or later. Take Rte. #33 and turn left on Vessup Lane. Red Hook Marina. (✆ **340/777-4552.**

Gay & Lesbian Nightlife

St. Thomas might be the most cosmopolitan of the Virgin Islands, but it is no longer the "gay paradise" it was in the 1960s and 1970s. The major gay scene in the U.S. Virgins is now on St. Croix (see chapter 5). That doesn't mean that gay men and lesbians aren't drawn to St. Thomas. They are, but many attend predominantly straight establishments, such as **the Greenhouse** (see "Bars & Clubs," above).

ST. CROIX

I f St. Thomas is the seasoned older sibling and St. John the dewy beauty, St. Croix is the region's cultural heart. It's an old soul with a lilting bohemian spirit. It also has a population so diverse and multicultural it's been called a "cultural callaloo."

At 84 square miles, St. Croix is certainly the largest U.S. Virgin Island, but it has a small-town feel. That may be because the "plantation island" is a place of bucolic delights, with acres of rural farmland and roads draped in a canopy of mahogany trees. The island's agricultural heritage is undergoing a renaissance: Organic farms in the northwest highlands are flourishing, and a celebrated Agricultural Fair draws thousands of visitors annually. Tied in with this trend is the island's growing reputation as a health-and-wellness destination: St. Croix has more vegan cafes, juice bars, and organic farms than all the other Virgins combined.

But perhaps more than anything, St. Croix is a living museum of the region's tangled past. Much of the architecture from the 18th-century Danish occupancy remains enshrined in picturesque Christiansted, on the island's west end. The colorful Victorian buildings facing the scenic waterfront of the island's second-largest town, Frederiksted, have been revitalized—a fetching welcome mat for the cruise-ship crowds that arrive weekly at the Frederiksted dock.

St. Croix is the most remote and least-visited of the Virgin Islands, separated from St. Thomas and St. John by one of the deepest ocean trenches in the Atlantic. But the island itself is protected by a natural necklace of coral reef, encircling gentle bays and powdery white-sand beaches. If R&R is at the top of your vacation criteria, this may be the spot for you; just ask U.S. Vice-President Joe Biden, who often spends his Christmas holidays in restorative serenity on the island of St. Croix.

ESSENTIALS

Getting There
BY PLANE
Currently, the best way to reach the island by plane, but a fast ferry was said to be in the works at press time. Most flights to St. Croix land at the small international **Henry E. Rohlsen Airport,** Estate Mannings Bay (© 340/778-1012; www.viport.com/airports.html; airport code STT), 6 miles southwest of Christiansted on the island's southern coast. **Seaplane flights** with Seaborne Airlines (see below) from St. Thomas land right at the seaport on the Christiansted waterfront.

American Airlines (© 800/433-7300; www.aa.com) no longer offers frequent service to St. Croix. American has one direct flight daily from Miami, with one stop (but no change of plane) in St. Thomas. **US Airways**

(☎ **800/428-4322**; www.usairways.com) offers a nonstop flight from Charlotte in the high season. Most visitors arrive via connecting service through Puerto Rico or St. Thomas. **Seaborne Airlines** (☎ **888/359-8687** or 340/773-6442; www.seaborne airlines.com) offers several flights daily, some on seaplanes that fly "downtown to downtown" between St. Thomas and the Christiansted waterfront (flight time: 25 min.). **Cape Air** (☎ **800/227-3247** in the U.S. and U.S.V.I.; www.capeair.com) flies between St. Croix and San Juan, Vieques Island, or St. Thomas. **JetBlue** (☎ **800/538-2583**; www.jetblue.com) has daily afternoon connections from San Juan.

A number of major car-rental firms maintain kiosks at the airport, including **Avis** (☎ 340/778-9355), **Hertz** (☎ **888/248-4261**), and **Budget** (☎ **888/264-8894**). At the Christiansted seaport, **Avis** (☎ **340/713-1347**) is located at 1210 Watergut St. The oldest independent car agency in St. Croix, **Olympic Rent-A-Car** (☎ **888/USVICAR;** www.olympicstcroix.com) offers free airport dropoff and pickup. Otherwise, taxis are on call at the airport and in downtown Christiansted to transfer you to your destination.

Travel time to St. Croix from St. Thomas is 25 minutes; between St. Croix and San Juan 50 minutes; and between St. Croix and Vieques 25 minutes. There are no direct flights to St. Croix from Canada or the United Kingdom; connections are made via Miami.

BY BOAT

The SeaTrans fast ferry that traveled sporadically between St. Thomas and St. Croix was out of commission at press time (it ran aground on one of the small cays between the islands a couple of years ago), but government plans are in the works for the introduction of spiffy new catamaran ferries to travel between St. Thomas and St. Croix. Special ferries do run between St. Thomas and St. Croix in April for the St. Thomas Carnival and again in December around St. Croix's Carnival. It's a 1-hour trip over one of the world's deepest oceans, and when the seas are up, it can be rough passage for those with motion sickness.

BY CRUISE SHIP

The island's main cruise ship pier, the **Ann E. Abramson Pier,** on the Fredricksted waterfront, was upgraded and now has the capacity to accommodate two mega-ships at a time. The dock enhancements have already upped cruise-ship visitation from one ship every 3 weeks to one or two ships making port stops weekly.

Visitor Information

The **St. Croix Visitor Bureau,** 53A Company St., in Christiansted (☎ **340/773-0495**), is located in a yellow building across from the open-air market. It's open Monday to Friday 8am to 5pm.

The **U.S. Virgin Islands Tourism** also has an office at the Customs House Building, Strand Street (☎ **800/372-8784** or 340/772-0357; www.visitusvi.com), in Frederiksted. A local independent website, **www.stcroixtourism.com**, offers lots of good information. Another website to check is **www.visitstcroix.com**.

Tourist offices provide free maps to the island. "St. Croix This Week," distributed free to cruise-ship and air passengers, has detailed maps of Christiansted, Frederiksted, and the entire island, pinpointing individual attractions, hotels, shops, and restaurants and listing the week's events and happenings.

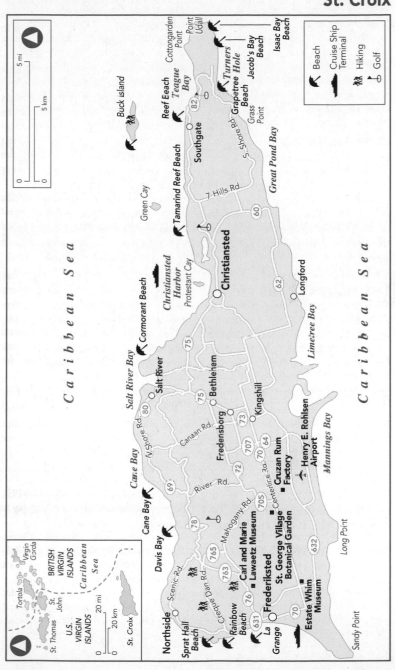

Caribbean Sea

Caribbean Sea

Buck Island

Green Cay

Cottongarden Point

Point Udall

Isaac Bay Beach

Jacob's Bay Beach

Turners

Grapetree Hole Beach

Grass Point

82

Teague Bay

Reef Beach

Southgate

Tamarind Reef Beach

Great Pond Bay

7 Hills Rd.

60

Christiansted Harbor

Protestant Cay

Cormorant Beach

Christiansted

62

Longford

Salt River Bay

Salt River

75

Limetree Bay

Cane Bay

N. Shore Rd.

80

Bethlehem

75

Kingshill

Canaan Rd.

Fredensborg

73

707

70 64

Henry E. Rohlsen Airport

Mannings Bay

72

89

River Rd.

12

Cruzan Rum Factory

Cane Bay

78

Centerline Rd.

705

Mahogany Rd.

Davis Bay

765

Carl and Marie Lawaetz Museum

St. George Village Botanical Garden

Long Point

Northside

Scenic Rd.

763

Rainbow Beach

Creque Dan Rd.

76

631

Frederiksted

La Grange

Estate Whim Museum

70

632

Sprat Hall Beach

Sandy Point

U.S. VIRGIN ISLANDS

BRITISH VIRGIN ISLANDS

Tortola

Virgin Gorda

St. Thomas

St. John

Caribbean Sea

St. Croix

20 mi

20 km

Beach

Cruise Ship Terminal

Hiking

Golf

5 mi

5 km

Island Layout

St. Croix has only two sizable towns: **Christiansted** on the northcentral shore and **Frederiksted** in the southwest. The Henry E. Rohlsen Airport is on the south coast, directly west of the former HOVENSA oil refinery, for many years the island's main industry (at press time, the refinery was closed and up for sale). No roads circle St. Croix's coast.

To continue east from Christiansted, take Rte. 82 (also called the E. End Rd.). Route 75 will take you west from Christiansted through the central heartland. Melvin H. Evans Highway, Route 66, runs along the southern part of the island. You can connect with this route in Christiansted and head west all the way to Frederiksted.

CHRISTIANSTED

The historic district of Christiansted has four main streets leading toward the water: Strand Street, King Street, Company Street, and Queen Street. Because the city is compact, it can easily be explored on foot. All streets start at the harbor and go up slightly sloped hillsides, and each street heads back down the hill to the port so you can't get lost. The **visitor information center** is located at 53A Company St. The center of Christiansted can get very congested, and driving around is difficult because of the one-way streets. It's usually more practical to park your car and cover the small district on foot. You will find open-air parking on both sides of Fort Christiansvaern. See the "Walking Tour: Christiansted" map, on p. 112, to orient yourself.

THE NORTH SHORE

This coastal strip that stretches from Cottongarden Point, the eastern tip of the island, all the way west past Christiansted and up and around Salt River Bay, comes to an end as it reaches the settlement of Northside in the far west. It is the most touristy region of St. Croix, site of the best beaches, the most hotels, and the densest shopping. It is also the takeoff point (at Christiansted Harbor) for excursions to Buck Island, St. Croix's most popular attraction. Many visitors confine their stay in St. Croix entirely to the north coast. The northern coastline is not only long but also diverse, going from a lush tropical forest that envelops most of the northwest to the eastern sector, which is dry with palm-lined beaches.

THE EAST END

The East End begins immediately east of Christiansted, the capital, taking in Tamarind Reef Beach and Reef Beach before it reaches Teague Bay, coming to an end at Cottongarden Point, the far eastern tip of St. Croix. This section of St. Croix is linked by Rte. 82 (also called E. End Rd.). The Buccaneer, the major resort of St. Croix, is found here, along with the Tamarind Reef Hotel. The area is far less congested than the section immediately to the west of Christiansted, and many visitors prefer the relative isolation and tranquility of the East End. This section of St. Croix is somewhat dry, the landscape a bit arid, but its compensating factor is a number of palm-lined beaches. The best place for a beach picnic is Cramer Park at the far eastern tip, a U.S.V.I. territorial beach popular with islanders.

FREDERIKSTED

Little Frederiksted has a storied past. It was established in 1751, but its colonial architecture was destroyed by fire in 1878 during a legendary labor revolt. The town was rebuilt in the Victorian style, and its historic waterfront today has been revitalized, a boon for the big cruise ships that arrive at the town's deep-water pier weekly.

In both Christiansted and Frederiksted, in St. Croix, buildings are numbered consecutively on one side, stretching all the way across town; then the numbers "cross the street" and begin consecutively on the opposite side. That means that even and odd numbers appear on the same side of the street. The numbering system begins in Christiansted at the waterfront. In Frederiksted, the first number appears at the north end of town for streets running north-south and at the waterfront for streets running east-west.

The two major streets, both of which run parallel to the water, are Strand Street and King Street.

Getting Around

If you plan to do some serious sightseeing on the island, you'll need to rent a car, as getting around by public transportation is a slow, uneven process.

BY CAR

Remember to *drive on the left.* In most rural areas, the speed limit is 35 mph; certain parts of the major artery, Route 66, are 55 mph. In towns and urban areas, the speed limit is 20 mph. Keep in mind that if you're going into the "bush country," you'll find the roads very difficult. Sometimes the government smoothes the roads out before the rainy season begins (often in Oct or Nov), but they rapidly deteriorate.

St. Croix offers moderately priced car rentals, even on cars with automatic transmissions and air-conditioning. However, because of the island's higher-than-normal accident rate (which is partly the result of visitors who forget about driving on the left-hand side of the road), insurance costs are a bit higher than elsewhere. **Avis** (© **800/331-1212** or 340/778-9355; www.avis.com), **Budget** (© **800/472-3325** or 340/778-9636; www.budget.com), and **Hertz** (© **800/654-3131** or 340/778-1402; www.hertz.com) all maintain headquarters at the airport; look for their kiosks near the baggage-claim areas. Collision-damage insurance costs $14 per day, depending on the company and size of car, and we feel that it's a wise investment. Some credit card companies grant you collision-damage protection, if you pay for the rental with their card. Verify coverage before you go.

BY TAXI

At Henry E. Rohlsen International Airport, official taxi rates are posted. From the airport, expect to pay about $16 to $36 to Christiansted and about $12 to $24 to Frederiksted. Even though taxi rates are standardized, cabs are unmetered, so agree on the rate before you get in. Taxis line up at the docks in Christiansted and Frederiksted.

We highly recommend the following taxi drivers (who double as wonderful tour guides): **Ames Joseph** (© **340/277-6133**) and **Francis M. Vazquez** (© **340/690-4045**). If they aren't available, contact the **St. Croix Taxicab Association** (© **340/778-1088**).

More and more drivers are employing multi-passenger **taxi vans** and **open-air safaris** (converted truck beds with open-air seating), ideal for transporting cruise-ship passengers arriving weekly on island excursions.

BY BUS

Air-conditioned **buses** run between Christiansted and Frederiksted about every 45 minutes daily between 5:30am and 8pm. They start at Tide Village, to the east of

Christiansted, and go along Route 75 to the Golden Rock Shopping Center. They transfer along Route 70, with stopovers at the Sunny Isle Shopping Center, La Reine Shopping Center, St. George Village Botanical Garden, and Whim Plantation Museum before reaching Frederiksted. The fare is $1, or 55¢ for seniors. For more information, call ✆ **340/773-1664.**

[FastFACTS] ST. CROIX

Banks FirstBank Virgin Islands (✆ **340/773-0440;** www.firstbankvi.com) has full-service locations in Christiansted (12–13 King St. and Orange Grove); in Frederiksted (6A Strand St.); and at Sunny Isle Shopping Center. **Scotiabank** (✆ **340/693-2966;** www.scotiabank.com) has a full-service locations in Sunny Isle Shopping Center. **Banco Popular** ✆ **800/724-3655;** www.popular.com/vi) has full-service locations in Christiansted (Orange Grove) and Sunny Isle. Most are open Monday to Thursday 9am to 3pm and Friday 9am to 4pm; both Scotiabank and FirstBank have Saturday-morning hours.

Business Hours Typical business hours are Monday to Friday 9am to 5pm, Saturday 9am to 1pm. **The V.I. Dental Center,** 2024 Estate Mt. Welcome, Ste. 15–16 (✆ **340/772-6000;** http://videntalcenter.com), has a team of dentists that are members of the American Dental Association. Call for information or an appointment.

Doctors For a referral, call **Sunny Isle Medical Center** (✆ **340/778-0069**) or the **Beeston Hill Medical Complex** (www.vihealth.com).

Drugstores Try the **Golden Rock Pharmacy,** Golden Rock Shopping Center (✆ **340/773-7666**), open Monday to Saturday 8am to 7pm and Sunday 8am to 3pm.

Emergencies To reach the police, fire department, or an ambulance, call ✆ **911.**

Hospitals The main facility is **Governor Juan F. Luis Hospital & Medical Center,** 4007 Estate Diamond Ruby (✆ **340/778-6311**).

Maps See "Visitor Information," in "Orientation," above.

Newspapers & Magazines St. Croix has its own online newspaper, "St. Croix Source" (http://stcroixsource.com). "The Virgin Island Daily News" (http://virginislandsdailynews.com) covers all the Virgin Islands. A good source of local information is "St. Croix This Week," which is distributed free by the tourist offices to hotels, restaurants, and most businesses.

Police Police headquarters is on Market Street in Christiansted. In case of emergency, dial ✆ **911;** for nonemergency assistance, call ✆ **340/778-2211.**

Post Office The post office is on Company Street (✆ **340/773-3586**), in Christiansted. The hours of operation are Monday to Friday 8:30am to 5:30pm.

Safety St. Croix is safer than St. Thomas. Although there have been random acts of violence against tourists in the past, even murder, most crime on the island is petty theft, usually of possessions left unguarded at the beach while vacationers go into the water for a swim, or muggings (rarely violent) of visitors wandering the dark streets and back alleys of Frederiksted and Christiansted at night. Exercise caution at night by sticking to the heart of Christiansted and not wandering around in Frederiksted. Avoid night strolls along beaches. Night driving in remote parts of the island can also be risky; you might be carjacked and robbed at knifepoint.

Taxes The only local tax is an 10 percent surcharge added to all hotel rates.

Telephone You can dial direct to St. Croix from the mainland by using the 340 area code. Omit the 340 for local calls. Make long-distance, international, and collect calls as you would on the U.S. mainland by dialing 0 or your long-distance provider.

Toilets There are few public restrooms, except at the major beaches and the airport. In Christiansted, the National Park Service maintains some restrooms within the public park beside Fort Christiansvaern.

Tourist Offices See "Visitor Information," above.

WHERE TO STAY

St. Croix's deluxe resorts lie along the North Shore; its old waterfront inns are mostly in Christiansted. You may also choose to stay in a villa or condo, which offers privacy and the chance to save money by preparing your own meals. A location in Christiansted or Frederiksted puts you close to shops and nightlife, but away from the beach. Most resorts are either on the beach or a short walk from it but isolated from towns. You'll have to drive for a shopping binge or to dine out in restaurants and clubs.

In general, rates are steep, but in summer, hotels slash prices by as much as 50 percent; some close altogether in late summer and early fall. All rooms are subject to a 10 percent hotel tax, not included in the rates given below.

Note: If you need a hair dryer, pack your own. Apparently, a lot of visitors have packed up hotel hair dryers upon departure, and some innkeepers are reluctant to provide them.

North Shore
EXPENSIVE

The Buccaneer ★★★ Family-run since the 1940s, this gracious resort is St. Croix's premier lodging. It's also steeped in the island's colonial plantation heritage. Three hundred years ago this was one of the island's biggest producers of sugarcane, and its crumbling stone sugar mill is but one of its historic touchstones (it's fun exploring the place to see the others). On the more modern side of the equation, the sprawling 340-acre resort is big enough to encompass a par-70 18-hole golf course, a 2-mile jogging path, two freshwater pools, and eight Laykold tennis courts (with a pro shop). The baronial-arched Great House has a restaurant, the open-air **Terrace;** and a full array of spa treatments is available at the newly renovated **Hideaway Spa & Salon.** The free daily Kid's Camp (ages 4–12) is available year-round, and introductory scuba lessons are complimentary. As for accommodations, they're either up in the hilltop Great House main building or dotted along the beach (it's a short but steep walk between the two). Rooms are big and comfortable, many outfitted in colorful floral prints, and those along the beachside are luxuriously over-sized—particularly the Doubloons, which come with whirlpool tubs and patios overlooking the sea. The resort also has a handful of luxury suites, which range from roomy family cottages to swank honeymoon-ready units with four-posters and whirlpool tubs. A handful of former slave quarters have been turned into hotel rooms. It also has a **beach house** to rent at Whistle Point.

© **800/255-3881** in the U.S., or 340/712-2100. www.thebuccaneer.com. 138 units. Winter $300–$782 double, $495–$1,943 suite; off season $260–$559 double, $443–$1,338 suite. Children 2–17 $60 per night Dec–Apr. Extra person $80 per night. Tax and energy surcharge 21%. Rates include full American breakfast and welcome cocktails. **Amenities:** 3 restaurants; bar; babysitting; children's program; health club and spa; 2 pools (outdoor); room service; 8 tennis courts (2 lit); watersports equipment; Wi-Fi (free).

St. Croix Hotels

Christiansted

Arawak Bay: the Inn at Salt River **7**
The Buccaneer **13**
Carringtons Inn **11**
Chenay Bay Beach Resort **14**
Club St. Croix Beach & Tennis Resort **10**
Colony Cove **12**
Company House Hotel **17**
Cottages by the Sea **1**
Divi Carina Bay All-Inclusive
Resort & Casino **16**

King's Alley Hotel **18**
Mount Victory Camp **3**
The Palms at Pelican Cove **8**
Rattan Inn **9**
Ridge to Reef Farm **4**
Renaissance Carambola Beach Resort & Spa **5**
Sand Castle on the Beach **2**
Tamarind Reef Resort, Spa & Marina **13**
Villa Madeleine **15**
Waves at Cane Bay **6**

94

Divi Carina Bay All-Inclusive Resort & Casino ★   This all-inclusive resort brought gambling to the U.S. Virgin Islands—and today remains the only casino in the island chain. But that's not its only perk (or downside, depending on your point of view). Opening onto a sugar-white beach, the Divi Carina's guest rooms and villa suites all offer unobstructed views of the Caribbean. Rooms are done in standard tropical décor, yes, but offer plenty of room to move around as well as kitchenettes and balconies. Note that 20 hillside villas are across the street, but they're still just a 3-minute walk to the sands—and they still offer those glorious ocean views. The most up-to-date building contains 50 oceanfront accommodations with balconies. Be sure to sign up for regular e-mail blasts touting money-saving specials.

ⓒ **800/823-9352** in the U.S., or 340/773-9700. www.diviresorts.com. 180 units. Winter $448–$470 double; off season $350–$412 double. Rates are all inclusive, 7-night minimum. Children 15 and under stay free in parent's room. **Amenities:** 4 restaurants; 4 bars; babysitting; casino; health club and spa; mini-golf; 2 freshwater pools (outdoor); spa; tennis court (lit); watersports equipment/ rentals; Wi-Fi (free in lobby and public areas).

The Palms at Pelican Cove ★★   Water-lovers take note: This elegant but casual boutique resort is not only set on 7 acres of gorgeous beachfront property, it boasts one of the largest pools on the island. Guest rooms are spacious, too, with private balconies or patios with ocean views. Social life revolves around an open-air lounge, bar, and restaurant with sea views (see the Palms, p. 105). The coral reef is just 100 feet offshore, making The Palms a particular favorite of snorkelers.

ⓒ **800/548-4460** or 340/718-8920. www.palmspelicancove.com. 35 units. Winter $240–$350 double, $360–$650 suite; off season $210–$310 double, $340–$590 suite. **Amenities:** Restaurant; bar; Internet (free); pool (outdoor); watersports (scuba).

Renaissance Carambola Beach Resort & Spa ★★   The third in the triumvirate of RockResorts built in the U.S. Virgin Islands by the Rockefellers, this 28-acre resort lies 30 minutes west of Christiansted along a sugary-sand beach on the island's north shore. The jumble of red-roofed buildings overlooks Davis Bay from a forested bluff. The island's second-largest resort (after Divi; see below), it is well-known for its outstanding golf course, the **Carambola Golf & Country Club ★★★**, adjacent to the resort. Many golfers fly over from the other Virgins just to tackle the course, designed by Robert Trent Jones, Jr., in 1966. The resort itself is comprised of 26 two-story buildings, each with six units, all furnished in Spanish colonial style (with Caribbean Creole touches) and dark (some say too dark) mahogany woodwork. Each room has its own screened porch, with garden or sea views, and many have full, modern kitchens with granite countertops and porcelain-top stoves.

ⓒ **888/503-8760** in the U.S., or 340/778-3800. www.carambolabeach.com. 150 units. Winter $349–$549 double; off season $249–$379 double. **Amenities:** 2 restaurants, including Saman; bar; exercise room; golf course; spa; pool (outdoor); 2 tennis courts (lit); Wi-Fi (free in public areas).

MODERATE

Chenay Bay Beach Resort ★   Set on one of the island's finest beaches for watersports activities (swimming, snorkeling, windsurfing)—a mile of talcum powder white sand—these barefoot-casual West Indian–style cottages are tucked into a terraced hillside just 3 miles east of Christiansted. Chenay Bay's a low-key boutique property, with just 50 cottages (each with its own charming front porch), and set on grounds that once held a sprawling sugar plantation. Chenay has a nimble versatility, its spacious cottages appealing both to honeymooners and families, the latter thanks to children's programs and adjoining units, one that sleeps 8. Plus, kitchenettes here include full-size refrigerators. Cottages are neat and clean and simply furnished, most with an understated tropical palette. Those numbered 21-50 are bigger than the older ones. The resort often offers money-saving online packages, so check out the resort website before booking.

Estate Chenay Bay. ✆ **866/357-2970** in the U.S., or 340/718-2918. www.defenderresorts.com/chenaybay. 50 cottages. Year-round $70–$300 cottage for 1 or 2. Extra person $25. Children 17 and under stay free in parent's room. $50 per person for all meals. **Amenities:** Restaurant; bar; babysitting; children's program; pool (outdoor); 2 tennis courts (lit); 2 tennis courts (unlit); watersports equipment/rentals; Wi-Fi (free).

Tamarind Reef Resort, Spa & Marina ★

You don't come to this modest, two-story property for top-end lodging. You come to be just steps away from a lovely, sandy beach with shade from thatched palapas and excellent snorkeling along the reef. You come to swim in the big oceanfront pool, or just sip cocktails at the poolside bar and grill, with the blue seas stretched out on the horizon before you. You pick the Tamarind Reef to take advantage of island-hopping trips offered by day-sail and charter-boat operators at the adjoining Green Cay Marina. And about the rooms: They're just fine—clean, comfortable, roomy, if done in an uninspired tropical motif. Hey, they even have ocean-facing patios or terraces so you can be reminded of why you picked the Tamarind in the first place.

✆ **800/619-0014** in the U.S., or 340/773-4455. www.tamarindreefhotel.com. 38 units. Winter $275–$325 double; off season $200–$250 double. Extra person $35–$50. Children 6 and under stay free in parent's room. Ask about dive, golf, and honeymoon packages. **Amenities:** 2 restaurants; bar; pool (outdoor); spa; 4 tennis courts (lit); watersports equipment/rentals; Wi-Fi (free).

INEXPENSIVE

Arawak Bay: The Inn at Salt River ★

Travelers praise this two-story North Shore B&B for its sweeping views of Salt River Bay; warm, accommodating staff; and its hearty, delicious home-cooked breakfasts (guaranteed to start your day off right). Each room has a king bed or two doubles, with top-quality bedding and vintage-style quilts; you step out of your room onto a long, shared balcony with sea views (the second-floor balcony has better sightlines). Help yourself to a nice glass of wine in the kitchen honor bar or take a dip in the (miniscule) pool. You will have to drive to reach the beach or nearby restaurants.

✆ **340/772-1684.** http://arawakbayinn.com. 14 units. Winter $160 double; off season $130 double. Rates include island breakfast. **Amenities:** Bar; outdoor pool; Wi-Fi (free).

Waves at Cane Bay ★

This intimate 12-room property is set alongside the sea at one of the island's best beaches, Cane Bay Beach. It's an ideal spot to hang your hat if you're a diving or snorkeling aficionado: Cane Bay is one of the island's top scuba and snorkeling beaches; the coral reef is just off the shoreline here, and you can even scuba dive right off the beach. You can rent all the equipment you need next door at the **Cane Bay Dive Shop** (www.canebayscuba.com). Rooms are high ceilinged, large and colorfully outfitted, each with a well-equipped kitchenette, tiled floors, and a private veranda.

✆ **800/545-0603** in the U.S., or 340/718-1815. www.canebaystcroix.com. 12 units. Winter $175–$200 double; off season $150–$175 double. Extra person $20. From the airport, go left on Rte. 64; after 1 mile, turn right on Rte. 70; after another 1 mile, go left at the junction with Rte. 75; after 2 miles, turn left at the junction with Rte. 80; follow for 5 miles. **Amenities:** Restaurant; bar; pool (outdoor); watersports equipment/rentals; Wi-Fi (free).

Christiansted

MODERATE

King's Alley Hotel ★   A location directly on the Christiansted waterfront within walking distance of the seaplane base makes this well-managed inn a convenient choice for business folk. The amenities are admittedly sparse (no pool, for one), but the small-to-mid-sized rooms have been nicely refreshed in a sunny palette of pale greens and yellows and feature better-than-normal beds (at least in this price range). Some overlook the hotel's tropical courtyard, while others offer views of the Christiansted harbor.

✆ **800/843-3574** or 340/773-0103. 35 units. Winter $180 double, $240 suite; off season $160 double, $220 suite. **Amenities:** Wi-Fi (free).

INEXPENSIVE

Company House Hotel ★   Just a block or two from the downtown Christiansted waterfront, this good-value three-level inn is located in a vintage warehouse that once served the West Indies Company. It's within walking distance of the town's National Historic Site district. Although the public rooms have a historical elegance, the accommodations have a more generic feel, simply outfitted in earth tones, tile floors, and wicker furniture. Two suites, one on the third floor with balcony views overlooking Christiansted, have full kitchens, a perk for budget-minded travelers. The pool is small and narrow, but at these rates, who's complaining? From Friday through Tuesday, the **Victor Borge Piano Bar** offers live piano music from 6pm to 11pm—and the first drink is on the house.

✆ **340/773-1377.** www.companyhousehotel.com. 35 units. Winter $125 double, $160 suite; off season $85 double, $150 suite. Children 12 and under stay free in parents' room. Rates include continental breakfast. **Amenities:** Piano bar; freshwater pool (outdoor); Wi-Fi (free).

Frederiksted

MODERATE

Cottages by the Sea ★   This hospitable and meticulously managed family-run resort is the kind of relaxing, laidback place where everyone is either digging their feet in the sand or curling up in some nook with a good book. Just outside Frederiksted (within walking distance), its set on a palm-fringed beach and consists of 21 nicely furnished cottages in tropical hues, each with its own private beachfront patio (and patio table) and fully equipped kitchen. Some are cinderblock, some wood, but all are well-maintained. It's an excellent value for St. Croix, especially for families—up to two children 17 and under stay for free in their parent's cottage—and the pretty beachfront locale gives it some real oomph.

✆ **800/323-7252** or 340/772-0495. http://caribbeancottages.com. 21 units. Beachside cottages $95–$185 double; beachfront cottages $165–$225 double. Extra person $15. Up to 2 children 17 and under stay free in parent's cottage; $10 per night for each additional child **Amenities:** Watersports equipment/rentals; Wi-Fi (free).

Sand Castle on the Beach ★   This 21-room hotel right on Frederiksted Beach has long had a gay and lesbian following, but it's welcoming to all, with friendly service and splendid sunset views. It has plenty of sociable public spaces, including two freshwater swimming pools (one being clothing optional) and the alfresco resort restaurant, **Beach Side Café** (p. 119), a lively place to eat and drink that's set right in the soft white sand. It's a popular spot for live music on Saturday nights and meltingly lovely sunsets. Accommodations range from luxury beachfront villas with full kitchens and terra-cotta-tile floors to roomy courtyard suites around a private pool. Budget travelers will appreciate the good-value garden or queen studios—they may lack views (and full kitchens and elbow room), but they're close to all the resort action.

(800/524-2018 or 340/772-1205. www.sandcastleonthebeach.com. 21 units. Winter $149–$199 double, $259–$349 suite, $319–$449 villa for up to 4 people; off season $109–$219 double, $235–$339 suite, $269–$399 villa for up to 4 people. Rates include continental breakfast. **Amenities:** Restaurant; exercise room; high-speed Internet (free in lobby); 2 pools (outdoor); watersports equipment/rentals.

Villas, Condos & Cottages

Renting a villa, condo, or house on St. Croix is an excellent option for vacationing groups and families, and couples. Most offer full kitchens and nailing down the details to rent is usually a snap.

One primo source of rentals is **Vacation St. Croix** ((**877/788-0361** or 340/718-0361; www.vacationstcroix.com), which offers some of the best accommodations on the island, specializing in lodgings directly on the beach (villas, condos, and private homes). Two- to seven-bedroom units are available, with prices from $1,000 to $15,000 per week.

With 54 apartments, the **Club St. Croix Beach & Tennis Resort,** 3280 Estate Golden Rock, Christiansted ((**800/524-2025** or 340/718-4800; www.clubstcroix.com; $140–$285; children 12 and under stay free in parent's room) has an enviable location on a lovely quarter-mile, palm-fringedbeach; additional perks include a pool and three tennis courts.

The all-suites **Colony Cove** ★, 3221 Estate Golden Rock ((**800/524-2025** or 340/718-1965; www.colonycove.com; $140–$255; children 11 and under stay free in parent's unit) offers 60 units and is 1 mile west of Christiansted on the same beach as Club St. Croix (see above). Of all the condo complexes on St. Croix, Colony Cove is most like a full-fledged hotel, with a large staff on hand, an on-site watersports desk, and a swimming pool.

The 43-unit **Villa Madeleine** ★★, off Rte. 82, Teague Bay (www.villamadeleine-stcroix.com; (**800/533-6863** or 340/690-3465; weekly: $1,700–$2,000 double, $2,300–$2,450 quad), is a real hideaway, with beautifully furnished two-story condo villas in a lush tropical setting. Each condo has its own private courtyard and pool, many with views of the bay.

Ridge to Reef Farm Stay

A creative alternative to the typical seaside resort is a stay on an organic rain-forest farm on the island's lushly forested western coast. **Ridge to Reef Farm** ((**340/220-0466;** www.ridge2reef.org) offers a range of lodging from tent camps ($35/night) to private stilted cabanas or treehouses ($125/night) to the lofty Hawk's Nest villa ($275/night), with views out over the tropical landscape. You can volunteer for farm work (like feeding the chickens) or simply relax and enjoy the bucolic setting.

Bed & Breakfasts

Carringtons Inn ★★   This peaceful, handsome five-room B&B just a 10-minute drive from Christiansted makes for an idyllic romantic escape. Rooms are sizeable and individually decorated, some with gleaming fourposters and pretty wicker chairs, and all with plump linens. After inhaling the fab home-cooked breakfasts (French toast, fresh fruit, pancakes), you can lounge around the tiled pool, framed in rounded stone arches and tropical greenery. A festive atmosphere prevails. Sorry, the inn does not accept children.

℗ **877/658-0508** in the U.S., or 340/713-0508. www.carringtonsinn.com. 5 units. Winter $125–$200 double; off season $100–$160 double. Rates include breakfast. **Amenities:** Breakfast room; health club (nearby); outdoor pool; tennis courts (nearby); Wi-Fi (free).

Rattan Inn ★   Set, literally, amid the ruins of an old sugarcane plantation, this inn has five elegantly appointed private residences, ideal for extended vacations. All but the Pool House have full kitchens, and three have their own laundry facilities (the Pink and Green houses share a laundry facility). The Main House has its own private court-yard, and the Master Suite has a private plunge pool and balcony.

℗ **340/718-5098.** www.rattaninnstx.com. 5 units. Cottages $150–$250; Main House $4,500/ month. **Amenities:** Outdoor pool; Wi-Fi (free).

Camping

Mount Victory Camp ★★   Just a 10-minute drive north of Frederiksted, this beautifully landscaped eco-resort gives visitors an opportunity to immerse themselves in one of St. Croix's lesser-known natural environments: the forested farm valley of the wild western coast, where nights bring cooling tradewinds and the island's agricultural riches are being tapped once more. It's a refreshing departure from the beach scene, although you're only a 2-mile drive down the hill to a comely white sand beach.

Four of the five camp lodgings are rustic Arts-and-Crafts-style bungalows hand-crafted by a shipwright using salvaged tropical hardwoods. The lone **Schoolhouse Apartment ★★** was built around the ruins of a historic old schoolhouse (ca. 1841); it's a wonderful mix of tropical hardwoods and native stone walls. Both the bungalows and the apartment accommodate four to six adults. You can also do tent camping, but you'll have to bring your own gear. Each dwelling has basic cooking and eating facilities, and open-air showers use solar-heated water collected from a solar flat-plate thermal collector. A shady, breezy pavilion is the beating heart of the resort, its pitched slats fashioned from mahogany (using wood harvested from dead or dying trees—mahogany is a protected species). The resort has its own orchard; you can also buy fresh organic fruit and produce from the celebrated Ridge to Reef farm, just a 10-min-ute stroll away. Outdoor activities include guided hikes in the rainforest and mountain biking (the camp has mountain bikes for rent)—and feeding the gentle red-footed land tortoises in the resident tortoise colony.

℗ **340/201-7983** or 340/772-1651. http://mtvictorycamp.com. 5 dwellings. Winter $85–$95 dou-ble; off season $75–$85 double. Extra person $15. Credit cards through PayPal only. **Amenities:** Public phone; picnic tables; Wi-Fi.

WHERE TO EAT

St. Croix has an amazing diversity of restaurants and cuisines, so don't limit yourself to your hotel for dining. The issue for most visitors—particularly those staying outside

The Chicken Shack ★★

It's Martha Stewart's favorite restaurant on island, and after you sample one of the shack's spit-roasted barbecued chickens, it might be yours too. The La Reine Chicken Shack is known for its juicy, fall-off-the-bone chicken, but it also serves up exemplary ribs, johnny-cakes, conch fritters, and specials like shrimp in butter sauce and curry chicken. It's good value, too; at press time you could get half a chicken and a couple of johnnycakes for $5.50! Eat in, or do as Martha does and take out. The Chicken Shack is located mid-island, on Centerline Road across from the old La Reine Shopping Plaza. It's open Monday through Wednesday 10:30am until 6pm, Thursday through Saturday 10:30am through 8pm, and Sunday 10:30am to 4pm (© **340/778-5717**).

of Christiansted and Frederiksted—is often simply getting around at night. Many roads in St. Croix are badly lit, and driving on the left (for those used to driving on the right) can be challenging even during daylight hours. Don't let that deter you, though: Taxi drivers are happy to deliver you to a restaurant and return for you when your meal is done. Have your hotel call a taxi for you, and be sure to confirm the rate there and back with the driver before you set out.

If you're staying at one of the small hotels or guesthouses in and around Christiansted, you'll likely be able to walk to your restaurant of choice. If you're at a hotel in Frederiksted, the night is yours. The cruise-ship crowds will have departed, and the small dining rooms here have an earthier, more laid-back (and less expensive) feel than those in Christiansted.

The **St. Croix Food & Wine Experience,** is a highlight of the year, a weeklong food party on St. Croix in mid-April, when the island's food is highlighted with city food crawls, wine events, sunset BBQs, and the chance to sample local creations at the "Taste of St. Croix." Go to www.stcroixfoodandwine.com to learn more.

North Shore
EXPENSIVE

The Galleon ★★ FRENCH/NORTHERN ITALIAN   Overlooking the sea, this upscale marina restaurant and bar is a special-occasion favorite. It serves northern Italian and French cuisine, occasionally including handmade pastas, osso buco, local fish—wahoo, tuna, swordfish, or mahimahi—or fresh Caribbean lobster. Order the beef tenderloin chateaubriand, and they will carve it right at your table. The wine list is extensive.

E. End Rd. © **340/718-9948.** www.galleonrestaurant.com. Reservations recommended. Main courses $22–$40. Sun brunch $11–$22 Mon–Fri 4–10pm (happy hour 4–6pm, dinner 6–10pm), Sun 10am–2pm. Go east on Rte. 82 from Christiansted for 5 min.; after going 1 mile past the Buccaneer, turn left into Green Cay Marina.

Flamboyant Beach Bar ★ AMERICAN   Seating up to 100 guests beneath a vaulted cathedral ceiling, this informal open-air enclave is located in the Renaissance Carambola Beach Resort. It's one of the island's best hotel restaurants, offering fresh, creative takes on American classics and Caribbean seafood. Friday nights feature a Pirate's Buffet, with a Moko Jumbies show (6:30–9:30pm; $30).

In the Renaissance Carambola Beach Resort (p. 95), Estate Davis Bay. © **340/778-3800.** Main courses $22–$35. Daily 11:30am–4pm and 5–10pm.

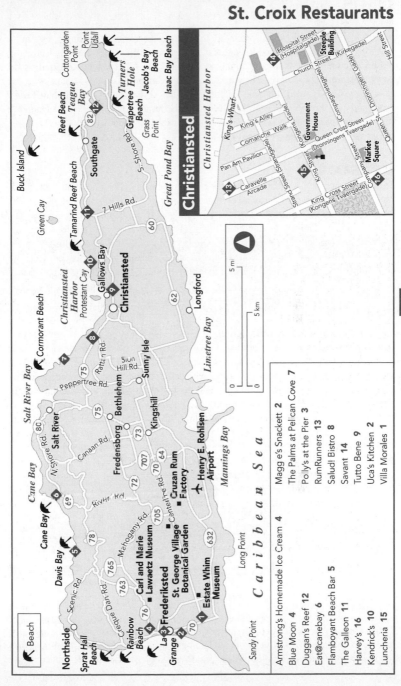

Christiansted Harbor

Christiansted

Hospital Street (Hospitalgade)
Steeple Building
Church Street (Kirkegade)
14
King's Wharf
King's Alley
Comanche Walk
Queen Cross Street (Compagniesgade)
Government House
Pan Am Pavilion
(Droningens Tvaergade)
15
King St. (Dronningers Gade)
Market Square
16
Caravelle Arcade
13
King Cross Street (Kongens Tvaergade)
Company Street
Hill Street

Point Udall
Cottongarden Point
Reef Beach
Teague Bay
Grapetree Hole
Turners Hole
Jacob's Bay Beach
Isaac Bay Beach
Grass Point
82
12
Southgate
Great Pond Bay
Buck Island
Green Cay
Tamarind Reef Beach
7 Hills Rd.
11
60
Gallows Bay
10
Christiansted Harbor
Protestant Cay
9
Christiansted
62
Longford
Cormorant Beach
Salt River Bay
8
Limetree Bay
7
Ratten Rd.
75
Sion Hill Rd.
Sunny Isle
Peppertree Rd.
Mannings Bay
75
Bethlehem
Kingshill
Salt River
80
N.Shore Rd.
Fredensborg
73
Canaan Rd.
707
Henry E. Rohlsen Airport
Cane Bay
Cane Bay
6
69
River Rd.
72
70
64
Cruzan Rum Factory
Caribbean Sea
Davis Bay
5
78
Mahogany Rd.
705
St. George Village Botanical Garden
632
Estate Whim Museum
Scenic Rd.
765
Carl and Marie Lawaetz Museum
1
Long Point
763
76
Frederiksted
Rainbow Beach
Creque Dan Rd.
4
3
La Grange
2
70
Sprat Hall Beach
Northside
Sandy Point

5 m
5 km

Beach

Christiansted

EXPENSIVE

Kendrick's ★★ FRENCH Some say this is the island's best fine-dining restaurant, and it's certainly has the good looks for it, with a beautiful courtyard and a setting in the historic Quin House cottage complex, built in 1762. Chef David Kendrick's food is memorable as well, with a seasonally changing menu. You might start with the exemplary Caesar salad, mussels steamed in white wine, or the sweet potato ravioli with pine nuts. For an entrée, if its offered, try the pecan-crusted pork tenderloin or a filet in a port-wine demi-glace. Service is impeccable.

2132 Company St. ℂ **340/773-9199.** Main courses $26–$39. Tues–Sat 6–10pm. Closed Mon Sept–Oct.

MODERATE

RumRunners ★ CARIBBEAN This is an easy-breezy choice, an open-air restaurant that sits right on the boardwalk with sunset views of the Christiansted harbor. The ambience is pure Caribbean—with waves rolling in in the background and pelicans wheeling above. During Sunday brunch a steel band plays. As for the food, it's surf and turf, from grilled New York strip steak to broiled whole lobster to meltingly tender baby-back ribs slow-cooked in island spices and Guinness. The bartender whips up some minxy drinks, or you may want to stop by for the $2 beer deals at happy hour.

In the Hotel Caravelle, on the boardwalk at Queen Cross St. ℂ **340/773-6585.** www.rumrunners stcroix.com. Reservations recommended. Main courses $10–$30. Mon–Fri 7–10:30am, 11:30am–3pm, and 5:30–9:30pm; Sat 8–10:30am and 11:30am–3pm; Sun brunch 8am–2pm.

Salud! Bistro ★★ MEDITERRANEAN/WINE BAR A buzzy, modern Mediterranean bistro and wine bar, Saludi has real local flavor, but not in the old-school-Caribbean sense. It's just a hopping place with a stylish local clientele, a window on the wide and wonderful diversity of folks who call St. Croix home. They come for the small plates, the expertly mixed mojiots and margaritas, the good wines and the warm ambience (walls are painted in richly saturated hues and hung with artwork). They also come for the expertly mixed mojitos and margaritas. Personal favorites among the starters: the platter of Mediterranean-style dips and spreads and the truffle mac 'n' cheese. The creative mains include lamb tagine, conch bolognese, and a zucchini pappadelle. Saludi is located 4 minutes west of Christiansted.

Princess Plaza, 9A Northside Rd. ℂ **340/718-7900.** http://saludbistro.com. Reservations recommended. Main courses $20–$35. Mon–Sat 5:30–10pm.

Savant ★★ CARIBBEAN/THAI/MEXICAN/FUSION Just like St. Croix itself, a "cultural callaloo," as one person put it, this is fusion on steroids. But it works, and this stylish bistro is a delightful place to dine, as the chefs take the food seriously. You can pinball from Thai curries to grilled fajitas to housemade egg rolls to fish tacos to maple-teriyaki pork tenderloin and not go wrong with any of it. Savant has only 20 candlelit tables, so call for a reservation as far in advance as you can.

4C Hospital St. ℂ **340/713-8666.** www.savantstx.com. Reservations required. Main courses $14–$39. Mon–Sat 6–10pm.

Tutto Bene ★★ ITALIAN A favorite among locals and visitors alike, this place has the warm, casual feel of a cantina, which meshes with the laidback island vibe. The food is simple and uncomplicated, the kind of hearty peasant dishes that built the

Roman empire. They also happen to be delicious and built from the freshest ingredients. You'll dine in a warehouselike setting just east of Christiansted, amid warm colors and, often, lots of hubbub. The menu is written on oversize mirrors against one wall. You might begin with a grilled flatbread pizza and go on to one of the pastas, like spaghetti bolognese, traditional carbonara with pancetta, or the vegetarian-friendly rasta pasta: penne in a pesto cream sauce. Fresh fish, steak, and pork chops round out the menu.

Boardwalk Building, Hospital St. ⓒ **340/773-5229.** www.tuttobenerestaurant.com. Reservations recommended. Main courses $23–$32. Wed–Sun 6–10pm.

INEXPENSIVE

Harvey's ★★ CARIBBEAN   Good, honest, utterly delicious Crucian food—that's what island matriarch Sarah Harvey delivers at her namesake restaurant. But Harvey's has plenty of fans, so you need to get here early for lunch....before the food runs out! We'd recommend you start with one of her homemade soups, or an appetizer of conch in butter sauce. Entrees will be barbecue chicken, goat stew, fried grouper, and, sometimes, even lobster. A side of cornmeal fungi comes with just about everything. Wash it all down with a fresh juice from exotic island fruits like gooseberry or tamarind. This is power eating, island style, so dig in.

11B Company St. ⓒ **340/773-3433.** Main courses $6–$22. Mon–Sat 11:30am–4pm.

In & Around Frederiksted
MODERATE

Blue Moon ★ INTERNATIONAL/CAJUN   Frederiksted's best little bistro is set in a 200-year-old stone house on the waterfront. It's a lively little café that becomes a hot spot when live jazz is on tap Wednesday and Friday nights and during Sunday brunch. The atmosphere is casual and welcoming, abetted by a New Orleans–influenced menu, featuring such classics as gumbo, jambalaya, and "Jazzy Shrimp": peel-and-eat shrimp with butter, garlic, and Cajun spices. There's also the usual array of fish, steak, and chicken dishes.

17 Strand St. ⓒ **340/772-2222.** www.bluemoonstcroix.com. Reservations recommended. Main courses $20–$29. Tues–Fri 11am–10pm; Sat 6–10pm; Sun 10am–2pm.

Villa Morales ★ SPANISH/CARIBBEAN   Family run for more than 60 years, this is St. Croix's top Puerto Rican restaurant. It's only open 3 nights a week, so if you have a craving for home-cooked Latino classics, check the opening times and book well in advance. Nightly specials might be stewed or roasted goat, barbecue ribs, or roast pork served with boiled rice and fungi. Seafood is a house specialty, especially the excellent steamed red snapper, conch, or lobster. Sides, as you might expect, are rice and beans, johnnycakes, and fried plantains. Villa Morales also has a budget-friendly **guest house** adjacent to the restaurant ($55 double; extra person $10).

Plot 82C, Estate Whim (off Rte. 70 about 2 miles from Frederiksted). ⓒ **340/772-0556.** http:// villamorales.fsted.com. Reservations recommended. Main courses $9–$35. Thurs–Sat 10am–10pm.

INEXPENSIVE

Armstrong's Homemade Ice Cream ★★ ICE CREAM   Since 1900, this family-run store has been making ice cream with local fruits, and it remains a must-visit. Flavors range from mango and soursop to guava, passionfruit and even gooseberry (not to mention basic choices like vanilla and chocolate). The recipes have been handed down in the family over three generations. The store makes a special guava-berry ice cream at Christmas.

78-B Whim. ℂ **340/772-1919.** Ice cream $2–$5. No credit cards. Tues–Sat 7am–7pm; Sun 11am–7pm.

Maggie's Snackett ★ CARIBBEAN   This welcoming local lunch spot, painted in buttery yellow, is a haven of home cooking. Maggie's menu changes every day, but expect such Caribbean classics as smoked mackerel and goat or chicken stew and fresh-baked island breads.

65 King St. ℂ **340/772-5070.** Breakfast $6–$7; main courses $12–$15. No credit cards. Daily 8am–3pm.

Polly's at the Pier ★★ COFFEE/INTERNATIONAL   This popular Art Deco spot is many things: an Internet café with free Wi-Fi; a gourmet coffee shop; a break-fast and lunch café (making fresh and delicious salads, sandwiches, burgers, soups); a mini-microbrewery selling Polly's Pale Ale; and an ice cream shop selling Armstrong's Homemade Ice Cream. It has a rotating art gallery. It even has the original Polly, an English bulldog for whom the shop is named, stopping in on occasion for photo ops.

#3 Strand St. ℂ **340/719-9434.** Sandwiches, salads, and platters $10–$30. Cash only. Mon–Fri 7am–7pm; Sat–Sun 8am–5pm.

Uca's Kitchen ★ VEGETARIAN   Just off the cruise dock, Uca's serves island-style vegetarian fare. The kitchen is a creative wonder, offering up such tantalizing and unusual dishes as barbecued tofu kebab or callaloo (a local spinach) with a fungi polenta or even gooseberry stew. The house specialty is a tasty mushroom lasagna. Don't leave without sampling one of the fresh tropical fruit juices.

King St. ℂ **340/772-5063.** Reservations not required. Main courses $10–$15. No credit cards. Daily 11:30am–7pm.

Out on the Island

Duggan's Reef ★ CONTINENTAL/CARIBBEAN   This popular open-air spot overlooks the placid blue seas of Reef Beach, where windsurfers and sailboats skim the water. Fresh lobster is a star here, from the fried johnnycakes and lobster salad to the lobster spring roll to Duggan's formidable Irish whiskey lobster. You'll find plenty of American classics here as well (burgers, steak, fried chicken). Set in an expansive green-and-white wood-frame structure with wraparound views, Duggan's is an island favorite.

E. End Rd. ℂ **340/773-9800.** http://dugganssreef.com. Reservations required for dinner in winter. Main courses $23–$39; pastas $19–$30. Mon–Sat 6–9:30pm; Sun brunch 11am–2pm.

MODERATE

Eat@canebay ★★ INTERNATIONAL   From the folks at the now-defunct Bac-chus, this hot spot on the island's northwest end is getting raves for its fizzy beach atmosphere and solid food. The breakfast and lunch menus feature a build-your-own premise—build your own burgers, salads, omelettes—along with sandwiches (pulled pork, Cane Bay Reuben), peel-your-own shrimp, and a nifty roster of sides, including smoked-duck chili, sweet potato fries, roasted beets. At night the menu goes uptown with a handful of elegantly prepared entrees listed on the blackboard. You might try pan-seared tuna, grilled steak, or linguine with scallops, mushrooms, and spinach in a garlicky cream sauce. The Sunday reggae brunch rocks the house; it's served from 11am to 4pm, and the music plays on till sunset.

groceries, markets & more: **ST. CROIX**
PROVISIONING

On St. Croix, everyone should take advantage of the island's farm-fresh fruit and produce. You can do so at the following places, whether you're stocking a kitchen or just looking for a snack or pre-prepared meal. *Note:* Beyond the resources listed below, the restaurant **Blue Water Terrace,** Cotton Valley, on the island's East End, has a market and deli selling sandwiches, cheeses, wine, picnic foods and lunch boxes; it also caters (*©* **740/692-2583**). Here are some essential St. Croix resources:

Groceries: Plaza Extra (*©* **340/719-1870;** http://plazaextra.com), with two locations on island, is stocked to the gills with, well, everything.

Fresh Seafood: Buy fresh fish (bluefish, tuna, alewife), Caribbean lobster, and conch at the **fish market** on the end of Strand Street on the Fredriksberg waterfront when the fishermen come in from 8:30am to 11am.

Fresh Meat: The family-run **Annaly Meat Market** (*©* **340/778-2229**) sells cut-to-order custom cuts of

meat, including local free-range organic Senepol beef, as well as U.S. choice beef, pork, lamb, and more. It's located on Route 72 on the way to the Carambola golf course. **Sejah Farms** (see below) raises chickens, goats, rabbits, and duck (the latter two to order) and sells fresh cuts from Thursday to Saturday at their farmstand.

Fresh Produce/Fruit: The roads of St. Croix are dotted with **farmstands.** Look for farmers selling fat avocadoes, bananas, papayas, beans, and more along Centerline Road and on roads in Estate Upper Love. **Sejah Farms** (*©* **340/773-8065;** http://sejahfarm.com) sells organic vegetables, eggs, honey, and chicken Monday to Friday 10am to 5pm and Saturday 7am to 5pm; it's on Casper Holstein Drive, near Fredriksted (they even accept farm volunteers). **ARTFarm** (*©* **340/514-4873;** www.artfarmllc.com), a unique organic farm/art gallery, sells organic produce and herbs every Saturday from 10am to noon The **La Reine Farmers' Market** is held on Saturday from 6:30am till 11am.

1110c Cane Bay. *©* **340/718-0360.** http://eatatcanebay.com. Reservations recommended. Main courses lunch $11–$16, dinner $22–$28. Wed–Mon 11am–9pm; Sun reggae brunch 11am–4pm.

The Palms at Pelican Cove ★★ CARIBBEAN/INTERNATIONAL The food is good and fresh and prepared with a lot of TLC at the signature restaurant of the Palms at Pelican Cove, but the setting is sheer enchantment: You're right on the beach with tall palms rustling and lights twinkling in the cove. Yes, you can plant yourself in the indoors dining room, but we prefer the terrace, and if you're lucky you can find a seat there too. The food is called "Caribbean-inspired" and it's mighty fine, with an emphasis on the catch of the day, but the restaurant is often lauded for its perfectly char-broiled ribeye. Monday is the restaurant's **Caribbean Night,** with an all-you-can-eat buffet featuring ribs, fish, chicken, johnnycakes, sweet potato stuffing, and more ($30 adults, $15 children 11 and under) and Carnival entertainment.

In the Palms at Pelican Cove (p. 95), 4126 La Grande Princesse. *©* **340/718-8920.** www.palms pelicancove.com. Reservations recommended. Main courses $12–$30. Daily 7:30–11am, 11:30am–2:30pm, and 6–9pm; Sun brunch 10am–2pm.

EXPLORING ST. CROIX

Beaches

Beaches are St. Croix's big attraction. Getting to them from Christiansted, however, home to most of the hotels, isn't always easy. It can also be expensive, especially if you want to beach it each day of your stay. From Christiansted a taxi will cost about $30 for two people to Davis Bay, $24 to Cane Bay, and $20 to Rainbow Beach. One solution is to rent a condo or stay in a hotel right on the water. Barring that, renting a car is a great way to hit the beaches—and see the island's attractions.

The most celebrated beach is offshore **Buck Island ★★★**, part of the U.S. National Park Service network. Buck Island is actually a volcanic islet surrounded by some of the most stunning underwater coral gardens in the Caribbean. The white-sand beaches on the southwest and west coasts are idyllic and the snorkeling is superb. The islet's interior is filled with cactus, wild frangipani, and pigeonwood. A number of operators runs excursions to Buck Island, leaving from Kings Wharf in Christiansted; the ride takes a half-hour. For details, see "A Side Trip to Buck Island," later in this chapter.

Your best choice for a beach in Christiansted is the one at the **Hotel on the Cay ★**. This white-sand strip is on a palm-shaded island. To get here, take the ferry from the fort at Christiansted; it runs every 10 minutes from 6am to midnight. The 4-minute trip costs $3 round-trip, free for guests of the timeshare resort Hotel on the Cay. Five miles west of Christiansted is the **Palms at Pelican Cove ★★**, where some 1,200 feet of white sand shaded by palm trees attracts a gay and mixed crowd. Because a reef lies just off the shore, snorkeling conditions are ideal.

Recommended highly are **Davis Bay ★** and **Cane Bay ★★**, each with swaying palms, white sand, and good swimming. Because they're on the north shore, these beaches are often windy, and as a result their waters are not always calm. The snorkeling at Cane Bay, however, is truly spectacular; you'll see elkhorn and brain corals, all some 750 feet off the Cane Bay Wall. Cane Bay adjoins Route 80 on the north shore. Close to the Renaissance Carambola Beach Resort, Davis Beach doesn't have a reef; it's more popular among bodysurfers than snorkelers.

On Route 63, a short ride north of Frederiksted, lies **Rainbow Beach ★**, with white sand and ideal snorkeling conditions. Nearby, also on Route 63, about 5 minutes north of Frederiksted, is another good beach, called **La Grange ★**. Lounge chairs can be rented here, and there's a bar nearby.

Sandy Point ★★★, directly south of Frederiksted, is the largest beach in all the U.S. Virgin Islands, but it's open to the public only on weekends from 10am to 4pm. Its waters are shallow and calm, perfect for swimming. Zigzagging fences line the beach to help prevent beach erosion. Sandy Point is protected as a nesting spot for endangered sea turtles. Continue west from the western terminus of the Melvin Evans Highway (Rte. 66). For more on visiting the refuge, see p. 115.

The island's East End has an array of beaches; they're somewhat difficult to get to, but much less crowded. The best choice here is **Isaac Bay Beach ★**, ideal for snorkeling, swimming, or sunbathing. Windsurfers like **Reef Beach,** which opens onto Teague Bay along Route 82, East End Road, a half-hour ride from Christiansted. You can get food at **Duggan's Reef** (p. 104). **Cramer Park** is a special public park operated by the Department of Agriculture. It's lined with sea-grape trees and has a delightful picnic area, a restaurant, and a bar. **Grapetree Beach** is off Rte. 60 (S. Shore Rd.), wide and sandy, with calm water. The beach is flanked only by a few private homes, although the beach at the Divi Carina is a short walk away.

Watersports & Outdoor Adventures

St. Croix offers many outdoor adventures. In the east, the terrain is rocky and arid, getting little water. But the western part of the island is lush, including a small "rain forest" of mango, tree ferns, and dangling lianas. Between the two extremes are beautiful sandy beaches, rolling hills and pastures, and roads lined with mahogany trees and colorful flamboyant trees. Watersports galore abound, including boating, sailing, diving, snorkeling, fishing, hiking, and windsurfing.

BICYLING St. Croix has miles of relatively flat roadways that make it ideal for biking, but it also has lush hills for the more adventurous. Contact **Freedom City Cycles,** 2E Strand Square, 2 Strand St., Frederiksted (☏ **340/227-2433;** www.freedomcity cycles.com), which, in addition to offering bike rentals, can arrange guided bike tours of the island. A 2- to 3-hour mountain bike tour begins at sea level and climbs through the rain forest on both paved and unpaved roads, costing $60 per person.

FISHING The fishing grounds at **Lang Bank** are about 10 miles from St. Croix. Here you'll find kingfish, dolphin fish, and wahoo. Using light-tackle boats to glide along the reef, you'll probably turn up jack or bonefish. At **Clover Crest,** in Frederiksted, local anglers fish right from the rocks. For more information on legal shore-fishing spots around the island, contact the tourist office in Christiansted or Frederiksted. Serious sport fishermen can head out with **St. Croix Deep Blue Charters** (☏ **340/643-5514;** www.stcroixdeepbluecharters.com), on a 38-foot Bertram special anchored at Silver Bay Dock on the Christiansted waterfront. Reservations can be made by calling during the day. The cost for up to six passengers is $650 for 4 hours and $850 for 6 hours with bait and tackle and drinks included.

GOLF St. Croix has the best golf in the Virgin Islands. Guests staying on St. John and St. Thomas often fly over for a round on one of the island's three courses.

Carambola Golf & Country Club, on the northeast side of St. Croix (☏ **340/778-5638;** www.golfcarambola.com), adjacent to the **Carambola Beach Resort** (p. 95), was created by Robert Trent Jones, Sr., who called it "the loveliest course I ever designed." It's been likened to a botanical garden. The par-3 holes here are known to golfing authorities as the best in the Tropics. The greens fee of $95 in winter, or $65 in the off season, allows you to play as many holes as you like. Carts are included.

The **Buccaneer,** Gallows Bay (☏ **340/712-2144;** p. 93), 3 miles east of Christiansted, has a challenging 5,685-yard, 18-hole course with panoramic vistas. Non-guests pay $110 in winter or $70 off season, including use of a cart.

The **Reef,** on the east end of the island at Teague Bay (☏ **340/773-8844**), is a 3,100-yard, 9-hole course, charging greens fees of $20 for 9 holes and $35 for 18 holes. Golf carts can also be rented at an additional $15 for 9 holes or $20 for 18 holes. The longest hole here is a 465-yard par 5.

HIKING Scrub-covered hills make up much of St. Croix's landscape. The island's western district, however, includes a dense, 15-acre forest known as the **"Rain Forest"** (although it's not a real one). The network of footpaths here offers fantastic nature walks. The area is thick with mahogany trees, kapok (silk-cotton) trees, and *samaan* (rain) trees. Sweet limes, mangoes, hog plums, and breadfruit trees, all of which have grown in the wild since the days of the plantations, are here. The "Rain Forest" is private property, but visitors are welcome to go inside to explore. To experience its charm, some people simply opt to drive along Route 76 (also known as Mahogany Rd.), stopping beside the footpaths that meander off on either side of the highway into dry riverbeds and glens. Stick to the most worn footpaths.

Our favorite trail in the "Rain Forest," **Creque Dam Road** (Rte. 58/78), takes about 2½ hours one-way. From Frederiksted, drive north on Route 63 to Creque Dam Road, where you turn right, park the car, and start walking. A mile past the Creque Dam, you'll be deep within the forest's magnificent flora and fauna. Continue on the trail until you come to the Western Scenic Road. Eventually, you reach Mahogany Road (Rte. 76), near St. Croix LEAP Project. The trail is moderate in difficulty.

To reach some of the most remote but scenic places on St. Croix, take a walking tour with **Crucian Heritage & Nature Tourism** (CHANT; ☏ 340/772-4079; http://chantvi.org). Its "Ay Ay Eco-Hike Tours" include a steep walk down the mountainside to the crystalline tidal pools and saltwater baths of Annaly Bay, and a stroll along scenic Maroon Ridge, established by runaway slaves in the 17th century ($50 per person).

The **St. Croix Environmental Association** (☏ 340/773-1989; www.stxenvironmental.org) also offers interesting hikes, including a Butler Bay Falls guided hike to study the traditional cultural and medicinal uses of plants along the way. **Buck Island** (see the section "A Side Trip to Buck Island," later in this chapter), just off St. Croix, also has nature trails.

HORSEBACK RIDING **Paul & Jill's Equestrian Stables,** 2 Sprat Hall Estate, Rte. 58 (☏ 340/772-2880; www.paulandjills.com), the largest equestrian stable in the Virgin Islands, is known throughout the Caribbean for its horses. It's set on the sprawling grounds of the island's oldest plantation great house, Sprat Hall. The operators lead scenic trail rides through the forests, along the beach, and past ruins of abandoned 18th-century plantations and sugar mills. Beginners and experienced riders alike are welcome. A 1½-hour trail ride costs $99. Tours usually depart daily in winter at 10:30am and 3pm, and in the off-season at 4pm, with slight variations according to demand. Reserve at least a day in advance.

KAYAKING The beauty of St. Croix is best seen from a **kayak.** You can explore the waters of Sandy Point, Shell Island, and Salt River Bay National Park or kayak over the steep underwater wall at Cane Bay on half-day, full-day, and weeklong tours offered by **Virgin Kayak** (☏ 340/718-0071; www.virginkayaktours.com). The tour, lasting 3 hours, costs $45 per person and includes water and a light snack.

Seeing St. Croix's magical **bioluminescent bays** ★★★ is a nighttime thrill on moonless nights. Both Virgin Kayak and **Sea Thru Kayaks VI** (☏ 340/244-8696; http://seathrukayaksvi.com) explore the island's two bioluminescent bays by kayak. See Thru Kayaks VI's see-through kayaks make the trip that much more memorable. Cost for an average 90-minute tour is $50 per person.

KITEBOARDING **Kite St. Croix** (☏ 340/643-5824; www.kitestcroix.com), in Cotton Valley on the north shore of the island's East End, offers kiteboarding lessons ($100–$225) and rentals ($50/half-day) on-site. The times for good kiteboarding winds are December through March and June through August.

SCUBA DIVING & SNORKELING ★★★ Sponge life, black coral (the finest in the West Indies), and steep drop-offs near the shoreline make St. Croix a snorkeling and diving paradise. The island is protected by the largest living reef in the Caribbean, including the fabled north-shore wall that begins in 25 to 30 feet of water and drops to 13,200 feet, sometimes plunging straight down.

Buck Island ★★ is a major scuba-diving site, with a visibility of some 100 feet. It also has an underwater snorkeling trail. Practically all outfitters on St. Croix offer scuba and snorkeling tours to Buck Island. For more information on the island, see the section "A Side Trip to Buck Island," later in this chapter.

Other favorite dive sites include the historic **Salt River Canyon ★★** (northwest of Christiansted at Salt River Bay), for advanced divers. Submerged canyon walls are covered with purple tube sponges, deepwater gorgonians, and black coral saplings. You'll see schools of yellowtail snapper, turtles, and spotted eagle rays. We also like the gorgeous coral gardens of **Scotch Banks** (north of Christiansted) and **Eagle Ray** (also north of Christiansted), the latter so named because of the rays that cruise along the wall there. **Cane Bay ★★** is known for its coral canyons.

Frederiksted Pier ★, near the historic area of Frederiksted, is the jumping-off point (literally) for a scuba voyage into a world of sponges, banded shrimp, plume worms, sea horses, and other creatures.

Davis Bay is the site of the 12,000-foot-deep Puerto Rico Trench. **Northstar Reef ★★**, at the east end of Davis Bay, is a spectacular wall dive, recommended for intermediate or experienced divers only. The wall here is covered with stunning brain corals and staghorn thickets. At some 50 feet down, a sandy shelf leads to a cave where giant green moray eels hang out.

At **Butler Bay,** to the north of Frederiksted on the west shore, there are the submerged ruins of three ships: the *Suffolk Maid,* the *Northwind,* and the *Rosaomaira,* the latter sitting in 100 feet of water. These wrecks form the major part of an artificial reef system that also contains abandoned trucks and cars. This site is recommended for intermediate or experienced divers.

A top outfitter is the **Cane Bay Dive Shop** (✆ **800/338-3843** or 340/773-9913; www.canebayscuba.com), with four locations around the island. The numerous locations means there's a variety of dive sites to choose from without having to take a long boat ride. A beginner's lesson goes for $60, and packages go all the way up the scale to a six-tank dive package for $295.

See "Beaches," above, for the best snorkeling spots. Most beachside resorts offer complimentary snorkling equipment. You can also rent everything you need at all four locations of rthe Cane Bay Dive Shop (see above).

STANDUP PADDLEBOARDING Kite St. Croix (✆ 340/643-5824; www.kite stcroix.com) offers paddleboard rentals ($35/per hour and $60/per day) as well as beginner lessons ($50–$75).

TENNIS Some authorities rate the tennis at the **Buccaneer ★★**, Gallows Bay (✆ 340/773-3036), as the best in the Caribbean. The resort offers a choice of eight courts, two lit for night play, all open to the public. Nonguests pay $18 daytime, $22 nighttime per hour; you must call to reserve a court at least a day in advance. A tennis pro is available for lessons, and if you're looking for tennis partners, they are happy to match you up for singles or doubles.

Taxi Tours

One of the best ways to explore St. Croix is on a **taxi tour ★★** with a local driver. We give our unqualified seal of approval to the following drivers, both of whom do wonderful and erudite sightseeing tours: **Ames Joseph** (📞 **340/277-6133**) or **Francis M. Vazquez** (📞 **340/690-4045**). In general, a 3½-hour island tour for one to four persons costs around $150; a 6-hour tour is $300. The fare should be negotiated in advance. Extra fees may be charged for the following sights: $10 for the botanical gardens, $10 for the Whim Estate House, and $8 for the rum distillery. *Note:* You may want to concentrate on the island's East End for one trip and the West End on another.

Heritage & Cultural Tours

St. Croix's cultural riches are explored on tours run by **Crucian Heritage & Nature Tourism (CHANT;** 📞 **340/772-4079;** http://chantvi.org). In addition to **historic walking tours** ★★ of the colonial towns of Christiansted and Frederiksted, CHANT offers a fascinating **Ridge to Reef Farm Tour,** showcasing the island's agricultural heritage and burgeoning farm-to-table movement with a tour of a 200-acre working tropical farm in a lush forest valley. The 3-hour tour is $55 per person.

The **St. Croix Landmarks Society** (📞 **340/772-0598;** www.stcroixlandmarks.com) offers a terrific roster of Sunday-afternoon **"Places that Matter/Ruins Rambles"** ★★: historic walking tours that let you "walk in the footsteps of people" who lived and worked here. A recent ramble took in the old slave market in Christiansted. It also holds **Annual House Tours** in February. Check the website for dates and hours.

Seeing the Sights

Christopher Columbus named the island Santa Cruz (Holy Cross) when he landed on November 14, 1493. He anchored his ship off the north shore but was quickly driven away by the spears, arrows, and axes of the Carib Indians. The French laid claim to the island in 1650; the Danes purchased it from them in 1733. Under their rule, the slave trade and sugarcane fields flourished until the latter half of the 19th century. Danish architecture and influence can still be seen on the island today. In a shrewd purchase deal with the Danes, the U.S. acquired the islands in 1917.

Although the 21st century has definitely invaded St. Croix, with subdivisions, condo complexes, shopping centers, and modern strip malls, evidence of the past is everywhere across its 84 square miles. St. Croix contains the nostalgic ruins of some 100 slave-driven plantations where sugarcane was once grown.

Today, the past is visible everywhere you go in St. Croix, from Fort Christiansvaern to Fort Frederick. Take the time to explore Christiansted and Frederiksted, where the island's Danish roots can be seen everywhere.

In His Footsteps: Alexander Hamilton (1755–1804)

Alexander Hamilton was an American statesman from the West Indies who served brilliantly in the American Revolution. He wrote many of the articles contained in the Federalist Papers and became secretary of the Treasury under George Washington. He was noted for both his literary and oratorical skills. Although he was born on the island of Nevis, Hamilton spent his adolescence in St. Croix.

o **Birthplace:** The British-held island of Nevis, on January 11, 1755

o **Residences:** Nevis, St. Croix, various cities in the United States

o **Final Days:** In a duel fought with Aaron Burr, Hamilton was mortally wounded and died on July 12, 1804.

WALKING TOUR: CHRISTIANSTED

START:	**The Visitors Bureau.**
FINISH:	**Christiansted's harborfront.**
TIME:	**1½ hours.**
BEST TIMES:	**Any day from 10am to 4pm.**
WORST TIMES:	**Monday to Friday 4 to 6pm.**

The largest town on St. Croix, Christiansted still has many traces of its Danish heritage. Constructed by the Danish West India Company, the heart of town is still filled with many imposing old buildings, mostly former warehouses, from the 18th century. Today they are registered as a U.S. National Historic Site. Across a small park stands **Fort Christiansvaern,** which the Danes built on the fortifications of a 1645 French fort. From its precincts, some of the best views of the harbor can be seen. Christiansted is best seen by walking tour.

---

1 The Old Scale House

This yellow-sided building with a cedar-capped roof is located near the harborfront. It was originally built as the Old Scale House in 1856 to replace a similar structure that had burned down. In its heyday, all taxable goods leaving and entering Christiansted's harbor were weighed here. In front of the building lies one of the most charming squares in the Caribbean. Its old-fashioned asymmetrical allure is still evident despite the mass of cars. Inside is an information center and a bookstore and gift shop.

With your back to the scalehouse, turn left and walk through the parking lot to the foot of the white-sided gazebo-like band shell that sits in the center of a park named after Alexander Hamilton, who spent his adolescence on St. Croix. The yellow-brick building with the ornately carved brick staircase is the:

2 Old Danish Customs House

This is currently the headquarters of the National Park Service. The gracefully proportioned 16-step staircase was added in 1829 as an embellishment to an older building dating back to 1734. During the island's Danish occupancy, this is where merchants paid their taxes. (There are public toilets on the ground floor.)

Continue climbing the hill to the base of the yellow-painted structure, which is:

3 Fort Christiansvaern

This is the best-preserved colonial fortification in the Virgin Islands. It's maintained as a historic monument by the National Park Service. Its original four-sided, diamond-shaped design was in accordance with the most advanced military planning of its era. The fort is the site of the St. Croix military museum, which documents police work on the island from the late 1800s to the present with photos, weapons, and other artifacts. The admission price of $3 also includes admission to the Steeple Building (see below). The fort is open Monday through Friday from 8am to 5pm. For information, call © **340/773-1460.**

Walking Tour: Christiansted

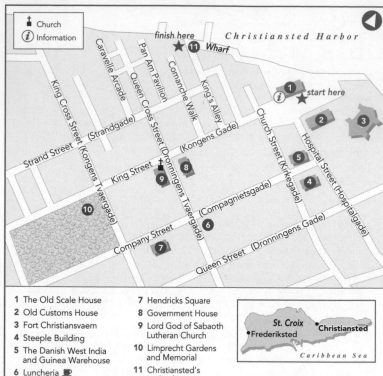

Exit from the fort, and head straight down the tree-lined path toward the most visible steeple in Christiansted. It caps the appropriately named:

4 Steeple Building

Completed in 1753, the Steeple Building was embellished with a steeple between 1794 and 1796. For a time it served as the headquarters of the Church of Lord God of Sabaoth, the island's first Lutheran church. The original structure can still be visited (see below). Inside is a National Park Service museum with exhibits on plantation life on the island. Admission is included in the $3 ticket for Fort Christiansvaern.

Across Company Street from the Steeple Building is a U.S. post office.

5 The Danish West India & Guinea Warehouse

The building that houses the post office was built in 1749 as the warehouse for the Danish West India and Guinea Company. The structure was once three times larger than it is today and included storerooms and lodging for staff. Go to the building's side entrance, on Church Street, and enter the rear courtyard. For many years, this was the site of some of the largest slave auctions in the Caribbean.

From the post office, retrace your steps to Company Street and head west for 1 block. On your left, you'll pass the entrance to Apothecary Hall, 2111 Company St., which contains a charming collection of shops and restaurants.

6 Luncheria ☕

If you need refreshment, try **Luncheria,** Apothecary Hall Courtyard, 2111 Company St. (📞 **340/773-4247**). The bar's tables are grouped in a courtyard shaded by trees. The owners are margarita specialists, stocking more types of tequila (15-plus) than any other bar in the neighborhood. Luncheria serves burritos, tostadas, enchiladas, and tacos, as well as daily specials and vegetarian meals.

Exit Apothecary Hall and turn left onto Company Street. Walk across Queen Cross Street (Dronningens Tvergade). A half-block later, you'll arrive at the island's largest outdoor market:

7 Hendricks Square

The square was rebuilt in a timbered, 19th-century style after the 1989 hurricane. Fruits and vegetables are sold here Monday through Saturday from 7am to 6pm.

Retrace your steps a half-block along Company Street, then turn left onto Queen Cross Street. Head downhill toward the harbor, walking on the right-hand side of the street. Within a half-block, you'll reach an unmarked arched iron gateway, set beneath an arcade. Enter the charming gardens of:

8 Government House

This grand Danish Colonial building was formed from the union of two much older town houses in the 1830s. It was used as the Danish governor's residence until 1871, when the Danish West Indies capital was moved to Charlotte Amalie, on St. Thomas. The European-style garden here contains a scattering of trees, flower beds, and walkways. The gardens are open Monday to Friday 8am to 5pm. The Virgin Islands Tourism Office is located downstairs.

Exit the same way you entered, turn right, and continue your descent of Queen Cross Street. At the first street corner (King St.), turn left and you'll see:

9 Lord God of Sabaoth Lutheran Church

This neoclassical church was built sometime before 1740 and was originally the site of the Dutch Reformed Church; it was turned over to the Lord God of Sabaoth congregation in 1834, when a Gothic Revival tower was added. Much inside predates the Lutheran occupation, including the tower bell, cast in Copenhagen in 1793, and an impressive 18th-century picture frame fashioned of local mahogany that resides behind the altar.

Continue walking southwest along King Street. Within 2 blocks is the:

10 Limprecht Gardens & Memorial

For 20 years (1888–1908), Peter Carl Limprecht served as governor of the Danish West Indies. Today, an occasional chicken pecks at seedlings planted near a Danish-language memorial to him.

At the end of the park, retrace your steps to Queen Cross Street, and go left. One very short block later, turn right onto Strand Street, which contains some interesting stores, including at least two different shopping arcades. The streets will narrow, and the pedestrian traffic will be more congested. Pass beneath the overpass belonging to a longtime bar and restaurant, the **Club Comanche.**

A trail that leads into the past, **St. Croix Heritage Trail** traces the island's Danish colonial heritage. All you need are a brochure and map, available at the tourist office in Christiansted (p. 88). This 72-mile itinerary includes a combination of asphalt-covered roadway, suitable for driving, and narrow woodland trails which must be navigated on foot. Many aficionados opt to drive along the route whenever practical, descend onto the footpaths wherever indicated, and then return to their cars for the continuation of the tour. En route, you'll be exposed to one of the Caribbean's densest concentrations of historical and cultural sites. Consisting largely of existing roadways, the route connects Christiansted and Frederiksted, going past the sites of former sugar plantations, and traverses the entire 28-mile length of St. Croix. The brochure identifies everything you're

seeing: cattle farms, suburban communities, even industrial complexes and resorts. It's not all manicured and pretty, but much is scenic and worth the drive. Allow at least a day for this trail, with stops along the way, including **Point Udall,** the easternmost point under the U.S. flag in the Caribbean, and the two highlights of the trail: the **Estate Mount Washington** (p. 116), a strikingly well-preserved sugar plantation; and **Estate Whim Plantation Museum** (p. 114), one of the best of the restored great houses, with a museum and gift shop. Of course, you'll want to stop and get a refreshment break. We recommend **Smithens Market.** Vendors at this market, which lies off Queen Mary Highway, offer freshly squeezed sugarcane juice and sell locally grown fruits and homemade chutneys.

Continue down the meandering curves of King's Alley. Within 1 block you'll be standing beside:

11 Christiansted's Harborfront

End your tour here by strolling the boardwalk of the waterside piers and watching the sailboats bob in the harbor (and perhaps a seaplane touching down).

Frederiksted ★

This former Danish settlement at the western end of the island, about 17 miles from Christiansted, is a sleepy port town that comes to life when a cruise ship docks at its pier—which is happening more frequently these days. Frederiksted was destroyed by a fire in an 1878 labor revolt, and the citizens rebuilt it by putting Victorian wood frames and clapboards on top of the old Danish stone and yellow-brick foundations.

Most visitors begin their tour at russet-colored **Fort Frederik,** at the northern end of Frederiksted next to the cruise-ship pier (𝄯 **340/772-2021**). This fort, completed in 1760, is said to have been the first fort in the Caribbean to salute the flag of the new United States. An American brigantine, anchored at port in Frederiksted, hoisted a crudely made Old Glory. To show its support for the emerging American colonies, the head of the fort fired a cannonball in the air to honor the Americans and their new independence. Such an act violated the rules of Danish neutrality. It was at this same fort, on July 3, 1848, that Governor-General Peter von Scholten emancipated the slaves in the Danish West Indies, in response to a slave uprising led by a young man named Moses "Buddhoe" Gottlieb. In 1998, a bust of Buddhoe was unveiled here. The fort has been restored to its 1840 appearance and today is a national historic landmark. You can explore the courtyard and stables. A local history museum has been installed in what was once the Garrison Room. Admission is $3, free for children 15 and under; it's open Monday through Friday from 8:30am to 4pm.

The **Customs House,** just east of the fort, is an 18th-century building with a 19th-century two-story gallery. To the south of the fort is the **visitor bureau** at Strand Street (© **340/772-0357**), where you can pick up a free map of the town.

SANDY POINT WILDLIFE REFUGE ★★

St. Croix's rarely visited southwestern tip is composed of salt marshes, tidal pools, and low vegetation inhabited by birds, turtles, and other wildlife. More than 3 miles of ecologically protected coastline lie between Sandy Point (the island's westernmost tip) and the shallow waters of the West End Salt Pond. This national wildlife refuge is one of only **two nesting grounds of the leatherback turtle** in the United States—the other is on Culebra, an offshore island of Puerto Rico. It's also home to colonies of green and hawksbill turtles, and thousands of birds, including herons, brown pelicans, Caribbean martins, black-necked stilts, and white-crowned pigeons. As for flora, Sandy Point gave its name to a rare form of orchid, a brown/purple variety. The area consists of 360 acres of subtropical vegetation, including the largest salt pond in the Virgin Islands.

The wildlife refuge is only open to the public on Saturday and Sunday from 10am to 4pm (admission is free). Park rangers are determined to keep the area pristine, and in doing so they have to face such problems as the poaching of sea turtles and their eggs, drug smuggling, dumping of trash, and the arrival of illegal aliens. Even the mongoose and feral dogs are a menace to the nesting female turtles.

If Sandy Point's rules and regulations seem a little stringent, then you haven't met a leatherback sea turtle. It's the largest of its species and can measure some 6 feet in length and weigh more than 1,000 pounds. Every 2, perhaps 3 years, the turtles come back to this refuge to nest from March to July. The average female will deposit anywhere from 60 to 100 eggs in her nest. The survival rate is only 1 in 1,000 hatchlings. The refuge is also home to the green sea turtle, which can grow to a maximum of 4 feet and weigh about 400 pounds. These turtles come here only from June to September, when the females lay from 75 to 100 eggs.

Birders also flock to Sandy Point to see some **100 species of birds,** five of which are endangered. Endangered brown pelicans, royal terns, Caribbean elaenias, bananaquits, and yellow warblers are among the birds that call Sandy Point home.

To reach the refuge, drive to the end of the Rte. 66 (Melvin Evans Hwy.) and continue down a gravel road. For guided weekend visits, call © **340/773-4554** to make arrangements.

SIGHTSEEING AROUND THE ISLAND

North of Frederiksted, you can drop in at **Sprat Hall,** the island's oldest plantation, or continue along to the "Rain Forest" (see above). Most visitors come to the area to see the jagged estuary of the northern coastline's **Salt River.** The Salt River was where Columbus landed on November 14, 1493. Marking the 500th anniversary of Columbus's arrival, former President George H. W. Bush signed a bill creating the 912-acre **Salt River Bay National Historical Park and Ecological Preserve** (www.nps.gov/sari). The park contains the site of the original Carib village explored by Columbus and his men, including the only ceremonial ball court ever discovered in the Lesser Antilles. Also within the park is the largest mangrove forest in the Virgin Islands, sheltering many endangered animals and plants, plus an underwater canyon attracting divers

The rocky promontory of Point Udall, jutting into the Caribbean Sea, is the easternmost point of the United States. Diehards go out to see the sun rise, but considering the climb via a rutted dirt road, you may want to wait until there's a bit more light before heading here. Once at the top, you'll be rewarded with one of the best scenic views in the U.S. Virgin Islands. Point Udall is reached along Rte. 82 (it's signposted).

from around the world. If you visit on your own, a taxi from Christiansted will cost $22. See "Watersports & Outdoor Adventures," earlier in the chapter, for suggestions on kayak and scuba tours to this very special park.

Carl and Marie Lawaetz Museum ★ MUSEUM This 1750 La Grange valley farmstead was built as a sugar plantation, but was converted to a cattle ranch after it became the home of Danish cattle farmer Carl Lawaetz in 1896. Here he and his wife, Marie, raised Senegal cattle and seven children. Today you can tour the house, filled with turn-of-the-20th-century antiques and family heirlooms. The grounds also hold the ruins of the plantation's old sugar mill, as well as flowers and tropical trees and bushes. Inside, touchingly, Marie's paintings still hang in almost every room.

Mahogany Rd., Rte. 76, Estate Little La Grange. ℂ **340/772-0598.** www.stcroixlandmarks.com. Admission $10 adults, $8 students and seniors, $5 children 6–12, free for children 5 and under. Tues, Sat, and cruise-ship days 10am–4pm.

Cruzan Rum Factory ★ FACTORY This vintage factory distills the famous Virgin Islands rum that some consider the finest in the world, although the stuff now detours through the Jim Beam bottling factory in the U.S.A. before it reaches your favorite beach bar. The grounds are quietly bucolic, with offices now ensconced in the 18th-century plantation house and a magnificent ficus tree spreading its wings on the lawn. The charmingly low-tech guided tours include a visit through the factory and the chance to peer into giant vats of bubbling molasses—the scent is pure sugar perfume. Call ahead for reservations.

Estate Diamond 3, W. Airport Rd., Rte. 64. ℂ **340/692-2280.** www.cruzanrum.com. Admission $5 adults, $1 children 18 and under. Tours given Mon–Fri 9–4pm and Sat 10am–2pm.

Estate Mount Washington Plantation ★ MUSEUM St. Croix's best-preserved sugar and cotton plantation was an island workhorse from 1780 to 1820, when sugar was king on St. Croix, then the second-largest sugar producer in the West Indies. The nine-bedroom great house is a private home and closed to the public, but you can go on a self-guided stroll of the 13 acres, where you'll see the stone ruins of the plantation's sugar factory, as well as the "cockpit" animal mill, where donkeys or horses would be utilized to crush the sugarcane.

At the very southwestern tip of the island, off Rte. 63, a mile inland from the highway that runs along the Frederiksted coast. Free admission.

Estate Whim Plantation Museum ★ MUSEUM The beautifully restored great house of the island's oldest sugar plantation was built to last, with 3-foot-thick walls of coral, stone, and molasses. All around, tropical greenery threatens to swallow up the plantation structures—which include a sugar factory and restored windmill—and before the estate became a landmark, it almost did. Inside, the great house has only three rooms, but each is filled with antiques from the era. You can tour the house and

12-acre grounds, and look for special ongoing events held here by the St. Croix Land-marks Society, such as evening concerts and arts and crafts shows. Check the website (www.stcroixlandmarks.com) to see what's happening. It also has a fabulous **museum store** (p. 118) on the premises, selling all manner of original island souvenirs.

Centerline Rd. (2 miles east of Frederiksted). ℂ **340/772-0598.** Admission $10 adults, $8 seniors, $5 children. Wed–Sat and cruise-ship days 10am–4pm.

St. George Village Botanical Garden ★ GARDEN This 16-acre garden of tropical trees, shrubs, vines, and flowers was built around the ruins of a 19th-century sugarcane workers' village. Self-guided walking-tour maps are available at the entrance to the garden's great hall. The gardens feature a lively roster of year-round events. Facilities include restrooms and a gift shop.

127 Estate St., 1 St. George (just north of Centerline Rd.), 4 miles east of Frederiksted. ℂ **340/692-2874.** www.sgvbg.org. Admission $8 adults, $6 seniors, $1 children 12 and under; donations welcome. Daily 9am–5pm.

SHOPPING

Christiansted is the shopping hub of St. Croix, though it pales in comparison to the turbo-charged shopping in Charlotte Amalie on St. Thomas. But may we venture to say that the goods sold on St. Croix often are more interesting and more original, and reflect the local, artisanal, handmade spirit of the island. Most of the shops are compressed into a half-mile or so; look for hole-in-the-wall boutiques selling handmade goods. Between Company Street and the harbor are many courtyards, antique buildings, arcades, and walkways riddled with shops, many of which are smaller branches of parent stores on St. Thomas. Along the boardwalk is the **King's Alley Complex,** a pink-sided compound filled with the densest concentration of shops on St. Croix.

In recent years, **Frederiksted** has also become a popular shopping destination. Many of its mall shops appeal to cruise-ship passengers arriving at Frederiksted Pier, but you can find a few gems among the cookie-cutter offerings.

Keep in mind that shopping in St. Croix is duty-free, and U.S. citizens enjoy a $1,600 duty-free allowance (even children) per person every 30 days.

St. Croix Shopping A to Z
ARTS & CRAFTS
Many Hands ★★ ART This shop has been selling local artworks for almost 50 years. The collection of local one-of-a-kind paintings is intriguing, as is the pottery and handmade jewelry. 110 Strand St. ℂ **340/773-1990.** http://manyhands.stcroixtravelusvi.com.

St. Croix LEAP ★★ HOUSEWARES If you're on western St. Croix, near Frederiksted, St. Croix LEAP makes an offbeat adventure. Inside this open-air shop are stacks of rare salvaged native wood being fashioned into serving boards, tables, wall hangings, clocks, you name it (the protected mahogany is from trees felled in storms or that needed to be trimmed). The St. Croix Life and Environmental Arts Project is dedicated to manual work, environmental conservation, and self-development. St. Croix LEAP is located 2 miles up Mahogany Road from the beach north of Frederiksted. Look for large mahogany signs and sculptures flanking the driveway. Visitors will need to bear to the right to reach the woodworking area and gift shop. The site is open Monday to Friday 9am to 5pm and Saturday 10am to 5pm. Mahogany Rd., Rte. 76. ℂ **340/772-0421.**

GIFTS

Franklin's on the Waterfront ★ GIFTS   This terrific gift and home-furnishing emporium stands out amid the mall clutter nearby. Franklin's sells a thoughtfully curated selection of beautiful things, including works made by local artisans (we got a charming Moko Jumbie Christmas ornament made by local artist Sandra Michael here), high-end candles, Caribbean bath and body products, and more. 4 Strand St. *©* **340/643-3830.**

Royal Poinciana ★ GIFTS   This gift shop has the look of an antique apothecary. You'll find such local items as hot sauces, Sunny Caribee spices, island herbal teas, Antillean coffees, and an array of scented soaps, toiletries, lotions, and shampoos. 1111 Strand St. *©* **340/773-9892.**

Whim Museum Store ★★ GIFTS   The Whim Museum Store has some intriguing gifts and souvenirs, both imported and local, including table linens, Madras cloth, jewelry, art prints, books, and local Guavaberry liqueur. Monies from the gift-store sales go toward the upkeep of the museum and the grounds (p. 116). An associated store in downtown Christiansted, with different inventory, is at 58 Queen St. (*©* **340/713-8102**). 52 Estate Whim Plantation Museum, east of Frederiksted on Centerline Rd. *©* **340/772-0598.**

JEWELRY

Crucian Gold ★ JEWELRY   This small West Indian cottage holds the gold and silver creations of island-born Brian Bishop. His most popular and distinctive item is the Crucian bracelet with a "true lovers' knot" design. Pendants framed in gold or silver encase shards of china dating from the 1600s or 1700s and found along the beaches of St. Croix. The shards were once collected by island kids who called them "China money" or "chiny." Strand St. *©* **340/773-5241.** www.cruciangold.com.

ib Designs ★ JEWELRY   Local metalsmith Whealan Massicott crafts beautiful Caribbean-inspired jewelry in delicately wrought designs at his shop in downtown Christiansted. Corner of Queen Cross and Company sts. *©* **340/773-4322.** www.islandboy designs.com.

Joyia ★ JEWELRY   The working studio of local jewelry artist Joyia Jones is filled with her fine handcrafted pieces of gold, silver, copper, and precious stones. 3A Queen Cross St. *©* **340/713-4569.** www.joyiajewelry.com.

Sonya Ltd. ★ JEWELRY   Sonya Hough makes sterling silver or gold versions of her original design, the C-clasp bracelet. There's some symbolism to the design: If the

---

Roll the Dice

In 1996, U.S. senators agreed to allow the opening of gambling casinos in the U.S. Virgin Islands. In a bow to the islanders, senators agreed that majority ownership of the casino hotels would be reserved for locals. It hasn't exactly been a casino bonanza since then, as only one casino is spinning its gambling wheels:

St. Croix's **Divi Carina Bay Casino** (Divi Carina Bay Resort; *©* **340/773-7529;** www.divicarina.com). The 10,000-square-foot casino has 20 gaming tables and 300 slot machines. No passport is needed to enter, but you do need some form of ID. It's open Sunday to Thursday 10am to 4am and Friday to Sunday 10am to 6am.

"C" is turned inward, toward your heart, it means you have a significant others. Those on the hunt wear the "C" turned out (and many locals won't leave the house without putting on this piece of jewelry just right). She also sells rings, earrings, and necklaces. 1 Company St. ✆ **877/766-9284** or 340/773-8924. www.sonyaltd.com.

PERFUME

Violette Boutique ★ PERFUME   This small department store sells exclusive fragrances and hard-to-find toiletry items. A selection of children's gifts, Montblanc pens, and other brand names are also found here. In the Caravelle Arcade, 38 Strand St ✆ **800/544-5912** or 340/773-2148.

ST. CROIX AFTER DARK

St. Croix doesn't have the nightlife of St. Thomas. Find out what's happening while you're on island with "St. Croix This Week," distributed free and available at hotels, restaurants, and the tourist office.

Try to catch a performance of the **Quadrille Dancers** ★★★, a genuine cultural treat. The Quadrille dances have changed little since plantation days. The women wear long dresses, white gloves, and turbans, and the men wear flamboyant shirts, sashes, and tight black trousers. When you've learned their steps, you're invited to join the dancers on the floor. Ask at your hotel if and where they're performing.

Note: Women (or men, for that matter) entering bars alone at night in Christiansted or Frederiksted should not leave the bar alone and walk the lonely streets to your hotel. Take a taxi back—it's worth the investment.

The atmospheric waterfront bistro **Blue Moon,** 7 Strand St., Frederiksted (✆ **340/ 772-2222**), is also known as a hip local stop for visiting jazz musicians. It's a live-jazz hotspot on Wednesday and Friday nights and at Sunday brunch. 7 Strand St.

The **Terrace Lounge** at the **Buccaneer Resort** (✆ **340/712-2100**), near Christiansted, features live music nightly, from calypso to jazz to steel pan, from 6 or 7pm till 10pm.

The **Beach Side Café** at **Sand Castle on the Beach** (✆ **340/772-1205**) offers live music every Saturday from 6:30 to 9:30pm.

The **Palms at Pelican Cove** (✆ **340/718-8920**) has live music from 6pm to 9pm on Saturday night and a steel-pan sounds during Sunday brunch (10am–2pm).

SIDE TRIP TO BUCK ISLAND ★★★

The crystal-clear waters and white-coral sands of **Buck Island Reef National Monument,** a satellite of St. Croix, are legendary. Some call it the single-most-important attraction of the Virgin Islands. Only about a half-mile wide and a mile long, Buck Island lies 1½ miles off the northeastern coast of St. Croix. A vibrant barrier reef here shelters a wealth of reef fish, including queen angelfish and smooth trunkfish.

Buck Island's greatest attraction is its underwater **snorkeling trails,** which ring part of the island and are maintained by the National Park Service. This 850-acre isle features a snorkeling trail through a forest of elkhorn coral. Equipped with a face mask, swim fins, and a snorkel, you'll be treated to some of the most beautiful underwater views in the Caribbean. Plan on spending at least two-thirds of a day at this famous ecological site.

You can hike the trails that twist around and over the island; circumnavigating the island takes only a couple of hours. Trails meander from several points along the

5

ST. CROIX

Side Trip to Buck Island

Buck Island

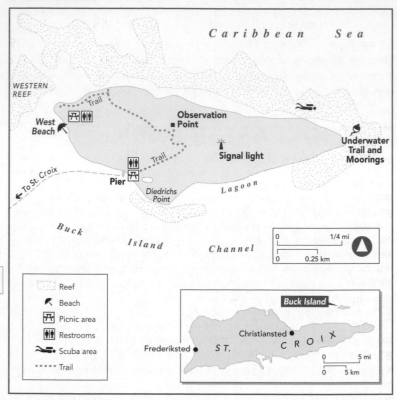

coastline to the sun-flooded summit, affording views over nearby St. Croix. *Warning:* The island's western edge has groves of poisonous manchineel trees, whose leaves, bark, and fruit cause extreme irritation when they come into contact with human skin. Plus, always bring protection from the sun's merciless rays—including a hat and sun block. The sandy beach has picnic tables and barbecue pits, as well as restrooms and a small changing room. There are no concessions on the island.

A number of reliable tour operators offer regular excursions to Buck Island, providing snorkeling equipment, drinks, and all-you-can-eat island barbecues. We recommend National Park Service–sanctioned **Big Beard's Adventure Tours,** in Christiansted (*©* **340/773-4483;** http://bigbeards.com), which offers full- and half-day Buck Island excursions. Rum punch and other libations are served, but these are no music-thumping St. Maarten–style booze cruises. The 42-foot catamaran *Renegade* can accommodate up to 39 passengers. Big Beard's full-day Adventure Tours go from 9:30am to 3:30pm and cost $99 adults, $80 children 6 to 12, and $26 children 5 and under.

ST. JOHN

I t may be the smallest of the U.S. Virgin Islands, but St. John is a natural wonder of luminous crescent bays and perfumed forest groves. It's got miles of pristine parkland, fresh-scented hiking trails, and mossy peaks with panoramic views. It's got probably the best beaches per capita of any Virgin Island. It's got a sleepy, secluded feel—if you can't chill out here, well, then better get thee to an apothecary. In fact, St. John is where St. Thomas locals come to "plug out. They don't call it "Love City" for nothing.

St. John is no mere pretty face, however. It has in the ruins of 18th-century sugar plantations a landscape dotted with its own trail of tears. It's got churches: 18 at last count.

St. John has no airport and no cruise-ship pier. Nonetheless, it is a favorite day-trip destination from nearby islands and a popular ferry excursion for cruise-ship passengers from St. Thomas. But the day-tripper and cruise-ship crowds that stream over in the morning are generally gone before nightfall.

ESSENTIALS

Getting There

BY PLANE

A number of major airlines have regularly scheduled nonstop air service from cities all over North America into St. Thomas—the major international gateway to the Virgins. From St. Thomas you'll take a ferry to St. John.

BY FERRY

Public ferries between St. Thomas and St. John run at regular times all day long. Ferry services link the ferry terminal at **Red Hook,** on the East End of St. Thomas, with **Cruz Bay** in St. John.

The Red Hook ferry dock is approximately 10 to 12 miles from the St. Thomas airport. If you've just landed on St. Thomas, your best bet is to take a taxi from the airport. Depending on the traffic, the cab ride on St. Thomas could take 30 to 45 minutes, at a fare between $20 and $22. Build taxi time into your schedule when planning your itinerary.

Ferries to St. John (© **340/776-6282**) leave every hour on the hour from Red Hook ($6 per person) and last only 15 to 20 minutes; you can also catch less frequent ferries from the Charlotte Amalie ferry terminal ($12 per person).

Car ferries also run between Red Hook and Cruz Bay, traveling from 7am to 7pm daily every half-hour; book ahead on one of three carriers: Boyson (© **340/776-6294**); Love City (© **340/779-4000**); or Global

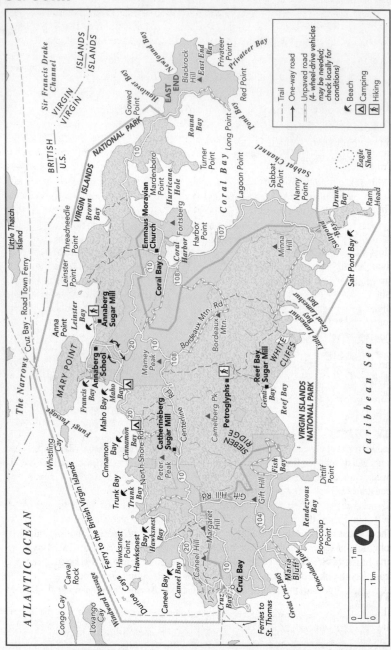

Marine (📞 **340/779-1739**). Car-ferry rates run from $42 to $50 round-trip; arrive at least 15 minutes before departure.

You can also get to St. John via **private water-taxi service.** Contact **Dohm's Water Taxi** (📞 **340/775-6501;** www.watertaxi-vi.com; St. Thomas to Red Hook, St. John: $25–$50 per person, five-person minimum), a private, full-service (pickup and transfer) inter-island water taxi service in custom-built catamaran powerboats. Dohm's also offers direct water-taxi service between St. John and the Ritz and Marriott Frenchmans Reef on St. Thomas ($30–$50 per person; five-person minimum).

Visitor Information

The **tourist office** (📞 **340/776-6450**) is located near the Battery, a 1735 fort that's a short walk from the St. Thomas ferry dock in Cruz Bay. It's open Monday to Friday from 8am to 5pm. A **National Park visitor center** (📞 **340/776-6201**) is also found at Cruz Bay, offering two floors of information and wall-mounted wildlife displays, plus a video presentation about the culture of the Virgin Islands; it's open daily 8am to 4pm.

You can pick up a map of the island from the tourist office and also a copy of "St. Thomas + St. John This Week," distributed free throughout the islands.

Island Layout

Most visitors will arrive on St. John at **Cruz Bay,** on a ferry from St. Thomas. This charming little village, with its few restaurants and shops, is quite the departure from the bustle of Charlotte Amalie. Cruz Bay is also the first stop on any trip to **Virgin Islands National Park,** which sprawls through the interior and encompasses almost all the coastline. The park service runs an information center in town. Route 20 leads north out of Cruz Bay, and passes the beaches at Caneel, Hawksnest, Trunk, Cinnamon, and Maho bays.

At the far north, Route 20 leads to the start of the **Annaberg Trail,** a historic hike through the ruins of 18th-century sugar plantations. Route 10 cuts through the center of the island. Dozens of foot trails lead off this road, making for easy exploration of the peaks and mountains.

On the east end of the island is **Coral Bay,** the island's original settlement. It's a favorite among yachties and home to a smattering of small restaurants and bars. Crumbling ruins of forts and plantations also dot the coastline here. The far east end is undeveloped and pales in comparison to the lush greenery of the park. The **south coast** is a favorite hideaway for locals, but little known by visitors. The coastline here is sweeping and tranquil, yet rocky in parts and punctuated with a handful of small protected bays.

Getting Around

The 20-minute ferry ride from St. Thomas will take you to **Cruz Bay,** the capital of St. John, which seems a century removed from the life you left behind. Cruz Bay is so small that its streets have no names, but it does have a couple of shopping centers, seaside restaurants and cafes, and a small park.

BY BUS

The local **Vitran** (📞 **340/774-0165**) service runs buses between Cruz Bay and Coral Bay, along Centerline Road about once an hour, costing $1 for adults and 75¢ for children.

BY TAXI

You'll have no trouble finding taxis to take you anywhere in St. John. Between midnight and 6am, fares are increased by 50 percent. Taxis meet the ferries as they arrive in Cruz Bay, or you can hail one if you see one. **Taxi rates** are set by the island's Taxi Association and fares are widely posted, even in taxis; check out the official fares in the free magazine "This Week" offered in most businesses. Typical fares from Cruz Bay are $8 to Trunk Bay, $9 to Cinnamon Bay, and $18 to Maho Bay. Waiting charges are $1/minimum per minute after the first 5 minutes.

Many taxi drivers operate multi-passenger **taxi van shuttles** or open-air **safari taxis** (converted truck beds with open-air seating). Taxi vans are equipped to transport approximately 8 to 12 passengers to multiple destinations on the island, while safaris can often fit up to 25 people. It's cheaper to hop on a van or safari than ride a taxi on your own if you're going between your hotel and Cruz Bay, but keep in mind you will be making stops along the way.

If you don't plan to rent a car, it's easy to find taxi drivers (who also double as tour guides). We highly recommend taxi driver **Kenneth Lewis** (© 340/776-6865), who will meet you at the ferry terminal in St. John for hotel or villa transfer and is also a wonderful **sightseeing guide.** Expect to pay about $50 for a single-passenger tour or $25 per person for two or more passengers for 2 hours of sightseeing in a shared car. Kenneth's vehicle can accommodate up to 18 passengers.

BY CAR OR JEEP

One of the best ways to see St. John is by a car, in particular a four-wheel-drive vehicle, which you can rent in town (reserve in advance in winter). The steep roadside panoramas are richly tinted with tones of forest green and turquoise and liberally accented with flashes of silver and gold from the strong Caribbean sun. *Remember:* Drive on the left and follow posted speed limits, which are generally very low.

There are only two gas stations on St. John, one of which is often closed. The more reliable of the two stations is in the upper regions of Cruz Bay, beside Route 104.

Unless you need to carry luggage, which should probably be locked away in a trunk, you might consider one of the sturdy, open-sided, jeeplike vehicles that offer the best view of the surroundings and are the most fun way to tour St. John. They cost around $76 to $84 a day.

A recommended local car-rental agency on St. John is **St. John Car Rental,** across from the Catholic church in Cruz Bay (© 340/776-6103; www.stjohncarrental.com), operating on the island since 1974. They have two- and four-door Jeep Wranglers, Dodge Nitros, Nissan Pathfinders, and Dodge Durangos.

[FastFACTS] ST. JOHN

Banks FirstBank Virgin Islands (© 340/776-6882; www.firstbankvi.com) has full-service bank and ATM in Cruz Bay. **Scotiabank** (© 340/776-6552; www.scotiabank.com) has a full-service location in Marketplace.

Business Hours Stores are generally open Monday to Friday 9am to 5pm, Saturday 9am to 1pm.

Dentists The **Virgin Islands Dental Association** (© 340/775-9110) is a member of the American Dental Association and is also linked with various specialists.

Doctors Call © **911** for a medical emergency. Otherwise, go to **Myrah Keating Smith Community Health Center,** 3B Sussanaberg

((℅ **340/693-8900**), which has a helipad for serious emergencies. The nearest hospital is in St. Thomas.

Drugstores Chelsea Drug Store, Marketplace Shopping Center, Route 104, Cruz Bay (℅ **340/776-4888**), is open Monday to Saturday 8:30am to 6:30pm and Sunday 9:30am to 4:30pm.

Emergencies For the police, an ambulance, or in case of fire, call ℅ **911.**

Maps See "Visitor Information," p. 123.

Newspapers & Magazines "What to Do: St.

Thomas + St. John," the official guidebook of the St. Thomas and St. John Hotel Association, is available at the tourist office (see "Visitor Information," p. 123) and at hotels. The Virgin Island Daily News covers the news in all the U.S. Virgin Islands.

Post Office The **Cruz Bay Post Office** is at Cruz Bay (℅ **340/779-4227**).

Safety There is some crime here, but it's relatively minor compared to St. Thomas. Most crime against tourists consists of muggings or petty theft, but rarely violent attacks.

Precautions, of course, are always advised. You are most likely to be the victim of a crime if you leave valuables unguarded on Trunk Bay, as hundreds of people seem to do every year.

Taxes The only local tax is an 10 percent surcharge added to all hotel rates.

Telephone All island phone numbers have seven digits. It is not necessary to use the 340 area code when dialing within St. John. Make long-distance, international, and collect calls as you would on the U.S. mainland by dialing 0 or your long-distance provider.

WHERE TO STAY

The number of accommodations on St. John is limited, and that's how most die-hard fans would like to keep it. There are four basic types of choices here: resorts, condominiums and villas, guesthouses, and campgrounds. Prices are often slashed in summer by 30 percent to 60 percent.

Chances are that your location will be determined by your choice of resort. However, if you're dependent on public transportation and want to make one or two trips to St. Thomas by ferry, Cruz Bay is the most convenient place to stay. It also offers easy access to shopping, bars, and restaurants if you want to walk.

Important: Keep in mind that lodgings tack on a government room tax of 10 percent.

Resorts

Caneel Bay ★★★ As a friend said, "Caneel Bay is not fancy, it's just perfect." Though it's one of the top luxury resorts of the Caribbean, Caneel Bay shuns showy glitz and high-tech toys. If that means no phones or TVs in the rooms, so be it. The happy guests (many of them families) who keep this place booked solid aren't complaining.

Mega-millionaire Laurance S. Rockefeller opened this, the Caribbean's first eco-resort, in 1956. It was once the Pieter Duerloo plantation, where white settlers defended themselves against a slave revolt. It's a sprawling, lushly landscaped property, some 170 acres, with seven stunning beaches and low-rise buildings fronting the bays or set back near the tennis complex. Wild donkeys with a laidback, languid demeanor stroll the grounds, as do white-tailed deer. The bays are a snorkeler's dream; on Hawksnest you are almost guaranteed to see turtles, and the clear, placid waters of Honeymoon and Scott Beach feature fish in a rainbow of hues.

The room decor is thoroughly updated but feels timeless, with dreamy bedding, Indonesian wood furnishings, and vintage-style tropical fabrics. Bathrooms are fashioned with native stone. Touches like beds turned down with beautiful helmet shells left on the pillows make this a constant delight. Caneel Bay's public lobby areas have a more modern feel; here, the big breakfast buffet in the open-air **Caneel Bay Beach Terrace** is one of the island's best. Up in ruins of a sugar mill, **ZoZo's** (p. 133) is serving exemplary Northern Italian in a splendid space, and on the resort's northern end, the magnificent **Turtle Bay Estate House**—the site of Rockefeller's private estate—has a lovely 4pm tea on the terrace and offers a new steakhouse menu on limited evenings.

(C) **888/767-3966** or 340/776-6111. www.caneelbay.com. 166 units. Winter $539–$1,179 double; off season $459–$999 double. MAP (breakfast and dinner) $90 per person per day extra. Extra person $80 per day. 1 child 5–11 $40 per day; children 4 and under stays free in parent's room. Service charge 10%. Private transfer from St. Thomas airport $110 adults, $55 children 5–11. **Amenities:** 4 restaurants; 2 bars; babysitting; children's center; concierge; health center and spa; pool (outdoor); room service; 11 tennis courts; Wi-Fi (free).

Concordia Eco-Resort ★

This 20-year-old eco-resort is a pioneer in sustainable tourism, drawing electricity from photovoltaic power and collecting (and filtering) water in cisterns. Shower tanks are solar-heated, and eco-tents use composting toilets. But most don't stay here to be virtuous, they do so because the views are wonderful (Concordia's elevated structures cling to 50 acres of cliffside), the staff lovely and the prices reasonable (for St. John). Doubles come in a range of lodging styles, from eco-tents to full-kitchen lofts to resort-style studios. The wood-framed, soft-sided eco-tents (and premium eco-tents) are set on the hillsides and have a treehouse feel, with cooling breezes (no A/C, of course) and those phenomenal views. Eight new eco-studios sleep four each with a queen bed and a queen futon. Some units come with full kitchens. For information on the on-site **Concordia Eco-Tents,** see "Campgrounds," below.

(C) **800/392-9004** in the U.S. and Canada, or 340/693-5855. www.concordiaeco-resort.com. 42 units. Winter $175–$289 double, $268–$289 quad; off season $126–$232 double, $175–$185 quad. **Amenities:** Restaurant (seasonal); laundry; pool (outdoor); watersports equipment rentals; Wi-Fi (free).

Gallows Point Resort ★

This well-run resort is a short stroll from Cruz Bay. All rooms are sunny, spacious one-bedroom suites with full kitchens and terraces with ocean or harbor views. And each can accommodate up to 5 people, making this a great choice for families. You can stay on the one-story lower floors or duplex upper floors, but we'd recommend the latter, as the duplex living rooms are bright, airy, and high-ceilinged. All suites are furnished in wicker and soft island hues. Two negatives: Harborside villas can be noisy and the beach nearby is small and rocky (so you likely want to go farther afield for the sands).

3 AAA Gallows Point Rd. *(C)* **800/323-7229** or 340/776-6434. www.gallowspointresort.com. 60 units. Winter $495–$695 suite; off season $265–$495 suite. **Amenities:** Restaurant; bar; pool (outdoor); sundecks; Wi-Fi (free).

Grande Bay Resort & Residence Club ★

Set above Cruz Bay and the harbor, these handsome condo suites come in studio and one- and two-bedroom configurations (with one three-bedroom suites) and lockout capability, making this a good choice for groups or families. Of the 54 units, only 19 are hotel rooms (these are studio doubles with kitchenettes with blenders); the rest are timeshares in the rental pool. Each is

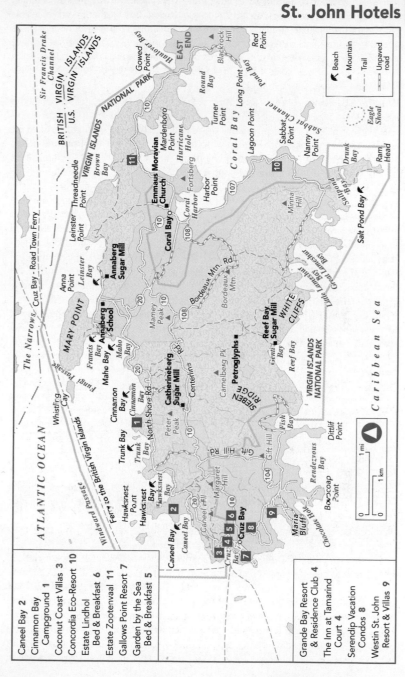

Caneel Bay **2**
Cinnamon Bay Campground **1**
Coconut Coast Villas **3**
Concordia Eco-Resort **10**
Estate Lindhol Bed & Breakfast **6**
Estate Zootenvaal **11**
Gallows Point Resort **7**
Garden by the Sea Bed & Breakfast **5**

Grande Bay Resort & Residence Club **4**
The Inn at Tamarind Court **4**
Serendip Vacation Condos **8**
Westin St. John Resort & Villas **9**

Key
Beach
Mountain
Trail
Unpaved road

ATLANTIC OCEAN

Caribbean Sea

127

individually decorated, so you never quite know what the decor will look like, but all are nicely laid out, complete with full kitchens, balconies, and washer-dryers. Kitchens are state of the art, with granite countertops and induction cooktops.

3 AAA Gallows Point Rd. ℂ **340/693-4668.** www.grandebayresortusvi.com. 73 units. Winter $646–$800 studio/1-bedroom, $810–$890 2-bedroom; off season $595 studio/1-bedroom, $695–$750 2-bedroom, Minimum-stay requirements in high season. **Amenities:** Gym; pool (heated); Wi-Fi (free).

Westin St. John Resort & Villas ★★ Fronting its own gentle bay and a sprawling 34 acres, this is a big, American-style resort. Which means it's not for everyone: The grounds are so spread out that the mobility-challenged need golf carts to get around, and the air-conditioned rooms are hermetically sealed off from the balmy tradewinds. None of the rooms are on the beach (admittedly, it's not St. John's best beach). But now that the **grandest pool** ★★ on St. John has reopened after a huge renovation, the resort's beating heart is back in business. The "hotel" side of the Westin has actually been slowly shrinking—a resort whose rooms once numbered in the hundreds now has 96 (renovated) hotel rooms. The others have been converted to villas (Westin Vacation Ownership timeshare units, to be specific), some 172 fully equipped units that move in and out of the rental pool. More villas are in the works. The beautifully renovated Bay Vista Villas, up on the hillside, are virtually apartments, with full (state-of-the-art) kitchens, washer/dryers, dining tables, and patios overlooking the bay. But back to that pool: It's a 3-quarter-acre beaut, with four chic cabanas and towering palm trees. It fronts the bay, which is dotted with sailboats and excursion boats; **Cruz Bay Water Sports** has a location right here for all your island-hopping needs. The resort has a small deli-grocery (look for Mango the resident cat), but you can also walk to the much better (and less pricey) **St. John Market,** on Chocolate Hole Road. The resort features excellent kids programs, though most require an extra outlay (boo! Hiss!).

Chocolate Hole Rd. ℂ **866/716-8108** in the U.S., or 340/693-8000. www.westinresortstjohn.com. 367 units. Winter $379–$1,069 double, $489–$1,349 villa; off season $305–$600 double, $415–$889 villa. Resort fee $50 per day. Round-trip shuttle and private ferryboat transfers from St. Thomas airport $120 per person, $80 ages 4–12. **Amenities:** 2 restaurants; 2 bars; deli; children's playground; children's programs; concierge; golf nearby; pool (outdoor); room service; 6 lit tennis courts; extensive watersports equipment/rentals; Wi-Fi (free).

Condos & Villas

Travelers who want a home away from home are in luck on St. John. There are actually more villa and condo beds available on island than there are hotel beds. What you get is spaciousness and comfort, as well as privacy and freedom, and most come with fully equipped kitchens, dining areas, patio grills, and more. Rentals range from large multiroom resort homes to simply decorated one-bedroom condos.

Caribbean Villas & Resorts (ℂ **800/338-0987** or 340/776-6152; www.caribbean villa.com), the island's biggest real estate agency, is an excellent choice if you're seeking a villa, condo, or private home. Most condos go for between $100 and $295 per night, though private homes are often much more expensive. Villa rentals begin at $1,750 per week. You can also look at such international sources as VRBO.com, Homeaway.com and FlipKey.com, all of which cover St. John.

EXPENSIVE

Coconut Coast Villas ★ Just a 10-minute stroll from Cruz Bay, this family-run boutique villa complex offers renovated studio doubles and two- and three-bedroom condos. Each unit faces the waterfront and is fully equipped with kitchens, private ensuite baths, private balconies, grills, and as a special perk, all you need to go beach-hopping: beach chairs, coolers, and beach towels. You will likely be beach-hopping as Coconut Coast's beach is rocky. But its just a 5-minute walk to nearby Frank Bay, where you can swim and snorkel off the sandy beach. The condos can be on the small-ish side, and the kitchens, while fully equipped, are far from updated (let's just say they have a New York apartment coziness).

Turner Bay. ✆ **800/858-7989** or 340/693-9100. www.coconutcoast.com. 9 units. Winter $289 studio, $389 2-bedroom condo, $559 3-bedroom condo; off season $189–$229 studio, $289–$329 2-bedroom condo, $349–$439 3-bedroom condo. Minimum of 3 days required in high season. **Amenities:** Internet (free); outdoor pool.

Estate Zootenvaal ★ With four seaside houses, this longtime family-owned Hurricane Hole property is a wonderful place to unplug and unwind. "Zoot" is very private, and you can cook in the full kitchen and swim and snorkel in the sparkling seas around Hurricane Hole. Each cottage has been crisply freshened in seaglass and earth colors, with wood and rattan furnishings and tile floors. Three of the cottages (Sunrise, Mangrove, and Spinnaker) have one bedroom, and Turtle Watch has two bedrooms and two baths, but each one can accommodate four people.

Hurricane Hole, near Coral Bay. ✆ **340/776-6321** or 216/861-5337. www.estatezootenvaal.com. 4 units. Winter $290–$380 1-bedroom unit, $580 2-bedroom unit; off season $190–$260 1-bedroom unit, $380 2-bedroom unit. Extra person $30 per day.

MODERATE

Serendip Vacation Condos ★ This well-managed, good-value hideaway offers 10 clean, newly updated and cheerfully decorated condo apartments, each with a fully equipped kitchen and covered veranda. It's not on the beach, but set on a hillside above Cruz Bay, with smashing sunset views. Book here early; Serendip gets a lot of repeat business.

9–7 Serendip Rd. ✆ **888/800-6445** in the U.S. and Canada, or 340/776-6646. www.serendipstjohn.com. 10 apts. Winter $225 studio, $295 1-bedroom apt; off season $135 studio, $170 1-bedroom apt. Extra person $25; $15 children ages 3–10; children 2 and under stay free in parent's apt. **Amenities:** Pool (outdoor); Wi-Fi (free).

Inns & Bed & Breakfasts

Estate Lindholm Bed & Breakfast ★★ Overlooking Cruz Bay harbor, this is the island's best B&B. It was part of an 18th-century sugar estate, and is set fetchingly among the Danish ruins. An elegant guesthouse, it boasts 14 guest rooms, each with private covered balconies and many with four-poster beds, Tiffany-style lamps, and big wooden armoires. Some have garden views; others have harbor views. Many have wooden rockers on their private balconies. On the property is **Asolare,** one of the island's best (p. 132) restaurants.

✆ **800/322-6335** in the U.S., or 340/776-6121. www.estatelindholm.com. 10 units. Winter $390–$595 double; off season $240–$550. Rates include continental breakfast. **Amenities:** Restaurant; exercise room; pool (outdoor); Wi-Fi (free).

Garden by the Sea Bed & Breakfast ★★ Overlooking the blue Caribbean, this colorful and quaint three-suite B&B is just a 10-minute walk from Cruz Bay. A classic West Indian cottage, it's done up in green and lavender hues, with a veranda shaded by genip trees and palm fronds. Both the Garden Suite and the Wild Ginger Room have fabulous outdoor tropical garden showers, with shower walls made of native stone. The Terrace View Room is upstairs, with views of the sea and a private veranda. (White-sand Frank Bay is a minute's walk from the B&B.) You can also rent the **Rendezvous by the Sea villa ★**, a charming three-bedroom villa overlooking the Caribbean (winter $4,950–$5,350; summer $2,900–$3,900). The inn only accommodates adults 18 and older.

✆ **340/779-4731.** www.gardenbythesea.com. 3 units. Winter $250–$275 double; off season $160–$200 double. No credit cards. Closed Sept. **Amenities:** Wi-Fi (free).

The Inn at Tamarind Court ★★ For casual comfort at economical rates, a warm, friendly welcome, and a convenient Cruz Bay location, you can't beat this 20-room inn. An effort has been made to give these rooms a little pizzazz, with bamboo-style furniture, buttery yellow walls, colorful linens, and tile floors. The Grand Suite and the Apartment can sleep four people comfortably. Standard rooms have twin or queen beds and private bathrooms. The inn has six rooms for single travelers that share two baths.

Cruz Bay. ✆ **800/221-1637** in the U.S., or 340/776-6378. www.tamarindcourt.com. 20 units, 14 with bathroom. Winter $75 single without bathroom, $148 double with bathroom, $240 apt for 4 with bathroom; off season $60–$65 single without bathroom, $110–$120 double with bathroom, $170–$190 apt for 4 with bathroom. Rates include continental breakfast. **Amenities:** Restaurant; bar; Wifi (free in the courtyard).

Campgrounds

Along with the listing below, consider the eco-tents solar- and wind-powered tent-cottages at **Concordia Eco-Tents** (see above under "Resorts"). (***Note:*** Sadly, two of the most popular campgrounds on the island, **Maho Bay,** along with **Harmony Studios,** closed in 2013.)

Cinnamon Bay Campground ★★ This National Park Service property is a dream of a campground, set right on the beach, with lush forests at your back and the serene blue seas of Cinnamon Bay before you. Choose from cottage, platform tent, or bare site. Cottages are more or less a room with two concrete walls and two screen walls. Canvas tents come with a floor and all cooking equipment. Bring your own tents and camping equipment to the primitive bare sites. Lavatories and showers are in separate buildings nearby. In winter, guests can camp for a maximum of 2 weeks; the rest of the year camping is limited to 30 days. The campground is closed to nonguests at 10pm. Onsite, the **Cinnamon Bay Watersports Center** (✆ **340/513-6330;** www.cinnamonbay.com; see p. 137) offers rentals, lessons, you name it.

✆ **340/776-6330.** www.cinnamonbay.com. 126 units, none with bathroom. Winter $126–$163 cottage for 2, $93 tent site, $37 bare site; off season $87–$105 cottage for 2, $67 tent site, $37 bare site. Extra person $20. Closed Sept. **Amenities:** Restaurant; extensive watersports equipment/rentals.

WHERE TO EAT

St. John has some pretty posh dining, particularly at luxury resorts like Caneel Bay, but it also has casual West Indian restaurants with plenty of local color and flavor. It's

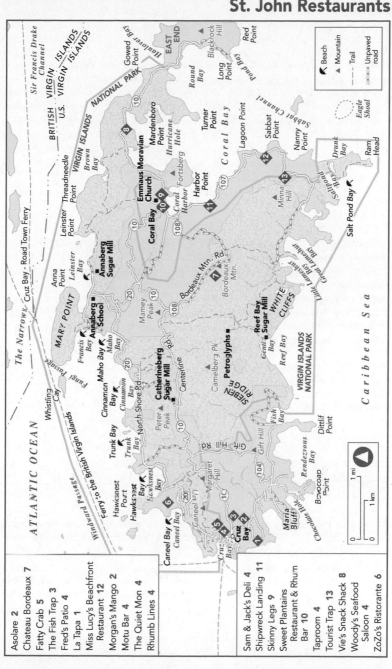

Asolare **2**
Chateau Bordeaux **7**
Fatty Crab **5**
The Fish Trap **3**
Fred's Patio **4**
La Tapa **1**
Miss Lucy's Beachfront Restaurant **12**
Morgan's Mango **2**
Motu Bar **4**
The Quiet Mon **4**
Rhumb Lines **4**

Sam & Jack's Deli **4**
Shipwreck Landing **11**
Skinny Legs **9**
Sweet Plantains Restaurant & Rhum Bar **10**
Taproom **4**
Tourist Trap **13**
Vie's Snack Shack **8**
Woody's Seafood Saloon **4**
ZoZo's Ristorante **6**

expensive to eat out anywhere you go, but you can sample the good spots at lunch at reasonable rates.

Cruz Bay
EXPENSIVE

Asolare ★★ ASIAN FUSION   A new culinary team is bringing creative—and determinedly locavore—Asian fusion cuisine to the Asolare. Which means that a nice Caribbean ceviche is made with the day's catch and served with a passionfruit vinaigrette. A pan-roasted mahi drawn from local waters comes with curried local pumpkin, and the restaurant's signature shrimp and grits come with sesame-crusted shrimp over stone-ground grits (with goat cheese and star anise), sauteed local peppers, and sour collard greens. It's a beautiful concept, neatly realized, and we look forward to seeing where the muse takes them. The restaurant is set in the Estate Lindholm Bed & Breakfast, perched atop a hill with Cruz Bay spread out below.

In the Estate Lindholm Bed & Breakfast. ℭ **340/779-4747.** www.asolarestjohn.com. Reservations required. Main courses $19–$45. Tues–Sun 6–9pm.

Fatty Crab ★★★ ASIAN/MALAYSIAN   This New York transplant has not been lost in translation in its West Indies adventure. In fact, in no time it's become one of the more popular dining spots on the island. Look for Fatty Crab classics like Fatty Sliders (mini spiced beef and pork burgers) and Green Mango & Papaya Salad, but also look for new dishes with local spins (and a menu that speaks the local lingo, with appetizers listed under "T'ings," and so forth). So you might order a very delicious local sauteed vegetable dish with smokey pork jus and a dash of chili or an island roti, here filled with local vegetables in a sassy green curry sauce. Pork ribs, smoked inhouse, are irresistible. Fatty Crab is so dellish it's upping the ante, we think, for the island's other eateries, and that's all for the good.

18–11A Enighad, Cruz Bay. ℭ **340/775-9770.** www.fattycrab.com. Reservations recommended. Main courses $30–$41. Wed–Mon 5–10pm; Sun brunch 11am–3pm.

La Tapa ★★ INTERNATIONAL/MEDITERRANEAN   A candlelit restaurant, set in a vintage West Indian structure, La Tapa features a smart, inventive menu with a locavore bent. The food is cooked to order by the talented chef/owner, and is heavy on small plate dishes (as the name implies). We've been particularly impressed with the grilled shrimp in a passionfruit-cilantro aioli, the bacalao cakes with avocado lime crème fraîche and the braised pork belly with fennel apple slaw—all can be ordered for the table and shared. You also can't go wrong starting with appetizer like gazpacho or organic greens grown in Coral Bay. Big plates—*platos grandes*—might be a classic paella or linguine tossed with shrimp, lobster, chanterelle mushrooms, and eggplant. Live jazz is on tap on Tuesdays.

Centerline Rd. (across from FirstBank). ℭ **340/693-7755.** www.latapastjohn.com. Reservations recommended. Tapas $15–$18; main courses $35–$41; paella $68. Daily 5:30–10pm.

Rhumb Lines ★ CARIBBEAN/PACIFIC RIM   Don't expect views at this Asian-Caribbean spot, set in an alfresco courtyard in a shopping complex. They make up for it with twinkling lights, swaying palm trees, and a reliably good Asian fusion menu. Do not resist the shrimp and corn fritters, a match made in culinary heaven. Heady and aromatic, the kaffir-lemongrass bouillabaisse is also primo, a Thai-style version of the French classic. Other faves include spicy Asian fusion entrees like sesame-crusted Szechuan tuna, with a bok choy stir-fry, and chicken glazed in a plum-ginger sauce.

groceries, markets & more: ST. JOHN
PROVISIONING

If you're doing any cooking on the island, you'll want to know where to stock your pantry and source fresh local food. But even if you don't have a kitchen, you'll want to know where to buy snacks, drinks, and prepared foods The restaurant **Blue Water Terrace,** on the East End, also has a market and deli selling sandwiches, cheeses, wine, picnic foods and lunch boxes; they also cater (© **740/692-2583**). Here are some essential St. Croix resources:

Deli/Prepared Foods: Sam & Jack's Deli (© **340/714-3354;** http://sam andjacksdeli.com) offers gourmet deli sandwiches, grab-and-go dinners, house-roasted meats and breads, pastas and ravioli, even homemade cookies. It's on the third floor of the Marketplace shopping complex in Cruz Bay.

Groceries: Starfish Market (© **340/779-4949**) is the island's largest grocery store; it's located on the first floor of the Marketplace in Cruz Bay; it also has a large selection of wine, liquor, and beer. A well-stocked grocery, **St. John Market** (© **340/779-6001**) is located on Chocolate Hole Road near the Westin resort.

Fresh Seafood: The **Seafood Market** at the Fish Trap restaurant (www.thefishtrap. com) in Cruz Bay sells fresh fish, shellfish, prepared foods, and salads; it's open noon to 6pm daily. Buy fresh fish (bluefish, tuna, alewife), Caribbean lobster, and conch at the **harbor at Cruz Bay** direct from the fishermen early in the morning from 9am to 11am.

Fresh Produce/Fruit: You can find vendors selling local fruits (papaya, bananas) and vegetables (tomatoes, okra) around the island. One vegetable stand is close to the Cruz Bay ferry connections.

Meada's Plaza. © **340/776-0303.** www.rhumblinesstjohn.com. Reservations recommended. Main dishes $22–$35. Wed–Mon 5:30–10pm; Sun brunch 10am–2:30pm.

ZoZo's Ristorante ★★★ ITALIAN   This 2013 marriage of superstars installed the island's best restaurant in one of the island's most beautiful locations: atop the ruins of an 18th-century sugar mill at Caneel Bay resort. It's a thrilling mashup, where colonial Caribbean meets Frank Lloyd Wright, and yet you feel as if you're in a technicolor James Bond film. Got that? And did we mention views? Get here for mind-blowing sunsets or to see lights shimmer across the bay in the blue-black night. The food and service are better than ever. Squid-ink linguine comes with diver scallops, broccoli rabe, and a garlic pomodoro sauce. Pork comes three ways: a center-cut loin with fennel, rosemark, and Tuscan kale stuffing; crispy pork belly; and hot Italian sausage in a white bean ragout. Classics like osso buco, house-aged steaks, and Caribbean lobster tail round out the straightforward, but wonderful, menu.

Caneel Bay, just outside Cruz Bay. © **340/693-9200.** www.zozos.net. Reservations recommended. Main courses $38–$46. Daily 5:30–9pm.

MODERATE

The Fish Trap ★ SEAFOOD   This casual spot is an easy walk from the ferry dock. It's an open-air affair, with tables on a breezy covered patio. Start with the signature seafood chowder, creamy and with a touch of peppery heat. Fish dishes include local catches like mahi or wahoo or farmed fish like tilapia and salmon. The sides are generally island-style, from sweet potato mash to rice and beans to fried plantains. You can even buy fresh seafood and pre-prepared Fish Trap dishes to take home to cook at the restaurant's **Seafood Market** (noon–6pm).

Cruz Bay, next to Our Lady of Mount Carmel Church. ℂ **340/693-9994.** www.thefishtrap.com. Reservations required for groups of 6 or more. Main courses $19–$59. Tues–Sun 4:30–9pm.

Morgan's Mango ★★ NEO-CARIBBEAN This open-air spot has a sociable drink scene, with a big bar and a lengthy list of frozen concoctions, many made with the juice from fresh island fruits. But Morgan's gets a lot of love for its gourmet Caribbean food as well, covering a broad range of island styles. That might include Anegada lobster and crab cakes, a nod to the lobster-rich B.V.I. island of Anegada, or the homemade Caribbean soup special. The St. John yellowfin tuna salad comes with local organic baby greens and local tuna. We also like the Island Fish Pot, a bouillabaisse-style French-Caribbean seafood mélange, or Poppas Pickapepper Steak, marinated in peppercorn-infused Pickapeppa sauce (the famous Jamaican condiment).

Cruz Bay (across from the National Park dock). ℂ **340/693-8141.** www.morgansmango.com. Reservations recommended. Main courses $16–$35. Daily 5:30–10pm.

INEXPENSIVE

The Quiet Mon ★ AMERICAN In a song called "Be as You Are," country singer Kenny Chesney sings about hanging with the locals at the Quiet Mon. Chesney continues to pop up at this atmospheric Irish pub from time to time. Does he come for the food? Hmmm. The menu is, kindly put, limited, with stuff like hot dogs, chili and french fries. But the atmosphere is funky and fun, so it still makes our list.

Cruz Bay. ℂ **340/779-4799.** http://quietmon.com. Lunch plates $4–$7. No credit cards. Lunch specials Mon–Fri 12:30–6pm. Bar daily 10am–4am.

Coral Bay

EXPENSIVE

Sweet Plantains Restaurant & Rhum Bar ★★ CARIBBEAN/CREOLE Fresh, seasonal, gourmet-global—all of these adjectives can be applied to the cuisine of Sweet Plantains, which offers a wide-spanning taste of the tropics. Chefs here marry West Indian home cooking—saltfish cakes with sweet mango puree, say or honey-jerked chicken drumettes—with international flavors and techniques. It gives this Coral Bay favorite a real sizzle. Wednesday and Thursday nights are Latin Nights, where you might sample *arroz con pollo* (chicken and rice), *carnes* Latino (beef stew), or ceviche. Saturday is given over to "Indo-Caribbean" curries, and Sundays and Mondays the place goes Gallic by way of the West Indies with such dishes as duck a la Sweet Plantains (sauteed duck breast with a black currant chutney confit) or a Creole ragout. The West Indian cottage is done up in richly saturated colors and is set between the road and the bay.

16118 Little Plantation. ℂ **340/777-4653.** www.sweetplantains-stjohn.com. Reservations recommended. Main courses $21–$34. Wed–Mon 5:30–9pm.

MODERATE

Miss Lucy's Beachfront Restaurant ★★ CARIBBEAN This legendary spot is worth the wait—and in high season or for Sunday brunch, you will likely have a wait before you. But the views of Friis Bay are lovely, so settle in and have a drink. You'll be glad you did. Pioneering Miss Lucy was St. John's first female taxi driver before she started this beloved eatery. If you're here for lunch or dinner, traditional conch fritters or callaloo soup are the starters to try followed by excellent grilled mahi. Main dishes come with sides like fried plantains, rice and peas, or fungi, a cornmeal side dish, here paired with okra. Her Sunday brunch, accompanied by a jazz duo, is fab: crab cakes Benedict, *pain perdu,* conch fritterdict. Every full moon, Lucy hosts Full Moon pig roasts (6–9pm; $18 per person), and that's something you won't want to miss. A new bar has 15 waterfront seats right by the sea.

Salt Pond Rd., near Estate Concordia. ℂ **340/693-5244.** Reservations recommended. Main courses $13–$30. Tues–Sat 11am–4pm (limited menu 4–5pm) and 5–9pm; Sun 10am–2pm.

Shipwreck Landing ★ SEAFOOD/CONTINENTAL   A local hot spot, Shipwreck Landing serves a good but limited menu in a palm-shaded spot with water views off Route 107. Sandwiches are Caribbean inspired, like the grilled mahi served with citrus herb butter on a Kaiser roll. Conch fritters or coconut-crusted golden-fried shrimp to starters to get. If you want something more substantial, get one of the entrees that focus on local fish—curry-nut-crusted grouper (with chopped peanuts) served with mango chutney, say, or a teriyaki grilled mahimahi marinated in Caribbean jerk spice and Asian teriyaki. Live music is on tap on Wednesday evenings and weekend nights, with no cover.

34 Freeman's Ground, Rte. 107. ℂ **340/693-5640.** http://shipwrecklandingstjohn.com. Reservations requested. Lunch $9–$17; main courses $16–$26. Daily 11am–9pm. Bar daily until 11pm. Closed Sept–Oct.

Around the Island

Chateau Bordeaux ★ CARIBBEAN   Dine to breathtaking views from your table at the Chateau Bordeaux, high atop Bordeaux mountain, overlooking Coral Bay and the British Virgin Islands. Under new ownership, this colorful spot located 5 miles east of Cruz Bay now serves casual island cuisine and is open for breakfast and lunch Monday to Friday (dinner is offered 3 nights a week). Start your St. John day with delicious French toast stuffed with mango, amaretto pancakes, or omelets served with yummy home fries that put the home in homemade. Lunch features island favorites like chicken roti, mahi mahi (grilled with pineapple sauce or in a sandwich), and conch with fungi and rice. Caribbean lobster stars at dinner. Stop by after a day of sightseeing for a fresh smoothie or ice-cream cone in the **Bordeaux Mountain Shop and Ice Cream and Smoothie Store.** It also has a shop selling local gifts, **Hibiscus Jazz.**

Junction 10, Bordeaux Mountain. ℂ **340/776-6611.** www.chateaubordeaux.net. Reservations required for dinner. Main courses lunch $10–$20, dinner $28–$38. Mon–Fri 7am–3:30pm (until 2:30 Fri); Tues–Thurs 5:30–9:30pm.

Vie's Snack Shack ★ WEST INDIAN   No, it's nothing fancy; in fact, it's little more than a hut cobbled out of plywood plunked down on a shady stretch of road. But don't judge by looks alone. This little lunch spot on the island's East End is the domain of one very talented home-style cook—actually, that would be *two* cooks: St. John native Vie (Violet) Mahabir, for whom the Snack Shack is named, and her daughter. Its many fans think the Snack Shack serves some of the best native food on island, including favorites such as garlic chicken, honey-drizzled johnnycakes, curried stew, conch fritters, and coconut pie. It's across the road from Hansen Bay beach and next to Vie's beachfront Hansen Bay Campground.

E. End Rd., Rte. 10 (13 miles east of Cruz Bay). ℂ **340/693-5033.** Main courses $5–$12. No credit cards. Tues–Sat 10am–5pm (but call first). Closed Oct.

EXPLORING ST. JOHN

The best way to see St. John quickly, especially if you're on a cruise-ship layover, is to take a 2-hour **taxi tour.** But if you aren't renting a car, arrange ferry pickup and transfer—and an island tour!—with a local taxi driver. We highly recommend **Kenneth Lewis** (② 340/776-6865), a former cop from Dominica who is one of the best guides on the island. If he can't accommodate you, he can refer you to someone who can. You can also contact the **St. John Taxi Association** (② 340/693-7530).

The ferries dock at **Cruz Bay,** St. John's main village. It's a jumble of waterfront bars, restaurants, boutiques, farmstands, and pastel-painted cottages. It's a bit sleepy, but relaxing after the fast pace of St. Thomas.

Much of the island is taken up with the **Virgin Islands National Park ★★** (② 340/776-6201; www.nps.gov/viis), with the lushest concentration of flora and fauna in the U.S. Virgin Islands. The park totals 12,624 acres, including submerged lands and water adjacent to St. John, and has more than 20 miles of hiking trails to explore. From pelicans to sandpipers, from mahogany to bay trees, the park abounds in beauty, dotted with colorful accents from the blooms of tamarind and flamboyant trees. The mongoose also calls it home. Park guides lead nature walks through this park that often take you past ruins of former plantations. See "Watersports & Outdoor Adventures," below, for information on trails and organized park activities.

Other major sights on the island include **Trunk Bay** (see "Beaches," below), one of the world's most beautiful beaches, and **Fort Berg** (also called Fortsberg), at Coral Bay, which served as the base for the soldiers who brutally crushed the 1733 slave revolt. Finally, try to make time for the **Annaberg Sugar Plantation Ruins** on Leinster Bay Road, where the Danes maintained a thriving plantation and sugar mill after 1718. It's located off Northshore Road, east of Trunk Bay. Admission is free. On certain days of the week (dates vary), guided walks of the area are given by park rangers. For information on the **Annaberg Historic Trail,** see "Watersports & Outdoor Adventures," below.

Beaches

St. John has so many delicious beaches it's hard to find a favorite. But the picture-perfect shoreline of **Trunk Bay ★★** is one of St. John's biggest attractions. Administered by the Virgin Islands National Park Service (NPS), this heart-shaped bay has a bathhouse, snorkel-gear rental, a snack bar, lifeguards on duty, and a souvenir shop. When conditions are optimal, the beach is ideal for diving, snorkeling, swimming, and sailing. But erosion can be a problem in spots, and crowds can inundate the beach especially when cruise-ship passengers from St. Thomas arrive en masse. Among the beach's many wonderful aspects is the underwater marked snorkeling trail near the shore, great for beginners: The **National Park Underwater Trail** (② 340/776-6201) stretches for 650 feet and helps you identify what you see—everything from false coral to colonial anemones. Trunk Bay is the only St. John beach that has an admission fee: It's $4 for adults 17 and over, and the beach is open from 7:15am to 4pm.

> ### St. John's Mascot
>
> The mongoose (plural *mongooses*) was brought to St. John to kill rats. It has practically been adopted as the island mascot—watch for mongooses darting across roads.

Caneel Bay resort, the stomping ground of the rich and famous, has seven beautiful beaches on its 170 acres. All are open to the public, but nonguests can only access two beaches from inside the resort: **Caneel Bay Beach** ★ and **Honeymoon Beach** ★★★. (Otherwise you have to visit by boat.) **Caneel Bay Beach** is the resort's main beach and easy to reach from the main entrance of the Caneel Bay resort. You'll need to bring your own beach chairs and gear for Caneel Beach. Bring your own chairs and watersports equipment to Honeymoon Beach or take advantage of the package **Honeymoon Day Pass** offered through **Virgin Islands Ecotours** (ⓒ 340/779-2155; http://viecotours.com). It's $49 per adult ($10 children 12 and under) for chairs, lockers, and all watersports equipment (snorkel gear, paddleboards, kayaks) at the beach's Honeymoon Hut. Honeymoon has a secluded feel, and the waters are calm and clear and ideal for snorkeling and kayaking.

One of the most beautiful beaches near Caneel Bay, **Hawksnest Beach** ★★ is administered by the NPS, with changing rooms, 24-hour restrooms, grills, and picnic tables. It's also near Cruz Bay, where the ferry docks, it can be crowded, especially when cruise-ship passengers come over from St. Thomas. Safari buses and taxis from Cruz Bay will take you along Northshore Road.

Cinnamon Bay ★★ is one gorgeous strip of white sand, complete with hiking trails, great windsurfing, and laidback wild donkeys (don't feed or pet them). Administered by the NPS, the beach has a **campground** right on the beach; see "Where to Stay," above, for contact information. It also has a water-sports center, the **Cinnamon Bay Watersports Center** (ⓒ 340/513-6330; www.cinnamonbay.com; see rates below), where you can rent watersports equipment (snorkel gear, kayaks). Snorkeling is popular here; you'll often see big schools of purple triggerfish. This beach is best in the morning and at midday, as afternoons can be windy. A marked **nature trail,** with signs identifying the flora, loops through a tropical forest on even turf before leading up to Centerline Road.

In 2014, **Maho Bay Beach** ★★ and its forested hillsides became the newest addition to the National Park Service collection of St. John beaches through a $2.5 million deal made by the nonprofit conservation group Trust for Public Lands. It's just east of Cinnamon Bay. With calm green waters, it's ideal for standup paddleboarding, and snorkelers are almost always guaranteed to see turtles grazing on the grassy bottom. It's a popular beach with visitors and cruise-ship passengers.

Traveling eastward along St. John's gently curving coastline, you'll come to **Francis Bay Beach** ★ and **Leinster Bay** ★★, the latter ideal for those seeking the solace of a private sunny retreat. You can swim in the bay's shallow water or snorkel over the spectacular and colorful coral reef, perhaps in the company of an occasional turtle or stingray. A tiny cay in one of the Leinster's inner bays, **Waterlemon Cay Beach** ★★ has some of the island's best snorkeling, with hawksbill turtles dining on seagrass and big starfish stretching along the sea bottom. You can walk along the Leinster Bay Trail to reach the island

Remote **Salt Pond Bay** ★★ lies on the beautiful coast in the southeast, adjacent to **Coral Bay.** The bay is tranquil, but the beach is somewhat rocky. It's a short walk down the hill from a parking lot. The snorkeling is good along the bay's eastern shore, and the bay has some fascinating tidal pools. Facilities are limited but include an outhouse and a few tattered picnic tables.

If you want to escape the crowds, head for **Lameshur Bay Beach** ★★, along the rugged south coast, west of Salt Pond Bay and accessible only via a bumpy dirt road.

The sands are beautiful and the snorkeling is excellent. You can also take a 5-minute stroll down the road past the beach to explore the nearby ruins of an old plantation estate that was destroyed in a slave revolt.

Watersports & Outdoor Adventures

St. John offers some of the best snorkeling, scuba diving, swimming, fishing, hiking, sailing, and underwater photography in the Caribbean. Scuba connossieurs know that the diving here is highly rewarding, with a natural wall just 15 minutes offshore. The island is known for the Virgin Islands National Park, as well as for its coral-sand beaches, winding mountain roads, hidden coves, and trails that lead past old, bush-covered sugar-cane plantations. If you've come for golf, you'll have to travel to sister islands St. Thomas and St. Croix to get your rounds in.

WATERSPORTS

DAY SAILING & BOAT EXCURSIONS   Island-hopping by boat is one of the top activities in the Virgins. You can take half- and full-day boat trips, including a full-day excursion to the Baths at Virgin Gorda. **Cruz Bay Watersports** (© 340/776-6234; www.divestjohn.com) offers trips to the British Virgin Islands. Trips to the Baths, in Virgin Gorda, for example, cost $140 per person ($70 children 7 and under), including food and beverages. *Note:* Be sure to bring your passport for any excursions to the British Virgin Islands.

   Sail Safaris (© 866/820-6906; www.sailsafaris.net) offers guided and custom sailing and snorkeling trips with a captain, sailing lessons, and sailboat rentals of their fleet of Hobie catamarans. Right on the beach in Cruz Bay, close to the ferry dock, this outfitter cruises in catamarans to remote spots in the Virgin Islands and features a range of destinations not available by charter boat or kayak, including trips to uninhabited islands. On guided tours, passengers can go island-hopping in the B.V.I. Sail Safaris also offers sailing lessons for those with an interest in sailing as a hobby. Half-day tours cost $79 to $90 per person; full-day jaunts, including lunch, go for $120 to $140; a 1-hour sailing lesson is $95 per person.

FISHING   The boats of **Offshore Adventures** (© 340/775-0389; www.sportfishingstjohn.com) leave from the dock at the Westin resort and the National Park Dock in Cruz Bay. Count on spending from $600 to $700 per party for a half-day of fishing. Fisherman can use hand-held rods to fish the waters in Virgin Islands National Park. Stop in at the tourist office at the St. Thomas ferry dock for a listing of fishing spots around the island.

KAYAKING ★★   **Arawak Expeditions,** based in Cruz Bay (© 800/238-8687 in the U.S., or 340/693-8312; http://arawakexp.com), provides kayaking gear, healthful meals, and experienced guides for full- and half-day kayak and snorkel outings. Trips cost $110 and $75, respectively. Multiday excursions with camping are also available;

Watersports Rentals

The most complete line of watersports equipment available, including rentals for windsurfing, snorkeling, kayaking, and sailing, is offered at the **Cinnamon Bay Watersports Center,** on Cinnamon Bay Beach (© 340/513-6330; www.cinnamonbay.com). One- and two-person sit-on-top kayaks rent for $20 to $30 per hour. You can also sail away in a Hobie mono-hull **sailboat** for $55 per hour.

call their toll-free number if you'd like to arrange an entire vacation with them. These 5-day trips range in price from $1,250 to $1,450.

SCUBA DIVING ★★   St. John is a diving paradise, with some 25 dive sites within a 15-mile radius. One of the best dive operators on island is PADI five-star **Low Key Watersports,** Wharfside Village, Cruz Bay (© **800/835-7718** in the U.S., or 340/693-8999; www.divelowkey.com). All wreck dives offered are two-tank/two-location dives and cost $100 with rental gear, with night dives going for $95. Snorkel and sail trips are also available; full-day trips on a Seabiscuit power vessel or 40-foot catamaran at $115 to $125, respectively, per person. The center also rents watersports gear, including masks, fins, snorkels, and dive skins, and arranges kayaking and fishing excursions.

Cruz Bay Watersports, Cruz Bay (© **340/776-6234;** www.divestjohn.com), is a PADI and NAUI five-star diving center. Open-water certifications can be arranged through a dive master, for $450 to $750. Beginner scuba lessons start at $120. Two-tank reef dives with all dive gear cost $100, and wreck dives, night dives, and dive packages are available. In addition, half-day snorkel tours are offered daily for $60.

SNORKELING ★★★   St. John has so many great snorkeling sites it's impossible to list them all. The most popular spot for snorkeling is **Trunk Bay** (see "Beaches," above), for its Underwater Snorkel Trail. Snorkeling gear can be rented from the Cinnamon Bay Watersports Center (see above) for $5, plus a $25 deposit. Other choice **snorkeling spots** around St. John are **Leinster Bay/Waterlemon Cay** ★★ and **Haulover Bay** ★★. Usually uncrowded Watermlemon Cay offers some of the best snorkeling in the U.S. Virgins. The water is calm, clear, and filled with brilliantly hued tropical fish. Haulover Bay is often deserted, and the waters are often clearer than in other spots around St. John.

Another amazing spot to snorkel are the mangrove stands at **Hurricane Hole.** Here coral grows in abundance on the mangrove roots—attended by huge starfish, sponges (and the hawksbills that eat them), and anemones. Seas are calm and gin-clear, and it's magical. It's best reached by boat. **SerenaSea** runs **snorkeling and sightseeing tours** out of Coral Bay to Hurricane Hole (http://serenasea.com) in a 30-foot vintage touring yacht; half-day tours are $60 per perons. A guided **kayak and snorkel tour** of the Hurricane Hole mangroves is offered by **Arawak Expeditions,** based in Cruz Bay (© **800/238-8687** in the U.S., or 340/693-8312; http://arawakexp.com); the full-day trip, including picnic lunch, is $120 per person.

WINDSURFING   The windsurfing at Cinnamon Bay is some of the best anywhere, for either the beginner or the expert. The **Cinnamon Bay Watersports Center** (see above) rents high-quality equipment for all levels, even for kids. Boards cost $25 to $65 an hour; a 2-hour introductory lesson costs $80.

OUTDOOR ADVENTURES

HIKING ★★★   Carved into St. John's rocky coastline are beautiful crescent-shaped bays and white-sand beaches. But the interior is no less impressive. The variety of wildlife is the envy of naturalists around the world. And there are miles of **hiking trails,** leading past the ruins of 18th-century Danish plantations to panoramic views. At scattered spots along the trails, you can find mysteriously geometric petroglyphs of unknown age and origin incised into boulders and cliffs. The terrain ranges from arid and dry (in the east) to moist and semitropical (in the northwest). Many of the trails wind through the grounds of sugar plantations, past ruined schoolhouses, rum distilleries, molasses factories, and great houses wrapped in lush, encroaching vines and

sustainable ST. JOHN:
A ROCKEFELLER DREAM

In 1956 multimillionaire Laurance Rockefeller sailed around the island with friends on his yacht. Rockefeller was so enchanted that he established his own resort here (Caneel Bay) and donated 9,500 acres of rolling green hills and an underwater preserve to the federal government to be set aside as a national park that would be here for future generations to enjoy. Thanks to the efforts of Rockefeller and others, today two-thirds of the island's surface area and the island's shoreline waters (the **Virgin Islands Coral Reef National Monument**) make up the **Virgin Islands**

National Park (© **340/776-6201;** www. nps.gov/viis). The hundreds of coral gardens that surround St. John (some 12,708 undersea acres) are protected rigorously—any attempt to damage or remove coral is punishable with large and strictly enforced fines.

Today St. John is the most tranquil, unspoiled island in the U.S. Virgin Islands. Sustainable tourism programs and eco-friendly practices keep the island clean and pristine. St. John, more than any other island in the Caribbean, works to ensure the preservation of its natural resources and ecosystems.

trees. The island boasts some 800 species of plants, 160 species of birds, and more than 20 trails maintained in fine form by the island's crew of park rangers.

At least 20 clearly marked walking paths originate from Northshore Road (Rte. 20) or from the island's main east-west artery, Centerline Road (Rte. 10). Each is marked at its starting point with a preplanned itinerary; the walks can last anywhere from 10 minutes to 2 hours. Trail maps are available from the **National Park Service Cruz Bay Visitor Center** (© **340/776-6201,** ext. 238; daily 8am–4:30pm), right at the ferry docks in Cruz Bay. Be sure to carry a lot of water and wear sunscreen and insect repellent when you hike.

REEF BAY HIKE   One of the most popular ranger-guided hikes on St. John is the guided 2.5-mile Reef Bay Hike. Many people think it's one of the best hikes in the Caribbean. This 6-hour hike includes a stop at the only known petroglyphs on the island and a tour of sugar-mill ruins, with a park ranger discussing the island's natural and cultural history along the way. The hike is from 9:30am to 3pm on Monday, Tuesday, Thursday, and Friday and costs $30 per person. Reservations are required and can be made by phone at least 2 to 3 weeks in advance © **340/779-8700**).

ANNABERG HISTORIC TRAIL   A short but terrific hike is the Annaberg Historic Trail (identified by the U.S. National Park Service as trail no. 10), about a .5-mile stroll. The Annaberg Historic Trail leads pedestrians around the ruined buildings of the best-preserved plantation on St. John. During the 18th and 19th centuries, the island was a sugarcane salt mine, with some 118 sugar plantations and 18 factories. The Danes brought slaves to the islands to work the plantations, and the smell of boiling molasses permeated the air. About a dozen NPS plaques identify and describe each building within the compound. The site has a sprinkling of onsite interpreters, including Miss Olivia in the small cookhouse, cooking and offering samples of traditional "dumb" bread (along with a glass of fresh passionfruit juice) and a gardener offering slices of fresh coconut. The walk takes about 30 minutes. From a terrace near the ruined windmill, a map identifies the British Virgin Islands to the north, including Little Thatch, Tortola, Waterlemon Cay, and Jost Van Dyke. Visiting the ruins is free.

LEINSTER BAY TRAIL If you want to prolong your hiking experience from the Annaberg Historic Trail (above), take the Leinster Bay Trail (trail no. 11), which begins near the point where trail no. 10 ends. It leads past mangrove swamps and coral inlets rich with plant and marine life; markers identify some of the plants and animals.

CINNAMON BAY TRAIL/CINNAMON BAY LOOP TRAIL Both of these trails begin at the Cinnamon Bay Campground. The half-mile Cinnamon Bay Loop Trail is a marked nature trail, with signs identifying the flora. It's a relatively flat, shady walk through plantation ruins and forest. The 1.1-mile Cinnamon Bay Trail starts out steeply but leads into shaded forest along the rutted cobblestones of a former Danish road, past ruins of abandoned plantations, and eventually leading to Centerline Road.

SHOPPING

Compared to St. Thomas, St. John's shopping isn't much, but what's here is interesting. The boutiques and shops of Cruz Bay are individualized and quite special. Most of the shops are clustered at **Mongoose Junction** (North Shore Rd., Cruz Bay), in a woodsy area beside the roadway, about a 5-minute walk from the ferry dock. Also in Cruz Bay, **Wharfside Village** (© 340/693-8210; www.wharfsidevillage.com), just a few steps from the ferry departure point, is a low-rise complex of courtyards, alleys, and seaside cafes with some unique boutiques. The **Marketplace of St. John** (© 340/776-6455; http://stjohnmarketplace.com) has St. John's biggest grocery store (Starfish Market), a pharmacy (Chelsea Drug Store), a hardware store (St. John Hardware), and a sprinkling of retail shops and cafes.

   Awl Made Here ★ (© 340/777-5757; www.awlmadehere.com), the Coral Bay studio of several enterprising island artisans, is owned by leather maker Tracey Keating, who makes handsome hand-tooled leather bags, cuffs, wallets, journals, and more.

   Bajo El Sol ★, Mongoose Junction (© 340/693-7070; www.bajoelsolgallery.com), is a cooperative gallery begun by a group of St. John artists in 1993. It's a wonderful place with lots of interesting pieces in a range of mediums, from paintings to glass and metal sculpture to jewelry, photography, and wood turning. This is the place to find a genuine St. John collectible.

   Bamboula ★, Mongoose Junction (© 340/693-8699; www.bamboulastjohn.com), is full of color and artisanal flavor, offering art (paintings from Haiti), unique homewares (hand-crafted wood bowls), world music, and African instruments. It also sells clothing, from flirty, sparkly skirts to jaunty straw hats.

   Bougainvillea ★, Mongoose Junction (© 340/693-7190; www.shoppingstjohn.com), sells a good selection of tropic wear and beachwear for men and women, with such brands as Tommy Bahama, Canovas, Gottex, and La Perla, along with shoes, bags, hats, and sarongs.

   Coconut Coast Studios, Frank Bay (© 800/887-3798 or 340/776-6944; www.coconutcoaststudios.com), is the studio of artist Elaine Estern, who paints colorful Caribbean landscapes, seascapes, and beneath-the-sea-scapes. Her seaside studio is a 5-minute walk along the waterfron from Cruz Bay. Every Wednesday evening from November through April the artist hosts a Sunset Cocktail Party from 5:30 to 7pm.

   Donald Schnell Studio ★, next to the Texaco gas station, Cruz Bay (© 340/776-6420; www.donaldschnell.com), is the working studio and gallery of Mr. Schnell, who

CORAL BAY: ST. JOHN'S first settlement

This was the site of the first plantation on St. John, which was established in 1717 and abandoned long ago. Claimed by the Danes in the 1600s and used to unload Danish ships, the bay still contains a crumbling stone pier. Follow the posted signs to see the remains of **Fort Berg,** which stationed the soldiers that suppressed the 1733 slave revolt. Today, this charming little village shelters a close-knit community of yachting enthusiasts, artists, and expats. Like folks in St. Thomas who come to St. John to "plug out," so people from Love City head to rustic Coral Bay to relax and chill out. Ringing the bay's perimeter is a handful of restaurants and bars. You can spend a day in Coral Bay hiking the

area's beautiful trails (see above) and swimming and snorkeling in **Salt Pond Bay** (p. 137), where the mud is thought to be rejuvenating for the skin. Have lunch or an early dinner at one of the village's quintessentially laidback cafes and beach shacks, whether **Miss Lucy's** (p. 134), **Shipwreck Landing** (p. 135), **Skinny Legs** (p. 143), or the tiny treasure that is **Tourist Trap ★**, 14B John's Folly (© **340/774-0912**), a roadside shack that can pack in maybe 15 diners and serves cold beer and hot nachos. Also on the menu are tacos, hot dogs, good sandwiches (blackened grouper, pulled-pork), and it's pretty cheap and all delicious. Be on the lookout for Buster, the colorful resident rooster.

fashions beautiful hand-crafted ceramics: planters, tableware, even fountains. The studio also sells the works of other artisans.

R&I PATTON Goldsmithing ★, Mongoose Junction (© **340/776-6548;** http:// pattongold.com), is the shop of "designer goldsmiths" Rudy and Irene Patton, who have been making and selling jewelry here since 1973. The island provides the jewelers with a wellspring of inspiration; their gold and sterling-silver petroglyph pieces are based on a petroglyph carved on a rock in Reef Bay. They also make molds of sea shells and sealife found on the beach to make earrings, pendants, and charms.

St. John Spice ★, Cruz Bay (© **877/693-7046;** http://stjohnspice.com), is located right at the ferry dock and up a set of brick stairs. It's *the* place to come for all things saucy and spicy, with a fantastic and comprehensive selection of locally made Virgin Islands hot sauces—from Blind Betty's to Anna's to Jerome's—as well as barbecue rubs, signature-blend spices, and Caribbean-made. It's a great place to stock up on hot sauce gifts to carry back home with you.

Steinworks ★ (© **340/776-8355;** http://sandisteinworks.com), on Coral Bay, is the studio and shop of Sandi Stein, who makes custom-designed jewelry in gold, silver, gemstones, and seaglass.

ST. JOHN AFTER DARK

Bring a good book or two. When it comes to nightlife, St. John is no St. Thomas, and everybody here seems to want to keep it that way. Although you can hear live music most any night of the week at venues around the island, many people are content to have a leisurely dinner and call it a day. But check out the "Live Music Scene" section on the **See St. John website** (www.seestjohn.com) for an updated schedule of live music offerings around the island.

Cruz Bay

The newest hot spot in town is the **Taproom,** the sunny brewpub of new microbrewery **St. John Brewers** (℃ 340/715-7775; www.stjohnbrewers.com), the brainchild of a couple of University of Vermont grads. Located in Mongoose Junction in Cruz Bay, the Taproom already feels rooted, and when you visit you'll sit elbow to elbow with locals and visitors sampling from the Caribbean-pub menu and swigging the brewpub's craft beers and homemade sodas. We very much like their Virgin Islands Summer Ale. It's open Monday to Saturday 11am to midnight and Sunday noon to midnight.

The **Motu Bar** (℃ 407/758-6924; www.motubar.com) is an upscale departure from the corrugated beach shack bar model. It's still pretty casual—St. John is no Miami—but with dark wicker loungers plumped with blue cushions and a roster of designer cocktails, it's definitely got an uptown vibe. It's on the deck of the Low Key Watersports building across from Cruz Bay beach.

Those who prefer their drinks *à la* hole in the wall, should check out the action at **Fred's Patio** (℃ 340/776-6363), across from the Lime Inn in Cruz Bay. This little West Indian restaurant has bands on Wednesday and Friday nights that get folks up and dancing. It's open 10am to 5pm, but stays open until Saturday morning.

Just 150 from the ferry dock in Cruz Bay, **Woody's Seafood Saloon** (℃ 340/779-4625) has a happening happy hour scene from 3pm to 6pm when drinks are dirt-cheap ($1 beers) and the crowd spills out onto the street.

St. John's one and only Irish pub, the **Quiet Mon** (p. 134), is adjacent to Woody's and located in a West Indian cottage with walls crammed with photos, memorabilia, and shamrock-themed tchotchkes. Four large-screen TVs are on hand for your sporting-event viewing pleasure.

Coral Bay

Skinny Legs, Emmaus, Coral Bay, beyond the fire station (℃ 340/779-4982; http://skinnylegs.com) is little more than a laidback island shack made of tin and wood. It's also the place to bring the kids for the island's **best burgers ★★**. Skinny Legs has live music on Thursday, Friday and Saturday nights during high season when it stays open until 10pm or later.

Another laidback spot in Coral Bay, **Shipwreck Landing** (℃ 340/693-5640; www.shipwrecklandingstjohn.com; p. 135), which has live music on Wednesday evenings and weekend nights, with no cover.

THE BRITISH VIRGIN ISLANDS

7

With its turquoise bays and hidden coves, once havens for pirates, the British Virgin Islands are among the world's loveliest cruising areas. The islands attract sailors and yachties aplenty, but the secluded white-sand beaches and laidback geniality make this an escapist's paradise.

The British Virgin Islands embrace 60-odd islands, some no more than spits of rock jutting out of the sea. Only four islands are of any significant size: Virgin Gorda, Tortola, Anegada, and Jost Van Dyke. The smaller islands and cays have colorful names, such as Fallen Jerusalem. Norman Island is said to have been the prototype for Robert Louis Stevenson's novel "Treasure Island." On Deadman's Bay, Blackbeard reputedly marooned 15 pirates and a bottle of rum.

These craggy and remote volcanic islands are just 15 minutes by air or 45 minutes by ferry from St. Thomas. Even though they are part of the same archipelago, the British Virgin Islands and the U.S. Virgin Islands have their differences. Where St. Thomas can sometimes seem like Hustle City, deep into mega-resort tourism, it's still a bit sleepy over in the B.V.I. Here the pace is much slower and development is less frenetic. Even the capital, Tortola, seems to exist in a bit of a time capsule.

Then there's the seclusion. Tortola has its share of private retreats, and most of the high-end resorts on Virgin Gorda are so isolated from one another you'll feel your hotel has the island to itself. On the even smaller, more remote islands like Guana Island, Peter Island, and Necker Island, you *will* have the island to yourself (and your fellow guests). These rustically private hideaways are the ultimate in laidback luxury. Barefoot minimalists on a budget can do rustic, too, without spending a fortune. At modest beachside inns on Jost Van Dyke and Anegada, you'll get all the seclusion you want—but you'll still probably end up knowing all the locals after a week. Forget casinos, splashy entertainment, TVs, and sometimes even air-conditioning: Who needs them when the balmy tradewinds blow, the rum is flowing, and sunlight dances like diamonds on the water?

ESSENTIALS

Getting There

BY PLANE

Your gateway to the B.V.I. will most likely be Tortola or Virgin Gorda, although currently there are no direct flights from North America or Europe to any of the British Virgin Islands (American Eagle discontinued

The British Virgin Islands

ATLANTIC OCEAN

Necker Island

Eustatia

South Sound

Prickly Pear Island

North Sound

Mosquito Island

To Anegada

Virgin Gorda

Spanish Town

Copper Mine Pt.

Seal Dogs

George Dog

Great Dog

Little Dix Bay

Virgin Gorda Yacht Harbour

Little Trunk Bay

Spring Bay

West Dog

Round Rock

Fallen Jerusalem

Ginger Island

Caribbean Sea

Scrub Island

Marina Cay

Long Bay

Beef Island

Cooper Island

Salt Island

The Rhone

Great Camanoe

Channel

Salt Island Passage

Little Camanoe

EAST END

Guana Island

Drake

Peter Island

Sir

Francis

Tortola

Road Town

Nanny Cay

The Indians

Pelican Island

Norman Island

Flanagan Passage

BRITISH VIRGIN ISLANDS
U.S. VIRGIN ISLANDS

Brewers Bay

East End Harbour

Little Harbour

Cane Garden Bay

Carrot Bay

Apple Bay

WEST END

Cove

Frenchmans Cay

Little Jost Van Dyke

Great Harbour

Jost Van Dyke

White Bay

Great Thatch Smugglers Island

Little Thatch Island

To St. Thomas

St. John (USVI)

Ferry Routes

Shipwreck

3 mi

3 km

0

0

Anegada

The Settlement

Anegada is 16 miles north of Virgin Gorda

all service to the island in 2013). Most visitors arrive into the international airports in St. Thomas or San Juan, Puerto Rico, and then fly or ferry to the B.V.I. A handful of regional airlines also offer service between Tortola or Virgin Gorda and islands like St. Croix and St. Maarten/St. Martin.

Air Sunshine (✆ **800/327-8900** in the U.S. or Canada, or 284/495-8900 in the B.V.I.; www.airsunshine.com) offers direct flights between San Juan (or St. Thomas) and both Tortola and Virgin Gorda; direct flights between Vieques, Puerto Rico, and both Tortola and Virgin Gorda; and direct flights between St. Croix and Virgin Gorda. **Cape Air** (✆ **800/227-3247** in the U.S. and U.S.V.I., or 284/495-2100 in the B.V.I.; www.capeair.com) flies between San Juan and Tortola or Virgin Gorda and between St. Thomas and Tortola. **Seabourne Airlines** (✆ **866/359-8784,** or 340/773-6442 in the U.S.V.I.; www.seaborneairlines.com), which moved its headquarters from St. Croix to San Juan in late 2013, offers regularly scheduled flights between San Juan and both Tortola and Virgin Gorda, as well as service between St. Croix (and St. Thomas) and the B.V.I.

Flying time between Tortola (or Virgin Gorda) and San Juan is 30 to 40 minutes; between Tortola and St. Thomas, 15 minutes; and between Tortola and St. Croix, 45 minutes.

Beef Island, the site of the major airport serving the British Virgins, the **Terrence B. Lettsome Airport (EIS),** is connected to Tortola by the one-lane **Queen Elizabeth Bridge.** Supplies and services on the other islands are extremely limited.

BY FERRY

Many B.V.I.–bound visitors who arrive in St. Thomas via the island's international airport then travel on by **public ferry.** (The more upscale resorts offer direct transfer from the airport by private ferry—for a fee, of course.) Public ferries connect to the B.V.I. via St. Thomas's two ferry terminals (Charlotte Amalie and Red Hook). It's essential to **plan your flights around ferry connections.** The last ferries from St. Thomas to the British Virgin Islands leave around 4:30 or 5pm. If you're arriving on a late flight into St. Thomas or your flight arrives late it's likely you'll need to overnight on the island. If you're just a little bit late, you can arrange a private water taxi. However—and this is a big however—the B.V.I. Customs on Tortola's West End closes at 6pm, so any water-taxi ride will have to leave by, at the very latest, 5:30pm.

In addition, it's important to **build time into your schedule for the taxi ride** from the St. Thomas airport to the closest ferry terminal, Charlotte Amalie—it's about a 15-minute trip, but traffic gridlock can make it longer—and so can stops for other passengers along the way (most airport taxi vans load up with passengers no matter where the destination). If time is tight, consider hiring a **private water-taxi service,** which includes transfers from the airport in private taxis (see information below); it's pricier than public ferries, but it's also a hassle-free, crowd-free way to make your connections.

Tortola has two main ferry terminals, **Road Town** and **West End. Beef Island (Trellis Bay),** off Tortola's East End, also gets ferry traffic and is where many of the Virgin Gorda and private island resorts have water launches for connecting guests. Public ferries from the other islands have regular runs to both the Road Town and West End terminals, so plan your itinerary around the terminal (and the departure time) that's most convenient for you. If you're staying on the island's West End, for example, it makes sense to take a ferry to the West End.

You can also get direct ferry service from St. Thomas to Virgin Gorda, but runs are infrequent (and only operate on certain days of the week)—so you may need to ferry to Tortola first (most likely Road Town) and then catch another ferry to Spanish Town, Virgin Gorda.

For those traveling on to the North Sound in Virgin Gorda, here's another option: Take a taxi ride from the Road Town ferry to Trellis Island, on Tortola's East End, and hop aboard the **North Sound Express** (✆ **284/495-2138**), which has daily connections to Spanish Town, Leverick Bay, and the Bitter End Yacht Club on Virgin Gorda; round-trip fares are $40 to $55 adults, $20 to $32 children.

Public ferries making runs between the U.S. Virgins and the B.V.I. include **Native Son** (✆ **284/494-5674;** www.nativesonferry.com), **Smith's Ferry Services** (✆ **284/ 495-4495;** www.smithsferry.com), and **Inter-Island Boat Services** (✆ **284/495- 4166**). (The latter specializes in somewhat roundabout routing—that is, you may find yourself traveling to St. John or Jost Van Dyke before you arrive in Tortola.) One-way and round-trip fares range from $25 to $49.

B.V.I. Public Ferries: Sample Travel Times

St. Thomas (Charlotte Amalie) to **Tortola** (Road Town): 50 min.

St. Thomas (Red Hook) to **Tortola** (West End): 35 min.

St. John to **Tortola** (West End): 20 min.

Tortola (Road Town) to **Virgin Gorda** (Spanish Town): 25 min.

Tortola (West End) to **Jost Van Dyke:** 20 min.

Tortola (Road Town) to **Anegada:** 60 min.

If you prefer **private water-taxi service,** contact **Dohm's Water Taxi** (✆ **340/775-6501;** www.watertaxi-vi. com; St. Thomas to Tortola: $325–$625, five-person minimum; $65 each additional person), a private, full-service (pickup and transfer) inter-island water taxi service that offers travel anywhere in the Virgin Islands in custom-built catamaran powerboats; or **Dolphin Water Taxi** (✆ **340/774-2628;** www.dolphinshuttle.com), which includes private taxi airport pickup to Red Hook with its private boat transfers to Tortola ($79–$95 per person, four-person minimum). Dolphin also offers water-taxi services throughout the Virgin Islands and day-trip charters to Jost Van Dyke ($55 per person one-way).

Visitor Information

On island, the **British Virgin Islands Tourist Board** (✆ **800/835-8530;** www.bvitourism. com) is located in downtown Road Town, Tortola, in the AKARA building, 2nd Floor, De Castro St. (✆ **284/494-3134**). Its New York branch is at 1 West 34th St., Suite 302, New York, NY 10001 (✆ **212/563-3117**). In the United Kingdom, contact the **B.V.I. Tourist Board,** 15 Upper Grosvenor St., London W1K 7PJ (✆ **207/355-9585**).

Getting Around
BY FERRY
A number of ferry services offer regularly scheduled trips within the British Virgin Islands.

TORTOLA & VIRGIN GORDA Both **Smith's Ferry** (✆ **284/495-4495;** http:// bviferryservices.com) and **Speedy's** (✆ **284/495-5235;** www.bviferries.com) operate daily ferry service between Tortola (both Road Town and Beef Island) and Virgin

7

Essentials

THE BRITISH VIRGIN ISLANDS

○**Christopher Fleming (1851–1935):** Born in the East End of Tortola, Fleming spent most of his life at sea and may even have been a smuggler. In 1890, a B.V.I. Customs officer seized a native boat, and in protest, Fleming led a group of armed men to the commissioner's house. Danish soldiers from St. Thomas put down the rebellion, and Fleming was sentenced to 6 months in jail. Today, islanders look upon Fleming as a hero who protested poverty and unfair economic conditions.

○**John Coakley Lettsom (1744–1815):** Born into a Quaker family on Jost Van Dyke, Lettsom was educated in England and completed his medical education in Edinburgh, Scotland. Rising rapidly and brilliantly, he founded the Royal Human Society of England, the Royal Seabathing Hospital at Margate, and the London Medical Society. Regrettably, he is mainly remembered today for this famous but libelous doggerel: "I John Lettsom . . . Blisters, bleeds, and sweats 'em. If,

after that, they please to die . . . I, John Lettsom."

○**Frederick Augustus Pickering (1835–1926):** Born in Tortola, Pickering became a civil service worker who, by 1884, had risen to become the first black president of the British Virgin Islands. He held the post until 1887 and was the last man to be known as president, as the job title after his presidency was changed to commissioner.

○**John Pickering (1704–68):** Born into a fervent Quaker family in Anguilla, Pickering moved in the 1720s to Fat Hogs Bay in Tortola. In 1736, he became the leader of a congregation of Quakers, and by 1741 he was named first lieutenant governor of the island. Fearing the Virgin Islands would be drawn into war between Spain and Britain, he resigned his post because of his Quaker beliefs. Apparently, he was an "enlightened" plantation owner, as hundreds of slaves, islandwide, mourned his death—or perhaps they feared their new master.

Gorda (both Spanish Town and Bitter End/Leverick Bay); round-trip fares are $30 to $65 adults, $28 children 5–11. The **North Sound Express** (© 284/495-2138), near the airport on Beef Island, has daily connections to Spanish Town, Leverick Bay, and the Bitter End Yacht Club on Virgin Gorda; round-trip fares are $40 to $55 adults, $20 to $32 children.

TORTOLA & ANEGADA The **Road Town Fast Ferry** (© 284/495-2323) operates daily trips on Monday, Wednesday, and Friday between Tortola, Virgin Gorda, and Anegada; round-trip fares are $55 adults, $35 children.

TORTOLA & JOST VAN DYKE New Horizons Ferry (© 284/495-9278) makes daily runs between Tortola and Jost Van Dyke; round-trip fares are $25 adults, $15 children (free children 5–11).

TORTOLA & NORMAN ISLAND A **Norman Island ferry** (© 284/494-0093) runs from Hannah Bay, Tortola, to Pirate's Bight restaurant (www.piratesbight.com). Call for schedules and fares.

TORTOLA & PETER ISLAND The **Peter Island Ferry** (© 284/495-2000) shuttles passengers between Road Town on Tortola and Peter Island at least five times a day; non-guests pay round-trip fares of $20 adults; $10 children.

Christmas Winds

The year-round weather in the British Virgin Islands is generally temperate, with few variations in temperature and winds usually out of the east. In late November and December, however, cold fronts in North America push cold air down from the north, bringing the so-called "Christmas winds" to the islands. While temperatures are minimally affected, Christmas winds can bring 25- to 30-knot blows to the islands for days at a time, making seas choppy and roiling placid bays that are generally calm for snorkeling. Christmas winds generally dissipate by January or early February.

NORTH SOUND, VIRGIN GORDA

The private resorts around Virgin Gorda's North Sound offer complimentary daily ferry service from Gun Creek, Virgin Gorda, to the resorts, including **Bitter End** (© 284/494-2746), **Biras Creek** (© 284/394-3555), and **Saba Rock** (© 284/495-7711). Call for schedules.

BY CAR, BUS, OR TAXI

There are car-rental agencies on Tortola, Virgin Gorda, Anegada, and Jost Van Dyke; numerous taxis also operate on these islands, as well as on some of the smaller ones; taxi rates are set by the government and posted on the BVI tourism website and in the free "Welcome Guide" tourist publication distributed everywhere. Bus service is available on Tortola and Virgin Gorda only. See the "Orientation" section for each island for further details.

TORTOLA ★★

There's no better place to launch your own sailing adventure than in the bareboat capital of the world: Tortola, the biggest (19×5km/12×3 miles) and most populous of the British Virgin Islands. But you don't have to be a sailor to appreciate the quiet, understated beauty of Tortola and its warm, laidback soul. Unwind to the soft caress of tradewinds, the gentle green hills that slope down to sparkling waters, and the secluded white-sand beaches.

Orientation
VISITOR INFORMATION

The offices of the **British Virgin Islands Tourist Board** (© 800/835-8530; www.bvitourism.com) are located in downtown Road Town, Tortola, in the AKARA building, 2nd Floor, De Castro St. (© 284/494-3134). Here you'll find information about hotels, restaurants, tours, and more. Pick up a copy of the "Welcome Tourist Guide," which has a useful map of the island.

ISLAND LAYOUT

Tortola is the largest of the British Virgin Islands. **Road Town** is the capital, a scattered sprawl of modern buildings wrapped around the harborfront and tucked into the green hillsides. Here and there, particularly along the narrow lanes of old Main Street, you'll see historic landmarks and examples of the island's West Indian-style gingerbread architecture. Main Street has a number of shops and restaurants. Wickham's Cay (sometimes called Wickham's Cay I) and Wickham's Cay II together form a small Inner Harbor in Road Town. This harbor takes in the Moorings complex area with Fort Burt and Prospect Reef standing near the port entrance. The cruise ship pier juts out at the far right of the cay, and shops are within easy walking distance of the cruise ship dock.

Tortola

DINING ◆

1748 Restaurant **3**
Bananakeet **8**
Brandywine Estate Restaurant **15**
The Clubhouse at Frenchmans **2**
Cruzin' **7**
D'Best Cup **1**
The Last Resort **18**
Marché at Trellis Bar & Grill **17**
North Shore Shell Museum Bar & Restaurant **7**
Quito's Gazebo **13**
Sebastian's Seaside Grille **5**
Sugar Mill Restaurant **6**

ATLANTIC

Rough Point
Larmier Bay
Angilla Point
Cooper Bay

Shark Bay

Martin Point

Brewers Bay

MOUNT HEALTHY NATIONAL PARK

Du Bois Point

Cane Garden Bay Rd

Ridge Rd

Great Mountain Rd

14

13
12
11

FAHIE HILL

Cane Garden Bay

9 10

Ballast Bay

Road Town

8
8

Great Carrot Bay

Sage Mountain 1780 ft.

Apple Bay

7

Long Bay Beach (West)

6

MOUNT SAGE NATIONAL PARK

Hannah

Sea Cow Bay

Smugglers Cove

Long Bay

5 5

6

Steele Point

3 3

Sir Francis Drake Hwy

Fort Recovery

Sopers Hole

2

4

2

Frenchmans Cay

1

Sir Francis

St. John

ACCOMMODATIONS ■

Beef Island Guest House **16**
Cane Garden Bay Cottages **14**
Cooper Island Beach Club **19**
Fort Recovery Beachfront **4**
Frenchmans **2**
Heritage Inn **8**

Long Bay Beach Club **3**
Mongoose Apartments **12**
Myett's Garden Inn **9**
Quito's Ole Works Inn **11**
Rhymer's Beach Hotel **10**
Sebastian's on the Beach **5**
The Sugar Mill Hotel **6**

OCEAN

Little Camanoe

Great Camanoe

Elizabeth Beach

Lambert Bay

Little Bay

Rogue Point

Trunk Bay

Carrot Bay

Cooten Bay

WESLEY HILL

Beef Island Channel

Long Bay Beach (East)

Trellis Bay

Bellamy Cay

18

Parham Town

16 **17**

Ridge Rd.

Lambert Rd.

Belle Vue Rd.

Waterfront Dr.

Fat Hogs Bay

Bluff Bay

Beef Island

Baughers Bay

Blackburn Hwy.

Brandywine Bay

15

Half Moon Bay

Paraquita Bay

Buck Island

Road Bay

See Road Town map

D r a k e   C h a n n e l

Cooper Island

19

Salt Island

Dead Chest Island

Peter Island

0   1 mi
0   1 km

151

GETTING THERE

BY PLANE   On Tortola's eastern end is **Beef Island,** the site of the **Terrence B. Lettsome International Airport,** the main airport for all of the British Virgin Islands. This tiny island is connected to Tortola by the one-lane Queen Elizabeth Bridge. For information on flights into Tortola, see "Getting Around: By Plane" under the chapter "Orientation," above.

Both **Hertz** (*©* **800/654-3131** in the U.S., or 284/495-4405 on Tortola; www.hertz. com) and **National** (*©* **284/494-3197;** www.nationalcar.com) have locations at the airport.

Taxis, taxi vans, and multi-passenger safari buses meet every arriving flight. The fare from the Beef Island airport to Road Town is $15 for one to three passengers.

BY FERRY   Many people arrive by air into St. Thomas and ferry over on one of the many public (and private) ferries traveling between the U.S. and British Virgin Islands. See "Getting Around: By Ferry" under the chapter "Orientation," above.

BY CRUISE SHIP   Tortola recorded nearly 400,000 cruise passengers arriving in Road Harbour in 2012. Its pier in Road Town has the capacity to host two large cruise ships at a time; other cruise ships anchor just outside the harbor and tender in.

As we went to press, cruise ships scheduling stops in Road Harbour included Regent Seven Seas *(Windstar);* Costa Cruise Lines *(Costa Magica);* Crystal; Celebrity; Royal Caribbean *(Jewel of the Seas);* Cunard; Holland America; Silver Seas *(Silver Spirit);* and P&O Cruises *(Arcadia).*

GETTING AROUND

The roads in Tortola are steep and twisting—not for the faint of heart. The island is fairly small, so driving distances aren't long. Plan your Road Town travel around rush hours and cruise-ship embarkations: You can easily become ensnared in Road Town traffic during arrival and departure times (around 8am and 4pm), when scores of taxi drivers pick up or drop off cruise-ship passengers around the pier at Wickhams Cay 1.

BY TAXI   We highly recommend **Wayne Robinson** as both taxi driver and tour guide (*©* **284/494-4097** or 284/499-2251 [cell]). For other taxi options in Road Town, dial the **BVI Taxi Association** at *©* **284/494-3942;** on Beef Island, call *©* **284/495-1982.** Your hotel can also call a taxi for you; there is a taxi stand in Road Town, near the ferry dock. A typical fare from Road Town to Cane Garden Bay is $24; from Road Town to Josiah's Bay on the north coast, it's $25.

BY BUS   **Scato's Bus & Taxi Services** (*©* **284/494-2365;** www.scatosbusntaxi.com) offers airport pickup and dropoff, lodging and ferry transfers, private and group tours, events transportation, and shopping expeditions in modern, air-conditioned buses.

BY RENTAL CAR   Ask your hotel concierge to recommend a local rental-car agency; many resorts have relationships with rental franchises that will deliver cars right to your hotel. **Itgo** (*©* **284/494-2639;** www.itgobvi.com) is located at the Mill Mall, Wickham's Cay I, Road Town. **Denzil Clyne** (*©* **284/495-4900**) offers rentals (Jeeps) on Tortola's West End near the ferry terminal. **Avis** (*©* **800/331-1212** in the U.S., or 284/494-2193 on Tortola; www.avis.com) maintains offices opposite the J.R. Neal Botanical Gardens in Road Town; and **Hertz** (*©* **800/654-3131** in the U.S., or 284/495-4405 on Tortola; www.hertz.com) has locations in Road Town, near the airport, and on the island's West End, near the ferryboat landing dock. **National** (*©* **284/494-3197;** www.nationalcar.com) has locations on Long Bay, West End, Road Town, and near the airport.

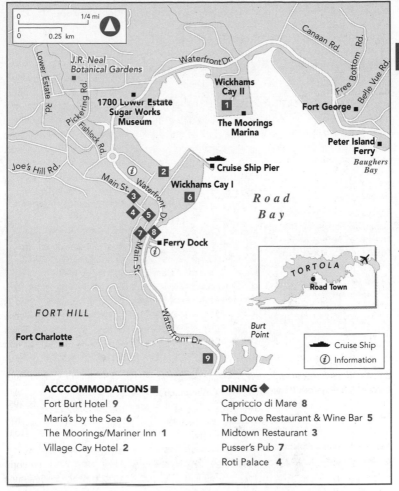

ACCCOMMODATIONS ■

Fort Burt Hotel 9
Maria's by the Sea 6
The Moorings/Mariner Inn 1
Village Cay Hotel 2

DINING ◆

Capriccio di Mare 8
The Dove Restaurant & Wine Bar 5
Midtown Restaurant 3
Pusser's Pub 7
Roti Palace 4

Rental companies will usually offer free hotel pickup. All require a valid driver's license and a temporary B.V.I. driver's license, which the car-rental agency will issue to you for $10; it's valid for 1 month. Because of the volume of tourism to Tortola, you should reserve a car in advance, especially in winter.

Remember: Drive on the left! Roads are pretty well paved, but they're often narrow, winding, and poorly lit, and they have few, if any, lines but plenty of speed bumps. Driving at night can be tricky. It's a good idea to take a taxi to that difficult-to-find beach, restaurant, or bar. If you're queasy about maneuvering mountainous corkscrew roads, day or night, take the **Sir Francis Drake coastal road,** which for the most part is flat and runs the length of the island. The other main road, **Ridge Road,** follows the mountainous spine of the island; this was the old roadway linking the island's many plantations.

ATMs/Banks The major B.V.I. banks are **Scotiabank** (www.scotiabank.com); **FirstBank** (www.firstbankvi.com), **First Caribbean** (www.cibcfcib.com); and **Banco Popular** (www.banco popular.com/vi). ATMs are less prevalent in the British Virgin Islands than in the U.S. Virgin Islands; all of the aforementioned banks have ATMs in Wickham Cay I, Road Town, Tortola. A First Caribbean ATM is located at Myett's beach bar in Cane Garden Bay, and Nanny Cay Marina has a FirstBank ATM. Most other small islands do not have ATMs, so if you're planning a visit, be sure to visit an ATM on Tortola to cash up first. Each machine charges around $2 to $3 for a transaction fee.

Bookstores The best bookstore is the **National Educational Services Bookstore,** Wickham's Cay I, in Road Town (📞 **284/494-3921**).

Business Hours Most offices are open Monday to Friday 9am to 5pm. Government offices are open Monday to Friday 8:30am to 4:30pm. Shops are generally open Monday to Friday 9am to 5pm and Saturday 9am to 1pm.

Dentists For dental emergencies, contact **Crown Dental** (📞 **284/494-2770**), or **Premier Dental** (📞 **284/494-8062**).

Drugstores Medicure Pharmacy is located in the Hodge Building, near Road Town Roundabout, Road Town (📞 **284/494-6189**).

Emergencies Call 📞 **999.** If you have a medical emergency, call **Peebles Hospital,** Porter Road, Road Town, Tortola (📞 **284/494-3497**). Your hotel can also put you in touch with the local medical staff.

Hospitals/Clinics Peebles Hospital, Porter Road, Road Town (📞 **284/494-3497**), has X-ray and laboratory facilities. The **B&F Medical Complex,** Mill Mall, Wickham's Cay I, Road Town (http://bfmedicalcomplex.com) is a public day clinic that accepts walk-ins. The **Eureka Medical Centre** (www.eurekamedicalclinic.com), Geneva Place, Road Town, Tortola, is a private-run urgent-care facility with both inhouse doctors and visiting specialists on call; call for an appointment.

Internet Access Internet and free Wi-Fi access is available all over the islands, including Nanny Cay Marina, Tortola, and Village Cay Marina, Road Town, as well as in many bars and restaurants. If you're in transit or your hotel's Internet access is weak or nonexistent, try **Serendipity Bookshop & Internet Cafe,** Main St., Road Town (📞 **284/494-5865**); the **Pub,** Waterfront Dr., Road Town (📞 **284/494-2608**); or **Trellis Bay Cybercafe,** Trellis Bay (📞 **284/495-2447**).

Newspapers "The BVI Beacon" (www.bvibeacon.com) is a weekly newspaper published on Thursday. The weekly "Island Sun" (www.islandsun.com) is published every Friday. Both are good sources of information on local entertainment. You can find these in most supermarkets and shops.

Police The main police headquarters is on Waterfront Drive near the ferry dock on Sir Olva Georges Plaza (📞 **284/494-2945**).

Post Office The main post office on Tortola is in Road Town (📞 **284/468-3701,** ext. 5160), and is open Monday to Friday 8:30am to 4:30pm. The beautiful and collectible B.V.I. stamps are sold here.

Safety The British Virgin Islands in general are quite safe, with a very low crime rate that many attribute to the illegality of owning guns. Minor robberies and muggings occur late at night outside bars in Road Town, especially in poorly lit areas around Wickham's Cay I and along Waterfront Drive. But outside of Road Town, Tortola is a very safe place to be.

Taxes The British Virgin Islands has no sales tax. It charges a departure tax of $15 per person for those leaving by boat or $20 if by airplane. Most hotels add a service charge of around 10 percent; there's also a 7 percent government room tax.

Most restaurants tack on an automatic 15 percent service charge.

Telephone All island phone numbers have seven digits. You can call the British Virgins from the United States by just dialing 1, the area code 284, and the number; from the U.K. dial 011-44, then the number. To call the U.S. from the B.V.I., just dial 1 plus the area code and the number; to call the U.K. from the B.V.I., dial 011-44, then the number.

Tipping Go to "Fast Facts," in Chapter 8 for tipping guidelines.

Toilets You'll find public toilets in restaurants, beach bars, at the ferry terminals, and at the airport.

Where to Stay

Tortola has few hotel-style lodgings. In fact, outside of villas, its accommodation choices are fairly stark. In addition to one or two topnotch boutique resorts, you have a sprinkling of modest marina hotels, informal guesthouses, and basic beach lodgings. None, however, is as big, splashy, and full service as the mega-resorts in the U.S. Virgin Islands—or as high-end luxe as the choices on Virgin Gorda—and many of the island's repeat visitors seem to like that just fine.

Many visitors rent villas for their Tortola stays. Most rent by the week. **Best of BVI** (© **1252-674878** from the U.K. and 011/44-1252-674878 from the U.S.; www.bestof bvi.com) represents properties listed nowhere else, including a one-bedroom cottage on Little Thatch Island, a privately owned isle minutes from Soper's Hole. Best of BVI also has a hugely informative trip-planning website, with an up-to-date ferry schedule. **Jewels of the BVI** (© **866/468-6284;** www.jewelsofthebvi.com) represents only BVI Islander–owned properties, including villas, condos, and resorts. Villas can range from $150 all the way to $750 per night, based on location, amenities and the number of bedrooms. For more villa options, go to Chapter 8.

Remember that most of Tortola's best beaches are on the northern shore, so guests staying elsewhere (at Road Town, for example) will have to drive or take a taxi to reach them. If you prefer to stay in a hotel or inn, we like the resorts on the island's leisurely West End best; not only do you have convenient access to West End ferry connections but you'll enjoy plenty of peace and serenity, few traffic woes, and easy proximity to the island's best beaches.

Note: All rates given within this chapter are subject to a 10 percent service charge and a 7 percent government tax. Rates are usually discounted significantly in summer. Note that some resorts offer all-inclusive dining plans, such as a "Modified American Plan," which means that the hotel provides meals (and sometimes additional amenities) for an extra charge.

IN ROAD TOWN

Business folks, yachties, and those who need to be near the center of the Tortola activity (such as there is) can opt for one of the basic hotels and inns in or around Road Town. Keep in mind that the daily arrival of two or more cruise ships into Road Harbour harbor can result in traffic gridlock. If you plan an extended stay on Tortola, we recommend combining a night here with a few other nights on a quieter, beachier part of the island.

Expensive

The Moorings/Mariner Inn ★ For those who love the buzz of a bustling marina, with a lively scrum of breezy bars and boaters ambling hither and thither, the Mariner Inn at the Moorings should fit the bill. Located right on Wickham's Cay II in Road Town, this full-service yachting resort offers not only support facilities and services but also better-than-average shoreside accommodations. It's a good way to sample Road Town life with fellow sailors and yachties. The rooms are nicely outfitted with dark wood furniture and tile floors; all have kitchenettes and balconies that open onto harbor or garden views.

Wickham's Cay II, Road Town. ☎ **800/535-7289** in the U.S., or 284/494-2333. www.bvimariner innhotel.com. 38 units. Winter $220–$455 double; off season $160–$420 double. **Amenities:** Restaurant; 2 bars; pool (outdoor); room service; watersports equipment/rentals; Wi-Fi (free).

Moderate

Fort Burt Hotel ★ This intimate hotel was built in 1960 on the ruins of a 17th-century Dutch fort (it was rebuilt in 1776 by the English but little is left of the old fort but a cannon). The hotel is blanketed in flowering vines, with spectacular vistas from private terraces of the harbor below (best views from rooms on the second floor). Rooms have a cheerful pastel palette, with wicker furnitures and touches of elegance here and there—plumped-up wingback chairs and high beamed ceilings—but the best thing about them are the big windows and sliding-glass doors opening onto the harbor. The hotel has a pool, but honeymoon and condo suites come with their own private pools. Steep stairs may make getting up and down tough for visitors with mobility issues.

☎ **888/692-0993** or 284/494-2587. www.fortburt.com. 18 units. Winter $115–$160 double, $200–$385 suite; off season $99–$120 double, $200–$310 suite. **Amenities:** Restaurant; bar; pool (outdoor); Wi-Fi (free).

Maria's by the Sea ★ This 38-room inn in central Road Town is a favorite of folks doing business in Tortola; it's close to the ferry and has little balconies that open right onto the harbor. Rooms have been updated and now add a modicum of stylish chic to their comfort (especially the enormous premium rooms in the hotel's new wing, sleekly outfitted in dark wood furniture, quality bedding, and rich buttery hues), but at night you may be too busy inhaling the sea breezes from your balcony and admiring the harbor lights to care. The hotel updates include a business center and fitness room. Sample excellent Caribbean cuisine at Maria's **on-site restaurant,** open for breakfast, lunch, and dinner on an alfresco patio overlooking Sir Frances Drake Channel.

☎ **284/494-2595.** www.mariasbythesea.com. 38 units. Winter $160–$200 double, $205 1-bedroom suite, $280 2-bedroom suite; off season $130–$170 double, $200 1-bedroom suite, $250 2-bedroom suite. Extra person $40/a night. **Amenities:** Restaurant; bar; fitness room; pool (outdoor); Wi-Fi (free).

Village Cay Hotel ★★ This small hotel overlooks the bustling 106-slip Village Cay Marina, and that's often reason enough for many people sailing through to stay here. Another is price: The one- and two-bedroom suites are nothing fancy but good value, each outfitted with gleaming wood-plank floors and colorful tropical linens; bathrooms are on the small side (some say cramped). Request one of the newly refurbished rooms, especially those with patios overlooking the harbor—that's good value plus. The hotel has a nice big pool as well as a buzzing restaurant, **Dockside Bar & Grille,** that serves Caribbean and continental classics and jumps to live music every Wednesday and Saturday nights. **Dockmasters' Deli** serves New York–style sandwiches and other tasty takeout fare, catnip to passing boaters. Just a 5-minute walk away are the shops of Wickham's Cay I and ferry service to other islands.

☎ **284/494-2771.** www.villagecayhotelandmarina.com. 23 units. Winter $125–$350 double; off season $100–$285. Children 11 and under stay free in parent's room. **Amenities:** 2 restaurants; bar; pool (outdoor); room service; watersports equipment/rentals; Wi-Fi (free).

COOPER ISLAND: eco-boutique RETREAT

On the northwest corner of Cooper Island, a 30-minute boat ride from Tortola, the **Cooper Island Beach Club ★★** opens onto Manchioneel Bay in a splendid setting of coconut palms. It's popular with divers—many of the Caribbean's most celebrated dive sites, including shipwreck-rich "Wreck Alley," are easily accessible—and snorkelers, who come to paddle around in the waters at the south end of Manchioneel Bay. It's a favorite of visiting yachties as well, who stop over to wine and dine in the resort's much-lauded **beachfront restaurant** and **bar.** (The resort's "pop-up rum bar" and artisanal coffee shop were in the works at press time and should be fully operational by the time you read this.) The on-site **Sail Caribbean Divers** offers snorkeling, kayaks, dinghy rentals, and full scuba services. This barefoot retreat has nine good-looking, smartly updated rooms (each with a private balcony), but it's far from luxurious, with an emphasis on simple, self-sufficient rusticity. To that end, Cooper Island is a local leader in green initiatives. It has no roads, no TVs,

no air-conditioning. Seventy percent of the island's energy comes from solar power. A cistern under each room collects fresh rainwater, which is heated by solar power. All toilets are flushed with seawater. The fryer oil used in the kitchen is recycled as bio-diesel fuel. Bar stools and lounge furniture are made from old fishing boats. Oh, and did we mention that the resort is a serious good deal, all year-round? And that full-board multi-stays are even better deals?

Cooper Island: www.cooper-island.com; ℭ **800/542-4624** or 284/495-9084; nightly room only: winter $265 double; off season $210 double; extra person $25.

Getting There: The resort does not operate a regular ferry service, but several (free of charge) boat trips are made each week to and from Hodges Creek Marina, Maya Cove, East End and Road Harbour Marina, Road Town, including the resort's supply boat. Otherwise, you'll have to pay for a private charter to the island.

WEST END & NORTH SHORE

Keep in mind that the island's most popular beach, **Cane Garden Bay,** has a few simple lodgings, often a modest (and modestly priced) assemblage of rooms above Cane Garden's popular beach bars—which means the musical entertainment below may rock well into the night. If you want a decent if frills-free place to hang your hat after a night of music and drinking on Cane Garden Bay, consider the following.

The east end of Cane Garden Bay is the domain of famed local musician Quito Rymer. Above Rhymer's Beach Bar, **Rhymer's Beach Hotel** (ℭ **284/495-4639;** www.canegardenbaybeachhotel.com; $90–$120 double) offers 21 simple accommodations with kitchenettes and private bathrooms.

Farther east, behind Quito's Gazebo, where you can hear the reggae star play 3 nights a week, is **Quito's Ole Works Inn** (ℭ **284/495-4837;** $85–$165 double, $150–$235 suite). The inn was undergoing renovations when we last visited but should be up and humming by the time you read this. Still, don't expect luxe: Rooms are cramped, but some have water views, even balconies.

Just west, the spacious and attractive suites in **Myett's Garden Inn ★** (ℭ **284/495-9649;** http://myetts.com; $150–$220 double) are set in the gardens of one of the most happening beachfront spots on the island.

An easy 3-minute stroll through a coconut grove leads you to **Mongoose Apartments** (© 284/495-4421; www.mongooseapartments.com; $135–$198 apt. for 2), where large, simply furnished one-bedroom apartments (with full kitchens and balconies) in a two-story building are one of the beach's best deals.

Another good deal: **Cane Garden Bay Cottages** (© 780/728-5934; www.canegardenbaycottages.com; $130–$195 double), with stand-alone four cottages in a shady coconut grove.

Expensive

Fort Recovery Beachfront Villas ★   Opening onto a lovely beach facing the Sir Francis Drake Channel and the Caribbean sea, this West End resort is built around what was once a 17th-century Dutch fort. The fort was actually rebuilt by the British in the late 1700s—and this is the structure that stands today. Nevertheless, it's a pretty impressive sight to see—the ruins of a large, squat stone tower from another era—as you noodle around on the beach. Unlike hillside Tortola resorts that offer views from above, this resort is right on a beach, with cottages leading right onto the sand and gentle seas that are perfect for swimming and snorkeling. It's very lush, nestled in a palm grove and about 12km (7½ miles) from Road Town and Choose from one-, two-, and three-bedroom suites or a spacious beach villa with up to eight bedrooms (can accommodate 30); most suites have full kitchens. Rooms are spacious and cheerfully decorated, with wood beamed ceilings and tile floors. The resort provides guests with a personal local cellphone with emergency and staff numbers, taxi contacts, and more. Ask about meal plans and special packages.

© 800/367-8455 or 284/541-0955. http://fortrecoverytortola.com. 30 units. Winter $310–$360 1-bedroom suite, $360 2-bedroom suite, $750 3-bedroom suite, $1,560–$3,120 villa; off season $210–$250 1-bedroom suite, $750 2-bedroom suite, $560 3-bedroom suite, $1,260–$2,520 villa. Extra person $50 per night; children 11 and under $35 per night. MAP (breakfast and dinner) $45 per day. **Amenities:** Restaurant; babysitting; bikes; exercise room; pool (outdoor); watersports equipment/rentals; Wi-Fi (free).

Frenchmans ★★★   This is the island's top lodging, a wonderful marriage of full-service resort and secluded villa. Comprised of nine pastel-hued cottages cunningly built into green bluffs overlooking Frenchmans Cay and the Caribbean Sea beyond, Frenchmans is the kind of place where you settle in for a few days to snorkel, swim, or simply do nothing but soak in the views.

All nine cottages face the blue sweep of Frenchman's Cay, with pelicans whirling and diving and terraces kissed by warm tradewinds. It's a quick drive (or leisurely stroll) to Soper's Hole marina, where you can shop or stock up on groceries in Harbour Market. The one- and two-bedroom cottages are outfitted with everything you need—including full modern kitchens, dining tables, living rooms, and beautiful rain-shower baths. All have big balconies with views of Sir Francis Drake Channel; at night you can watch the lights of vehicles on the coastal road rounding the dark green hills. Frenchmans has a pool and a small, pebbly beach (but excellent snorkeling around the rocks), but the island's storied north-shore beaches are just minutes away. The on-site **Clubhouse at Frenchmans** (p. 162) restaurant is magical, a wood-and-stone treehouse ablaze with warm light and real bonhomie, and its three-course Sunday brunches are legendarily delicious—don't miss the mango pancakes.

Frenchmans Cay. © 284/494-8811. www.frenchmansbvi.com. 9 units. Winter $398–$625 1-bedroom villa, $565–$985 2-bedroom villa; off season $245–$365 1-bedroom villa, $395–$525 2-bedroom villa. Rates include continental breakfast. Ask about provisioning services. **Amenities:** Restaurant; bar; concierge; pool (outdoor); tennis court (lit); watersports equipment; Wi-Fi (free).

Long Bay Beach Club ★★ A favorite of travelers since the 1960s, this resort has gone boutique, scaling down considerably in late 2013 from 156 units to 42 rooms and changing its name to Long Bay Beach Club. It has one of the nicest beachfront locales on Tortola, a 1½-mile-long stretch of sandy North Shore beach overlooking beautiful Long Bay. The low-rise complex has three lodging categories (beachfront rooms, beachfront deluxe suites, and beachfront cabanas), but all share that glorious ocean view (not to mention personal BBQ grills). Twelve suites have full kitchens and big two-person tubs; all other rooms have kitchenettes. The handsome beachfront deluxe rooms have big showers with seats and high wood-beamed ceilings. It's not swanky, but every room is pleasantly furnished, with state-of-the-art bedding, and the views from the patios or terraces are hard to beat. The resort has a dive shop on the premises, and a beachfront pool is in the works. And the snorkeling right off the beach is surprisingly rewarding (ask the manager to point you to the best spots).

The main restaurant is **1748** (p. 161), and the main lobby and bar are built within the ruins of an 18th-century sugar mill.

Long Bay. ℂ **866/237-3491** in the U.S. and Canada, or 284/495-4252. www.longbay.com. 42 units. Winter $385–$430 double, $465 junior suite; off season $255–$300 double, $325 junior suite. Extra person $35. Children 11 and under stay free in parent's room. All-inclusive plans available. **Amenities:** Restaurant; 2 bars; babysitting; pool (outdoor); 2 tennis courts (lit); limited watersports; Wi-Fi (free).

The Sugar Mill Hotel ★★ Historic ruins, fine dining, and intimate accommodations make this boutique inn, on the site of a 300-year-old sugar mill, a favorite among travelers. Built on a hillside sloping down the beach and nestled in grounds filled with vibrant tropical foliage and big fruit trees, the Sugar Mill has a natural serenity. It's across the two-lane road from the sea, with not much of a beach to speak of (but spectacular bird action, as big-beaked pelicans plunge into the sea for silver bonito all day long). The contemporary accommodations vary in quality, but all are furnished with topnotch beds and linens; the tight quarters of the pool suites (with one king bed and a sleeper couch) are balanced by nice terraces, big stone outdoor showers, and the evening lullaby of tree frogs. In fact, we turned off the A/C and slept like babies to the music of bird (and frog) song and hillside breezes. For a truly posh stay, opt for the luxury cottage, the deluxe villa, or the Plantation House suites—the latter have two 1,100-square-foot bedroom suites, a spacious porch, and charming West Indian architectural flourishes, like wood-beamed ceilings and gingerbread trim.

Lunch is served down by the beach at **Islands,** which features standard Caribbean specialties such as jerk ribs and stuffed crab. The acclaimed **Sugar Mill Restaurant** (p. 163) serves dinner in the old rum distillery's boiling house.

Apple Bay. ℂ **800/462-8834** in the U.S., or 284/495-4355. www.sugarmillhotel.com. 23 units. Winter $350–$385 double, $400 triple, $415 quad, $405 cottage, $300–$320 1-bedroom villa, $735 2-bedroom villa; off season $265–$320 double, $325–$350 triple, $350–$370 quad, $320–$355 cottage, $300–$320 1-bedroom villa, $565–$605 2-bedroom villa. Extra person $15/night. Children 11 and under not accepted in winter but stay free in parent's room Apr to Dec 20. MAP (breakfast and dinner) $100 per person per day extra. Closed Aug–Sept. **Amenities:** 2 restaurants; 2 bars; babysitting; concierge; pool (outdoor); Wi-Fi (free).

Moderate

Heritage Inn ★ Locals smartly book a room here to avoid driving the spiraling roads home after dinner at **Bananakeet** (p. 163), one of the best restaurants on island and reason enough to visit. It's not the only reason, though. The frills-free furnishings in this little seven-room inn are clean if motel-basic, but step onto your balcony, and a world of **panoramic views** ★★★ is laid out before you. Perched on top of Windy Hill, rooms command vistas out over three shimmering bays, including Carrot, Apple, and Long bays, and a dozen islands and cays, like Jost Van Dyke, Great Tobago, and Green Cay. Each of the (very modest) rooms (two two-bedroom, five one-bedroom) comes with a full kitchen—which, if you're smart, you'll only need for breakfast and lunch; otherwise you'll want to reserve a sunset-viewing spot at Bananakeet. Spring for the two-bedroom units, which have terraces that stretch the length of your suite. With balmy breezes and that hushed sweep of glittering blue sea, you may never want to leave.

Windy Hill. ⑦ **877/831-7207** or 284/494-5842. www.heritageinnbvi.com. 7 units. Winter $200 1-bedroom suite, $315 2-bedroom suite; off season $125 1-bedroom suite, $185 2-bedroom suite. Extra person $25. **Amenities:** Restaurant; bar; pool (outdoor); Wi-Fi (free).

Sebastian's on the Beach ★   This good-value hotel is a happening spot, with live music in the beach bar and a popular restaurant. It's located on the North Shore at Little Apple Bay, about a 15-minute drive from Road Town. The rooms are housed in three buildings, with only one, a two-story, right on the beach. All are done in a sunny tropical motif, with tile floors, but the most sought-after are the light and airy beach-front rooms, some mere steps from the surf, others with views from second-floor balconies. The rear accommodations ("tropical yard" rooms) feel like country cottages, with apple-green wainscotting and beamed ceilings, but lack sea views—but, really, nothing is farther than a short crawl to the beach. You can also stay in one of the seven spacious new **Seaside Villas** (winter $250–$350; off season $150–$250) all of which have stunning ocean views. **Sebastian's Seaside Grille** (p. 164) overlooks the bay and has a solid menu of island and continental favorites.

Little Apple Bay. ⑦ **800/336-4870** in the U.S., or 284/495-4212. www.sebastiansbvi.com. 39 units. Winter $135–$285 double; off season $85–$185 double. MAP $50 per person extra ($30 children). Children 12 and under stay free in parent's room. **Amenities:** Restaurant; bar, Wi-Fi (free in restaurant and courtyard).

EAST END

Beef Island Guest House ★   This little B&B has the lived-in feel of someone's neat little home. It's a convenient and congenial spot to stay if you have an early flight out of Beef Island or are traveling on to Virgin Gorda in the morning. The converted cottage is set right on the sands at Trellis Bay, its doors and trim done in a happy salmon-pink. It offers four clean, private rooms with private bathrooms and a communal living room and sun room. Throughout, filmy curtains blow with the breezes (it has no air-conditioning). Join your neighbors for a drink on the tables and chairs on the beach, and watch sailboats coming in and out of the harbor.

Trellis Bay. ⑦ **284/495-2303.** www.beefislandguesthouse.com. 4 units. Winter $130 double; off season $100 double. Extra person $25. Rates include continental breakfast. **Amenities:** Restaurant; bar; limited watersports; Wi-Fi (free on patio).

Where to Eat

If you're in the British Virgin Islands around Thanksgiving, take advantage of the island-wide **Restaurant Week,** where some 40 participating restaurants throughout the B.V.I. feature discounted prix-fixe dinners. It's usually held the last week in November. Go to www.bvitourism.com to learn more.

IN ROAD TOWN
Expensive
The Dove Restaurant & Wine Bar ★★★ FRENCH/ASIAN   Set in an old West Indian cottage in Road Town, the Dove has its elegant, ambitious way with haute cuisine, with an eye to seasonality and exceptional ingredients. It's probably the best dining you'll do in Tortola. You might start with tomato and artichoke soup with a dollop of basil cream, or a braised beef rib with a yellow curry glaze. Entrees include pan-roasted duck with a red-wine raspberry ginger glaze, or a pork tenderloin with fried garlic honey glaze and cheddar bacon potato rosti. It's an intimate, romantic place, with a candlelit interior and a deck beneath a mango tree.

67 Main St. ☎ **284/494-0313.** http://thedovebvi.com. Reservations recommended. Main courses $23–$33. Daily 6–10pm.

Inexpensive
Capriccio di Mare ★ ITALIAN   Right on Waterfront Drive across from the ferry dock is this casual cafe, serving spot-on Italian and terrific pizzas in a sea of Caribbean eateries. The pastas are Italian favorites—carbonara, pesto, amatrriciana—but the execution is satisfying. Convenience to the ferry docks doesn't hurt.

196 Waterfront Dr. ☎ **284/494-5369.** Main courses $10–$18. Mon–Sat 11:30am–9pm.

Midtown Restaurant ★ CARIBBEAN   This ultra-local café in the heart of Road Town serves homemade island specialties. It's a great breakfast spot as well. Here is where you find classic island dishes: souse, curried chicken, stewed beef ribs, jerk chicken, and chicken roti. Sides are as good as the entrees, including fungi (a cornmeal polenta), plantains, and rice and peas.

Main St. ☎ **284/494-2764.** Main courses $5–$14. No credit cards. Daily 7am–10pm.

Pusser's Pub ★ CARIBBEAN/ENGLISH   Yes, this is Tortola's original Pusser's, standing proudly on the waterfront across from the ferry dock in Road Town. The storied pub still serves a few British standards like shepherd's pic and fish & chips—but Caribbean influences have seeped in and now the menu is awash in conch, jerk chicken and pork, and grilled local fish. Take home Pusser's Navy mug filled with Pusser's Rum—the classic "single malt of rum" favored by the British Royal Navy since the mid-1600s.

Waterfront Dr. and Main St. ☎ **284/494-3897.** www.pussers.com. Reservations recommended. Main courses $7.95–$22. Daily 11am–10pm.

Roti Palace ★ CARIBBEAN   Set on Road Town's historic old main street, this colorful West Indian cottage is the place to come for state-of-the-art roti. If you don't know roti, it's an East Indian transplant by way of Trinidad: a soft tortilla-like flatbread folded and filled with curry sauce and vegetables, fish, chicken, or meat. Be sure to have yours with a little hot pepper or mango sauce.

Old Main St. ☎ **284/494-4196.** Main courses $8–$25. No credit cards. Mon–Sat 10am–6pm.

WEST END & NORTH SHORE
Expensive
1748 Restaurant ★ CONTINENTAL   This beachfront restaurant in the **Long Bay Beach Club** (p. 159) is set on the covered outside deck of an 18th-century sugar mill. It's a breezy spot to sample upscale continental classics like chicken cacciatore while watching the waves ripple onto Long Bay beach. Start with the popular white

groceries, markets & more:
PROVISIONING RESOURCES ON TORTOLA

Tortola is a prime provisioning stop for boaters, but many people who rent houses, villas, condos and hotel rooms with full kitchens need to stock their pantries. Even if you're staying in a resort without self-catering facilities, it's always good to know where to buy snacks, drinks, and prepared foods. If you're in Road Town, consider a visit to **Ample Hamper,** Villa Cay Marina, Wickham's Cay I, Road Town (℅ **284/494-2494;** www.amplehamper.com), which stocks packaged food, cheeses, and bottled wines.

Gourmet Deli: The **French Deli** ★★, on Wickham's Cay II (℅ **284/494-2195**) sells high-end French and European gourmet prepared foods (including plats du jour and hearty soups), sandwiches, salads, wine, and pastries.

Groceries: Shop in the store or provision online with **RiteWay** (℅ **284/437-1188;** www.rtwbvi.com), the B.V.I.'s biggest grocery store chain, with seven locations on the islands (six on Tortola) including its flagship store in Pasea on Wickham's Cay II (with a Cash & Carry next door for bulk purchases). **Bobby's Marketplace** (℅ **284/494-2189;** www.bobbys marketplace.com), Wickham's Cay I, Road Town, delivers groceries straight to the ferry docks, marinas, and boat charters. The West End has **Harbour Market** (℅ **284/495-4541**) at Soper's Hole Marina.

Fresh Seafood: Buy fresh fish, Caribbean lobster, and conch at the **BVI Fishing Complex** on Baughers Bay (℅ **284/494-3491**). Another source for Caribbean lobster is Wayne Robinson (℅ **284/494-4097** or 284/499-2251)—he can hook you up with fishermen who go out daily filling orders for local restaurants.

Fresh Produce/Fruit: Look for Movienne Fahie's **farmstand** set up across from Craft Alive village in Road Town on Fridays. The West End village of Sea Cow Bay has a **Saturday vegetable market. Prophy's Farm** sells organic eggs, fruit and vegetables and fresh salt from Salt Island (℅ **284/496-7190**). **Good Moon Farm** (http://goodmoonfarm.com) will deliver fresh organic produce and fruit anywhere in the B.V.I., with free delivery offered in Tortola. A **farmer's depot** on old Main Street in Road Town sells local cow's milk, sweet potatoes, pumpkin, papaya, and cashew punch, peanut punch and passionfruit punch (℅ **284/544-6587**). Call the **BVI Dept. of Agriculture** for more contacts (℅ **284/495-2110**).

Organic Meat: L&C Poultry & Pig Plus, in Road Town (℅ **284/494-1310**), sells pork, mutton, and eggs.

---

bean and sage soup and don't pass up the barbecued shrimp—it's killer. The menu also includes a range of pastas and risottos.

In the Long Bay Beach Club. ℅ **284/495-4252.** www.longbay.com. Reservations recommended. Main courses $15–$27. Daily 7:30–10am, noon–3pm, and 6:30–9pm.

The Clubhouse at Frenchmans ★★★ CONTINENTAL   The Clubhouse boasts a beautiful setting, up in the treetops in a round stone-and-wood aerie with wood-beamed ceilings and open-air views of the blue Caribbean. But we'd say the elegant food, overseen by Chef Paul Mason) is equal to the setting, as is the convivial atmosphere—the place feels lit from within. The service is warm as well, with a small staff that cheerfully juggles a range of responsibilities. They might direct you to the grilled shrimp and black bean gateau, served with spicy mango salsa, to start. In a nod to French country cooking, Chef prepares a fine slow-roasted organic chicken Grand-mère, but then goes native with a gussied-up Caribbean lobster in saffron broth, fennel, and garlic. The island's most popular **Sunday brunch** is served here from 11am to 2pm ($27 three-course prix-fixe), with a menu that may include Belgian waffles with strawberry compote, a Boston beer bagel with house-made smoked salmon spread, and a Caribbean broiled steak marinated with Bajan herbs and served with Bernaise sauce.

Frenchmans Cay Resort. (C) **284/494-8811.** Reservations recommended. Main courses $15–$27. Daily 5:30–9:30pm.

Sugar Mill Restaurant ★★ CONTINENTAL/CARIBBEAN   Set in the ruins of an 18th-century sugarcane plantation, the Sugar Mill serves food that is immaculately and expertly prepared. No, it's not the cutting-edge California-fresh food that years ago set off fireworks at the Sugar Mill, won awards and spun off cookbooks—that, in effect, brought the world to its door. Maybe the world caught up with the Sugar Mill playbook. At any rate, you can expect a quiet, gracious dining experience and often great food. And that setting! It's hard to believe that this romantic candlelit space was once the old rum distillery's superheated boiling house—a place of misery in a tropical climate—and that the mottled stone walls are made of cobblestone and rock slab wrenched from the streets of Liverpool nearly 400 years ago to use as ballast in trading ships on their way to the Americas. The walls were likely fashioned by slaves, who strengthened the cornerstones with brain and star coral drawn from the seas 200 yards away.

In the Sugar Mill Hotel (p. 159). (C) **284/495-4355.** www.sugarmillhotel.com/restaurant. Reservations required. Main courses $26–$40. Daily 7–9pm. Closed Aug–Sept. From Road Town, drive west 11km (6¾ miles), turn right (north) over Zion Hill, and turn right at the T-junction opposite Sebastian's on the Beach; Sugar Mill is .8km (½ mile) down the road.

Moderate

Bananakeet ★★★ CARIBBEAN FUSION   With some of the best food on the island, a truly warm and friendly staff, and views to kill for, this is a winner high above the North Shore on Windy Hill. The not-so-good news: It's located in the crook of a steep corkscrew road and a bit of a challenge to reach. The good news: You can call a taxi. Just don't miss a meal here—or a sunset on the deck either, which is where you'll find the locals at quitting time. The specialty is seafood (the coconut shrimp is divine), but the menu also has a variety of other options, savory meat entrees like spicy grilled jerk pork loin with banana chutney, or a grilled steak topped wth caramelized onions, mushrooms, and Gorgonzola cheese. Live music is played on Sunday, Wednesday, and Friday.

Heritage Inn, Windy Hill (p. 159). (C) **284/494-5842.** Reservations required. Main courses $15–$35. Daily 11:30am–midnight.

North Shore Shell Museum Bar & Restaurant ★ CARIBBEAN   Above the strange and wonderful North Shore Shell Museum, this laidback spot catches the breezes above Carrot Bay through big windows. This is as local as it gets, which means a homecooked vibe, overseen by Egberth Donovan, proprietor (and folk artist) of the museum on the first floor. Seafood is the highlight here, lobster and cracked conch are the house specialties. Call to reserve a table.

Little Carrot Bay. (C) **284/495-4714.** Reservations required. Main courses $18–$35. Daily 11:30am–midnight.

Sebastian's Seaside Grille ★ CARIBBEAN/INTERNATIONAL With wooden tables scattered indoors and out, you dine just feet from the waves. Which makes this casual spot a popular place to eat, though to be fair, it does island style food very well. Try the Anegada conch stew as a main course, served with Caribbean-style rice and peas. Other deftly done mains include shrimp Creole, ginger chicken, and jerk chicken, but if you're tired of island cuisine, know you can also get a solid grilled filet mignon here. The after-dinner treat: a small sample of Sebastian's rum.

Sebastian's on the Beach (p. 160). © **284/495-4212.** http://sebastiansbvi.com. Reservations required for dinner. Main courses $20–$38. Daily 8–11:30am, noon–2:30pm, and 6:30–9:30pm.

Inexpensive

If you're looking for a good cup of espresso, head to Soper's Hole Marina to the **D'Best Cup** ★ (© **284/494-1096**), where you can also get a range of other gourmet coffee drinks, sandwiches, and gelato.

Cruzin' ★ PIZZA/CARIBBEAN For those looking for a satisfying pizza escape from all that conch and fish, this casual alfresco spot on Carrot Bay should do the trick. The specialty of the house is grilled pizza, and it comes in toppings that sound offbeat but execute nicely: shrimp curry, BLT, and BBQ chicken. You can also order grilled local lobster, rotis, and tacos.

Little Carrot Bay. © **284/340-3566.** Main courses $13–$16; pizza $18–$25. Tues–Sun 11:30am–10pm.

Quito's Gazebo ★★ CARIBBEAN/INTERNATIONAL In an open-air wooden "gazebo" built right on the beach, this restaurant is one of two Cane Bay beach bars owned by Quito Rymer, the island's most famous musician. It's a gem hidden in plain sight. Not only does Rymer play here 3 nights a week (solo Tues and Thurs 8pm; Fri 9:30pm with a full band), but the kitchen serves up some of the island's best West Indian food, made to order by a real homestyle cook. The conch fritters are the finest on island. The curry roti, many think, ranks up there with the tops in Road Town. Grilled fish and jerk chicken come with superlative island slaw and fried plantains.

Cane Garden Bay. © **284/495-4837.** Main courses $18–$32; lunch platters, sandwiches, and salads $6–$14. Tues–Sun 11am–3pm and 6:30–9pm. Bar Tues–Sun 11am–midnight.

EAST END

At press time, locals were celebrating the reopening of **The Last Resort** (© **284/495-2520**) on Bellamy Cay in Trellis Bay; this fun, popular spot, only reachable by boat, has good food and many fans. Another recommended spot to dine while you're waiting for a boat transfer on Trellis Bay is **Marché at Trellis Bar & Grill** (© **284/542-0586**), with a surprisingly tasty roster of breakfast and lunch items, including a creamy conch chowder and grilled shrimp salad.

Expensive

Brandywine Estate Restaurant ★★★ MEDITERRANEAN BISTRO Set on a cobblestone garden terrace along Tortola's south shore, overlooking Sir Francis Drake Channel, this is easily one of the island's most beautiful restaurants. You can sit inside the elegant dining room, on a pretty patio with sea views, or back in the shady garden—it's all alfresco, cooled by gentle tradewinds and tropical plantings. Although the menu changes seasonally, your meal might include a traditional Spanish paella; perfectly seared scallops served with a bacon and pea sauce; and a mahimahi and salmon "braid," where the two filets are entwined and served with a savory saffron sauce.

Brandywine Estate, Sir Francis Drake Hwy. ℂ **284/495-2301.** www.brandywinerestaurant.com. Reservations required. Main courses $26–$38. Wed–Mon noon–11pm.

Exploring Tortola
BEACHES

Tortola's wide, sandy beaches are rarely crowded, unless a cruise ship is in port. The best beaches are on the northern coast, especially Cane Garden Bay with its silky stretch of sand and gin-clear waters. Apple Bay is best for surfers, and Long Bay West is a dazzling strip of white sand running for a mile. Reached down a horrible road, riddled with pot holes, Smugglers Cove, with its palm-fringed beach, is worth the trouble to get there. *Note:* If you take a taxi to the sands, don't forget to arrange a time to be picked up.

Tortola's finest beach is **Cane Garden Bay ★★★**, on the aptly named Cane Garden Bay Road, directly west of Road Town. You'll have to navigate some roller-coaster hills to get there, but these fine white sands, with sheltering palm trees and gentle surf, are among the most popular in the B.V.I. Outfitters here rent Hobie Cats, kayaks, and sailboards, and it's easy to rent beach chairs and umbrellas for $5. The calm seas make this a wonderful spot for standup paddleboarding (you can rent paddleboards here, as well). Beach bars line the sand, including Myett's and Quito's Gazebo. It's a real scene when cruise-ship passengers arrive in big safari vans, bringing vendors and hair braiders out of the woodwork. Still, with sparkling sapphire seas and forested hills and Jost Van Dayke on the horizon, it's quite a fetching place to be. Surfers like **Josiah's Bay** (for longboard surfing) and **Apple Bay** (locally known as Cappoons Bay), which is west of Cane Garden Bay along North Shore Road. There isn't much beach at Apple Bay, but that doesn't diminish activity when the surf's up — so watch the locals take to the waves after 5pm. After enjoying the white sands here, you can have a drink at the **Bomba Surfside Shack,** a classic dive of a beach bar at the water's edge (p. 171). Conditions all over the island are best in January and February. **Smugglers Cove ★★**, known for its tranquility and for the beauty of its sands, lies at the extreme western end of Tortola, opposite the offshore island of Great Thatch, and just north of St. John. It's a lovely crescent of white sand with calm turquoise waters. A favorite with locals, Smugglers Cove is also popular with snorkelers, who appreciate the fact that the reef is close to shore. The beach is located at the end of bumpy road through a grove of lush coconut palms. You can see the remains of the old set for the TV-movie remake of "Old Man and the Sea," filmed here in 1990, but the long-standing honor bar is gone, replaced by a couple of enterprising fellows selling drinks and snacks out of the back of their cars.

East of Cane Garden Bay, **Brewers Bay ★★**, accessible via the long, steep Brewers Bay Road, has calm, clear waters that are ideal for snorkelers and small children. (When winter swells from the north kick up, it's a good surfing spot.) The only gold-sand beach on island is a great place to stroll or just sip a rum punch from the Bamboo beach bar and watch the world go by. It even has a sprinkling of plantation ruins. A bare-bones campground is tangled in the tropical foliage along the beach—sometimes operational, sometimes not.

The 2km-long (1¼-mile) white-sand beach at **Long Bay ★★**, reached along Long Bay Road, is one of the most beautiful in the B.V.I. Joggers run along the water's edge, and spectacular sunsets make this spot perfect for romantic strolls. The Long Bay

Beach Resort stands on the northeast side of the beach; many visitors like to book a table at the resort's restaurant overlooking the water.If you'd like to escape from the crowds at Cane Garden Bay and Brewers Bay, head east along Ridge Road until you come to **Josiah's Bay Beach** on the north coast. This beach lies in the foreground of Buta Mountain. If you visit in winter, beware: On many days there's a strong undertow, and there are no lifeguards.

On the island's south shore, **Brandywine Bay** is a pretty sweep of crescent beach right next to the highway and is rarely touristed. It was rebuilt with dredged sand and may see some development in the coming years.

TOURING THE ISLAND

A **taxi tour** of the island is a must and a great way to get the lay of the land before you tackle the driving yourself. But the best taxi tours are even more than that, giving you an overview and insight into the island's culture, history, and sociology. Taxi drivers are great resources for insider travel tips as well, like tapping into a network of local fishermen for fresh lobster, or finding the beach that's just right for you. We highly recommend **Wayne Robinson** (© **284/494-4097** or 284/499-2251) as a warm, reliable, and erudite guide. Expect to pay around $110 for two persons for a 2-hour tour; extra persons are $20. Wayne's van can hold up to 14 passengers.

A taxi tour of the island might include a visit to **Soper's Marina,** on the island's West End; a sweep of the beautiful **North Shore beaches** (including Cane Garden Bay), also on the West End; a drive along historic **Main Street** in Road Town (and a retail expedition to the **Craft Alive Village** shops; see below); and a stop at **Sage Mountain National Park** (see below). Serious shoppers of local art and gifts should definitely include a trip to **Aragorn's Local Arts and Crafts Center** in Trellis Bay, on the island's East End (see below). If you want to dig deeper into the culture and history of island life, ask your driver to include the following little gems, all fascinating.

Callwood Rum Distillery ★ DISTILLERY With 400 years of history, this, the last distillery still standing on Tortola (once there were 53!), continues to blend and bottle its own rum in an 18th-century stone structure, the very picture of beautiful decay, all tangled in tropical greenery. The ramshackle interior has a tobacco patina, and you can sample the rums, of which 50 gallons are produced every day. Buy a bottle or two; they're well-priced and make a nice souvenir.

Cane Garden Bay. Free admission.

Fahie Hill Murals ★ PUBLIC ART A series of colorful murals done by different local artists follows the narrow, sinuous curves of mountainous Ridge Road. Each mural is a vignette of an old way of island life, from "banking" (terracing) crops on the island's steep hills to cutting sugarcane to telling ghost stories by lantern light. Pull over to give the murals a good look (you may be joined by safari buses filled with cruise-ship passengers).

Fahie Hill, Ridge Rd., btw. Great Mountain Rd. and Johnson's Ghut Rd. Free admission.

J.R. Neal Botanical Gardens ★ GARDEN This little 1.6-hectare (4-acre) park in the middle of Road Town was created by the B.V.I. National Parks Trust and is becoming an increasingly important repository of endangered and threatened island species. It has an orchid house, a small rainforest, and a palm grove. The aptly named flamboyant tree, with its brilliant scarlet flowers, is one of the highlights here.

Botanic Rd. © **284/494-2069.** www.bvinpt.org. Free admission; donations taken.

island-hopper DAY-TRIPPING

If you'd like to island-hop, seeing as many of the different British Virgins as you can on your trip, your best bet is to base yourself in Tortola and take day-trips from there. A number of public ferries (and airlines) offer regular trips from Tortola to the larger islands. **Speedy's** (www.bvi ferries.com) travels between Road Town and Spanish Town. **Virgin Gorda. New Horizons Ferry Service** (✆ 284/495-9278) runs the 25-minute trip between Tortola and **Jost Van Dyke.** Spend the day at the beach and lunch at one of the local eateries, such as Foxy's, before returning to Tortola. **Road Town Fast Ferry** (www.roadtownfastferry.com) travels from Road Town to **Anegada** on Monday, Wednesday, and Friday. Once there, of course, you can have a taxi driver deliver you to the beach.

But many other hidden islets and tiny islands are only accessible by charter boat or yacht. We highly recommend taking a **customized sailing, snorkeling, or island-hopping trip** while you're on island. The following day-sail operators come highly recommended:

- **Aristocat Day Sails** (✆ 284/499-1249;** http://aristocatcharters. com): Hop aboard luxury 48-foot catamarans for intimate swimming and snorkeling island excursions. The Aristocat runs full-day swimming, snorkeling, and lunch trips out of Soper's Hole marina to Norman Island and Jost Van Dyke. The Lionheart has full-day excursions from Road Town's Village Cay to Peter, Salt, and Cooper islands as well as Virgin Gorda's the Baths. Cost is $120 per person, half-price for children, lunch included.

- **Kuralu** (✆ 284/495-4381; www. kuralu.com): Swim, snorkel, and sail on uncrowded, all-inclusive day sails on this 50-foot cruising catamaran out of Soper's Hole. Kuralu goes to places like Norman Island and the Indians, Jost Van Dyke, and Green Cay and Sandy Spit. Full-day sails cost $110 per person, half-price for children, lunch included.

- **White Squall II** (✆ 284/541-2222; www.whitesquall2.com): Sail in a circa-1936 day-sail schooner on full-day excursions of magical spots like Norman Island and the Caves, the Baths, and Cooper Island. Cost is $110 per person; the boat leaves from Road Town.

North Shore Shell Museum ★ MUSEUM   There may be no one manning the "museum" when you visit, but you're welcome to explore on your own. The folk artist/ poet/proprietor/chef Egberth Donovan has created this splendidly cluttered, open-air assemblage of shells. Shells comprise floors and walls and have been made into shell boats and shell mobiles. Lots of wise words scribbled on boards and surfaces are scattered about as well. The museum even has a restaurant on the second floor, serving local lobster and regional dishes to those who call and reserve a table.

North Coast Rd. Free admission; donations taken.

1780 Lower Estate SugarWorks Museum ★★ MUSEUM   Built by 18th-century slaves, this original 1780 sugar works structure was once part of a thriving harborside sugar plantation. Inside is a treasure trove of island artifacts, including old muskets, coal irons, bedding stuffed with banana leaves, woven baskets; a maritime display; a native folk medicine exhibit (slate bush is good for the kidneys, and angelica works for cataracts and colds); and a rotating art gallery.

Station Ave. ℂ **284/494-9206.** Free admission.

WATERSPORTS & OUTDOOR ADVENTURES

Most visitors come to Tortola not for historic sights but to explore the island's natural scenery, with its rugged mountain peaks, lush foliage, and wide, sandy beaches.

BOAT CHARTERING/BAREBOATING   Tortola boasts the largest fleet of bareboat sailing charters in the world. One of the best places to get outfitted is the **Moorings,** Wickham's Cay (ℂ **888/979-0153** in the U.S. and Canada, or 284/494-2331 in the B.V.I.; www.moorings.com). Depending on your nautical knowledge and skills, you can arrange a bareboat rental (with no crew) or a fully crewed rental with a skipper, staff, and a cook. Boats come equipped with a portable barbecue, snorkeling gear, dinghy, linens, and galley equipment. If you're going out on your own, expect to get a thorough briefing session on Virgin Island waters and anchorages. The cost for bareboat rentals varies depending on the season and the boat. Powerboats, daysailers, and catamarans can range from $385 to $1,700 per day.

HIKING   No visit to Tortola is complete without a trip to **Sage Mountain National Park ★**, rising to an elevation of 523m (1,716 ft.). Here, you'll find traces of a primeval rainforest, and you can enjoy a picnic while overlooking neighboring islets and cays. Covering 37 hectares (91 acres), the park protects the remnants of Tortola's original forests (those that were not burned or cleared during the island's plantation era). Go west from Road Town to reach the mountain. Before you head out, stop by the tourist office in Road Town and pick up the brochure "Sage Mountain National Park." It has a location map, directions to the forest and parking, and an outline of the main trails through the park. From the parking lot at the park, a trail leads to the park entrance. The two main trails are the Rainforest Trail and the Mahogany Forest Trail.

SCUBA DIVING   The region has a number of excellent dive operators, most of which also offer snorkeling excursions. Among them are **Sail Caribbean Divers** (ℂ **284/495-1675;** www.sailcaribbeandivers.com), with seven locations in the B.V.I. including three full-service scuba centers on Tortola alone; and **Blue Water Divers,** Road Town (ℂ **284/494-2847;** www.bluewaterdiversbvi.com), with dive-shop locations at Soper's Hole and Nanny Cay. A resort course costs around $105; a PADI open-water certification is $410.

SNORKELING   Many who stay on Tortola do snorkeling trips to neighboring islands, but you don't have to leave the island to enjoy a fine snorkel. Many think **Smugglers Cove** (p. 165) is swell. Another spot is **Long Bay,** with the best spots near the west end of the beach. **Brewer's Bay** has good spots along the reef. **Frenchmans Cay** has surprisingly good snorkeling around the rocks near Frenchmans resort. Another great place to snorkel is just offshore at **Norman Island** (see below) and its neighboring islands the **Indians,** four fingers of rock jutting out of sea at depths of between 10 and 50 feet. The Indians have no beach, just moorings to anchor, but if you break bread in the water, reef fish (like yellowtail snappers) will come up to meet you. Go to "Island-Hopper Day-Tripping " (p. 167) for a list of operators that go to Norman Isle and the Indians.

SURFING   **Apple Bay** is the island's top surfing spot. You can rent surfboards from **HIHO** (ℂ **284/494-0337;** www.go-hiho.com) in advance and pick them up at HIHO's Road Town store or have them delivered to you at your lodging (for a fee). At Soper's

B.V.I. FAVORITE scuba SITES

The British Virgin Islands have a wealth of world-class dive sites, including the area between Salt and Cooper islands known as "Wreck Alley," home to four shipwrecks. The following sites are just a sampling. Go to "Scuba Diving," above, for recommended dive operators.

o The **wreck of the RMS Rhone** ★★ sank in 1867 near the western point of Salt Island. "Skin Diver" magazine called it "the world's most fantastic shipwreck dive." The wreck was featured in the 1977 movie "The Deep."

o **Chikuzen** is another excellent dive site off Tortola. The 266-foot steel-hulled refrigerator ship sank off the island's eastern end in 1981 and is now home to yellowtail, barracuda, black-tip sharks, octopus, and drum fish.

o The newest wreck in Wreck Alley, the interisland cargo ship **Island Seal** went down in 2006 on a reef near Brandywine Bay near Salt Island. It was moved to Wreck Alley in 2013.

o South of Ginger Island, **Alice in Wonderland** is a deep-dive site with a wall that begins at around 3.6m (12 ft.) and slopes gently to 30m (98 ft.). It abounds with rainbow-hued fan coral and mammoth mushroom-shaped coral.

o **Spyglass Wall** is another offshore dive site dropping to a sandy bottom and filled with sea fans and large coral heads. The drop is from 3 to 18m (10–59 ft.). Divers here should keep an eye out for tarpon, eagle rays, and stingrays.

Hole marina, **Tortola Island Surf and Sail** (© 284/494-0123; www.bviwatertoys.com) rents shortboards, longboards, and standup paddleboards, among other watersports equipment.

Shopping

Unlike the U.S. Virgin Islands, the British Virgins have no duty-free shopping. British goods are imported without duty, though, and you can find some good buys among these imported items, especially in English china. In general, store hours are Monday to Saturday from 9am to 4pm.

ROAD TOWN

You'll find the densest concentration of shops and restaurants at **Wickham's Cay** in Road Town.

Bamboushay Pottery ★ HOUSEWARES   Bamboushay makes handsome kiln-fired stoneware—homeware, tableware, scones, and more—in its studio in Nanny Cay. In addition to pottery, this shop sells coffee and Island Roots homemade patties. 109 Main St. © **284/494-7752.** www.bamboushay.com.

Craft Alive Village ★★ GIFTS   This collection of colorful West Indian–style cottages has been newly landscaped and revamped, and amid the mass-produced clutter is a growing assemblage of BVI–made arts and crafts. Look for **Asante Studio,** where BVI master artist (and a founding member of the BVI Art Foundation) **Joseph Hodge** (© 284/53-0563) paints watercolors and acrylics (often genre scenes of local farming and fishing). **Locally Yours** sells homemade "lollies" made with the juice of local fruits like guava and Caribbean cherry. **Joan Wilson** makes embroidered

Exploring "Treasure Island"

Across Drake Channel from Tortola lies the former pirate den known as **Norman Isle**. Legend has it that Norman Isle was the inspiration for Robert Louis Stevenson's "Treasure Island," first published in 1883. You can row a dinghy into the southernmost cave of the island—with bats overhead and phosphorescent patches—where Stevenson's Mr. Fleming supposedly stowed his precious treasure. A series of other Norman Isle caves are some of the best-known snorkeling spots in the B.V.I., teeming with spectacular fish, octopuses, squid, and colorful coral. The lively island beach bar, **Pirate's Bight,** has been reborn after a 2013 fire. Intrepid hikers climb through scrubland to the island's central ridge, Spy Glass Hill. Many cruisers make Norman Isle a favorite stop, and **day-sail operators** offer swimming and snorkeling excursions here; see "Island-Hopper Day-Tripping," above.

children's dresses and hand-stitched linens. There is also a farmers' market on Saturday morning. Road Town Harbor.

Sunny Caribbee Spice Co. ★ FOOD   This quaint and colorful shop specializing in Caribbean spices and condiments in located in a historic West Indian building that was the first hotel on Tortola. It also sells potions, botanicals, soaps, teas, and coffees. The spices make wonderful gifts and are charmingly packaged, but the ingredients are sourced from all over the Caribbean and not necessarily B.V.I.-specific. 119 Main St. ✆ **284/494-2178.** www.sunnycaribbee.com.

Pusser's Company Store ★ FOOD/WINE   The little empire that is Pussers sells clothing, nautical tchotchkes, and gourmet food items including Pusser's famous Rum Cake, meats, spices, fish, and a nice selection of wines. Pusser's Rum is one of the best-selling items here. Main St. and Waterfront Rd. ✆ **284/494-2467.** www.pussers.com.

Virgin Islands Folk Museum ★ GIFTS   You might find a few interesting BVI-centric souvenirs at this museum in the Penn House, a charming West Indian cottage built by a shipwright in 1911. 98 Main St. ✆ **284/494-3701,** ext. 5055.

WEST END

You'll find shops at **Soper's Hole Marina,** including **Zenaida** ★ (✆ **284/495-4867**), an atmospheric little shop selling handblock fabrics and scarves, sarongs, and Moroccan lamps; outposts of both **Sunny Caribbee** and **Pusser's** (see above); the **Arawak Surf Shop** (✆ **284/494-5240**), selling island clothing, crafts, and gifts; and the **Harbour Market grocery** (✆ **284/347-1250**).

Green Glass Studio ★★ GIFTS   Founded by local nonprofit GreenVI, this outdoor glass-blowing studio on Cane Garden Bay in Tortola recycles the daily refuse from the local beach bars—beer and booze bottles—to fashion beautiful hand-blown glass delicacies, from starfish paperweights to turtle ornaments to flower glass sculptures. The GreenVI Glass Studio has trained a number of locals in the intricacies of glass-blowing, and a local octogenarian makes cloth bags out of donated clothing to carry them home in. It's open daily 9am to 5pm. Cane Garden Bay. ✆ **284/542-2266.**

EAST END

Aragorn's Local Arts and Crafts Center ★★★ ART/GIFTS   Aragorn's Studio is a showcase for the most talented artisans in the islands. Any search for wonderful local art should start at Aragorn's Studio. Tortola-born Aragorn is a printmaker, potter, and sculptor; his giant "fireballs"—silhouetted metal sculptures—are set ablaze during the monthly Fireball Full Moon Parties on Trellis Bay. Look for miniature fire balls (candle holders), beautiful original prints, pottery, jewelry, and gifts, the work of Aragorn, inhouse artisans, and regional artists. It also sells gourmet delicacies: organic produce and herbs from Aragorn's Good Moon Farm; salt raked from the old salt ponds on Salt Island; and traditional coconut bread and banana bread baked in the nearby Mangrove Bakery. Trellis Bay. Ⓒ **284/495-1849.** www.aragornsstudio. com.

HIHO ★★ CLOTHING Founded by two brothers who spent their childhood on Tortola, this clothing firm makes comfortable and stylish "Caribbean-inspired" clothing for men and women: cotton dresses and flirty tunics and sturdy T-shirts. It's several notches above your local T-shirt outlet. HIHO has three locations in Tortola, including this one in Trellis Bay, and also rents surfboards and paddleboards out of its Road Town shop. Trellis Bay. Ⓒ **284/494-7694.** http://shop.go-hiho.com.

Tortola After Dark

Ask around to find out which hotel might have entertainment on any given evening. Steel bands and fungi or scratch bands (musicians who improvise on locally available instruments) appear regularly. Pick up a copy of "Limin' Times," an entertainment magazine that lists what's happening locally; it's usually available at hotels.

Bomba Surfside Shack, Cappoons Bay (Ⓒ **284/495-4148**), is the oldest and most famous hangout on the island, a shack cobbled together with scrap driftwood, corrugated metal, rubber tires, and other flotsam and jetsam and plopped right on the beach near the West End. Undergarments swing in the breezes; graffiti covers the wood. Bomba Callwood is usually somewhere in attendance, a big man in overalls with a wreath of smoke around his head. Bomba's attracts a varied crowd, from surfers riding the swells at Cappoons to vans of cruise-ship passengers stopping for a photo op and a swig of Bomba's rum punch. Despite its makeshift appearance, the shack is quite a business enterprise, bringing in crowds of visitors every month for Bomba's Full Moon bashes, where Bomba's "herbal" mushroom tea simmers in a cauldron in the bushes. It's open daily from 10am to midnight (or later, depending on business).

Quito Rymer, one of the island's most well-known musicians, oversees his own mini-empire along the eastern stretch of Cane Garden Bay. The more touristy spot is the bar/restaurant **Rhymer's** ((Ⓒ **284/495-4639;** p. 157), where you can sip cold beer or tropical rum concoctions along with a casual menu of ribs, conch chowder, and more. The beach bar and restaurant is open daily 8am to 9pm. **Quito's Gazebo ★** (Ⓒ **284/495-4837;** p. 164) is where the guitarist plays solo on Tuesdays and Thursdays (8pm) and Friday with a full band (9:30pm). It serves any and every kind of alcoholic libation and excellent food from an open-air restaurant built almost directly above the waves.

Myett's ★ (Ⓒ **284/495-9649**) is another Cane Garden Bay hot spot, with a prime location right on the beach and regular live music; look for a Caribbean party every Wednesday night. In the same area, but not directly on the beach, visit **Columbus Sunset Bar,** Cane Garden Bay (Ⓒ **284/495-751**), where locals gather to drink, talk, and sample good island food (they also have clean rooms to rent).

Finally, over on Little Apple Bay, check out **Sebastian's** (Ⓒ **284/495-4212;** p. 164), especially on Sunday, when you can dance to live music under the stars, at least in winter.

VIRGIN GORDA ★★★

The second-largest island in the British cluster, Virgin Gorda has a population of some 3,000 people. It was named Virgin Gorda, or "Fat Virgin," by Christopher Columbus on his second voyage to the New World in 1493. It's located 19km (12 miles) east of Tortola and 41km (25 miles) east of St. Thomas.

Virgin Gorda was a fairly desolate agricultural community until Laurance Rockefeller established the resort of Little Dix here in the early 1960s, following his success with Caneel Bay on St. John in the 1950s. He envisioned a "wilderness beach," where privacy and solitude reigned. Other major hotels followed in the wake of Little Dix, but seclusion is still highly guarded and respected. Many visitors think Virgin Gorda is home to some of the most beautiful natural attractions in the British Virgins, including the boulders-strewn beach known as the Baths; the island's highest point, Gorda Peak; and the gin-clear bays of the Valley.

Essentials
GETTING THERE
BY PLANE   Air Sunshine (✆ 800/327-8900 in the U.S. or Canada, or 284/495-8900 in the B.V.I.; www.airsunshine.com) offers direct flights between San Juan (or St. Thomas) and Virgin Gorda; direct flights between Vieques, Puerto Rico, and Virgin Gorda; and direct flights between St. Croix and Virgin Gorda. **Cape Air** (✆ 800/227-3247 in the U.S. and U.S.V.I., or 284/495-2100 in the B.V.I.; www.capeair.com) flies between San Juan and Virgin Gorda. **Seabourne Airlines** (✆ 866/359-8784, or 340/773-6442 in the U.S.V.I.; www.seaborneairlines.com) offers regularly scheduled flights between San Juan and Virgin Gorda.

BY BOAT   Both **Smith's Ferry** (✆ 284/495-4495; http://bviferryservices.com) and **Speedy's** (✆ 284/495-5235; www.bviferries.com) operate daily ferry service between Tortola (both Road Town and Beef Island) and Virgin Gorda (both Spanish Town and Bitter End/Leverick Bay); round-trip fares are $30 to $65 adults, $28 children 5–11. The **North Sound Express** (✆ 284/495-2138), near the airport on Beef Island, has daily connections between Spanish Town, Leverick Bay, and the Bitter End Yacht Club on Virgin Gorda; round-trip fares are $40 to $55 adults, $20 to $32 children.

You can also get direct ferry service from St. Thomas to Virgin Gorda, but runs are infrequent (and only operate on certain days of the week)—so you may need to ferry to Tortola first (most likely Road Town) and then catch another ferry to Spanish Town, Virgin Gorda.

Most of the high-end resorts have their own boats to transfer guests from the airport on Beef Island to Virgin Gorda.

GETTING AROUND
BY TAXI   Taxis are widely available, and, much like everywhere else in the islands, drivers double as solid tour guides. Contact the good folks at **Potters' Taxi Service** for excellent taxi service and island tours (✆ 284/495-5329). The **Valley Taxi Association** is at ✆ 284/495-5539. The standard fee for traveling between Spanish Town and Gun Creek is $30. Many drivers operate open-sided **taxi safari buses** that can hold up to 22 passengers. These buses charge upwards of $3 to $5 per person to transport a passenger, say, from the Valley to the Baths.

BY CAR   If you'd like to rent a car, try one of the local firms, such as **Virgin Gorda Car Rental** (✆ 284/496-0383; www.virgingordacar.com) or **Mahogany Rentals**

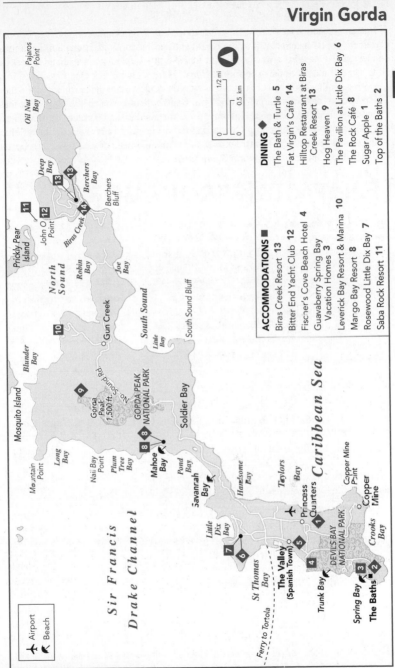

DINING ◆

The Bath & Turtle **5**
Fat Virgin's Café **14**
Hilltop Restaurant at Biras
    Creek Resort **13**
Hog Heaven **9**
The Pavilion at Little Dix Bay **6**
The Rock Café **8**
Sugar Apple **1**
Top of the Baths **2**

ACCOMMODATIONS ■

Biras Creek Resort **13**
Bitter End Yacht Club **12**
Fiscner's Cove Beach Hotel **4**
Guavaberry Spring Bay
    Vacation Homes **3**
Leverick Bay Resort & Marina **10**
Margo Bay Resort **8**
Rosewood Little Dix Bay **7**
Saba Rock Resort **11**

Airport
Beach

Pajaros
Point

Oil Nut
Bay

Deep
Bay

Berchers
Bay

Berchers
Bluff

John O
Point

Biras Creek

Prickly Pear
Island

North
Sound

Robin
Bay

Joe
Bay

South Sound

Gun Creek

South Sound Bluff

Little
Bay

Blunder
Bay

Mosquito Island

No Sound Rd.

Gorda Peak
1,500 ft.

GORDA PEAK
NATIONAL PARK

Soldier Bay

Mountain
Point

Long
Bay

Naii Bay
Point

Plum
Tree Bay

Mahoe
Bay

Pond
Bay

Savanrah
Bay

Handsome
Bay

Taylors
Bay

Princess
Quarters

Copper Mine
Point

Copper
Mine

Caribbean Sea

Little
Dix
Bay

The Valley
(Spanish Town)

DEVIL'S BAY
NATIONAL PARK

Crooks
Bay

Trunk Bay

Spring Bay

The Baths

St Thomas
Bay

Ferry to Tortola

Sir Francis
Drake Channel

1/2 mi
0.5 km

(© 284/495-5469; http://mahogany.nfshost.com), both in the Valley close to the yacht harbor. Both companies also offer taxi tours and transfers.

Remember: Drive on the left. Road conditions on Virgin Gorda range from good to extremely poor. An aerial view of the island shows what looks like three bulky masses connected by two very narrow isthmuses. The North Sound resorts are not even accessible by road at all, requiring ferryboat transfers from Gun Creek. One possibility for exploring Virgin Gorda by car is to drive from the southwest to the northeast along the island's rocky and meandering spine. This route will take you to the **Baths** (in the extreme southeast), to **Spanish Harbour** (near the middle), and eventually, after skirting the mountainous edges of **Gorda Peak,** to the most northwesterly tip of the island's road system, near **North Sound.** Here, a miniarmada of scheduled ferryboats runs between Gun Creek and North Sound resorts.

[FastFACTS] VIRGIN GORDA

Banks/ATMs Scotiabank (www.scotiabank.com) has a full-service bank in Spanish Town near the Yacht Harbour Shopping Centre. Both Scotiabank and **First Caribbean** (www.cibcfcib.com) have ATM locations at the Yacht Harbour Shopping Centre.

Dentists & Doctors Contact **Apex Medical**

Center, Millionaire Rd., the Valley (© **284/495-6557**).

Drugstore Go to **Island Drug Centre** at Spanish Town (© **284/495-5449**).

Emergencies Call © **999** or **911.**

Internet Access The **Bath & Turtle** restaurant, in Yacht Harbour Marina

(© **284/495-5239**), has free Wi-Fi.

Police There is a station in the Valley at Spanish Town (© **284/495-7584**).

Tourist Information The island's tourist office is in Virgin Gorda Yacht Harbour, Spanish Town (© **284/495-5181**).

Where to Stay

Many people who come to the island rent villas. One of the best sources for villa rentals is **Virgin Gorda Villa Rentals Ltd.,** P.O. Box 63, Leverick Bay, Virgin Gorda, B.V.I. (© **800/848-7081** or 284/495-7421; www.virgingordabvi.com). A 5-night minimum stay is required in the off season, and a 7-night minimum stay is requested in winter. Most accommodations have access to an outdoor pool, dining facilities, a spa, tennis courts, and extensive watersports. Wi-Fi is free in most rentals. Weekly rates range from $900 to whopping $9,000 for seriously luxe digs.

EXPENSIVE

Biras Creek Resort ★★★ Reachable only by boat, Biras Creek delivers a kind of luxurious serenity that's thoroughly rejuvenating. This is not where the action is—that would be next door at lively Bitter End, which you can reach by 20-minute hiking trail—but for a soulful immersion in the natural world, with all the creature comforts at your fingertips, Biras Creek delivers. This is the kind of place where you can truly unplug (there's no TV, and cellphone coverage is spotty); where studying the antics of chickens, iguanas, and hermit crabs becomes part of your daily routine; where you can reach up and almost pluck a thousand stars from the velvety night skies.

They get the details right here: Each suite comes with state-of-the-art bedding, complimentary bottle of rum, big picture windows, and sweet little flashlights to help you navigate the pathways in the dark. The décor is chic and modern, with each suite book-ended by ultra-private patios and garden showers. The resort has two Grand Suites, each with two master suites and private plunge pools. Ask for a room facing the open Atlantic, where the wild surf is deliciously dramatic. Each suite comes with two bikes, a fun and helpful transport to fully cover the sprawling, 140-acre property. Bike to the beach on the Caribbean side; it has soft white sand, but the water is a little grassy—still, it's a lovely spot to have the barbecue lunch. On the way you'll pass a paddock, home to the resort's five Paso Fino horses (rescued from Puerto Rico in 2009), ready to ride. Guests can also take the resort's little Boston Whaler boats out for 2-hour excursions to remote coves and beaches nearby—it's great fun to tootle around the blue expanse of North Sound and stop in at Prickly Pear Island or Saba Rock for lunch and a swim.

Hilltop at Biras Creek (p. 178), the on-site restaurant, is the best restaurant on the island, with magical views from its perch high above North Sound.

Biras Creek is ideal for couples but is becoming more family-friendly, particularly in the summer and spring breaks.

Ⓒ **877/883-0756** or 284/394-3555. www.biras.com. 32 units. FAP (Full American Plan) rates (all meals included, no drinks) winter $790–$1,960 suite; off season $660–$1,540 suite. You can also opt for room-only rates. Private motor launch from Beef Island airport $95 per person round-trip. No children ages 7 and under. **Amenities:** Restaurant; bar; babysitting; Boston whalers; exercise room; helipad; hiking trails; pool (outdoor); spa; 2 tennis courts (lit); watersports equipment/rentals, Wi-Fi (free).

Bitter End Yacht Club ★★★ What began in the 1950s as a primitive and ramshackle sailors' stop is now the liveliest of the B.V.I. resorts, a full-service sailing complex that opens onto the North Sound's gorgeous deepwater harbor, accessible only by boat. You almost expect a Somerset Maugham heroine to come waltzing through the lobby, a British Empire outpost of Balinese teak and whirring fans. Accommodations have a breezy-casual rustic elegance, with lots of burnished wood and old clocks and a vintage-yacht look. You can stay in hillside chalets (North Sound Suites) or in the resort's original cottages along the beachfront—either way, you'll have your own private patio or veranda to admire the views. True to its roots as a self-sustaining survivor, the Bitter End is an eco pioneer, generating its own electricity (much through solar power) and collecting and desalinating its own water.

There are activities aplenty at Bitter End, from movie screenings in the Sand Palace to sailing school lesson to Champagne cruises to snorkeling excursions. The resort has more shops than the rest of Virgin Gorda combined, practically. The pool is big and beautiful, enveloped in checkerboard tiles and coconut palms. The open-air **Clubhouse Steak & Seafood Grille** has front-row North Sound views, with high beamed ceilings hung with international nautical flags and Moroccan lamps; it's filled with happy chatter through breakfast, lunch, and dinner.

Ⓒ **800/872-2392** in the U.S. for reservations, or 284/494-2746. www.beyc.com. 85 units, 5 yachts. Winter (double occupancy) $700–$1,840 beachfront villa, suite, yacht, or hillside villa; off season (double occupancy) $500–$1,360 all units. Rates include all meals. Take the private ferry from the Beef Island airport, $30 per person one-way. **Amenities:** 3 restaurants; pub; babysitting; exercise room; pool (outdoor); watersports equipment/rentals; Wi-Fi (free).

Mango Bay Resort ★★   Nestled on lushly landscaped grounds, these resort villas are set on a ridiculously beautiful beach around a ridiculously beautiful blue lagoon. You can stay in suites in resort duplex villas or in your own private villa, enjoying all the comforts and conveniences of home, plus resort services. In fact, all units but studios have full kitchens. The lodgings are extremely adaptable and have many lockout capabilities for larger groups. Resort villa duplexes have high-ceilinged great rooms with furnishings in warm earth tones and tile patios with dining tables and rattan chairs. Big picture windows and doors open to the tradewinds and the golden sands of Mahoe Bay.

☏ **284/495-5672.** www.mangobayresort.com. 26 units. Winter $295 studio, $435/$495 1-bedroom suite/villa, $585/$755 2-bedroom suite/villa, $985 3-bedroom villa; off season $220 studio, $300/$360 1-bedroom suite/villa, $440/$580 2-bedroom suite/villa, $695 3-bedroom villa. **Amenities:** Restaurant; bar; pool (private villas only); limited watersports; Wi-Fi (free).

Rosewood Little Dix Bay ★★★   This palace of casual elegance is mighty fine in every way. In fact, with new management freshening up the place and turning to eco-conscious innovations, Little Dix has never been better. To the relief of many long-standing guests, that means more of the same. Endearingly, rooms have not had keys since the resort opened in 1964—Virgin Gorda is notable for its lack of crime—although you can lock yourself in securely at night.

Celebrating its 50th anniversary in 2014, this former RockResort holds a special place in the heart of many, and one big reason is the warm, insightful service from the best staff in the Virgin Islands. There is a wonderful sense of ownership by the staff, a good number of whom have worked here 20, 30, even 40 years (Little Dix is the island's second-largest employer, after the government). The setting doesn't hurt either: Little Dix is comfortably sandwiched between a half-mile of crescent beach and tropical forest. All of the bright, airy rooms face the beach, with private terraces that offer sea views. Trade winds breeze through wooden louvers and screens, and bathrooms are roomy and luxurious. The details matter, little touches like wooden walking sticks and complimentary bottles of rum in your room. Step outside and snorkel right off the beach; we saw hawksbill turtles chomping on seagrass and rays skimming the bottom. It's a quick boat ride (or 1.5-mile walk along a wooded trail) to the beautiful beach at Savannah Bay. Children are welcomed (kids under 5 eat free), and families generally stay at the Ocean Cottages, four buildings on the south end of the resort, close to the complimentary **Rose Buds** kids' activities club. Little Dix is also just a 20-minute stroll from Spanish Town, the island's main town. The **Sense Spa ★★★** is utterly fabulous, with a dreamy setting in a tropical glade on the resort's western flank. You await your spa treatment around an infinity pool, with spectacular views of the Dog islands below fringed in rustling palms. Nonguests can arrange spa treatments here as well. In the fall, Little Dix partners with Necker Island for the annual **Necker Cup,** a Pro-Am charity doubles tournament where big-name tennis players compete and run clinics. The **Pavilion** (p. 178) is one of the most romantic dinner spots on Virgin Gorda, serving themed buffets 6 nights a week.

☏ **888/767-3966** in the U.S., or 284/495-5555. www.littledixbay.com. 100 units. Winter $725–$950 double, from $1,200 suite; off season $380–$775 double, from $875 suite. Extra person $75. Private ferry from Beef Island airport: $115 per person round-trip (children 5–11 $58); air taxi transfers from St. Thomas also available. **Amenities:** 3 restaurants; 2 bars; babysitting; children's programs; exercise room; pool; room service; spa; 7 tennis courts (lit); watersports equipment; Wi-Fi (free).

MODERATE

Fischer's Cove Beach Hotel ★   Set on the white-sand Paradise Beach, this good-value, locally owned barefoot beach hotel has eight free-standing stone cottages, each with one or two bedrooms and a living/dining space, as well as 12 smallish hotel studio rooms with balconies to soak up the sea (or garden) views. Rooms have tile floors, gauzy curtains, and an oyster-shell palette. A food store near the grounds is a great place to stock up on provisions. An open-air restaurant onsite serves both Caribbean and Continental classics, not to mention live music twice weekly.

ⓒ **284/495-5252.** www.fischerscove.com. 20 units. Winter $165–$175 double, $245–$255 studio cottage, $370 family cottage; off season $145–$155 double, $125–$205 studio cottage, $255 family cottage. MAP (breakfast and dinner) $40 per person extra. **Amenities:** Restaurant; bar; babysitting; children's playground; watersports equipment/rentals; Wi-Fi (free in lounge).

Guavaberry Spring Bay Vacation Homes ★★   Just minutes from the Baths and a short stroll to the beach at beautiful Spring Bay, these handsome redwood "treehouses" on stilts are a throwback to a simpler time. Don't expect TVs or phones; air-conditioning is offered (for a fee) only in some cottages. Do expect fully outfitted cottages with a private feel, where screened and louvered walls let in the sea breezes. Each one-, two-, or three-bedroom house comes with a complete kitchen, dining and living areas, and a splendid sundeck overlooking Sir Francis Drake Passage. Interiors are modest, with rattan furniture and linens in tropical prints. A well-stocked on-site provisioning store, the commissary, has groceries, wines and beers, and kitchen staples, but Spanish Town and the Yacht Harbour Shopping Centre are just a mile away. You can even swim to the famous Baths from the Spring Bay beach.

ⓒ **284/495-5227.** www.guavaberryspringbay.com. 18 units. Winter $235–$420; off season $150–$320. Extra person $25. No credit cards. **Amenities:** Babysitting; watersports equipment/rentals; Wi-Fi ($2 per half-hour).

Saba Rock Resort ★★   A great escape, this idyllic retreat is perched on its own little 1-acre cay in the middle of North Sound; it's only accessible by free ferry or boat. The island belonged for 3 decades to the late legendary diver Bert Kilbride, who discovered some 90 shipwrecks in and around the B.V.I. and whose scuba-diving resort course is taught around the world. Bert's former private island has been transformed into a luxe complex of nine one- and two-bedroom suites. Today this boutique hotel is ideal for swimming, sailing, or exploring North Sound. But with a good restaurant and jaunty bar right on the property, you'll never have to leave. Look for the little nautical museum with shipwreck artifacts accumulated by Bert.

ⓒ **284/495-7711.** www.sabarock.com. 8 units. Winter $150–$295 double, $295 quad, $495–$550 2-bedroom suite; off season $140–$250 double, $250 quad, $475 2-bedroom suite. **Amenities:** Restaurant; bar; watersports equipment/rental; Wi-Fi (free).

INEXPENSIVE

Leverick Bay Resort & Marina ★   This good-value, happening spot is set along the southern edge of beautiful North Sound. The décor in the 14 colorful rooms may be in need of an update, but the seafront balcony or veranda makes up for any style issues. The complex offers a food market and two small beaches—but the beauteous Savannah Bay is a 10-min. drive away. The **Restaurant at Leverick Bay** ★ is a winner, serving fresh local seafood right on the beach.

ⓒ **800/848-7081** in the U.S., 800/463-9396 in Canada, or 284/495-7421. www.leverickbay.com. 14 units, 4 condos. Winter $149 double; off season $119 double. Extra person $36. **Amenities:**

Restaurant; bar; dive shop; pool (outdoor); tennis court (lit); watersports equipment/rentals; Wi-Fi (in some; free).

Where to Eat

EXPENSIVE

Hilltop Restaurant at Biras Creek Resort ★★★ INTERNATIONAL   For many people, this hilltop restaurant high above North Sound has the most beautiful setting on island. For others, Hilltop serves the island's best food. We fall in with both camps. The four-course prix-fixe menu changes nightly, but you may start with a curry lobster cake, served with homemade tartar sauce and move on to pan-seared salmon, grilled lobster, or steak. From 3 to 6pm, a cocktail menu is served, with daily 2-for-1 drink specials and snacks like Buffalo wings, burgers, and shellfish fritters. The breakfast buffet is delicious and often includes local delicacies like sauteed callaloo with onions, mushrooms, and cherry tomatoes.

In Biras Creek Resort (p. 174). (*) **284/494-3555.** www.biras.com. Reservations required. Fixed-price dinner $85–$125. Daily 8–10am, 12:30–2pm (Wed, Sat, Sun only), and 6:30–9pm.

The Pavilion at Little Dix Bay ★★★ INTERNATIONAL   The iconic Pavilion is magical place to dine, an open-air pavilion beneath handsome vaulted wooden rooftops with sea views and bay breezes. Six nights a week dinner is a themed buffet, from Italian to Asian to seafood. (You can also order a la carte if you like.) Standards are high here, and it shows: The buffets are innovative, fresh, and delicious, aided and abetted by the warm embrace of the staff and that soul-stirring setting.

In Rosewood Little Dix Bay (p. 176), 1km (⅔ mile) north of Spanish Town. (*) **284/495-5555.** www. littledixbay.com/dine2.cfm. Reservations required. Nightly buffets (some including a la carte menu items) $55–$100. Daily 11:30am–5:30pm and 6:30–9:30pm.

MODERATE

The Bath & Turtle ★ CARIBBEAN/INTERNATIONAL   The most popular pub in Spanish Town is located inside (and outside) the Yacht Harbour marina, serving such island delights as pepperpot soup, curried mutton, and conch. The beer-battered fish and chips is rightly famous (the menu doesn't lie). We also like the ginger pineapple ribs (in various degrees of "hurricane" heat), salads, and Anegada fish fingers. A Caribbean buffet ($25 per person) is offered every Wednesday. Grab a table right on the waterfront for a ringside view of yachts pulling into the harbor, turtles coming up for air, and colorful roosters ruling their little fiefdom ashore.

Virgin Gorda Yacht Harbour. (*) **284/495-5239.** Reservations recommended. Entrees $17–$24, burgers, wraps, and paninis $12–$17. Daily 7am–9pm.

The Rock Café ★★ ITALIAN/CARIBBEAN   Set between the big rocks of the Baths near Spanish Town, this cafe is one of the island favorites. There's something satisfyingly primal about dining among giant granite boulders to flickering candlelight and stars winking in the big night sky. It doesn't hurt that the Rock specializes in excellent Italian pastas and pizzas. Try the spaghetti Rock, with crispy bacon, peas, and cream, or the penne Boscaiola, with chicken and broccoli. You can also get steaks and local seafood, including fresh grilled Anegada lobster. At press time, the Rock Café folks had opened an intriguing new spot above called the **Treehouse,** literally housed in a custom-built treehouse (with crazy-good views) and big enough to accommodate just 20 people at a time.

The Baths. (*) **284/495-5482.** www.bvidining.com. Reservations recommended. Main courses $18–$40. Daily 4pm–late.

Top of the Baths ★ CARIBBEAN   This breakfast and lunch restaurant is one of the best in the Baths area. It overlooks the famous Baths beach and even has a nice pool to cool off in while you wait for your food. The setting is glorious, and the food—a mix of standard Americanized bar food and Caribbean homestyle cooking—is happily satisfying. You can order burgers, tuna salads, pastas, and wraps, or sample local cuisine like conch fritters, curried shrimp, and conch in butter sauce.

The Baths. ✆ **284/495-5497.** www.topofthebaths.com. Main courses $16–$25; sandwiches and salads $12–$18. Daily 8am–7pm.

INEXPENSIVE

Fat Virgin's Cafe ★ CARIBBEAN FUSION   This modest outdoor cafe on North Sound is good and local, with home-cooked meals whipped up right in front of you and a lively throng of visitors traversing the North Sound. Expect delicious chicken roti, barbecued ribs, and pan-fried fish—and pass the homemade pepper sauce, please. Even if you don't sample the fine fare, this is a fizzy spot to sip a rum drink and watch the shadows of big yachts slip into the harbor.

Marina Village, Biras Creek Resort.✆ **284/495-7052.** http://fatvirgin.com. Breakfast $7–$16; main courses lunch $10–$19, dinner $10–$24. Daily 7am–9pm.

Hog Heaven ★ BARBECUE   It's barbecue with a view at this lunch and dinner hilltop joint, with **sensational views** ★★★ of North Sound and beyond from the heights of Virgin Gorda and a hearty menu of pulled pork sandwiches, barbecue ribs, barbecue chicken, potato salad, and fried plantains.

Nail Bay Rd. 9:30am–closing.

Sugar Apple ★ CARIBBEAN   This bright new spot features local dishes like fish and johnnycakes; stewed chicken with rice and peas; oxtail and rice; saltfish and coconut dumplings, and "Okra Punch" for dessert.

South Valley. ✆ **284/545-4841.** $5–$10. No credit cards. Daily 10am–6pm.

Exploring Virgin Gorda

The northern side of Virgin Gorda is mountainous, with Gorda Peak reaching 417m (1,368 ft.), the highest spot on the island. In contrast, the southern half of the island is flat, with large boulders appearing at every turn.

The best way to see the island is on an **island tour.** Call **Andy Flax,** who runs the **Virgin Gorda Tours Association** (✆ **284/495-5252;** www.virgingordatours.com), which will give you a tour of the island. Cost is from $55 (1 hr.) to $220 (4 hr.) for one or two persons, adding $15 to $30 per person more depending on the group size. You can be picked up at the ferry dock if you give 24 hours' notice.

You should also see the island by water, and having a local take you on customized tours of hidden coves and bays in a small boat is pure pleasure. The genial **Avery Baptist** (averymbaptist@hotmail.com) runs small charters and customized beach-hopping trips to places like the Baths and lesser-known gems out of his base in the Valley.

BEACHES

Don't miss the beauty of the **Baths** ★★★, where giant boulders form a series of tranquil pools and grottoes flooded with seawater. Nearby snorkeling is excellent, and you can rent gear on the beach. Scientists think the boulders were brought to the surface eons ago by volcanic activity. The Baths and surrounding areas are part of a proposed system of parks and protected areas in the B.V.I. The protected area encompasses 273 hectares (675 acres) of land, including sites at Little Fort, Spring Bay, and Devil's Bay on the east coast.

Devil's Bay National Park ★★ can be reached by a trail from the Baths. A 15-minute walk through boulders and dry coastal vegetation ends on a secluded coral-sand beach.

Neighboring the Baths is **Spring Bay** ★★, one of the best of the island's beaches, with white sand, clear water, and good snorkeling. **Trunk Bay** is a wide, sandy beach reachable by boat or along a rough path from Spring Bay. **Savannah Bay** ★★★ is a sandy beach north of the yacht harbor, and **Mahoe Bay** ★★, fronting the Mango Bay Resort, has a gently curving beach with neon-blue water.

The white-sand beach at **Prickly Pear Island** ★★ in the North Sound, is protected national parkland and a sweet stopover for a dip in crystal-clear seas and lunch at the **Sandbox beach bar;** those staying in the North Sound area can call for free water taxi pickup and dropoff (© **284/342-3696**).

WATERSPORTS & OUTDOOR ADVENTURES

HIKING Virgin Gorda has some of the most breathtaking panoramic vistas in the Caribbean. A good way to see the sights from the heights is on a trek along the stairs and hiking paths that crisscross Virgin Gorda's largest stretch of undeveloped land, the **Gorda Peak National Park.** To reach the best departure point for your uphill trek, drive north of the Valley on the only road leading to North Sound for about 15 minutes of very hilly driving (using a four-wheel-drive vehicle is a very good idea). Stop at the base of the stairway leading steeply uphill. There's a sign pointing to the Gorda Peak National Park.

It should take between 25 and 40 minutes to reach the summit of Gorda Peak, the highest point on the island, where views out over the scattered islets of the Virgin Islands archipelago await you. There's a tower at the summit, which you can climb for even better views.

SCUBA DIVING & SNORKELING **Kilbrides Sunchaser Scuba** is located at the Bitter End Yacht Club at North Sound (© 800/932-4286 in the U.S., or 284/495-9638; http://sunchaserscuba.com). Kilbrides offers the best diving in the British Virgin Islands, at 15 to 20 dive sites, including the wreck of the ill-fated RMS *Rhone*. Prices range from $100 to $110 for a two-tank dive on one of the coral reefs. A one-tank dive in the afternoon costs $75. Equipment, except wet suits, is supplied at no charge. Hours are 7:45am to 5:30pm daily. **Dive BVI** (© 800/848-7078; www.divebvi.com) has four locations in and around Virgin Gorda and offers diving outings and snorkeling day-trips and island-hopper cruises.

Shopping

Shops are sparse here; most of the best shopping is found in the boutiques in the island's upscale resorts. The Bitter End Yacht Club's **Reeftique** (© 284/494-2745), has a good selection of sexy kurtas, cotton T's and henleys, and top-quality Bitter End beach bags. Also at the Bitter End, the **Trading Post** has great kids' gifts, including messages in the bottle.

Pusser's Company Store, Leverick Bay (© 284/495-7369), sells Pusser's usual lineup of rum products, sportswear, and gift and souvenir items.

In Spanish Town, stop in at the Yacht Harbour Shopping Centre, which has an out-post for **Dive BVI** (© 284/495-5513; www.divebvi.com), selling all sorts of scuba and snorkeling equipment, plus clothes and tchotchkes. You can buy interesting handmade Virgin glass gifts, straw baskets, and beautiful beaded bags at **Next Wave Designs** (📞 **284/495-5634**), also in the Yacht Harbour Shopping Centre.

Virgin Gorda After Dark

There isn't a lot of action at night. The **Bath & Turtle** pub, at Yacht Harbour (p. 178; 📞 **284/495-5239**), brings in local bands for dancing in the summer on Wednesday and Friday at 8:30pm. Check out the weekly "Welcome Guide to the British Virgin Islands" to see what's happening at the time of your visit.

JOST VAN DYKE ★★★

This rugged 10-sq.-km (4-sq.-mile) island (pop. 300) on the seaward (west) side of Tortola was named after a Dutch settler. In the 1700s, a Quaker colony settled here to develop sugarcane plantations. (One of the colonists, William Thornton, won a world-wide competition to design the Capitol in Washington, D.C.)

On the south shore are some fine, powdery beaches, especially at **White Bay** and **Great Harbour.** This tranquil island is a popular stopover point not only for the yachting set but also for many cruise ships.

Essentials

GETTING THERE   You can take the ferry to Jost Van Dyke's White Bay via St. Thomas, St. John, or Tortola. **New Horizon** (📞 **284/495-9278**) has daily 25-minute ferryboat shuttles from the West End; round-trip fares are $25 adults, $15 children 5–11. (Note that departure times can vary widely throughout the year, and often don't adhere very closely to the printed timetables.) If all else fails, negotiate a transportation fee with one of the handful of privately operated water taxis on Tortola. Fees start around $100 one-way.

GETTING AROUND   To get around the island, call **Bun Taxi** at 📞 **284/495-9281.** You can rent Jeeps from **Abe's by the Sea** (📞 **284/495-9329**) at $65 to $80 per day and **Paradise Jeep Rentals** (📞 **284/495-9477**) at $55 to $70 per day.

FAST FACTS   In a medical emergency, call **VISAR (Virgin Islands Search and Rescue)** at 📞 **284/494-4357;** you can be flown to Tortola. There are no banks, ATMs, or drugstores on the island. Stock up before you arrive here.

Where to Stay

Ivan's Stress Free Bar & White Bay Campground ★   Seventh-generation Jost Van Dyke native Ivan Chinnery oversees this campground right on White Bay Beach. It's got campsites and one-room plywood "cabins" outfitted with screens, ceiling fans, fridges, and big beds. The campground is simplicity itself, but it's also one of the livliest spots on Jost. Take your place in Ivan's Stress Free Bar at happy hour, downing sundowners with sailors and locals at your elbows. Ivan plays guitar in the White Bay International Ever-Changing All Star Band (the house band), which plays regularly here. Visiting musicians often drop in—yes, even Keith Richards or Jimmy Buffet.

📞 **284/495-9358.** www.ivanscampground.com. 8 cabins, 15 campsites, 5 tents. Year-round $65–$75 cabin, $40 tent, $20 bare site, $150–$260 studio. **Amenities:** Food service; Wi-Fi ($10).

Sandcastle Hotel ★   Joined at the hip to the legendary beach bar the **Soggy Dollar,** this barefoot retreat is for escapists who want total privacy. The six cottages are wrapped in lush tropical foliage and bougainvillea, with sweeping views of White Bay Beach. The roomy, breezy rooms are hung with local art and have king-size beds, rattan furniture, and tropical accents. Two units are air-conditioned, while all others have ceiling fans. You mix your own drinks at the Soggy Dollar, and keep your own tab—the resident drink is the famed Painkiller (see below)—and yes, cruise-ship passengers often flood the place for a few hours midday. The restaurant (see below) is an old standard on the island.

ⓒ **284/495-9888.** www.soggydollar.com/sandcastlehotel. 6 units. Winter $310 double, $285 cottage; off season $250 double, $210 cottage. Extra person $35–$45. 3-night minimum. Children 15 and under not permitted. **Amenities:** Restaurant; bar; watersports equipment/rentals; Wi-Fi (free).

Sandy Ground Estates ★   These happily oversized two- and three-bedroom villas sit on the edge of a beach on the eastern part of Jost Van Dyke. The "Castle" has two terraces with commanding views of other islands; The "Genip Tree House" is a three-level villa above the beach, with terraces that boast sparkling sea views. Each villa is equipped with a full kitchen, and each is individually owned, so interiors vary widely, from fashionable to more modest. The managers help guests with boat and watersports rentals. Diving, day sails, and other activities can be arranged, and there are dinghies available.

ⓒ **284/494-3391.** Fax 284/495-9379. www.sandyground.com. 7 units. Winter $1,950 villa for 2; off season $1,400 villa for 2. Extra person $500 per week in winter, $350 off season. Children 3–12 half-price. **Amenities:** Watersports equipment/rentals; Wi-Fi (free).

White Bay Villas & Seaside Cottages ★★   With its eye-candy sea views and easy access to a white-sand beach, this is a real find and a first-rate, secluded retreat. Perched above the sea, all of the cottages were built by owner John Klein. The property is comprised of several different fully equipped accommodations ranging from one- to two-bedroom houses to a three-bedroom, three-bathroom villa for up to eight guests. The Plantation Villa is the largest in the complex, with a great room and kitchen decorated with murals depicting the island's culture.

ⓒ **800/778-8066** or 410/571-6692. www.jostvandyke.com. 3 villas, 7 cottages. Weekly rates winter $1,995 1-bedroom, $3,045 2-bedroom, $4,095 3-bedroom; off season $1,595 1-bedroom, $2,435 2-bedroom, $3,275 3-bedroom. No credit cards.

Where to Eat

Abe's by the Sea ★ WEST INDIAN   This all-purpose sailors' stop serves lunch and dinner and specializes in seasonal local seafood like lobster and conch. "Casual"

The Infamous Painkiller

Don't leave the B.V.I. without sampling the notorious rum drink known as the Painkiller, which got its start at the Soggy Dollar Bar and has gone on to greater glory at all Pusser's outlets. An Englishwoman, Daphne Henderson, is said to have invented the drink in the

1980s, which is an orange-colored blend of island rum, orange juice, pineapple juice, cream of coconut, and a scraping of nutmeg on top. Today the Painkiller is probably the most popular drink among sailors in the B.V.I.

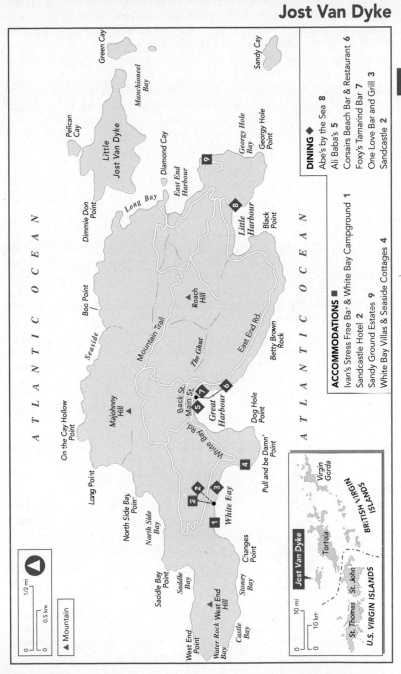

Jost Van Dyke

ATLANTIC OCEAN

Green Cay

Sandy Cay

Little
Jost Van Dyke

Pelican
Cay

Manchioneel
Bay

Diamond Cay

Georgy Hole
Bay

Georgy Hole
Point

Dimmie Don
Point

Long Bay

East End
Harbour

Little
Harbour

Black
Point

9

8

Seaside

Boc Point

Roach
Hill

Mountain Trail

The Chut

East End Rd.

Betty Brown
Rock

On the Cay Hollow
Point

Majohnny
Hill

Back St.

Main St.

Great
Harbour

Dog Hole
Point

ATLANTIC OCEAN

Lang Point

White Bay Rd.

5 7
6

North Side Bay
Point

Pull and be Damn'
Point

North Side
Bay

4

2
3

White Bay

1

Saddle Bay
Point

Saddle
Bay

Stoney
Bay

Changes
Point

West End
Point

Water Rock West End
Hill

Castle
Bay

▲ Mountain

1/2 mi
0.5 km

DINING ◆
Abe's by the Sea **8**
Ali Baba's **5**
Corsairs Beach Bar & Restaurant **6**
Foxy's Tamarind Bar **7**
One Love Bar and Grill **3**
Sandcastle **8**

ACCOMMODATIONS ■
Ivan's Stress Free Bar & White Bay Campground **1**
Sandcastle Hotel **2**
Sandy Ground Estates **9**
White Bay Villas & Seaside Cottages **4**

Virgin
Gorda

BRITISH VIRGIN
ISLANDS

Jost Van Dyke

Tortola

St. John

St. Thomas

U.S. VIRGIN ISLANDS

10 mi
10 km

doesn't begin to describe the low-key nature of this modest dockside spot, cobbled together with plywood and serving what fans say is the coldest beer on island.

Little Harbour. ℂ **284/495-9329.** Reservations recommended for groups of 5 or more. Dinner $20–$45; nightly barbecue $30. Daily 11:30–11pm.

Ali Baba's ★ CARIBBEAN   Fashioned from unvarnished beams and planks, this restaurant near the edge of the harbor, adjacent to the Customs house, has a breezy veranda right next to the Customs House. Expect well-executed version of island staples, such as conch chowder, conch fritters, and savory pumpkin soup. The fish is fresh and good, and you can get grilled lobster, mahimahi, and stewed conch. If you're on the island in time for breakfast, drop in to join the locals for a tasty wake-up meal.

Great Harbour. ℂ **284/495-9280.** Breakfast from $10; main courses lunch $9–$12, dinner $18–$22 Daily 9am–11pm.

Corsairs Beach Bar & Restaurant ★ SEAFOOD/CARIBBEAN   Open for breakfast, lunch, and dinner this convivial beach bar is a happening hangout for a hearty breakfast and a post–happy hour rib-sticking lunch and dinner. Start with conch fritters in a goat-cheese sauce, followed by seared tuna with a spicy mango-rum sauce or lobster Thai style in a coconut-and-pumpkin sauce. Four pastas, including fettuccine shrimp al pesto, are featured nightly.

Great Harbour. ℂ **284/495-9294.** www.corsairsbvi.com. Lunch from $10; dinner main courses $24–$39. Daily 8:30am–2pm and 6:30–9pm.

Foxy's Tamarind Bar ★★ WEST INDIAN   On an island chain known for its happening beach bars, this may be the most famous beach bar in the B.V.I. Sixth-generation Jost Van Dyke native Philicianno "Foxy" Callwood opened the place in the late 1960s and is a big part of the draw. Foxy plays the guitar and is deeply invested in preserving the environment and culture of his native Jost. In November 2013, several years after the Jost Van Dyke Preservation Society initiated the building of a traditional wooden "Tortola" boat behind Foxy's bar (with the help of the island children), the 32-foot *Endeavor II* was launched in Great Harbour to much fanfare among locals and visitors alike.

Most nights feature rock 'n' roll, reggae, or soca. The food and drink aren't bad, either—order up Foxy's Painkiller punch along with fish sandwiches, rotis, and burgers, lobster, ssteamed shrimp, or the catch of the day. Look for beach barbecues on the weekends and ongoing events all year-round, including **Foxy's Old Year's Night** celebration around New Year's.

Great Harbour. ℂ **284/495-9258.** www.foxysbar.com. Reservations recommended. Lunch $10–$15; dinner $18–$35. Daily 9am–11pm.

One Love Bar and Grill ★★ CARIBBEAN   Foxy's oldest son (see previous recommendation) operates one of the liveliest spots on the island. Seddy Callwood and his wife, Raquel, have a loyal following, and the house policy of "No Shoes, No Shirt, No Problem" is said to have inspired Kenny Chesney's hit song. The menu includes the catch of the day, kabobs, and tangy ribs—washed down with a knee-knocking Bushwhacker. One Love features live reggae music on Saturday and Sunday afternoons, but as soon as the sun sets, Seddy locks up and goes home.

White Bay. ℂ **282/495-9829.** www.onelovebar.com. Main courses $10–$15. Daily 11am–sunset.

Sandcastle ★ INTERNATIONAL   This hotel restaurant serves lunch in the open-air dining room, while lighter fare and snacks are available at the Soggy Dollar Bar. At night, guests settle in with a three-course dinner that may feature good soups, mahimahi Martinique (marinated in orange-lemon-lime juice and cooked with fennel, onions, and dill), and "Sandcastle hen": grilled Cornish hen that's been marinated in rum, honey, lime, and garlic! Meals are served with seasonal vegetables and a variety of salads.

At the Sandcastle Hotel (p. 182). ℂ **284/495-9888.** www.soggydollar.com. Reservations required for dinner by 4pm. Lunch main courses $10–$15; fixed-price dinner $22–$33. Daily 9am–3pm and 1 seating at 7pm.

ANEGADA ★★★

The most remote of the British Virgins, Anegada is the second-largest island in the B.V.I. chain. Yet is has a population of about 250, none of whom has found the legendary treasure from the more than 500 wrecks lying off notorious Horseshoe Reef. This is a remote little corner of the Caribbean: Don't expect a single frill, and be prepared to put up with a few minor hardships, such as mosquitoes.'

Located 30 miles east of Tortola and 15 miles north of Virgin Gorda, Anegada is different from the other British Virgins in many ways. First of all, in contrast to the voluptuous volcanic topography of the other islands, Anegada is a flat coral-and-limestone atoll. Its highest point only reaches 8m (26 ft.), and when you're sailing to it, it hardly appears on the horizon. (Its Spanish name doesn't mean "drowned island" for nothing.) At the northern and western ends of the island are some lyrical white-sand beaches, the main reason for coming here. Second, most of the island is reserved for birds and other wildlife. The B.V.I. National Parks Trust has established a flamingo colony here (they flock to the old salt ponds), and it's also the protected home of several varieties of heron, ospreys, and terns. The Trust has also designated much of the interior of the island as a preserved habitat for Anegada's animal population of some 2,000 wild goats, donkeys, and cattle.

Anegada is a fishing paradise and the lobster capital of the B.V.I., celebrating its famous catch yearly with the **Anegada Lobster Festival** in November. Anegada is a low key, friendly, unspoiled place to kick back and relax to the retro rhythms of the Caribbean. Come here for tranquility, not for posh pampering. But come soon: Ever so slowly, the modern world is coming to Anegada.

Essentials

GETTING THERE Fly BVI (ℂ **284/495-1747;** www.fly-bvi.com) operates an **"Anegada Day-Trip"** between Anegada and Beef Island off Tortola. It includes the round-trip airfare, round-trip taxi transfers on Anegada, and a lobster lunch at the Big Bamboo. Cost is $175 per person and up, depending on group size.

You can also take a day excursion to Anegada by ferry from Tortola. The **Road Town Fast Ferry** (ℂ **284/495-2323**) operates daily trips on Monday, Wednesday, and Friday between Tortola, Virgin Gorda, and Anegada; round-trip fares are $55 adults, $35 children. A number of day-sail operators also make full-day beach and snorkeling excursions to Anegada. **Dive BVI** (ℂ **800/848-7078** or 284/495-5513; www.divebvi. com) offers a full-day guided snorkeling tour of the island every Wednesday, leaving from Virgin Gorda. The cost is $95 per person ($75 children 12 and under) and does not include lunch.

Loblolly Bay: A Day at the Beach

Any trip to Anegada has to include a visit to the fantastic beach and reef at Loblolly Bay. If you're taking a day-trip from Tortola, make sure you call one of the taxi drivers mentioned under "Getting Around," above ahead of time, and have them take you across the island to the bay, with one quick stop to see the legendary pink flamingos en route. Once you pull up at Loblolly Bay, stake out a place on the beach and enjoy some of the most spectacular snorkeling in the B.V.I. Break for lunch at Big Bamboo (see below), and have a drink at the small thatched-roof bar where scrawled signatures on the bar and roof supports are from Cindy Crawford, Brooke Shields, and Andre Agassi (the bartender swears they're real).

GETTING AROUND   Taxi drivers offer both transfers and island tours. Recommended drivers include **Lawrence Wheatley** (② 284/495-8002); **Aubrey Levons** (② 284/443-9956); and **Rondell** at **Tony's Taxis** (② 284/495-8027). Taxi rates are standardized by the government; check the You can rent cars and scooters at **DW Car Rental** (② 284/495-9677) or **SnK Scooters & Jeep Rentals** (② 284/346-5658).

FAST FACTS   Anegada has a small fire department and a little library, but it has no banks, ATMs, or drugstores. Make adequate arrangements for supplies before coming here.

Where to Stay

The 15-room **Anegada Beach Club** (② 800/871-3551; www.anegadabeachclub.com), opened in late 2013 by Driftwood Resorts, is notable for its modern, upscale rooms and swimming pool—the island's only pool.

Anegada Beach Cottages ★   You'll feel like a castaway on your own curving slice of sugary sand at this unspoiled oceanfront hideaway. Set on the sands at Pomato Point, the three fully furnished one- and two-bedroom cottages are spread out, separated from one another by some 500 feet of sand and tropical brush. Each cottage is sweetly prim and neat as a pin, with beamed ceilings, louvered windows to let in the breezes, and a fully equipped kitchen. One cottage is actually two cottages built together and can be rented as a half or a whole. During the day, guests lounge about, snorkel, or go bonefishing.

② **284/495-9234.** www.anegadabeachcottages.com. 4 units. Year-round $140 double. 2-night minimum stay.

Anegada Reef Hotel ★   For nearly 40 years, this has been the island's main lodging, opened in 1976 by Lowell and Vivian Wheatley. Still owned and operated by the Wheatley family, the Anegada Reef sits right on a white-sand beach, about a 5-minute drive west of the airport. It's a friendly, casual place that has freshened up the rooms, and all come with private porches and garden or ocean views. The hotel's **restaurant** serves breakfast, lunch, and dinner daily; its evening specialty is Anegada spiny lobster, served up at alfresco tables beneath the stars. If you're visiting the island for the day, you can use the hotel as a base and arrange to go deep-sea fishing or bonefishing (it has a tackle shop). In addition, it's a good place from which to set up

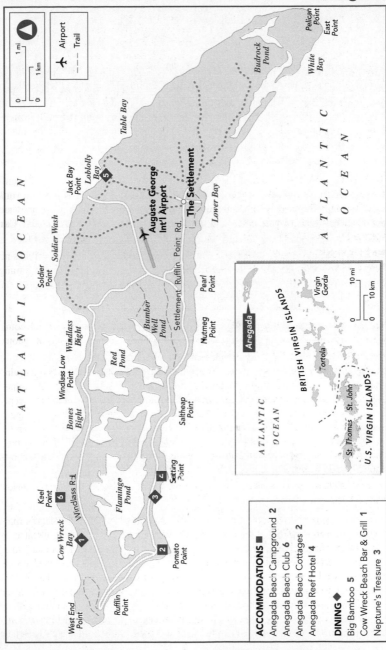

ACCOMMODATIONS ■

Anegada Beach Campground **2**

Anegada Beach Club **6**

Anegada Beach Cottages **2**

Anegada Reef Hotel **4**

DINING ◆

Big Bamboo **5**

Cow Wreck Beach Bar & Grill **1**

Neptune's Treasure **3**

snorkeling excursions and secure taxi service and jeep rentals. Call and they'll have a van meet you at the airport.

© **284/495-8002.** www.anegadareef.com. 20 units. Winter $265–$400 double; off season $240–$365 double. Rates include all meals. **Amenities:** Restaurant; bar; babysitting; Internet ($5 per 15 min.).

Where to Eat

Big Bamboo ★ CARIBBEAN   One of the most popular of the local beach bars and restaurants, the Big Bamboo has a large, open-air dining pavilion set right on gorgeous Loblolly Bay. Locals and daytrippers alike come for the famous fresh Anegada lobster (served with island sides like rice and vegetables) as well as locally caught conch. You can also order babyback ribs and spicy barbecue chicken. Chill out after a big meal in a nearby hammock beneath a coconut palm.

Loblolly Bay. *©* **284/499-1680.** Reservations recommended for large groups. Main courses $16–$40 lunch, $22–$45 dinner. Daily 9am–9pm.

Cow Wreck Beach Bar & Grill ★ WEST INDIAN   Don't miss a sunset sundowner at this family-run joint, a favorite among yachties anchoring at Anegada. Diners relax on a terrace where tables and plastic chairs feature a view of the water just steps away. If you go during lunch, you can snorkel in the clear seas until your food is ready. Fans claim the Cow Wreck serves the best lobster in the B.V.I., but it also offers tasty grilled steaks, ribs, chicken and local grilled fish.

Lower Cow Wreck Beach. *©* **284/495-8047.** http://cowwreckbeach.com. Reservations required for dinner. Main courses $18–$53. Daily 7am–6pm; dinner at 6pm but it can accommodate later reservations. Closing time for bar "when the last customer departs."

Neptune's Treasure ★ INTERNATIONAL   The funky family-run bar and restaurant on the island's southwestern shore is the heart of this lodging/dining establishment. Neptune's Treasure hosts a lively mix of yachties and locals. The Soares family (a legendary local fishing clan) serve heaping platters of lobster, fish, chicken, steaks, and ribs in the spacious indoor dining area, which also has a bar and scrapbooks of the family's record-breaking fishing catches. The family is happy to provide tips on local snorkeling sites and fishing spots, and deftly maintain order amid the festive atmosphere.

The restaurant also offers **nine guest rooms** and **two cottages,** all with beach views and air-conditioning. Depending on the season, rooms (with a private bathroom) rent for $97 to $150 per night, and cottages go for $300 to $370.

Btw. Pomato and Saltheap points. *©* **284/495-9439,** or shortwave channel 16. www.neptunes treasure.com. Reservations for dinner must be made by 4pm. Breakfast $8–$12; main courses lunch $12–$32, dinner $18–$49. Daily 8am–10pm.

PETER ISLAND ★★

Half of this island is devoted to the yacht club, with a good marina and docking facilities. The other part is deserted. A gorgeous beach is found at palm-fringed Deadman's Bay, which faces the Atlantic but is protected by a reef. All goods and services are at the one resort (see below).

The public **Peter Island Ferry** (*©* **284/495-2000**) shuttles passengers between Road Town on Tortola and Peter Island at least five times a day; nonguests pay round-trip fares of $20 adults; $10 children.

You can also get to the resort via a private Peter Island Ferry from the **airport in St. Thomas,** which includes taxi transport to the ferry terminal. It's a 90-minute trip and the round-trip cost is $199 per person; reservations must be made in advance. In addition, a private Peter Island ferry transports connecting guests between **Beef Island and Peter Island** (it includes the taxi ride from the airport to the Peter Island dock at Trellis Bay); the round-trip cost is $60 per person, and the trip takes 30 minutes.

Where to Stay & Eat

Peter Island Resort ★★   This 720-hectare (1,779-acre) tropical island is the domain of Peter Island Resort guests and those boat owners who moor their crafts here. The island is rimmed by five idyllic beaches, among them **Deadman's Beach** ★★, often voted one of the most romantic beaches in the world.

The resort itself is comprised of Oceanview Rooms in two-story, A-frame structures between the pool and the harbor and Beachfront Junior Suites at the far end of Deadman's Beach (and three villa "estates"). The Oceanview Rooms, with pitched ceilings, dark woods, and a blue-green palette, are the smallest and least expensive (and least desirable) units, although all rooms come with a balcony or terrace. A big step up are the luxuriously spacious and sunny Beachfront Junior Suites. More extravagant still are the ultra-swanky four- and six-bedroom villa estates, which come with private chef, valet, chauffeured vehicle, and housekeeper. The Crow's Nest, a posh four-bedroom villa, overlooks the harbor and Deadman's Bay, and features a private swimming pool. The Hawk's Nest villas are three-bedroom villas set on a tropical hillside. The resort has two restaurants. The more casual **Deadman's Beach Bar & Grill** is set right on the beach, enjoying a secluded setting amid sea-grape trees and fringing palms. It offers a Wednesday-night Caribbean buffet, accompanied by a steel-drum band. The **Tradewinds** restaurant hosts a Saturday-night Gala Buffet, featuring Caribbean seafood and meat-carving stations.

🅒 **800/346-4451** in the U.S., or 284/495-2000. www.peterisland.com. 52 units. Winter $800–$940 double, $1,280–$1,560 junior suite, $4,600–$14,500 villa; off season $400–$640 double, $750–$1,180 junior suite, $3,100–$12,500 villa. Rates include all meals and beverages, except in Ocean View Rooms and Beachfront Junior Suites. Children 11 and under stay in parent's room for $50 per night. **Amenities:** 2 restaurants; 2 bars; babysitting; health club and spa; pool (outdoor); 4 tennis courts (lit); watersports equipment/rentals; Wi-Fi (free in lobby and clubhouse).

GUANA ISLAND ★★★

This 340-hectare (840-acre) island resort is one of the most private hideaways in the Caribbean. Don't come here looking for action; do come if you seek serenity and rustic old-school luxury. Just off the north coast of Tortola, Guana has virgin beaches, nature trails, and rare and unusual species of plant and animal life, including iguana, red-legged tortoise, and the Caribbean roseate flamingo. Arawak relics have even been discovered here. You can climb 242m (794-ft.) Sugarloaf Mountain for a panoramic view. Guana Island sends a boat to meet arriving guests at the Beef Island airport (trip time is 10 min.).

Where to Stay & Eat

Guana Island ★★★   Guana Island was purchased in 1974 by dedicated conservationists Henry and Gloria Jarecki, and it's both a nature preserve and wildlife sanctuary. This is one stunning landscape: Upon your arrival by boat, a Land Rover meets you at the docks and transports you up one of the most scenic hills in the region. From above you can see an old salt pond dotted with pink flamingos and the lacy fringes of beautiful White Bay, the island's main beach. Guana even has the ruins of an old sugarcane plantation. The island is a model of self-sufficiency, with its own desalination plant and a private organic orchard, growing tropical fruits like papaya and key lime. The island has seven beaches in all, five of which require a boat to reach. All have sand as soft as baby powder, lapped by gin-clear sapphire seas.

The cluster of white stone cottages was built as a private club in the 1930s, on the foundations of a Quaker homestead. Each cottage has its own unique decor, but most have rustic wood-beam ceilings and New England–style wainscotting. The resort never holds more than 35 guests, and because the dwellings are staggered along a flower-dotted ridge overlooking the Caribbean and Atlantic seas, the sense of privacy is almost absolute. The Sea View pool cottage has its own private pool and three rooms. The North Beach villa has its own pool *and* beach. In fact, all four villas have infinity pools. Sixty percent of the cottages have air-condioning, but most guests find the hillside breezes plenty cooling. Hors d'ouevres are served nightly (6:30pm) in the stone living room, followed by 7:30pm candlelight dinner on the veranda's communal tables. A new chef from Spain was getting raves in the kitchen at press time. Kids 8 and under stay free at Guana during "Kids' Weeks" in July and August. The entire island can be rented by groups of up to 35 ($22,000 and up per day).

© **800/544-8262** in the U.S., or 284/494-2354. www.guana.com. 15 units. Winter $1,250–$2,125 cottage, $2,325–$6,500 villa; off season $695–$1,965 cottage, $1,535–$6,500 villa. Rates include all meals and drinks served with meals. Closed Sept–Oct. Children welcome certain times of year. **Amenities:** Restaurant; honor bar; babysitting; 2 tennis courts (lit); watersports equipment/rentals.

PLANNING YOUR TRIP TO THE VIRGIN ISLANDS

A little preparation is essential before you start your journey to the Virgin Islands, especially if you plan on making island-hopping a big part of your itinerary. This chapter tackles the how-tos of a trip to the Virgin Islands, including everything from finding the best airfare to deciding when to go to choosing the best tour or excursion. For on-the-ground resources, head straight to "Fast Facts," beginning on p. 201.

GETTING THERE

For American citizens, visiting the U.S. Virgin Islands is relatively easy and hassle-free: Because it's part of the U.S. territory, you won't even need a passport to enter the country on arrival. American citizens do need a passport to enter the British Virgin Islands, however. For complete information on passports and visas, go to "Fast Facts," later in this chapter.

By Plane

A number of major airlines have regularly scheduled nonstop air service from cities all over North America into St. Thomas—the major international gateway to the Virgins. But most flights include stopovers in Miami or San Juan. Currently, there are no direct flights from North America or Europe to any of the British Virgin Islands. Anyone planning to visit the B.V.I. will likely have to fly into St. Thomas, San Juan (Puerto Rico), or Miami and make a connection by ferry or air in lieu of a direct flight (there are also connections through St. Kitts and Antigua). Those traveling from overseas will also most likely make a connection in St. Thomas, St. Croix, or San Juan after first connecting in the mainland U.S.

The major airports in the Virgin Islands are the **Cyril E. King Airport** (© **340/774-5100;** www.viport.com/airports.html; airport code STT) in St. Thomas and the **Henry E. Rohlsen Airport,** Estate Mannings Bay (© **340/778-1012;** airport code STX), on St. Croix. From these airports, you can take ferries or small planes on to your destination in the Virgin Islands.

For more information on getting to each island, see the "Getting There" sections in the individual island chapters.

By Cruise Ship

The Virgin Islands are a popular stop for cruise ships traveling the Caribbean, in particular Charlotte Amalie in St. Thomas, one of the world's busiest cruise ports, which welcomed nearly 1,800,000 cruise passengers in 2012, and that number was expected to rise by 7.8 percent for the 2013/2014 season. In comparison, the historic waterfront of St. Croix saw the arrival of only 117,000 cruise passengers in 2012. Tortola recorded nearly 400,000 cruise passengers in 2012 but lost a big chunk of its market when Carnival Cruise Line announced in late 2013 that it would suspend travel to Tortola indefinitely while the island overhauls its docking facilities.

THE CRUISE SHIPS
St. Thomas

Most of the major cruise lines include regular stops in St. Thomas in their Caribbean itineraries, including the biggest cruise ships in the world, such as the Royal Caribbean's mega ships *Allure of the Sea* and *Oasis of the Sea,* each with a maximum passenger capacity of more than 6,000 people; Norwegian Cruise Line's *Epic;* and Princess Cruise Line's *Royal Princess.*

The port at Charlotte Amalie is one of the world's busiest cruise ports, welcoming nearly 1,800,000 cruise passengers in 2012 (the last date for which there are figures). Cruise ships dock at one of two major piers, each with room for two mega-ships at a time: **Havensight Pier** and **Crown Bay.** In high season for cruising, it's not unusual to have an additional one or two ships anchored in the harbor, delivering cruise-ship passengers to shore in tenders.

A number of smaller cruise ships visit the waters of the Virgin Islands without docking, including Club Med, Star Clipper, and Windsar Cruises.

St. Croix

Cruise lines that make stops in St. Croix included Celebrity *(Summit, Century);* Norwegian Cruise Line *(Jewel);* Royal Caribbean *(Vision, Adventure);* Holland America *(Maasdam);* and Silversea *(Silver Cloud).*

Tortola

Cruise lines that dock in Road Town, Tortola, include Regent Seven Seas *(Windstar);* Costa Cruise Lines *(Costa Magica);* Crystal; Celebrity; Royal Caribbean *(Jewel of the Seas);* Cunard; Holland America; Silver Seas *(Silver Spirit);* and P&O Cruises *(Arcadia).*

GETTING AROUND

By Plane

Regular flights are scheduled between St. Thomas and St. Croix, and between St. Thomas and Tortola. **Seaborne Airlines** (✆ **866/359-8784;** www.seaborneairlines. com) flies between St. Thomas and St. Croix on several runs daily; Seaborne also flies between St. Thomas and Beef Island, Tortola. **Cape Air** (✆ **866/227-3247** in the U.S. and U.S.V.I.; www.capeair.com) offers regularly scheduled flights between St. Thomas and both St. Croix and Tortola.

St. John has no airport; passengers usually land first at St. Thomas, then take the 20-minute ferry ride to St. John.

ferry COMPANIES: WHERE THEY GO

Ferry service is an essential transportation link in the Virgins, and most of the ferries get you where you want to go with speed and efficiency. But know that not all ferry companies are alike—boats vary from sleek high-speed catamarans (Road Town Fast Ferry) to older, no-frills models (pretty much all the rest). Some ferries are more reliably on time than others; also check to see if your ferry is "non-stop"—some ferries, like Inter Island, may make pit shops on the way to your final destination. Fares are not necessarily economical; in addition, nonresidents traveling by sea now have to pay a $15 passenger tax per person ($10 B.V.I. residents) anytime they depart the B.V.I. Still, we love the ferries—they're scenic bliss. Here is a breakdown of the various public ferry companies and where they go; keep in mind that itineraries are subject to change. Note that children and seniors pay discounted fares, and that some ferries charge an extra $2 per piece of luggage. And note that you'll save by buying round-trip tickets.

Inter Island Boat Services (📞 **284/495-4166;** www.interislandboatservices.com): Makes runs between Red Hook (St. Thomas), Cruz Bay (St. John), and the West End (Tortola), with stops on Virgin Gorda, Jost Van Dyke, and Anegada. Rates between St. Thomas and Tortola are $30 one-way; $45 round-trip.

Native Son (📞 **284/495-4617** in the U.S.V.I. or 340/774-8685 in the B.V.I.; www.nativesonferry.com): Makes daily runs between St. Thomas (both Red Hook and Charlotte Amalie) and Tortola (both West End and Road Town). Prices are $30 one-way; $50 round-trip.

Road Town Fast Ferry (📞 **340/777-2800** in the U.S.V.I or 284/494-2323 in the B.V.I.; www.roadtownfastferry.com): Offers daily runs between Charlotte Amalie and Road Town, Tortola, on sleek air-conditioned high-speed catamarans. Fares are $35 one-way; $60 round-trip; group rates available.

Smith's Ferry Service (📞 **340/775-5235;** www.bviferryservices.com): Known as the "Tortola Fast Ferry," Smith's operates daily service between Tortola and St. Thomas; between Tortola and Virgin Gorda; and charter service to outer B.V.I. islands. Prices $30 to $40 one-way; $50 to $60 round-trip.

Speedy's (📞 **284/495-7292;** www.bviferries.com): Speedy's operates routes between Charlotte Amalie (St. Thomas) and Tortola (Road Town); Charlotte Amalie and Virgin Gorda; Tortola (Road Town and Beef Island) and Virgin Gorda. B.V.I. domestic fares are $20 one-way, $30 round-trip. Fares for travel between the U.S.V.I. and the B.V.I. are $25–$40 one-way, $45–$70 round-trip.

By Boat

Ferry service is a vital link on the Virgin Islands and a wonderful, leisurely way to see these beautiful islands by water. On the U.S. Virgin Islands, public ferries between St. Thomas and St. John (private water taxis also operate on this route) run at regular times all day long. Launch services link Red Hook, on the East End of St. Thomas, with both Charlotte Amalie in St. Thomas and Cruz Bay in St. John (not to mention Tortola and Virgin Gorda). At press time, there was no regular ferry between St. Thomas and St. Croix (although plans were in the works at press time for a high-speed ferry service between the islands).

Ferries are also a vital link between the U.S. Virgins and the B.V.I.—and the inter-island public ferries are generally a more economical alternative to flying between the U.S. Virgins and the B.V.I. Ferries run from both ferry terminals on St. Thomas (Charlotte Amalie and Red Hook) to either West End or Road Town on Tortola, a 45- to 55-minute voyage. In the B.V.I., ferries and private boats link Road Town, Tortola, with the island's West End; there's also service to and from Virgin Gorda and some of the smaller islands, such as Anegada and Jost Van Dyke. Note that on some of the really remote islands, boat service may be only once a week. Many of the private island resorts, such as Peter Island, provide launches from Tortola or from the airport in St. Thomas.

For more details on specific ferry connections, including sample fares, see the "Getting Around" sections of the individual island chapters.

By Car

A rental car is often the best way to get around each of the Virgin Islands. Just remember the most important rule: In both the U.S. and the British Virgin Islands, *you must drive on the left.*

All the major car-rental companies are represented in the U.S. Virgin Islands, including **Avis** (*©* **800/331-1212;** www.avis.com), **Budget** (*©* **800/626-4516;** www. budget.com), and **Hertz** (*©* **800/654-3131;** www.hertz.com); many local agencies also compete in the car-rental market (for detailed information, see the "Getting Around" sections in individual island chapters). On St. Thomas and St. Croix, you can pick up most rental cars at the airport. On St. John, there are car-rental stands at the ferry dock. Cars are sometimes in short supply during the high season, so reserve as far in advance as possible.

Parking lots in the U.S. Virgin Islands can be found in Charlotte Amalie, on St. Thomas, and in Christiansted, on St. Croix (in Frederiksted, you can generally park on the street). Most hotels, except those in the congested center of Charlotte Amalie, have free parking lots.

Even though taxi service in the British Virgin Islands is readily available, we highly recommend renting a car, particularly in Tortola. Given that, you'll have to drive on the left along roads that can be hairy or feel like roller-coaster rides. (If you plan to stay in the B.V.I. longer than 30 days, you must purchase a temporary local driver's license for $10 from police headquarters or a car-rental desk in town.) You must be at least 25 years old to rent a car in the B.V.I. Most of the major U.S. car-rental companies are represented on these islands, but you'll find a number of reliable local companies as well, many conveniently located near the ferry docks and in the main towns. Vehicles come in a wide range of styles and prices, including Jeeps, Land Rovers, mini mokes, and even six- to eight-passenger Suzukis. Weekly rates are usually slightly cheaper.

Note: There are no car-rental agencies at the airports on Tortola or Virgin Gorda.

GASOLINE   St. Thomas has plenty of service stations, especially on the outskirts of Charlotte Amalie and at strategic points in the north and in the more congested East End. On St. Croix, most gas stations are in Christiansted, but there are also some along the major roads and at Frederiksted. On St. John, make sure your tank is filled up at Cruz Bay before heading out on a tour of the island.

Gas stations are not as plentiful on the British Virgin Islands. Road Town, the capital of Tortola, has the most gas stations; fill up here before touring the island. Virgin Gorda has a limited but sufficient number of gas stations. Chances are you won't be using a car on the other, smaller British Virgin Islands.

Taxes are already included in the printed price. One U.S. gallon equals 3.8 liters or .85 imperial gallons.

BREAKDOWNS   All the major islands, including St. Thomas, St. John, St. Croix, Tortola, and Virgin Gorda, have garages that will tow vehicles. Always call the rental company first if you have a breakdown. If your car requires extensive repairs because of a mechanical failure, a new one will be sent to replace it.

By Taxi

Taxis are the main mode of transport on all the Virgin Islands. On **St. Thomas,** taxi vans carry up to a dozen passengers to multiple destinations; smaller private taxis are also available. You'll find plenty of taxis on arrival at the airport. On **St. John,** both private taxis and vans for three or more passengers are available. On **St. Croix,** taxis congregate at the airport, in Christiansted, and in Frederiksted, where the cruise ships arrive. On all the islands, you'll see more and more **open-air safari "buses"** (more like retrofitted flat-bed trucks) capable of handling up to 30 passengers, which taxi drivers use largely to transport groups (for instance, cruise-ship passengers) on island tours and excursions. Increasingly, these safari buses are also used as pickup and dropoff taxis.

Throughout the U.S.V.I, standard per-person taxi rates are set by the local government (look for a complete rate listing at the St. Thomas airport or in free local magazines like "This Week") but it's always good to confirm the rate before the ride begins.

On the **British Virgin Islands,** taxis are readily available and, on some to the smaller islands, often the best way to get around. Service is available on Tortola, Virgin Gorda, and Anegada, and rates are fixed by the local government.

Tip: It's highly recommended that if you find a good taxi driver on the islands, get his or her card—not only will you have a reliable driver to drop you off and pick you up places but most drivers are smart and entertaining island guides. Rates for sightseeing taxi tours are also generally regulated by the government. The standard taxi tour on St. Thomas, for example, is $50 for one or two passengers and $25 per extra passenger.

By Bus

The only islands with recommendable bus service are **St. Thomas** and **St. Croix.** On St. Thomas, buses leave from Charlotte Amalie and circle the island; on St. Croix, air-conditioned buses run from Christiansted to Frederiksted. Bus service elsewhere is highly erratic; it's mostly used by locals going to and from work.

TIPS ON ACCOMMODATIONS

Throughout this book, we provide detailed descriptions of the lodging properties so that you get an idea of what to expect. Keep in mind that many of the more high-end island resorts charge a **daily resort fee** of between $35 and $50.

Resorts and hotels in the Virgin Islands offer money-saving package deals galore, and you can find land-air (and land-air-rental-car) packages on almost all of the online travel agencies (Expedia.com, Orbitz.com, Priceline.com, VacMart.com, Cheap Caribbean.com). Be sure to check the hotel's own websites: Many hotels offer terrific online-only multi-stay or theme deals (especially in the off season).

Like most Caribbean islands, the Virgins have high and low seasons, and properties are priced accordingly. The most exorbitant rates are charged during the Christmas and New Year's holidays. If you have flexibility in your travel times, keep in mind that during the off season (mid-Apr to mid-Dec), most hotels offer tremendous deals, often slashing 25 to 50 percent off their regular-season prices.

Renting Your Own Villa or Vacation Home

Another popular lodging alternative, and a smart money-saving option if you're traveling with a large party of family or friends, is renting a villa, condo, apartment, or cottage for your Virgin Islands vacation. Having your own self-catering facilities can be a big money-saver—dining out is chillingly pricey in the Virgin Islands. *Note:* If you're planning your trip for the high season, reservations should be made at least 5 to 6 months in advance.

Dozens of agencies throughout the United States and Canada offer rentals in the Virgin Islands. **Villas of Distinction** (𝒞 800/289-0900; www.villasofdistinction.com) offers "complete vacations," including car rental and domestic help. Its private luxury villas have one to seven-plus bedrooms, and many have swimming pools. Rates run from $500 a night and up.

Vacation St. Croix, 4000 La Grande Princesse, Christiansted (𝒞 877/788-0361 or 340/718-0361; www.vacationstcroix.com), offers some of the best properties on St. Croix, specializing in villas, condos, and private homes, many of which are on the beach. Two- to seven-bedroom units are available, with prices from $1,000 to $15,000 per week.

Best of BVI (𝒞 1252-674878 from the U.K. and 011/44-1252-674878 from the U.S; www.bestofbvi.com) handles properties you won't find anywhere else, including a one-bedroom cottage on Little Thatch Island, a privately owned island minutes from Soper's Hole; Best of BVI also has a hugely informative trip-planning website, with an up-to-date ferry schedule). **Jewels of the BVI** (𝒞 866/468-6284; www.jewelsof thebvi.com) represents only BVI Islander–owned properties, including villas, condos, and resorts.

At Home Abroad (𝒞 212/421-9165; www.athomeabroadinc.com) has a roster of private luxury homes, villas, and condos for rent in St. Thomas, St. John, Tortola, and Virgin Gorda; maid service is included in the price. In the U.K., browse the options offered through **Holiday Rentals** (𝒞 020/8846-3441; www.holiday-rentals.co.uk).

You can also find excellent deals on popular owner-rented vacation lodging websites, including **VRBO** (www.vrbo.com) and **HomeAway** (www.homeaway.com); both websites list numerous attractive villas and condos throughout the Virgins. What you will *not* get with these rentals is service (unless advertised) or even guarantees that the rental is what is appears to be. Both VRBO and HomeAway sell rental guarantee insurance ($39 and up) that guarantees your money back under certain circumstances (the property has been double-booked or grossly misrepresented, for example)—so you may want to weigh that extra fee against the low rental rates.

SPECIAL-INTEREST TRIPS & TOURS

There's no rule that says you have to confine yourself to a beach chair while visiting the Virgin Islands (although there's no rule against it, either). You will have endless opportunities to sit by the surf sipping rum drinks, but remember that these islands offer more than just ribbons of fetching white-sand beach. Coral reefs and deepwater channels provide backdrops for a variety of watersports, from snorkeling to sea kayaking to sailing, and the lush island interiors make ideal playgrounds for scenic hikes and breathtaking vistas. This section presents an overview of tours, special-interest trips, and outdoor excursions on the Virgin Islands. See individual chapters for more specific information on locations and outfitters. *Note:* During the low summer season, tours and excursions may not run regularly unless enough people book, so always call in advance to confirm.

Air Tours

It's a pricey option, but well-heeled visitors may want to see the Virgin Islands as the birds do. Helicopter sightseeing tours, island-hopping day-trips, and heli-adventures (heli-fishing in Anegada, for example) are available through **Caribbean Buzz Helicopters,** in St. Thomas (© **340/775-7335;** http://caribbean-buzz.com). A **Full Moon tour** takes you over St. Thomas and St. John on 15- or 30-minute jaunts by moonlight. Helicopters seat five passengers and a pilot and are also available to rent for island transfers.

If you can't afford such a luxury, you can get a panoramic aerial view from Paradise Point on St. Thomas (p. 73).

Adventure Trips

Dive in: The Virgin Islands is one big outdoor playground, with aquatic pleasures, rain-forest peaks, and breathtakingly scenic sightseeing. For general guided tours, contact the following three tour operators:

One of the best tour operators in the U.S.V.I. is **Adventure Center,** in the Marriott Frenchman's Reef Resort, Flamboyant Point, St. Thomas (© **340/774-2992;** www.adventurecenters.net). It offers a wide variety of tours, on both land and sea, and many tours of both St. Thomas and St. John depart right from the hotel's dock. Their 2½ hour "Scenic Island Drive" tour explores St. Thomas's highlights, including the Botanical

---

Sea Turtle Etiquette

These are some of the most highly endangered species in the oceans. Catching even a passing glimpse of one is a magical experience, but you'll blow the chance unless you heed some basic guidelines. When you first spot a sea turtle, resist the urge to move in and get a closer look; you will only scare it off and ruin the opportunity for others to see it. Instead, stay still and watch at a respectful distance as it goes about its business, searching for food or gliding along gracefully. Keep an eye out for identification tags on their flippers or shells—a sure sign these fellas are being closely studied and well protected. You should never approach a turtle or its nest, and never touch or try to touch one—for your safety and theirs. Although it seems harmless to humans, it is in fact quite stressful for the turtles (how'd you like to be chased around the grocery store by strangers all day?). *Warning:* Do not swim above the turtles; it will prevent them from surfacing to breathe and subject them to undue respiratory stress. And, of course, if someone offers you sea turtle shell, egg, or meat products, just say no.

—Christina P. Colón

Gardens, Drake's Seat, and Charlotte Amalie; this tour costs $49 per person. Their "St. John Land and Snorkel Safari" is a full-day tour that takes visitors through the beaches and national parks in St. John, including a snorkel stop in Trunk Bay, in open-air buses; it costs $95 per person. Adventure Center offers an array of other quality guided tours throughout the Virgin Islands.

Tan Tan Tours (© **340/773-7041;** www.stxtantantours.com) is a tour operator based in St. Croix that offers off-the-beaten-path jeep tours of the island. A 2½-hour guided swim in the Anally Bay tide pools costs $100 per person, while a full-day (8-hr.) tour of the island costs $160 per person; custom tours are also available.

B.V.I. Eco-Tours (© **284/495-0271;** www.bvi-ecotours.com) offers a variety of guided tours, including snorkeling, hiking, bird watching, sightseeing, diving, and general tours of the British Virgin Islands.

Virgin Gorda Tours (© **284/495-5240;** www.virgingordatours.com) offers guided taxi tours of Virgin Gorda, including stops at Savannah Bay, Gorda Peak, the historical Copper Mine ruins, and the famous Baths; tours vary, but a 1-hour tour (for two people) costs $55.

BICYCLE TOURS   Bike riding can be a wonderful way to explore the islands. **Water Island Adventures** (© **340/775-5770;** www.waterislandadventures.com) offers guided bike tours on Water Island, off of St. Thomas. Tours depart from the Crown Bay cruise-ship dock at St. Thomas, where you'll take a ferry to Water Island—from there the biking tour begins.

St. Croix has miles of relatively flat roadways that make it ideal for biking, but it also has lush hills for the more adventurous. Contact **Freedom City Cycles,** 2E Strand Sq., 2 Strand St., Frederiksted (© **340/227-2433;** www.freedomcitycycles.com), which, in addition to offering bike rentals, can arrange guided bike tours of the island. A 2- to 3-hour mountain bike tour begins at sea level and climbs through the rain forest on both paved and unpaved roads, costing $60 per person.

FISHING   The Virgin Islands are home to some of the best fishing grounds in the world. More than 20 sportsfishing world records have been set in the Virgin Islands in the last few decades, mostly for the big kahuna of the sea, blue marlin. Other abundant fish in these waters are bonito, tuna, wahoo, sailfish, and skipjack. Sport-fishing charters, led by experienced local captains, abound in the islands; both half-day and full-day trips are available. But you needn't go out to sea to fish. On St. Thomas, St. John, and St. Croix, the U.S. government publishes lists of legal shoreline fishing spots (contact local tourist offices for more information). Closer inshore, you'll find kingfish, mackerel, bonefish, tarpon, amberjack, grouper, and snapper.

On St. Thomas, many people line-fish from the rocky shore along Mandahl Beach, which is also a popular spot for family picnics. The shore here is not the best place for swimming, because the seafloor drops off dramatically and the surf tends to be rough. On St. John, the waters in Virgin Islands National Park are open to fishermen with hand-held rods. No fishing license is required for shoreline fishing, and government pamphlets available at tourist offices list some 100 good spots. Call © **340/774-8784** for more information.

HIKING TOURS   The best islands for hiking are **Tortola** and **St. John.** In Tortola, the best hiking is through **Sage Mountain National Park,** spread across 37 hectares (91 acres) of luxuriant flora and fauna. On St. John, the most intriguing hike is the **Annaberg Historic Trail,** which takes you by former plantation sites. Most of St. John is itself a national park, so there are dozens of opportunities for hiking.

St. Croix also has good hiking opportunities. To reach some of the most remote but scenic places on St. Croix, take a walking tour with **Crucian Heritage & Nature Tourism (CHANT; *Ⓒ* 340/772-4079;** http://chantvi.org). Its "Ay Ay Eco-Hike Tours" include a steep walk down the mountainside to the crystalline tidal pools and saltwater baths of Annaly Bay, and a walking trip along scenic Maroon Ridge, established by runaway slaves in the 17th century ($50 per person).

Buck Island, off the coast of St. Croix, is beloved by snorkelers and scuba divers but also fascinating to hike. You can easily explore the island in a day—it's just a half-mile wide and a mile long. While hiking in the Virgin Islands, you'll encounter many birds and flowers—but no poisonous snakes. Be sure to look for the trumpet-shaped Ginger Thomas, the U.S. Virgin Islands' official flower.

SAILING & YACHTING The Virgin Islands are a sailor's paradise, offering crystal-clear turquoise waters, secluded coves and inlets, and protected harbors for anchoring. The most popular cruising area around the Virgin Islands is the deep and lushly scenic **Sir Francis Drake Channel,** which runs from St. John to Virgin Gorda's North Sound. The channel is rimmed by mountainous islands and boasts steady tradewinds year-round. In heavy weather, the network of tiny islands shelters yachties from the brute force of the open sea. The waters surrounding St. Croix to the south are also appealing, especially near Buck Island. Outside the channel, the Virgin Islands archipelago contains reefy areas that separate many of the islands from their neighbors.

For details on arranging a multi-day boat charter—bareboat (on your own) or fully crewed—see "Chartering Your Own Boat," below. Most visitors, however, are content with **day sails,** which are easy to organize, especially at the harbors in St. Thomas, Tortola, and Virgin Gorda. Regardless of where you decide to cruise, you really shouldn't leave the islands without spending at least 1 day on the water, even if you have to load up on Dramamine or snap on your acupressure wristbands before you go. For sailing companies on each island, go to the individual chapters.

> ### Sailing, Sailing: Distances by Nautical Mile
>
> Except for Anegada, a low-lying atoll of coral limestone and sandstone, all the Virgin Islands are high and easily spotted. The shortest distance between St. Thomas and St. Croix is 35 nautical miles; from St. John to St. Croix, 35 nautical miles; from St. Thomas to St. John, 2 nautical miles; from Tortola to St. Thomas, 10 nautical miles; from Virgin Gorda to Anegada, 13 nautical miles; and from St. John to Anegada, 30 nautical miles. Virgin Gorda to St. Croix is about the longest run, at 45 nautical miles. (Specific distances between the islands can be misleading, however, because you often need to take round-about routes from one point to another.)

If you don't know how to sail but want to learn, there's no better place than the Virgin Islands. On Tortola, the **Tortola Sailing School (*Ⓒ* 800/390-7594;** http://tortolasailingschool.com) is an accredited American Sailing Association sailing school, with courses in both sailing and bareboating running out of Soper's Hole Marina on the island's West End. It offers a full-day "Learn the Ropes" basics course on a 36-foot monohull for $175 per person. It also offers multi-day live-aboard sailing and bareboating courses. On St. Croix, call **Jones Maritime Sailing School,** 1215 King Cross St., Christiansted (*Ⓒ* **340/773-4709;** www.jonesmaritime. com), which has three 24-foot day-sailors and charges $325 per person for a 2-day course, held on Saturdays and Sundays.

CHARTERING YOUR OWN boat

There may be no better way to experience the "Sailing Capital of the World" than on the deck of your own yacht. Impossible? Not really. No one said you had to *own* the yacht. Experienced sailors and navigators with a sea-wise crew might want to rent a **bareboat charter**—a fully equipped boat with no captain or crew, where you are the master of the seas, charting your own course, and do your own cooking and cleaning. If you're not an expert sailor but yearn to hit the high seas, consider a **fully crewed charter,** which includes a captain and chef. The cost of a crewed boat is obviously more than that of a bareboat, and varies according to crew size and experience.

Most boats, bareboat or crewed, are rented on a weekly basis and come equipped with a GPS system. Full-service crewed boats come in all shapes and sizes, from traditional sailboats to roomy multihulls to elegant motor yachts. Crewed charters generally come with a fully stocked kitchen (or a barbecue) and bar, fishing gear, and watersports equipment. For details on crewed yachts, go to **www.bvicrewedyachts.com**. Private boats are given up to 30 days to cruise

the B.V.I. and are required to pay a 30-day cruising fee based on tonnage (maximum fee $55). Contact the **British Virgin Islands Customs Department** (℡ 284/494-3475 or 284/468-3701, ext. 2533) for current cruising permit requirements.

Among the outfitters in the Virgin Islands, the **Moorings** in Tortola (℡ 888/952-8420; www.moorings.com) offers both bareboat and fully crewed charters equipped with such extras as a barbecue, snorkeling gear, a dinghy, and linens. The company even supplies windsurfing equipment for free with crewed boats (and for an extra cost with bareboats). The experienced staff of mechanics, electricians, riggers, and cleaners is extremely helpful, especially if you're going out on your own. They'll give you a thorough briefing about Virgin Islands waters and anchorages. If you're looking for bareboat and full-crew charter companies in St. Thomas, you'll find the craft you're looking for through **IGY: American Yacht Harbor** (℡ 340/775-6454; www.igy-americanyachtharbor.com), a full-service marina located in Red Hook and home to numerous charter companies.

The **Offshore Sailing School,** Prospect Reef Resort, Road Town (℡ 284/494-5119) is the official sailing school for the Moorings, the bareboat charter outfitter based in Road Town; it offers sailing instruction year-round (℡ 888/454-7015 or 239/454-1700; www.offshore-sailing.com).

SEA KAYAKING   Arawak Expeditions, Cruz Bay, St. John (℡ 800/238-8687 or 340/693-8312 in the U.S.; www.arawakexp.com), offers not only kayaking day-trips but multi-day sea-kayaking/island-camping excursions. The vessels with Arawak Expeditions are in two-person fiberglass kayaks, complete with foot-controlled rudders. The outfit provides all the kayaking gear, healthy meals, camping equipment, and experienced guides. The cost of a full-day trip is $110, half-day $75; you can also book longer expeditions, such as a 5-day excursion costing $1,195 per person or a 7-day trip going for $2,495 per person.

SNORKELING & SCUBA DIVING   St. John has spectacular snorkeling right offshore at beaches like **Trunk Bay, Maho Bay, Cinnamon Bay,** and **Hawksnest Beach.** A steep undersea wall just 15 minutes offshore makes for excellent scuba diving.

On St. Croix, the best site for both is **Buck Island,** easily accessible by day sails from the harbor in Christiansted. St. Croix is also known for its dramatic "drop-offs," including the famous Puerto Rico Trench.

On St. Thomas, all major hotels rent fins and masks for snorkelers, and most day-sail charters have equipment on board. Many outfitters, like the **St. Thomas Diving Club** (📞 **340/776-2381;** www.stthomasdivingclub.com), also feature scuba programs.

On the British Virgin Islands, some of the best snorkeling is around **Norman Island** and the **Indians; Smuggler's Cove,** in Tortola; and the **Baths,** Virgin Gorda's major attraction. **Anegada Reef,** which lies off Anegada Island, has been a "burial ground" for ships for centuries; an estimated 300 wrecks, including many pirate ships, have perished here. The wreckage of the **RMS _Rhone,_** near the westerly tip of Salt Island, is the most celebrated dive spot in the B.V.I. This ship went under in 1867 in one of the most disastrous hurricanes ever to hit the Virgin Islands.

Heritage & Cultural Tours

St. Croix's cultural riches are explored on tours run by **Crucian Heritage & Nature Tourism** (**CHANT;** 📞 **340/772-4079;** http://chantvi.org). In addition to **historic walking tours** of the colonial towns of Christiansted and Frederiksted, CHANT offers a fascinating **Ridge to Reef Farm Tour,** showcasing the island's agricultural heritage and burgeoning farm-to-table movement with a tour of a 200-acre working tropical farm in a lush valley amid the island's tropical forests. The 3-hour tour is $55 per person.

[FastFACTS] THE VIRGIN ISLANDS

Area Codes The area code for the U.S.V.I. is **340;** in the B.V.I., it's **284.** You can dial direct from North America; from outside North America, dial 001, plus the number for the U.S.V.I., and 011-44 plus the number for the B.V.I.

Business Hours See "Fast Facts" in individual island chapters for information on business hours.

Crime See "Safety," later in this section.

Customs Every visitor to the U.S.V.I. 21 years of age or older may bring in, free of duty, the following: (1) 1 liter of wine or hard liquor;

(2) 200 cigarettes, 100 cigars (but not from Cuba), or 3 pounds of smoking tobacco; and (3) $100 worth of gifts. These exemptions are offered to travelers who spend at least 72 hours in the United States and who have not claimed them within the preceding 6 months. It is altogether forbidden to bring into the country foodstuffs (particularly fruit, cooked meats, and canned goods) and plants (vegetables, seeds, tropical plants, and the like). Foreign tourists may carry in or out up to $10,000 in U.S. or foreign currency with no formalities; larger sums

must be declared to U.S. Customs on entering or leaving, which includes filing form CM 4790. For details regarding U.S. Customs and Border Protection, consult your nearest U.S. embassy or consulate, or **U.S. Customs** (📞 **800/232-5378;** www.cbp.gov).

Visitors to the B.V.I. can bring in food, with the exception of meat products that are not USDA-approved. Visitors can bring up to $10,000 in currency and 1 liter of alcohol per person.

Australian Citizens: A helpful brochure available from Australian consulates or

Customs offices is "Know Before You Go." For more information, contact the **Australian Customs Service,** Customs House, 5 Constitution Ave., Canberra City, ACT 2601 (✆ **1300/363-263,** or 61 2 9313 3010 from outside Australia; www.customs.gov.au).

Canadian Citizens: For a clear summary of Canadian rules, write for the booklet "I Declare," issued by the **Canada Border Services Agency,** Ottawa, Ontario, K1A 0L8 (✆ **800/461-9999** in Canada, or 204/983-3500; www.cbsa-asfc.gc.ca).

New Zealand Citizens: Most questions are answered in a free pamphlet available at New Zealand consulates and Customs offices: "New Zealand Customs Guide for Travellers, Notice no. 4." For more information, contact **New Zealand Customs Service,** the Customhouse, 1 Hinemoa St., Harbour Quays, Wellington 6140 (✆ **04/901-4500;** www.customs.govt.nz).

U.K. Citizens: From the B.V.I., U.K. citizens can bring back (duty-free) 200 cigarettes (250g of tobacco), 2 liters wine, 1 liter strong liquor, 60cc perfume, and £145 of goods and souvenirs. Larger amounts are subject to tax. For further information, contact **HM Revenue & Customs,** Crownhill Court, Tailyour Road, Plymouth, PL6 5BZ (✆ **0300 200 3700;** www.hmrc.gov.uk).

U.S. Citizens & Residents: From the U.S.V.I., U.S. citizens can bring back 5 liters of liquor duty-free, plus an extra liter of rum (including Cruzan rum) if one of the bottles is produced in the Virgin Islands. Goods made on the island are also duty-free, including perfume, jewelry, clothing, and original paintings; however, if the price of an item exceeds $25, you must be able to show a certificate of origin.

Be sure to collect receipts for all purchases in the Virgin Islands, and beware of merchants offering to give you a false receipt—he or she might be an informer to U.S. Customs. Also, keep in mind that any gifts received during your stay must be declared. For the most up-to-date specifics on what you can bring back **from the B.V.I.** and the corresponding fees, contact the **U.S. Customs & Border Protection (CBP),** 1300 Pennsylvania Ave. NW, Washington, DC 20229 (✆ **877/227-5511;** www.ct.gov/dcp.gov).

Disabled Travelers

For the most part, the accessibility of hotels and restaurants in the U.S.V.I. remains far behind the progress made on the mainland. Of the U.S. Virgins, St. Thomas and St. John remain the most difficult islands for wheelchair-bound visitors to maneuver because of their hilly terrain. St. Croix is flatter and is an easier place to get around.

Although most hotels in the Virgin Islands have a long way to go before they become a friend of a person with disabilities, some have made inroads. As of this writing, about a third of the major resorts in St. Thomas or St. Croix have the facilities to accommodate vacationers who have disabilities. Many inns, guesthouses, and villas terraced in the hills of Charlotte Amalie can present challenges to those with mobility issues—a number have steep steps and no elevators. Of the resorts in the U.S.V.I., the **Ritz-Carlton, St. Thomas** (p. 56), is the most hospitable to persons with disabilities. It maintains "accessible rooms"—rooms that can be reached without navigating stairs—in every price category. The Ritz also offers beach wheelchairs (resting on balloon tires).

Accessible Island Tours (✆ **340/344-8302;** http://accessvi.com) is a tour operator in St. Thomas that offers a land-based tour of St. Thomas in a custom wheelchair-accessible vehicle. Originating from Wico Dock at Havensight or Crown Bay at the Sub Base, tours stop at Magens Bay, Drakes Seat, and the Skyline Drive, and cost $37 per person (minimum of six passengers).

Doctors You should have no trouble finding a good doctor in the Virgin Islands. See "Fast Facts" in individual island chapters for information on doctors.

Drinking Laws In the U.S. Virgins, the legal age for purchase and consumption of alcoholic beverages is 18. Proof of age is required and often requested at bars, nightclubs, and restaurants, so it's always a good idea to bring ID when you go out. Do not carry open containers of alcohol in your car or any public area that isn't zoned for alcohol consumption. The police can fine you on the spot. Don't even think about driving while intoxicated. Although 18-year-olds can purchase, drink, and order alcohol, they cannot transport bottles back to the United States with them. If an attempt is made, the alcohol will be confiscated at the Customs check point. The same holds true for the B.V.I.

In the B.V.I., the legal minimum age for purchasing liquor or drinking alcohol in bars or restaurants is 18. Alcoholic beverages can be sold any day of the week, including Sunday. You can have an open container on the beach, but be you can be fined if you litter.

Driving Rules In both the U.S.V.I. and the B.V.I., you must drive on the left. See "Getting Around," earlier in this chapter.

Electricity The electrical current in the Virgin Islands is the same as on the U.S. mainland and Canada: 110 to 120 volts AC (60 cycles), compared to 220 to 240 volts AC (50 cycles) in most

of Europe, Australia, and New Zealand. Downward converters that change 220 to 240 volts to 110 to 120 volts are difficult to find in the United States, so bring one with you.

Embassies & Consulates There are no embassies or consulates in the Virgin Islands. If you have a passport issue, go to the local police station, which in all islands is located at the center of government agencies. Relay your problem to whomever is at reception, and you'll be given advice about which agencies can help you.

Emergencies Call ☎ **911** in the U.S.V.I. or **999** in the B.V.I.

Family Travel The Virgin Islands, both U.S. and British, are very family-friendly. **St. Thomas** and **St. Croix** have the most facilities and attractions for families. The British Virgin Islands have fewer attractions that cater specifically to children, although families who love watersports, boating, and nature activities will have a great time. When compared with some of the other major destinations in the Caribbean (such as Jamaica, where crime is high), the U.S. Virgins are generally safe, and the British Virgin Islands are even safer.

Gasoline Please see "Getting Around," earlier in this chapter, for information.

Health Other than the typical tropical environment health concerns, like sun

exposure and seasickness (see below), there are no major health concerns in the Virgin Islands.

St. Thomas has the best hospital in the U.S. Virgin Islands (**Schneider Regional Medical Center;** p. 48). St. Croix also has good hospital facilities (**St. Croix Regional Medical Center;** p. 204). There is only a health clinic on St. John; more serious cases are transferred to the hospital on St. Thomas.

The B.V.I. has one small general hospital, **Peebles Hospital** (p. 154) on Tortola. Day clinics are available on Tortola, Virgin Gorda, Anegada, and Jost Van Dyke. Both Tortola and Virgin Gorda are served by ambulances with paramedics. The **Eureka Medical Centre** (www.eurekamedicalclinic. com), Geneva Place, Road Town, Tortola, is a private-run urgent-care facility. There is also no hyperbaric chamber in the B.V.I. Patients requiring treatment for decompression illness are transferred to St. Thomas.

In very serious cases, patients in the U.S. Virgins and the B.V.I. are transported to Puerto Rico.

It is not difficult to get a prescription filled or find a doctor on St. Thomas, St. Croix, and Tortola. Pharmacies are few and far between on the smaller islands, so you should get any prescriptions refilled before you venture into more remote territory. Often it requires a phone call from the U.S.V.I. to a stateside pharmacy or to the doctor who prescribed the medicine in the first place. CVS and Wal-Mart are the best for contacting a stateside branch of those chains, if your prescription is on a computer file. To avoid possible hassles and delays, it is best to arrive with enough medication for your entire vacation.

o **BUGS & BITES** **Mosquitoes** do exist in the Virgin Islands, but they aren't the malaria-carrying mosquitoes that you might find elsewhere in the Caribbean. They're still a nuisance, though. **Sand flies,** which appear mainly in the evening, are a bigger annoyance. Screens can't keep these critters out, so use bug repellent.

o **DIETARY RED FLAGS** If you experience **diarrhea,** moderate your eating habits and drink only bottled water until you recover. If symptoms persist, consult a doctor. Much of the fresh water on the Virgin Islands is stored in cisterns and filtered before it's served. Delicate stomachs might opt for bottled water. Some say a nightly drink of **ginger ale and bitters** helps soothe tummies.

o **SEASICKNESS** The best way to prevent **seasickness** is with the scopolamine patch by Transderm Scop, a

prescription medication. Bonine and Dramamine are good over-the-counter medications, although each causes drowsiness. Smooth Sailing is a ginger drink that works quite well to settle your stomach. You might also opt for an acupressure wristband available at drugstores (www.sea-band.com). Some say a ginger pill taken with a meal and followed by Dramamine an hour before boating also does the job.

o **SUN EXPOSURE** The Virgin Islands' sun can be brutal. To protect yourself, consider wearing sunglasses and a hat, and use **sunscreen** (SPF 15 and higher) liberally. Limit your time on the beach for the first few days. If you overexpose yourself, stay out of the sun until you recover. If your sunburn is followed by fever, chills, a headache, nausea, or dizziness, see a doctor.

Hospitals The largest hospital in St. Thomas is the **Schneider Regional Medical Center** (p. 48), with 24-hour emergency-room service. Islanders from St. John also use this hospital, which is about a 5-minute drive from Charlotte Amalie. The other major hospital is the **St. Croix Regional Medical Center** on St. Croix (p. 204); it has a Level IV trauma center offering 24-hour emergency-room

service. Both offer air and ground-level support to hospitals with more extensive facilities. The payment of Medicare and Medicaid operates as it does in the United States. If you walk into a hospital without any coverage or insurance, you are expected to pay.

On Tortola, in the British Virgin Islands, the main hospital in the little country is **Peebles Hospital** (p. 154), with surgical, X-ray, and laboratory facilities. If you are on one of the out islands, you are generally taken to Tortola for treatment. In addition to these hospitals, there are a number of private doctors' offices throughout the islands, charging higher rates than the hospitals.

Internet & Wi-Fi Internet access is becoming increasingly available all around the Virgin Islands, but it can still be spotty on some of the more remote islands. Most hotels and resorts are ratcheting up their Internet capabilities. Many bars and cafes throughout the Virgin Islands have free Wi-Fi access.

If you're in transit and looking for a spot with Internet access, see the "Fast Facts" section of each island chapter for recommendations on where to go.

Language English is the official language of both the U.S. and British Virgin Islands.

Legal Aid While driving, if you are pulled over for a minor infraction (such as speeding), never attempt to pay the fine directly to a police officer; this could be construed as attempted bribery, a much more serious crime. Pay fines by mail, or directly into the hands of the clerk of the court. If accused of a more serious offense, say and do nothing before consulting a lawyer. In the U.S.V.I., the burden is on the state to prove a person's guilt beyond a reasonable doubt, and everyone has the right to remain silent, whether he or she is suspected of a crime or actually arrested. Once arrested, a person can make one telephone call to a party of his or her choice.

LGBT Travelers The Virgin Islands are some of the most gay-friendly destinations in the Caribbean. However, discretion is still advised. Islanders tend to be religious and conservative, and displays of same-sex affection, such as hand holding, are frowned upon.

St. Thomas is the most cosmopolitan of the Virgin Islands, but it is no longer the "gay paradise" it was in the 1960s and 1970s. Most gay vacationers now head for Frederiksted, in St. Croix, which has more hotels and other establishments welcoming to the gay market. In Charlotte Amalie, on St. Thomas, the most boisterous gay nightlife takes place in the Frenchtown section of the city.

Mail At press time, domestic postage rates in the U.S.V.I. were 33¢ for a postcard and 46¢ for a

letter up to 1 ounce. For international mail, a first-class postcard or letter stamp costs $1.10. For more information, go to **www.usps.com**. Always include zip codes when mailing items in the U.S. If you don't know your zip code, visit **www.usps.com/zip4**.

If you aren't sure what your address will be in the U.S. Virgin Islands, mail can be sent to you, in your name, c/o General Delivery at the main post office of the city or region where you expect to be. (Call ℓ **800/275-8777** for information on the nearest post office.) The addressee must pick up mail in person and must produce proof of identity (driver's license, passport, and so on). Most post offices will hold your mail for up to 1 month, and are open Monday to Friday 8am to 6pm, and Saturday 9am to 3pm.

Postal rates in the British Virgin Islands to the United States or Canada are 35¢ for a postcard (airmail), and 50¢ for a first-class airmail letter (½ oz.). Mailing a postcard to the U.K. costs 50¢ and a first-class letter via airmail costs 75¢ (½ oz.). **B.V.I. postage stamps** are beautiful and highly coveted; contact the **BVI Philatelic Bureau** (ℓ **284/494-7789**) for information about exhibitions.

Medical Requirements Unless you're arriving from an area known to be suffering from an epidemic (particularly cholera

or yellow fever), inoculations or vaccinations are not required for entry into the U.S. Virgin Islands or the British Virgin Islands.

If you have a medical condition that requires **syringe-administered medications,** carry a valid signed prescription from your physician; syringes in carry-on baggage will be inspected. Insulin in any form should have the proper pharmaceutical documentation. If you have a disease that requires treatment with **narcotics,** you should also carry documented proof with you—smuggling narcotics aboard a plane carries severe penalties in the U.S.

For **HIV-positive visitors,** requirements for entering both the U.S.V.I. and B.V.I. are somewhat vague and change frequently. Anyone who does not appear to be in good health may be required to undergo a medical exam, including HIV testing, prior to being granted or denied entry. For up-to-the-minute information, contact **AIDSinfo** (ℓ **800/448-0440** or 301/519-0459 outside the U.S.; www.aidsinfo.nih.gov) or the **Gay Men's Health Crisis** (ℓ **212/367-1000;** www.gmhc.org). Also see "Health."

Mobile Phones In the U.S. Virgin Islands: The two largest cellphone operators in the U.S.V.I. include Sprint PCS (www.sprint.com) and AT&T Wireless (www. att.com/wireless). Phones operating in the mainland

U.S. under those plans will usually operate seamlessly, and without any excess roaming charges, in the U.S.V.I. If your phone presently operates through some other carrier, it's wise to call them before your departure about signing up (at least temporarily) for one of their international plans, which will save you money on roaming charges during the duration of your trip. If your cellphone is not equipped for reception and transmission in the U.S.V.I., consider renting (or buying) a cheap cellphone for temporary use, or, less conveniently, head for a Sprint PCS or AT&T sales outlet (each maintains offices on all three of the U.S.V.I.'s major islands) for a substitute SIM card, a key operating component that can be inserted into your existing phone, making it operational. Throughout the U.S.V.I., the electrical system is the same as within the U.S. mainland (115 volts and female sockets which accept the U.S.-style "flat" plugs), so most U.S. residents won't need any special transformers or adaptors.

In the British Virgin Islands: The three largest cellphone operators in the B.V.I. are CCT Global Communications (www.cct wireless.com), LIME (www. lime.com), and Digicell BVI (www.digicelbvi.com), all with offices in Road Town and on Virgin Gorda. Other than that, the cellphone situation is roughly equivalent to what's described

immediately above in the U.S.V.I. The electrical system in the B.V.I. is the same as that within the U.S.V.I. and the mainland U.S. (115 volts), so British and European visitors may want to bring adaptors and transformers. Hotels in the B.V.I. often have the appropriate adaptors, and in some cases, those adaptors are physically built directly into the wall sockets.

Money & Costs The U.S. Virgin Islands and the British Virgin Islands both use the **U.S. dollar** as the form of currency. Frommer's lists exact prices in the local currency. The currency conversions quoted above were correct at press time. However, rates fluctuate, so before departing consult a currency exchange website such as **www.xe.com** to check up-to-the-minute rates.

Banks on the islands are your only option if you need to **exchange currency.** These rates can be expensive, and additional charges are often tacked on; it is best to change money before you arrive.

ATMs throughout the Virgin Islands dispense U.S. dollars. ATMs are most prevalent on St. Thomas in Charlotte Amalie (on the downtown streets, near the cruise-ship terminals, within the large resorts, and in shopping malls) and in Christiansted on St. Croix. You will also find several ATMs in Cruz Bay on St. John. ATMs are less prevalent in the British Virgin

Islands; you will find a cluster of banks in Wickham Cay I, Road Town, Tortola, and a couple in the harbor in Spanish Town, Virgin Gorda. The other islands do not have ATMs, so if you're planning a visit, be sure to visit an ATM to get some cash first (or have your resort front you some petty cash). Each machine charges around $2 to $3 for a transaction fee. Nearly all of the machines are operated by three banks: **Scotiabank** (www.scotiabank.com), **FirstBank** (www.firstbankvi. com), and **Banco Popular** (www.bancopopular.com/vi).

Most establishments in the Virgin Islands accept **credit cards;** we note in our reviews those places that accept cash only. MasterCard and Visa are widely accepted on all the islands that cater to visitors, especially Virgin Gorda, Tortola, St. John, St. Croix, and, of course, St. Thomas. In the past few years, there has been a tendency to drop American Express because of the high percentage it takes from transactions.

However, visitors should not rely solely on credit cards, as a number of establishments in the Virgin Islands accept only **cash.** You will want to arm yourself with cash while browsing the small boutiques and curio shops throughout the islands—many do not take credit cards. Most taxi drivers only deal in cash.

Beware of credit card fees while traveling. Check with your credit or debit card issuer to see what fees, if any, will be charged for overseas transactions. Recent reform legislation in the U.S., for example, has curbed some exploitative lending practices. But many banks have responded by increasing fees in other areas, including fees for customers who use credit and debit cards while out of the country—even if those charges were made in U.S. dollars. Fees can amount to 3 percent or more of the purchase price. Check with your bank before departing to avoid any surprise charges on your statement.

Passports   If you're a U.S. citizen and you travel directly to the U.S.V.I. and do not visit the British Virgin Islands, you do not need a passport—but you are highly encouraged to carry one. If you return to the mainland U.S. from the U.S.V.I. through another country (Mexico or Bermuda, for example), you will need a passport to get back home. For non–U.S. citizens, visiting the U.S. Virgin Islands is just like visiting the mainland United States: You need a passport and visa.

A passport is necessary for *all* visitors to the British Virgin Islands (including citizens of the U.K.).

For information on how to get a passport, contact your passport office (see below). Allow plenty of time before your trip to apply for a passport; processing normally takes 3 weeks but can take longer during busy periods. And keep in mind that if you need a passport

in a hurry, you'll pay a higher processing fee. When traveling, safeguard your passport in an inconspicuous, inaccessible place like a money belt, and keep a copy of the critical pages with your passport number in a separate place. There are no foreign consulates in the Virgin Islands, so if you lose your passport, go to the local police station.

Passport Offices
Australia   Australian Passport Information Service (✆ **131-232;** www. passports.gov.au).

Canada   Passport Office, Passport Canada Program, Gatineau QC K1A 0G3 (✆ **800/567-6868;** www. ppt.gc.ca).

Ireland   Passport Office, Frederick Buildings, Molesworth Street, Dublin 2 (✆ **353 1 671 1633;** www. dfa.ie).

New Zealand   Passports Office, Department of Internal Affairs, 109 Featherston St., Wellington, 6140 (✆ **0800 22 50 50** in New Zealand, or 64 4 463 9360; www.passports.govt.nz).

United Kingdom   Visit your nearest passport office, major post office, or travel agency, or contact the **HM Passport Office,** 4th Floor, Peel Building, 2 Marsham St., London, SW1P 4DF (✆ **0300 222 0000;** www. ips.gov.uk).

United States   To find your regional passport office, check the U.S. State Department website (http://travel.state.gov/passport) or call the **National Passport**

Information Center (✆ **877/ 487-2778**) for automated information.

Petrol   Please see "Getting Around," earlier in this chapter for information.

Pets   To bring your pet to the U.S.V.I., you must have a health certificate from a mainland veterinarian and show proof of vaccination against rabies. Very few hotels allow animals, so check in advance. If you're strolling with your dog through the national park on St. John, you must keep it on a leash. Pets are not allowed at campgrounds, in picnic areas, or on public beaches. Both St. Croix and St. Thomas have veterinarians listed in the Yellow Pages.

Your dog or cat is permitted entry into the B.V.I. without quarantine, if accompanied by an Animal Health Certificate issued by the Veterinary Authority in your country of origin. This certificate has a number of requirements, including a guarantee of vaccination against rabies.

Police   Dial ✆ **911** for emergencies in the U.S.V.I. The Crime Line phone number is ✆ **340/777-8700.** The main police headquarters is currently located in the Alexander Farrelly Criminal Justice Center in Charlotte Amalie (✆ **340/774-2211**). In the B.V.I., the main police headquarters is on Waterfront Drive near the ferry docks on Sir Olva George's Plaza (✆ **284/494-2945**) in Tortola. There are also police stations on Virgin Gorda (© **284/ 495-5222**) and on Jost Van Dyke (© **284/495-9345**). See individual island chapters for more detailed information.

Safety The Virgin Islands are a relatively safe destination. The small permanent populations are generally friendly and welcoming. That being said, **St. Thomas** is no longer as safe as it once was. Crime, especially muggings, is on the rise in Charlotte Amalie. Wandering the town at night, especially on the back streets (particularly on Back St.), is not recommended. Guard your valuables or store them in hotel safes if possible.

The same holds true for **St. Croix** and the back streets of Christiansted and Frederiksted. Although these areas are safer than St. Thomas, random acts of violence against tourists in the past, even murder, have been known to happen. Know that most crime on both these islands is petty theft aimed at unguarded possessions on the beach, unlocked parked cars, or muggings at night. Exercise the same amount of caution you would if you were traveling to an unfamiliar town on the mainland. Whether on St. Thomas or St. Croix, always take a taxi home after a night out.

St. John is a bit different, because there is no major town and most of the island is uninhabited. Muggings and petty theft do happen, but such occurrences are rarely violent. You are most likely to find your camera stolen if you leave it unattended on the beach.

The **British Virgin Islands** are very safe, with a very low crime rate that many attribute to the illegality of owning guns. Minor robberies and muggings do occur late at night outside bars in Road Town, especially in poorly lit areas around Wickham's Cay I and along Waterfront Drive. Car theft in Trellis Bay and by the Road Town ferry has also been on the rise. On Virgin Gorda, most resorts don't even have room keys (although you can lock yourself in at night), and some people have reported dropping off rental cars at the airport with the keys in the lock.

Driving safety: In general, the Virgin Islands' steep, curvy roads are often poorly lit at night; many are potholed or have been eroded by rain runoff. St. Croix's road network is composed of rocky, steep dirt roads through the interior. As a result, car-rental insurance is higher on this island than the others. St. John's national park roads are for the most part excellent. For those travelers who are unaccustomed to driving on the left, we suggest leaving the night driving up to a taxi driver. Do not attempt the most rural roads at night, as cellphone service is spotty at best and breakdowns (or worse) are an all-too-perfect way to ruin your Virgin Islands vacation; see "Getting Around," earlier in this chapter.

Smoking In the U.S.V.I, smoking is prohibited in restaurants and public buildings; bars may allow smoking outdoors as long as it's 20 feet from entrance and service areas. On the B.V.I., smoking is banned in public places (bars, restaurants, nightclubs, airports, offices, and sports facilities) and within 50 feet of any public space.

Student Travel St. Thomas has perhaps the most youth-oriented scene of any of the Virgin Islands, British or American. Many young people who visit St. Thomas stay in the guesthouses in and around Charlotte Amalie. Beyond St. Thomas, the island of St. Croix attracts a large array of young, single travelers, mainly to the inns in and around Christiansted and Frederiksted.

Taxes For the U.S. Virgin Islands, the United States has no value-added tax (VAT) or other indirect tax at the national level. The U.S.V.I. may levy their own local taxes on all purchases, including hotel and restaurant checks and airline tickets. These taxes will not appear on price tags. A 10 percent room tax is added to hotel bills.

The British Virgin Islands has no sales tax. It charges a departure tax of $15 per person for those leaving by boat or $20 if by airplane. Most hotels add a service charge of around 10 percent; there's also a 7 percent government room tax. Most restaurants tack on an automatic 15 percent service charge.

Telephones In the Virgin Islands, hotel surcharges on long-distance and local calls are usually astronomical, so you're better off using your **cellphone** or a **public pay telephone.** Many convenience stores, groceries, and packaging services sell **prepaid calling cards** in denominations up to $50; for international visitors these can be the least expensive way to call home. Many public pay phones at airports now accept American Express, MasterCard, and Visa credit cards. **Local calls** made from pay phones in most locales cost either 25¢ or 35¢ (no pennies, please). Many of the most rural or expressly private resorts and hotels in the Virgin Islands do not provide phones in the rooms, but have phones in their lobbies or common areas.

To make calls within the United States, including the U.S. Virgins, and to Canada, dial 1 followed by the area code and the seven-digit number. **For other international calls,** dial 011 followed by the country code, city code, and the number you are calling.

You can **call the British Virgins** from the United States by just dialing **1,** the area code **284,** and the number; from the U.K. dial **011-44,** then the number. **To call the U.S. from the B.V.I.,** just dial 1 plus the area code and the number; **to call the U.K. from the**

B.V.I., dial 011-44, then the number.

Calls to area codes **800, 888, 877,** and **866** are toll-free. However, calls to area codes **700** and **900** (chat lines, bulletin boards, "dating" services, and so on) can be very expensive— usually a charge of 95¢ to $3 or more per minute, and they sometimes have minimum charges that can run as high as $15 or more.

For **reversed-charge or collect calls,** and for person-to-person calls, dial the number 0, then the area code and number; an operator will come on the line, and you should specify whether you are calling collect, person-to-person, or both. If your operator-assisted call is international, ask for the overseas operator.

For **local directory assistance** ("information"), dial 411; for long-distance information, dial 1, then the appropriate area code and 555-1212.

Time The Virgin Islands are on Atlantic Standard Time, which is 1 hour ahead of Eastern Standard Time. However, the islands do not observe daylight saving time, so in the summer, the Virgin Islands and the East Coast of the U.S. are on the same time. In winter, when it's 6am in Charlotte Amalie, it's 5am in Miami; during daylight saving time it's 6am in both places.

Tipping In hotels, tip **bellhops** at least $1 per bag ($2–$3 if you have a lot of luggage) and tip the

chamber staff $1 to $2 per day (more if you've left a disaster area for him or her to clean up). Tip the **concierge** only if he or she has provided you with some specific service (obtaining difficult-to-get dinner reservations, for example). Tip the **valet-parking attendant** $1 every time you get your car.

Note that **many local restaurants tack on a service charge to the total bill,** often between 10 and 15 percent; you may want to add extra if the service was good. Otherwise tip waitstaff 15 to 20 percent of the check. In bars and nightclubs, tip **bartenders** 15 to 20 percent of the check; tip **checkroom attendants** $1 per garment, and tip **valet-parking attendants** $1 per vehicle.

As for other service personnel, tip **taxi drivers** 15 percent of the fare; tip **skycaps** at airports at least $1 per bag ($2–$3 if you have a lot of luggage); and tip **hairdressers** and barbers 15 to 20 percent. It's always a good idea to tip **tour guides** or **charter captains** at the end of an excursion, generally 15 to 20 percent of the cost.

Toilets You won't find public toilets or restrooms on the streets, but they can be found in hotel lobbies, bars, restaurants, museums, department stores, bus stations, and service stations. Large hotels are often the best bet for clean facilities.

Visas Non–U.S. visitors to the **U.S. Virgin Islands**

should have a U.S. visa; those visitors may also be asked to produce an onward ticket. In the **British Virgin Islands,** visitors who stay for less than 6 months don't need a visa if they possess a return or onward ticket.

For information about U.S. Visas, go to **http://travel.state.gov** and click on "Visas." Or go to one of the following websites:

Australian citizens can obtain up-to-date visa information from the **U.S. Embassy Canberra,** Moonah Place, Yarralumla, ACT 2600 (✆ **02/6214-5600**), or by checking the U.S. Diplomatic Mission's website at **http://canberra.usembassy.gov/visas.html**.

British subjects can obtain visa appointments the **U.S. Embassy Visa Appointment Line** (✆ **020-3608-6998** from within the

U.K., or ✆ **703/439-2367** from within the U.S.; **https://ais.usvisa-info.com/en-gb**). **Irish** citizens can obtain up-to-date visa information through the **U.S. Embassy Dublin,** 42 Elgin Rd., Ballsbridge, Dublin 4 (✆ **01 903-6255** from within the Republic of Ireland; **http://dublin.us embassy.gov.visas.html**).

Citizens of **New Zealand** can obtain up-to-date visa information by contacting the **U.S. Embassy New Zealand,** 29 Fitzherbert Terrace, Thorndon, Wellington (✆ **04 462 6000** from within New Zealand; **http://newzealand.usembassy.gov/visas.html**).

Visitor Information Go to the **U.S.V.I. Division of Tourism**'s website at www.visitusvi.com. The **British Virgin Islands Tourist Board** can be found at www.bvitourism.com.

Water Many visitors to both the U.S. and British Virgins drink the local tap water with no harmful effects. To be prudent, especially if you have a delicate stomach, stick to bottled water. Many hotels and resorts have their own desalination plant, making delicious and highly potable water out of seawater.

Women Travelers St. John and the British Virgin Islands have a low crime rate, while St. Thomas and St. Croix have the highest crime rate against women in the archipelago. To put that into context, however, you are far safer in the Virgin Islands than you would be walking the streets of any major U.S. city. Follow the usual precautions that you'd follow in any major U.S. city.

Index

See also Accommodations and Restaurant indexes, below.

General Index

A

Accessible Island Tours, 202
Accommodations, 3. *See also* Condo, apartment, and villa rentals; *and* Accommodations Index
Anegada, 186, 188
best resorts, 5–8
eco-friendly, 41
Jost Van Dyke, 181–182
Peter Island, 189
St. Croix, 93–99
St. John, 125–130
St. Thomas, 22, 49–59
tips on, 195–196
Tortola, 155–160
Virgin Gorda, 174–178
Accra, 35
Adventure Center (St. Thomas), 56, 71, 197
Adventure trips, 197–198
Agricultural & Cultural Food Fair (St. Thomas), 61
Agrifest: St. Croix Agricultural Fair, 37
Air Sunshine (British Virgin Islands), 146, 172
Air tours, 197
Air travel, 191–192
Anegada, 185
British Virgin Islands, 144, 146
Peter Island, 189
St. Croix, 87–88
St. John, 121
St. Thomas, 42, 44
Tortola, 152
Virgin Gorda, 172
Alice in Wonderland (deep-dive site, south of Ginger Island), 5, 169
American Airlines, 42, 87
American Yacht Harbor (St. Thomas), 19, 69
Ample Hamper (Tortola), 162
Anegada, 3, 4, 18, 185–188
Anegada Lobster Festival, 39, 185
Anegada Reef, 201
Annaberg Historic Trail (St. John), 5, 140–141
Annaberg Sugar Plantation Ruins, 14, 136
Annaberg Trail (St. John), 123
Annaly Meat Market (St. Croix), 105
Ann E. Abramson Pier (St. Croix), 88
Annual House Tours (St. Croix), 110
Annual St. Croix International Regatta, 39

Antilles Resorts (St. Thomas and St. Croix), 50
Antiques, St. Thomas, 82
Apple Bay (Tortola), 165, 168
Aqua Action Dive Center (St. Thomas), 68, 72
Aragorn's Local Arts and Crafts Center (Tortola), 166, 170–171
Arawak Expeditions (St. John), 138, 139, 200
Arawak Indians, 26
Arawak Surf Shop (Tortola), 170
Architecture, 30
Area codes, 201
Aristocat Day Sails (Tortola), 167
ARTFarm (St. Croix), 105
Art galleries
St. Croix, 117
St. John, 141–142
St. Thomas, 83
Art in the Garden Arts & Crafts Festival (St. Thomas), 39
Asante Studio (Tortola), 169
At Home Abroad, 196
Avis, 47, 88, 91, 152, 194
Awl Made Here (St. John), 141

B

Back Street (Charlotte Amalie), 45, 81
Bajo El Sol (St. John), 141
Bamboula (St. John), 141
Bamboushay Pottery (Tortola), 169
Banks/ATMs, 206–207
St. Croix, 92
St. John, 124
St. Thomas, 48
Tortola, 154
Virgin Gorda, 174
Baptist, Avery, 179
Bath & Turtle (pubbn), 181
The Baths (Virgin Gorda), 4, 16, 24, 179–180
Beaches
best, 2–4
Jost Van Dyke, 181
St. Croix, 106–107
St. John, 14, 136–138
St. Thomas, 67–69
Tortola, 165–166
Virgin Gorda, 179–180
Beach Side Café at Sand Castle on the Beach (St. Croix), 119
Bed & breakfasts (B&Bs), St. John, 129–130
Beef Island, 146
The Belgian Chocolate Factory (Charlotte Amalie), 84
Best of BVI, 155, 196
Bicycle tours, 198
Bicyling, St. Croix, 107
Big Beard's Adventure Tours, 14, 120
Bioluminescent bays, St. Croix, 108

Biras Creek (Virgin Gorda), 24
Birding, 2, 32, 115
Blue Moon (St. Croix), 119
Blue Water Divers (Tortola), 168
Blue Water Terrace (St. Croix), 105
Blue Water Terrace (St. John), market and deli, 133
Boating and sailing, 32, 199. *See also* Kayaking
chartering your own boat, 200
responsible travel, 40
St. John, 138
St. Thomas, 69–70
special events, 38, 39
Tortola, 23, 167, 168
Boat travel, 193–194. *See also* Cruise ships; Ferries; Water taxis
St. Croix, 88
St. John, 121, 123
St. Thomas, 44
Virgin Gorda, 172
Bobby's Marketplace (Tortola), 162
Bomba Surfside Shack (Tortola), 171
Books, 31–32
Bookstores, Tortola, 154
Boolchand's (St. Thomas), 82
Bordeaux farmer's market (Charlotte Amalie), 61
Botany Bay, Preserve at, 25, 61
Bougainvillea (St. John), 141
Boyson, 71
Brandywine Bay (Tortola), 166
Brewers Bay (St. Thomas), 69
Brewers Bay (Tortola), 165
British Virgin Islands, 144–190
brief description of, 23–24
history of, 24, 27–29
landmass, 19
suggested itineraries, 15–16
transportation, 147–149
traveling to, 144, 146–147
U.S. Virgin Islands compared to, 3
visitor information, 147
The Buccaneer (St. Croix)
golf course, 107
tennis, 109
Buck Island (off St. Croix), 1
beach, 106
nature trails, 108
scuba diving, 109
side trip to, 119–120
snorkeling, 4, 14, 119
Buck Island National Park, 22
Buck Island Reef National Monument (off St. Croix), 119
Budget car rentals, 47, 88, 91, 194
Bugs and bites, 204
Business hours
St. Croix, 92
St. John, 124
St. Thomas, 48
Tortola, 154

211

Accommodations

Restaurants